TABVLÆ
CORVORVM

TABVLÆ CORVORVM

CONTAINING
the
COMPLETE CURRICULUM
and
CABALISTIC COMPENDIA
for
CROWLEYAN CATECHESIS

THELEMA PUBLICATIONS

Helsinki · Washington D.C. · London

PROMVLGATIONES ALBA ALTA
Series Editor: Antti P. Balk

This volume first published in 2024 by
Thelema Publications, LLC
UK: BCM Agape, London WC1N 3XX
US: P.O. Box 10102, Washington, DC 20018-0102

Editorial enquiries should be addressed to: The Editors,
Promulgationes Alba Alta, P.O. Box 131, 02771 Espoo, Finland

British Library Cataloguing-in-Publication Data
A catalogue record for this book is available from the British Library.

Library of Congress Control Number: 2023947418

ISBN 978 952 5700 80 0

Printed on acid-free paper

In Memory of
William Emmet Heidrick
(1943–2023)

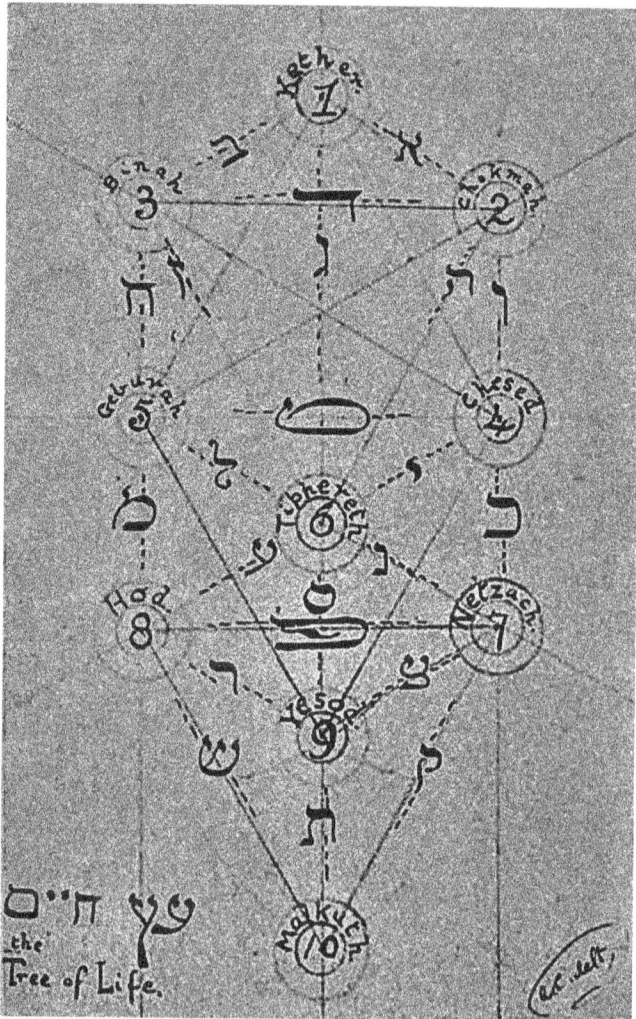

LIBER DCCLXXVII, col. xii. This arrangement is the basis of the whole system of this book. Besides the 10 numbers and the 22 letters, it is divisible into 3 columns, 4 planes, 7 planes, 7 palaces, &c. &c. See "The Temple of Solomon the King," Part V., for a full description and explanation of this whole matter. Note that some lines used in construction are not "paths." The figure is left purposely rough to show construction.

CONTENTS

בראשית

AN ESSAY IN ONTOLOGY
WITH SOME REMARKS ON CEREMONIAL MAGIC

O Man, of a daring nature, thou subtle production!
Thou wilt not comprehend it, as when understanding some common thing.
ORACLES OF ZOROASTER.

IN presenting this theory of the Universe to the world, I have but one hope of making any profound impression, viz.—that my theory has the merit of explaining the divergences between three great forms of religion now existing in the world—Buddhism, Hinduism, and Christianity, and of adapting them to ontological science by conclusions not mystical but mathematical. Of Mohammedanism I shall not now treat, as, in whatever light we may decide to regard it (and its esoteric schools are often orthodox), in any case it must fall under one of the three heads of Nihilism, Advaitism, and Dvaitism.

Taking the ordinary hypothesis of the universe, that of its infinity, or at any rate that of the infinity of God, or of the infinity of some substance or idea actually existing, we first come to the question of the possibility of the co-existence of God and man.

The Christians, in the category of the existent, enumerate among other things, whose consideration we may discard for the purposes of this argument, God, an infinite being; man; Satan and his angels; man certainly, Satan presumably, finite beings. These are not aspects of one being, but separate and even antagonistic existences. All are equally real: we cannot accept mystics of the type of Caird as being orthodox exponents of the religion of Christ.

The Hindus enumerate Brahm, infinite in all dimensions and directions—indistinguishable from the Pleroma of the Gnostics—and Maya, illusion. This is in a sense the antithesis of noumenon and phenomenon, noumenon being negated of all predicates until it becomes almost extinguished in the Nichts under the title of Alles. (*Cf.* Max Müller on the metaphysical Nirvana, in his Dhammapada, Introductory Essay.) The Buddhists express no opinion.

Let us consider the force-quality in the existences conceived of by these two religions respectively, remembering that the God of the Christians is infinite, and yet discussing the alternative if we could suppose him to be a finite God. In any equilibrated system of forces, we may sum and represent them as a triangle or a series of triangles which again resolve into one. In any moving system, if the resultant motion be applied in a contrary direction, the equilibrium can also be thus represented. And if any one of the original forces in such a system may be considered, that one is equal to the resultant of remainder. Let x, the purpose of the universe be the resultant of the forces G, S, and M (God, Satan, and Man). Then M is also the resultant of G, S and $-x$. So that we can regard either of our forces as the supreme, and there is no reason for worshipping one rather than another. All are finite. This argument the Christians clearly see: hence the development of God from the petty joss of Genesis to the intangible, but self-contradictory spectre of to-day. But if G be infinite, the other forces can have no possible effect on it. As Whewell says, in the strange accident by which he anticipates the metre of *In Memoriam:* "No force on earth, however great, can stretch a cord, a horizontal line that shall be absolutely straight."

The definition of God as infinite therefore denies man implicitly; while if he be finite, there is an end of the usual Christian reasons for worship, though I daresay I could myself discover some reasonably good ones. [I hardly expect to be asked, somehow.]

The resulting equilibrium of God and man, destructive of worship, is of course absurd. We must reject it, unless we want to fall into Positivism, Materialism, or something of the sort. But if, then, we call God infinite, how are we to regard man, and Satan?

(the latter, at the very least, surely no integral part of him). The fallacy lies not in my demonstration (which is also that of orthodoxy) that a finite God is absurd, but in the assumption that man has any real force.[1]

In our mechanical system (as I have hinted above), if one of the forces be infinite, the others, however great, are both relatively and absolutely nothing.

In any category, infinity excludes finity, unless that finity be an identical part of that infinity.

In the category of existing things; space being infinite, for on that hypothesis we are still working, either matter fills or does not fill it. If the former, matter is infinitely great; if the latter, infinitely small. Whether the matter-universe be 10^{10000} light-years in diameter or half a mile makes no difference; it is infinitely small—in effect, Nothing. The unmathematical illusion that it does exist is what the Hindus call Maya.

If, on the other hand, the matter-universe is infinite, Brahm and God are crowded out, and the possibility of religion is equally excluded.

We may now shift our objective. The Hindus cannot account intelligibly, though they try hard, for Maya, the cause of all suffering. Their position is radically weak, but at least we may say for them that they have tried to square their religion with their common sense. The Christians, on the other hand, though they saw whither, the Manichean Heresy[2] must lead, and crushed it, have not officially admitted the precisely similar conclusion with regard to man, and denied the existence of the human soul as distinct from the divine soul.

Trismegistus, Iamblicus, Porphyry, Boehme, and the mystics generally have of course substantially done so, though occasionally with rather inexplicable reservations, similar to those made in some cases by the Vedantists themselves.

Man then being disproved, God the Person disappears forever, and becomes Atman, Pleroma, Ain Soph, what name you will,

1   Lully, Descartes, Spinoza, Schelling. See their works.
2   The conception of Satan as a positive evil force; the lower triangle of the Hexagram.

infinite in all directions and in all categories—to deny one is to destroy the entire argument and throw us back to our old Dvaitistic bases.

I entirely sympathize with my unhappy friend Rev. Mansel, B.D.,[3] in his piteous and pitiful plaints against the logical results of the Advaitist School. But on his basal hypothesis of an infinite God, infinite space, time, and so on, no other conclusion is possible. Dean Mansel is found in the impossible position of one who will neither give up his premises nor dispute the validity of logical processes, but who shrinks in horror from the inevitable conclusion; he supposes there must be something wrong somewhere, and concludes that the sole use of reason is to discover its own inferiority to faith. As Deussen[4] well points out, faith in the Christian sense merely amounts to being convinced on insufficient grounds.[5] This is surely the last refuge of incompetence.

But though, always on the original hypothesis of the infinity of space, &c., the Advaitist position of the Vedantists and the great Germans is unassailable, yet on practical grounds the Dvaitists have all the advantage. Fichte and others exhaust themselves trying to turn the simple and obvious position that: "If the Ego alone exists, where is any place, not only for morals and religion, which we can very well do without, but for the most essential and continuous acts of life? Why should an infinite Ego fill a non-existent body with imaginary food cooked in thought only over an illusionary fire by a cook who is not there? Why should infinite power use such finite means, and very often fail even then?"

What is the sum total of the Vedantist position? " 'I' am an illusion, externally. In reality, the true 'I' am the Infinite, and if the illusionary 'I' could only realize Who 'I' really am, how very happy we should all be!" And here we have Karma, rebirth, all the mighty laws of nature operating nowhere in nothing!

There is no room for worship or morality in the Advaitist system. All the specious pleas of the Bhagavad-Gita, and the ethical

---

3   *Encyclopedia Britannica.* Art. Metaphysics.

4   "The Elements of Metaphysics."

5   Or as the Sunday-school boy said: "Faith is the power of believing what we know to be untrue." I quote Deussen with the more pleasure, because it is about the only sentence in all his writings with which I am in accord.

works of Western Advaitist philosophers, are more or less consciously confusion of thought. But no subtlety can turn the practical argument; the grinning mouths of the Dvaitist guns keep the fort of Ethics, and warn metaphysics to keep off the rather green grass of religion.

That its apologists should have devoted so much time, thought, scholarship, and ingenuity to this question is the best proof of the fatuity of the Advaitist position.

There is then a flaw somewhere. I boldly take up the glove against all previous wisdom, revert to the most elementary ideas of cannibal savages, challenge all the most vital premises and axiomata that have passed current coin with philosophy for centuries, and present my theory.

I clearly foresee the one difficulty, and will discuss it in advance. If my conclusions on this point are not accepted, we may at once get back to our previous irritable agnosticism, and look for our Messiah elsewhere. But if we can see together on this one point, I think things will go fairly smoothly afterwards.

Consider[6] Darkness! Can we philosophically or actually regard as different the darkness produced by interference of light and that existing in the mere absence of light?

Is Unity really identical with .9 recurring?

Do we not mean different things when we speak respectively of 2 sine 60° and of $\sqrt{3}$?

Charcoal and diamond are obviously different in the categories of colour, crystallisation, hardness, and so on; but are they not really so even in that of existence?

The third example is to my mind the best. 2 sine 60° and of $\sqrt{3}$ are unreal and therefore never conceivable, at least to the present constitution of our human intelligences. Worked out, neither has meaning; unworked, both have meaning, and that a different meaning in one case and the other.

We have thus two terms, both unreal, both inconceivable, yet both representing intelligible and diverse ideas to our minds (and

---

6   Ratiocination may perhaps not take us far. But a continuous and attentive study of these quaint points of distinction may give us an intuition, or direct mind-apperception, of what we want, one way or the other.

this is the point!) though identical in reality and convertible by a process of reason which simulates or replaces that apprehension which we can never (one may suppose) attain to.

Let us apply this idea to the Beginning of all things, about which the Christians lie frankly, the Hindus prevaricate, and the Buddhists are discreetly silent, while not contradicting even the gross and ridiculous accounts of the more fantastic Hindu visionaries.

The Qabalists explain the "First Cause"[7] by the phrase: "From 0 to 1, as the circle opening out into the line." The Christian dogma is really identical, for both conceive of a previous and eternally existing God, though the Qabalists hedge by describing this latent Deity as "Not." Later commentators, notably the illustrious[8] Mac-Gregor-Mathers have explained this Not as "negatively-existing." Profound as is my respect for the intellectual and spiritual attainments of him whom I am proud to have been permitted to call my master,[8] I am bound to express my view that when the Qabalists said Not, they meant Not, and nothing else. In fact, I really do claim to have re-discovered the long-lost and central Arcanum of those divine philosophers.

I have no serious objection to a finite god, or gods, distinct from men and things. In fact, personally, I believe in them all, and admit them to possess inconceivable though not infinite power.

The Buddhists admit the existence of Maha-Brahma, but his power and knowledge are limited; and his agelong day must end. I find evidence everywhere, even in our garbled and mutilated version of the Hebrew Scriptures, that Jehovah's power was limited in all sorts of ways. At the Fall, for instance, Tetragrammaton Elohim has to summon his angels hastily to guard the Tree of Life, lest he should be proved a liar. For had it occurred to Adam to eat of that Tree before their transgression was discovered, or had the Serpent been aware of its properties, Adam would indeed have lived and not died. So that a mere accident saved the remnants of the already besmirched reputation of the Hebrew tribal Fetish.

---

7   An expression they carefully avoid using.
8   I retain this sly joke from the 1st edition.

When Buddha was asked how things came to be, he took refuge in silence, which his disciples very conveniently interpreted as meaning that the question tended not to edification.

I take it that the Buddha (ignorant, doubtless, of algebra) had sufficiently studied philosophy and possessed enough worldly wisdom to be well aware that any system he might promulgate would be instantly attacked and annihilated by the acumen of his numerous and versatile opponents.

Such teaching as he gave on the point may be summed up as follows: "Whence whither, why, we know not; but we do know that we are here, that we dislike being here, that there is a way out of the whole loathsome affair—let us make haste and take it!"

I am not so retiring in disposition; I persist in my inquiries, and at the last the appalling question is answered, and the past ceases to intrude its problems on my mind.

Here you are! Three shies a penny! Change all bad arguments.

I ASSERT THE ABSOLUTENESS OF THE QABALISTIC ZERO.

When we say that the cosmos sprang from the 0, what kind of 0 do we mean? By 0 in the ordinary sense of the term we mean "absence of extension in any of the categories."

When I say "No cat has two tails," I do not mean, as the old fallacy runs, that "Absence-of-cat possesses two tails"; but that "In the category of two-tailed things, there is no extension of cat."

Nothingness is that about which no positive proposition is valid. We cannot truly affirm: "Nothingness is green, or heavy, or sweet."

Let us call time, space, being, heaviness, hunger, the categories.[9] If a man be heavy and hungry, he is extended in all these, besides, of course, many more. But let us suppose that these five are all. Call the man X; his formula is then $X^{t+s+b+h+h}$. If he now eat, he will cease to be extended in hunger; if he be cut off from time and gravitation as well, he will now be represented by the formula X^{s+b}. Should he cease to occupy space and to exist, his formula would then be X^0. This expression is equal to 1; whatever X may represent, if it be raised to the power of 0 (this meaning

---

9   I cannot here discuss the propriety of representing the categories as dimen-
    sions. It will be obvious to any student of the integral calculus, or to anyone
    who appreciates the geometrical signicance of the term x^4.

mathematically "if it be extended in no dimension or category"), the result is Unity, and the unknown factor X is eliminated.

This is the Advaitist idea of the future of man; his personality, bereft of all its qualities, disappears and is lost, while in its place arises the impersonal Unity, The Pleroma, Parabrahma, or the Allah of the Unity-adoring followers of Mohammed. (To the Musulman fakir, Allah is by no means a personal God.)

Unity is thus unaffected, whether or no it be extended in any of the categories. But we have already agreed to look to 0 for the Uncaused.

Now if there was in truth 0 "before the beginning of years," THAT 0 WAS EXTENDED IN NONE OF THE CATEGORIES, FOR THERE COULD HAVE BEEN NO CATEGORIES IN WHICH IT COULD EXTEND! If our 0 was the ordinary 0 of mathematics, there was not truly absolute 0, for 0 is, as I have shown, dependent on the idea of categories. If these existed, then the whole question is merely thrown back; we must reach a state in which the 0 is absolute. Not only must we get rid of all subjects, but of all predicates. By 0 (in mathematics) we really mean 0^n, where n is the final term of a natural scale of dimensions, categories, or predicates. Our Cosmic Egg, then, from which the present universe arose, was Nothingness, extended in no categories, or, graphically, 0^0. This expression is in its present form meaningless. Let us discover its value by a simple mathematical process!

$$0^0 = 0^{1-1} = 0^1/0^1 \text{ [Multiply by } 1 = n/n]$$
$$\text{Then } 0^1/n \times n/0^1 = 0 \times \infty.$$

Now the multiplying of the infinitely great by the infinitely small results in SOME UNKNOWN FINITE NUMBER EXTENDED IN AN UNKNOWN NUMBER OF CATEGORIES. It happened, when this our Great Inversion took place, from the essence of all nothingness to finity extended in innumerable categories, that an incalculably vast system was produced. Merely by chance, chance in the truest sense of the term, we are found with gods, men, stars, planets, devils, colours, forces, and all the materials of the Cosmos:

and with time, space, and causality, the conditions limiting and involving them all.[10]

Remember that it is not true to say that our 0^0 existed; nor that it did not exist. The idea of existence was just as much unformulated as that of toasted cheese.

But 0^0 is a finite expression, or has a finite phase, and our universe is a finite universe; its categories are themselves finite, and the expression "infinite space" is a contradiction in terms. The idea of an absolute and of an infinite[11] God is relegated to the limbo of all similar idle and pernicious perversions of truth. Infinity remains, but only as a mathematical conception as impossible in nature as the square root of -1. Against all this mathematical, or semi-mathematical, reasoning, it may doubtless be objected that our whole system of numbers, and of manipulating them, is merely a series of conventions. When I say that the square root of three is unreal, I know quite well that it is only so in relation to the series 1, 2, 3, &c., and that this series is equally unreal if I make $\sqrt{3}$, π, $\sqrt[3]{50}$ the members of the ternary scale. But this, theoretically true, is practically absurd. If I mean "the number of a, b, and c," it does not matter if I write 3 or $\sqrt[3]{50}$; the idea is a definite one; and it is the fundamental ideas of consciousness of which we are treating, and to which we are compelled to refer everything, whether proximately or ultimately.

So also my equation, fantastic as it may seem, has a perfect and absolute parallel in logic. Thus: let us convert twice the proposition "some books are on the table." By negativing both terms we get "Absence-of-book is not on the table," which is precisely my equation backwards, and a thinkable thing. To reverse the process, what do I mean when I say "some pigs, but not the black pig, are not in the sty"? I imply that the black pig is in the sty. All I have done is to represent the conversion as a change, rather than as merely another way of expressing the same thing. And "change" is

---

10 Compare and contrast this doctrine with that of Herbert Spencer ("First Principles," Pt. I), and see my "Science and Buddhism" for a full discussion of the difference involved.

11 If by "infinitely great" we only mean "indefinitely great," as a mathematician would perhaps tell us, we of course begin at the very point I am aiming at, viz., Écrasez l'Infini.

really not my meaning either; for change, to our minds, involves the idea of time. But the whole thing is inconceivable—to ratiocination, though not to thought. Note well too that if I say "Absence-of-books is not on the table," I cannot convert it into "All books are on the table" but only to "some books are on the table." The proposition is an "I" and not an "A" proposition. It is the Advaita blunder to make it so; and many a schoolboy has fed off the mantelpiece for less.

There is yet another proof—the proof by exclusion. I have shown, and metaphysicians practically admit, the falsity alike of Dvaitism and Advaitism. The third, the only remaining theory, *this* theory, must, however antecedently improbable, however difficult to assimilate, be true.[12]

"My friend, my young friend," I think I hear some Christian cleric say, with an air of profound wisdom, not untinged with pity, condescending to pose beardless and brainless impertinence: "Where is the *Cause* for this truly remarkable change?"

That is exactly where the theory rears to heaven its stoutest bastion! There is not, and could not be, any cause. Had 0^0 been extended in causality, no change could have taken place.[13]

Here, then, are we, finite beings in a finite universe, time, space, and causality themselves finite (inconceivable as it may seem) with our individuality, and all the "illusions" of the Advaitists, just as real as they practically are to our normal consciousness.

As Schopenhauer, following Buddha, points out, suffering is a necessary condition of this existence.[14] The war of the contending forces as they grind themselves down to the final resultant must cause endless agony. We may one day be able to transform the categories of emotion as certainly and easily as we now transform the categories of force, so that in a few years Chicago may be importing suffering in the raw state and turning it into tinned salmon: but at present the reverse process is alone practicable.

---

12 I may remark that the distinction between this theory and the normal one of the Immanence of the Universe, is trivial, perhaps even verbal only. Its advantage, however, is that, by hypostatising nothing, we avoid the necessity of any explanation. "How did nothing come to be?" is a question which requires no answer.

13 See the Questions of King Milinda, vol. ii, p. 103.

14 See also Huxley, "Evolution and Ethics."

How, then, shall we escape? Can we expect the entire universe to resolve itself back into the phase of 0^0? Surely not. In the first place, there is no reason why the whole should do so; x/y is just as convertible as x. But worse, the category of causality has been formed, and its inertia is sufficient to oppose a most serious stumbling-block to so gigantic a process.

The task before us is consequently of a terrible nature. It is easy to let things slide, to grin and bear it in fact, until everything is merged in the ultimate unity, which may or may not be decently tolerable. But while we wait?

There now arises the question of freewill. Causality is probably not fully extended in its own category,[15] a circumstance which gives room for a fractional amount of freewill. If this not be so, it matters little; for if I find myself in a good state, that merely proves that my destiny took me there. We are, as Herbert Spencer observes, self-deluded with the idea of freewill; but if this be so, nothing matters at all. If, however, Herbert Spencer is mistaken (unlikely as it must appear), then our reason is valid, and we should seek out the right path and pursue it. The question therefore not trouble us at all.

Here then we see the use of morals and of religion, and all the rest of the bag of tricks. All these are methods, bad or good, for extricating ourselves from the universe.

Closely connected with this question is that of the will of God. People argue that an Infinite intelligence must have been at work on this cosmos. I reply No! There is no intelligence at work worthy of the name. The Laws of Nature may be generalized in one—the Law of Inertia. Everything moves in the direction determined by the path of least resistance; species arise, develop, and die as their collective inertia determines; to this Law there is no exception but the doubtful one of Freewill; the Law of Destiny itself is formally and really identical with it.[16]

---

15 Causality is itself a secondary, and in its limitation as applied to volition, an inconceivable idea. H. Spencer, *op. cit.* This consideration alone should add great weight to the agnostic, and *à fortiori* to the Buddhist, position.

16 See H. Spencer, "First Principles," "The Knowable," for a fair summary of the facts underlying this generalization; which indeed he comes within an ace of making in so many words. It may be observed that this law is nearly if not quite axiomatic, its contrary being enormously difficult if not impossible to formulate mentally.

As to an *infinite* intelligence, all philosophers of any standing are agreed that all-love and all-power are incompatible. The existence of the universe is a standing proof of this.

The Deist need the Optimist to keep him company; over the firesides all goes well, but it is a sad shipwreck they suffer on emerging into the cold world.

This is why those who seek to buttress up religion are so anxious to prove that the universe has no real existence, or only a temporary and a relatively unimportant one; the result is of course the usual self-destructive Advaitist muddle.

The precepts of morality and religion are thus of use, of vital use to us, in restraining the more violent forces alike of nature and of man. For unless law and order prevail, we have not the necessary quiet and resources for investigating, and learning to bring under our control, all the divergent phenomena of our prison, a work which we undertake that at last we may be able to break down the walls, and find that freedom which an inconsiderate Inversion has denied.

The mystical precepts of pseudo-Zoroaster, Buddha, Çankaracharya, pseudo-Christ and the rest, are for advanced students only, for direct attack on the problem. Our servants, the soldiers, lawyers, all forms of government, make this our nobler work possible, and it is the gravest possible mistake to sneer at these humble but faithful followers of the great minds of the world.

What, then, are the best, easiest, directest methods to attain our result? And how shall we, in mortal language, convey to the minds of others the nature of a result so beyond language, baffling even imagination eagle-pinioned? It may help us if we endeavour to outline the distinction between the Hindu and Buddhist methods and aims of the Great Work.

The Hindu method is really mystical in the truest sense; for, as I have shown, the Atman is not infinite and eternal; one day it must sink down with the other forces. But by creating in thought an infinite Impersonal Personality, by *defining* it as such, all religions except the Buddhist and, as I believe, the Qabalistic, have sought to annihilate their own personality. The Buddhist aims directly at extinction; the Hindu denies and abolishes his own finity by the creation of an absolute.

As this cannot be done in reality, the process is illusory; yet it is useful in the early stages—as far, at any rate, as the fourth stage of Dhyana, where the Buddha places it, though the Yogis claim to attain to Nirvikalpa-Samadhi, and that Moksha is identical with Nirvana; the former claim I see no reason to deny them; the latter statement I must decline at present to accept.

The task of the Buddhist recluse is roughly as follows. He must plunge every particle of his being into one idea: right views, aspirations, word, deed, life, will-power, meditation, rapture, such are the stages of his liberation, which resolves itself into a struggle against the law of causality. He cannot prevent past causes taking effect, but he can prevent present causes from having any future results. The exoteric Christian and Hindu rather rely on another person to do this for them, and are further blinded by the thirst for life and individual existence, the most formidable obstacle of all, in fact a negation of the very object of all religion. Schopenhauer shows that life is assured to the will-to-live, and unless Christ (or Krishna, as the case may be) destroys these folk by superior power —a task from which almightiness might well recoil baffled!—I much fear that eternal life, and consequently eternal suffering, joy, and change of all kinds, will be their melancholy fate. Such persons are in truth their own real enemies. Many of them, however, believing erroneously that they are being "unselfish," do fill their hearts with devotion for the beloved Saviour, and this process is, in its ultimation, so similar to the earlier stages of the Great Work itself, that some confusion has, stupidly enough, arisen; but for all that the practice has been the means of bringing some devotees on the true Path of the Wise, unpromising as such material must sound to intelligent ears.

The esoteric Christian or Hindu adopts a middle path. Having projected the Absolute from his mind, he endeavours to unite his consciousness with that of his Absolute, and of course his personality is destroyed in the process. Yet it is to be feared that such an adept too often starts on the path with the hideous idea of aggrandising his own personality to the utmost. But his method is so near to the true one that this tendency is soon corrected, as it were automatically.

(The mathematical analogue of this process is to procure for yourself the realisation of the nothingness of yourself by keeping the fourth dimension ever present in your mind.)

The illusory nature of this idea of an infinite Atman is well shown by the very proof which that most distinguished Vedantist, the late Swami Vivekananda (no connection with the firm of a similar name[17] across the street), gives of the existence of the infinite. "Think of a circle!" says he. "You will in a moment become conscious of an infinite circle around your original small one." The fallacy is obvious. The big circle is not infinite at all, but is itself limited by the little one. But to take away the little circle, that is the method of the Esoteric Christian or the mystic. But the process is never perfect, because however small the little circle becomes, its relation with the big circle is still finite. But even allowing for a moment that the Absolute is really attainable, is the nothingness of the finity related to it really identical with that attained directly by the Buddhist Arahat? This, consistently with my former attitude, I feel constrained to deny. The consciousness of the Absolute-wala[18] is really extended infinitely rather than diminished infinitely, as he will himself assure you. True, Hegel says: "Pure being is pure nothing!" and it is true that the infinite heat and cold, joy and sorrow, light and darkness, and all the other pairs of opposites,[19] cancel one another out: yet I feel rather afraid of this Absolute! Maybe its joy and sorrow are represented in phases, just as 0^0 and finity are phases of an identical expression, and I have an even chance only of being on the right side of the fence!

The Buddhist leaves no chance of this kind; in all his categories he is infinitely unextended; though the categories themselves exist; he is in fact $0^{A+B+C+D+E+..+N}$ and capable of no conceivable change, unless we imagine Nirvana to be incomprehensibly divided by

17 The Swami Vive Ananda, Madame Horos, for whose history consult the Criminal Law Reports.

18 Wala, one whose business is connected with anything. *E.g.* Jangli-wala, one who lives in, or has business with, a jungle, *i.e.*, a wild man, or a Forest Conservator.

19 The Hindus see this as well as anyone, and call Atman *Sat-chit-ananda*, these being above the pairs of opposites, rather on the Hegelian lines of the re-conciliation (rather than the identity) of opposites in a master-idea. We have dismissed infinity as the figment of a morbid mathematic: but in any case the same disproof applies to it as to God.

Nirvana, which would (supposing the two Nirvanas to possess identical categories) result in the production of the original 0^0. But a further change would be necessary even then before serious mischief could result. In short, I think we may dismiss from our minds any alarm in respect of this contingency.

On mature consideration, therefore, I confidently and deliberately take my refuge in the Triple Gem.

Namo Tasso Bhagavato Arahato Samma-sambuddhasa![20]

Let there be hereafter no discussion of the classical problems of philosophy and religion! In the light of this exposition the antitheses of noumenon and phenomenon, unity and multiplicity, and their kind, are all reconciled, and the only question that remains of that of finding the most satisfactory means of attaining Nirvana—extinction of all that exists, knows, or feels; extinction final and complete, utter and absolute extinction. For by these words only can we indicate Nirvana: a state which transcends thought cannot be described in thought's language. But from the point of view of thought extinction is complete: we have no data for discussing that which is unthinkable, and must decline to do so. This is the answer to those who accuse the Buddha of hurling his Arahats (and himself) from Samma Samadhi to annihilation.

Pray observe in the first place that my solution of the Great Problem permits the co-existence of an indefinite number of means: they need not even be compatible; Karma, rebirth, Providence, prayer, sacrifice, baptism, there is room for all. On the old and, I hope, now finally discredited hypothesis of an infinite being, the supporters of these various ideas, while explicitly affirming them, implicitly denied. Similarly, note that the Qabalistic idea of a supreme God (and innumerable hierarchies) is quite compatible with this theory, provided that the supreme God is not infinite.

Now as to our weapons. The more advanced Yogis of the East, like the Nonconformists at home, have practically abandoned ceremonial as idle. I have yet to learn, however, by what dissenters have replaced it! I take this to be an error, except in the case of the very advanced Yogi. For there exists a true magical ceremonial,

---

20   Hail unto Thee, the Blessed One, the Perfect One, the Enlightened One!

vital and direct, whose purpose has, however, at any rate of recent times, been hopelessly misunderstood.

Nobody any longer supposes that any means but that of meditation is of avail to grasp the immediate causes of our being; if some person retort that he prefers to rely on a Glorified Redeemer, I simply answer that he is the very nobody to whom I now refer.

Meditation is then the means; but only the supreme means. The agony column of the *Times* is the supreme means of meeting with the gentleman in the brown billycock and frock coat, wearing a green tie and chewing a straw, who was at the soirée of the Carlton Club last Monday night; no doubt! but this means is seldom or never used in the similar contingency of a cow-elephant desiring her bull in the jungles of Ceylon.

Meditation is not within the reach of every one; not all possess the ability; very few indeed (in the West at least) have the opportunity.

In any case what the Eastern calls "one-pointedness" is an essential preliminary to even early stages of true meditation. And iron will-power is a still earlier qualification.

By meditation I do not mean merely "thinking about" anything, however profoundly, but the absolute restraint of the mind to the contemplation of a single object, whether gross, fine, or altogether spiritual.

Now true magical ceremonial is entirely directed to attain this end, and forms a magnificent gymnasium for those who are not already finished mental athletes. By act, word, and thought, both in quantity and quality, the one object of the ceremony is being constantly indicated. Every fumigation, purification, banishing, invocation, evocation, is chiefly a reminder of the single purpose, until the supreme moment arrives, and every fibre of the body, every force-channel of the mind, is strained out in one over-whelming rush of the Will in the direction desired. Such is the real purport of all the apparently fantastic directions of Solomon, Abramelin, and other sages of repute. When a man has evoked and mastered such forces as Taphtatharath, Belial, Amaimon, and the great powers of the elements, then he may safely be permitted to begin to try to stop thinking. For, needless to say, the universe, including the thinker, exists only by virtue of the thinker's thought.[21]

In yet one other way is magic a capital training ground for the Arahat. True symbols do really awake those macrocosmic forces of which they are the eidola, and it is possible in this manner very largely to increase the magical "potential," to borrow a term from electrical science.

Of course, there are bad and invalid processes, which tend rather to dispense or to excite the mind-stuff than to control it; these we must discard. But there is a true magical ceremonial, the central Arcanum alike of Eastern and Western practical transcendentalism. Needless to observe, if I knew it, I should not disclose it.

I therefore definitely affirm the validity of the Qabalistic tradition in its practical part as well as in those exalted regions of thought through which we have so recently, and so hardly, travelled.

Eight are the limbs of Yoga: morality and virtue, control of body, thought, and force, leading to concentration, meditation, and rapture.

Only when the last of these has been attained, and itself refined upon by removing the gross and even the fine objects of its sphere, can the causes, subtle and coarse, the unborn causes whose seed is hardly sown, of continued existence be grasped and annihilated, so that the Arahat is sure of being abolished in the utter extinction of Nirvana, while even the world of pain, where he must remain until the ancient causes, those which have already germinated, are utterly worked out (for even the Buddha himself could not swing back the Wheel of the Law), his certain anticipation of the approach of Nirvana is so intense as to bathe him constantly in the unfathomable ocean of the apprehension of immediate bliss.

AUM MANI PADME HOUM.

---

21 See Berkeley and his expounders, for the Western shape of this Eastern commonplace. Huxley, however, curiously enough, states the fact almost in these words.

NOTE.

A possible mystic transfiguration of the Vedanta system has been suggested to me on the lines of the Syllogism—

God   = Being (Patanjali).
Being = Nothing (Hegel).
∴ God   = Nothing (Buddhism).

Or, in the language of religion:

Every one may admit that monotheism, exalted by the introduction of the ∞ symbol, is equivalent to pantheism. Pantheism and atheism are really identical, as the opponents of both are the first to admit.

If this be really taught, I must tender my apologies, for the reconcilement is of course complete.—A. C.

A NOTE ON GENESIS
FROM THE PAPER WRITTEN
BY THE
V. H. Fra. I.A. 5 = 6

PREFATORY NOTE

THE following Essay is one of the most remarkable studies in the Hebrew Qabalah known to me.

Its venerable author was an adept familiar with many systems of symbolism, and able to harmonise them for himself, even as now is accomplished for all men in the Book 777.

In the year 1899 he was graciously pleased to receive me as his pupil, and, living in his house, I studied daily under his guidance the Holy Qabalah. Upon his withdrawal—whether to enjoy his Earned Reward, or to perform the Work of the Brotherhood in other lands or planets matters nothing here—he bequeathed to me a beautiful Garden, the like of which hath rarely been seen upon Earth.

It has been my pious duty to collate and comment upon this arcane knowledge, long treasured in my heart, watered alike by my tears and my blood, and sunned by that all-glorious Ray that multiplieth itself into an Orb ineffable.

In this Garden no flower was fairer than this exquisite discourse; I beg my readers to pluck it and lay it in their hearts.

It should be studied in connection with the Book 777, and with the Sepher Sephiroth, a magical dictionary of pure number which was begun by the author of this essay, carried on by myself, and now about to be published as soon as the MS. can be prepared.

The reader who is at all familiar with the sublime computations of the Qabalah will find no difficulty in appreciating this Essay to

1

the full; but all will gain benefit from the study of the ratiocinative methods employed. These methods, indeed, are so fine and subtile that they readily sublime into the Intuitive. This study is truly a Royal Magistry, an easy and sure means of exalting the consciousness from Ruach to Neschamah.

PART I

IN the First Verse of the First Chapter of the First Five Books of the Holy Law: it is written:—B'RAShITh Ba RA ALoHIM ATh HaShaMaIM VaATH HaAReTz, or in Aramaic script

בראשית ברא אלהים את השמים ואת הארץ

Such are the Seven Words which constitute the Beginnings or Heads of One Law; and I propose to show, by applying to the Text the Keys of the Qabalah, that not merely the surface meaning is contained therein.

In the Beginning, created, God, the Essence of the Heavens, and the Essence, of the Earth.

In the Beginning		God		
In Wisdom	Created	The Elohim	the Essence[2]	of the
In the Head[1]		The Holy Gods		Heavens

and the Essence { of the Earth

Contained therein also are the Divine, Magical, and Terrestrial Formulæ of the Passage of the Incomprehensible Nothingness of the Ain Soph to the Perfection of Creation expressed by the Ten Voices or Emanations of God the Vast One—Blessed be He!—even the Holy Sephiroth.

And the Method whereby I shall work shall be the One Absolute and inerratic Science: the Science of Number: which is that single Mystery of the Intellect of Man whereby he

---

1   *I.e.*, the White Skull. *Vide* Idra Zutra Qadisha, cap. ii. Distinguish from the skull of Microprosophus.

2   אח = the First and Last—Alpha and Omega—Aleph and Tau.

2

becometh exalted unto the Throne of Inflexible and Unerring Godhead.

As it is written, "Oh, how the World hath Inflexible Intellectual Rulers" (Zoroaster).

But before I may proceed unto the Qabalistical[3] enumeration and analysis of the Text, a certain preamble in the fruitful fields of that Science will become necessary. The Evolution of the Numbers is the Evolution of the Worlds, for as it is written in the Clavicula Salomonis, "The Numbers are Ideas; and the Ideas are the Powers, and the Powers are the Holy Elohim of Life." That which is behind and beyond all Number and all thought (even as the Ain Soph with its Mighty Veils depending back from Kether is behind and beyond all Manifestation) is the Number 0. Its symbol is the very Emblem of Infinite Space and Infinite Time.[4] Multiply by it any active and manifested number; and that number vanishes—sinks into the Ocean of Eternity. So also is the Ain Soph. From It proceed all Things: unto It all will return, when the Age of Brahman is over and done, and the day of Peace-Be-with-Us is declared by Thoth, the Great God, and the Material Universe sinketh into Infinity.

The first Number, then, is ONE; emblem of the All-Father; the Unmanifest Mind behind all Manifestation: the First Mind. Multiply by It any other Number—for the Multiplication of the Numbers is a Generation, as is the Multiplication of Men and Gods—and behold! the *Resultant* is a replica of the Number taken. So is One the All-Father, the All-begetter— generating and producing all.

The next step is the division into TWO. Thus was manifested the Great Dual Power of Nature. As above, so

---

3   Here used in its true meaning of "the marshalling forth by number." Qabalah, קבלה, by Tarot, "The Mystery shown forth in balanced disposition by Command."

4   "Hidden behind my Magic Veil of Shows,
    I am not seen at all—Name not my Name."

below. And thus we find that the simple division into two is the method of multiplication of the Amœba, the lowest, simplest, and most absolute form of physical life that we know.

The Dual Power of Nature is the Great Mother of the Worlds.

Again, to draw an analogy from the Material World, consider the Moon, our Mother. Behold in her the Typic representative of the Powers of the Two. Light and Darkness, Flux and Reflux, Ebb and Flow—these are her manifested Powers in Nature—where also she binds the *Great Waters* to her Will.

Now in the Yetziratic Attribution is the second number, Beth (*i.e.*, a House), an Abode, the Dwelling of the Holy One, shown to be equivalent to the Sphere of Kokab and his lords. And the symbolic weapon of ☿ is the Caduceus, whose Twin Serpents show again the Dualistic Power. (*Note.*—Woden, the Scandinavian Mercury, was the All-Father, as it is written in the Ritual of the Path of the Spirit of the Primal Fire ש. "For all things did the Father of All Things perfect, and delivered them over unto the *Second Mind; whom all Races of Men call First.*") Behold, then, in these two great Numbers 1 and 2 the Father and the Mother of the Worlds and of Numbers.

Now these twain being Conjoined and manifest in ONE, produce the Number 3; as it is written: "For the Mind of the Father said that 'All Things should be cut into Three,' Whose Will[5] assenting All Things were so divided. For the Mind of the Father said *Into three,* governing All Things by Mind. And there appeared in it the Triad, Virtue and Wisdom and Multiscient Truth." Thus floweth forth the form of the Triad.[6] Thus is formulated the Creative Trinity which is, as it were, the essential preliminary to Manifestation.

---

5   ב, the Magus of Power in Taro = Will.

6   Ritual of the Path of the Daughter of the Firmament.

This Mystic Son of the Eternal Parents, having for his number 3, is typified in all the sacred scripts by that number. Thus it is written of the manifestation of the Son of God upon the Earth, "Shiloh shall come" (the initial of which Mystery-Name is ש = 300). And in the Grecian tongue it is written: "In the beginning was the *Word*," &c., which is λόγος (λ = 30). But the best of all the Examples is found in the Holy Tetragram יהוה. For we may regard this venerable name as typical of the Father and the Mother, and so divided into וה and יה.[7] Now if into the midst of this divided Name we cast the triple fire of the Holy letter ש = 300, we get the name of the Godhead Incarnate upon Earth, יהשוה. But 1 + 2 + 3 = 6, which is the number of ו, the third letter of the Venerable Name: Microprosopus and the Son of God.

We are now, therefore, arrived at the Great Mystery of the Tetractys, and to go further we must resort to the Twin Sister of the Science of Number—which, indeed, is but Number made Flesh: Geometry, or Absolute Symbolism. Even as it was spoken by the holy Pythagoras: "God geometrises."

Let us behold the Work of His Fingers!

---

7   For it is written (Genesis v. 1, 2):
:ברא אלהים אדם בדמות אלהים עשה אתו קבר ונקבה בראם
"And the Elohim created Mankind: in the Likeness of the Elohim created they them: Male and Female created they them." Now if ADAM be in the similitude of the Elohim: and are male and female, then must the Elohim be also male and female. Now in the first of those mysterious three verses in Exodus xiv. wherein the divided name is hidden it is written, "and went the Angel of the Elohim before the Camp," &c. And this Angel of the Elohim, מלאך אלהים, is the Manifestations of their presence. Now מלאך hath the numeration 91, which also is the number of יהוה אדני, wherefore by Gematria "Tetragrammaton our Lord" is the Angel of the Elohim of the Divided Name. Therefore is the Tetragrammaton symbolic of the Manifested Presence of the Elohim; and if the Elohim be Male and Female, so also must be the Tetragram. Also is the number of אמן (also 91) by Aiq Bekar 1 + 4 + 5 = 10—the Perfection of the Sephiroth.

One Son Incomprehensible.

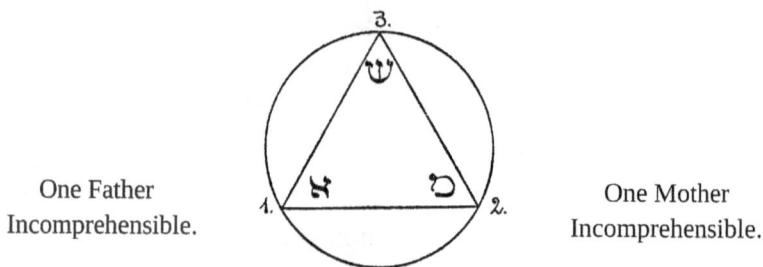

One Father
Incomprehensible.

One Mother
Incomprehensible.

FIG. I.—THE TRINITY UNMANIFEST.

One Son Eternal.

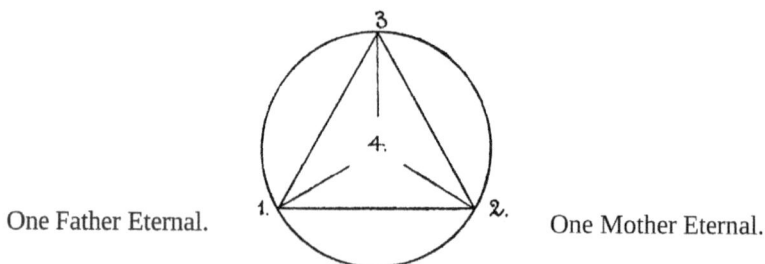

One Father Eternal.

One Mother Eternal.

FIG. II.—THE TRINITY IN MANIFESTATION.

In both of these Symbols the all-including circle represents the underlying idea of the Number 0: the Infinite: Parabrahman: the Ain Soph. In the first is shown the Mystic Trinity before manifestation; as it were unlimited, unbound, and unbounded, inoperative because of its diffusiveness and dispersion. In the second figure we behold their concentration: focalisation: producing by their joint action the number of manifestation—4. In the worlds—Assiah: in the Taro, the Princess—the throne of the Spirit: in the Tetragram, the Hé final, and in symbolic language—the Daughter: in the Cycle of Life (Birth, Life, Death, Resurrection), the forth; in the Keys of the Book Universal, the Empress, Κορη Κοσμου, the Virgin of the World, Venus, Aphrodite: Centrum in Trigonis Centri—by whatsoever of a myriad names we call Her, still the same in Spirit, the same in Number and in form! And this number is herein formulated by the Concentration of the Three in One. 3 + 1 = 4. Now in this Figure II. we behold six certain Paths; and in six days did God create the Heavens and the Earth. And the total numeration of its numbers is the Perfect Number, even the Decade of the Sephiroth. (1 + 2 + 3 + 4 = 10.)

Thus can our Science teach us wherefore the Door[8] of ♀, ר, is the Gateway of Initiation: that one planet whose symbol alone embraceth the 10 Sephiroth; the Entrance to the Shrine of our Father C.R.C., the Tomb of Osiris; the God Revealer, coming, moreover, by the Central Path of ס through the midst of the Triangle of Light. And the Lock which guards that Door is as the Four Gates of the Universe. And the Key is The Ankh, Immortal Life—the Rose and Cross of Life; and the Symbol of Venus ♀.

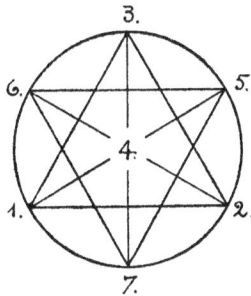

FIG. III. THIRD SYMBOL.

By producing the Paths whereby the Forces of the Three (*see* Second Symbol) were concentred into four, we find they read 1 + 4 = 5, 2 + 4 = 6, 3 + 4 = 7. And thus is revealed the Second Triangle of the Hexagram of Creation.[9]

8 As above, so below; wherefore saith the Holy Qabalah that alone amongst the Shells is Nogah, the Sphere of Venus, exalted unto Holiness. (Venus is the Goddess of Love.)

9 As it is written in the Path of the Child of the Sons of the Mighty: "And the Chaos cried aloud for the unity of Form and the Face of the Eternal arose. ... That Brow and those Eyes formed the △ of the Measureless Heavens: and their Reflection formed the ▽ of the measureless Waters. And thus was formulated One Eternal Hexad: and this is the Number of the Dawning Creation."

Further, this Reflected Triangle showeth forth the evolution of the four Worlds and their Consolidation: for

$1 + 2 + 3 + 4 = $ י $=$ Atziluth

$1 + 2 + 3 + 4 + 5 = 15 = $ יה $=$ Briah

$1 + 2 + 3 + 4 + 5 + 6 = 21 = $ יהו $=$ Yetzirah

$1 + 2 + 3 + 4 + 5 + 6 + 7^{10} = 28 = 2 + 8 = 10$ Assiah

The Number 28, the total numeration, therefore represents Malkuth, the Tenth Sephira: Assiah made manifest—the Work of Creation accomplished: wherefore God rested on the *Seventh* Day. And 28 is 7 × 4, the seven stars shining throughout the four Worlds.

One thing is significant, indeed. Let us take the Primal Three and convert those Numbers into Colours. So we get א, the Father, the Yellow Ray of the Dawning Sun of Creation; מ, the Mother, the Blue Ray of the Great Primaeval Waters; ש, the Son, the Red Ray: the Ruach Elohim,[11] symbol of the Red Fire of God, which brooded (v. 2) upon the Face of the Waters: or like the Red Glory that lights up the Heavens at Dawn, when the Golden Sun illumines the Waters above the Firmament. Now this Red Glory is the IGNIS DEI: which is also the AGNUS DEI, or Lamb of God that destroyeth (literally *burns out*) the Sins of the World. As it is written in the Ordinary of the Mass: the Priest goeth unto the South of the Altar and prays: "O Agnus Dei! qui tollis—qui tollis Peccata Mundi—Dona Nobis Pacem!" And this Fire, this Lamb of God, is *Aries*, Symbol of the Dawning Year: whose colour also is as the Red Fire, and which is the head of the Fiery Triplicity in the Zodiac. So also in the Grade of Neophyte in the Order of the Golden Dawn the Hierophant weareth a robe of flame-scarlet as symbolic of the Dawn.

---

10   But herein is the Fall, that there were only six numbers, so that for the seventh was 5 repeated. Hence $1 + 2 + 3 + 4 + 5 + 6 + 5 = 26$ יהוה. Assiah; Tetragrammaton as the Elemental Limitation, the Jealous God.—P.

11   Remember that the numeration of the Name רוח אלהים is 300 = ש.

NOTE.—It may be objected to this enunciation of the colours that ', the Father, is Fire; that ה, the Mother, is Water; that ו, the Son, is Air, and Yellow instead of Red. This also is true, but it relates to the governance of the Elemental Kingdoms, which are in the Astral Worlds, and whose monads are on the descending arc of Life, whilst Man is on the Ascending; that scale is therefore inverted. For by the mighty sacrifice of the Man Made Flesh and by His Torturous Pilgrimage is evolved that Glorified Son Who is Greater than His Father. In Alchemy we have again the descending arc, for we find that the *red* powder cast upon the Water of the Metals produceth the Golden Sol. But it is important not to confuse. The Christians have terribly muddled their Trinity by making the Son the second instead of the third Principle; whilst with them the Holy Spirit at one Time symbolises the Mother and at another the Son.

Thus at the Annunciation and at the Baptism of the Christ the S.S. appeareth as a Dove, emblem of ♀ and the Mother: whilst the S.S. that descended upon the Apostles at Pentecost was in reality the Spirit of the Christ, and therefore symbolised by the ש (*see* Lecture on Microcosmos in MSS. of R.R. et A.C.).

In Theosophical nomenclature this latter was the M anas or Jeheshuah: the third Principle.

For the same reason I have drawn the triangle with the 3 uppermost instead of it.

PART II

IT was necessary that I should go thus somewhat at length into this Mystery of the Opening of the Numbers, because without this explanation much of the meaning of the verse must necessarily remain obscure.

Now let us consider this most Mystic Verse!

The first thing that strikes us is that it contains *Seven Words*: the Second that the number of its letters is *twenty-eight*. Thus does it perfectly symbolise in its entirety the third Symbol in the numerical evolution.

Before proceeding to a detailed analysis, and following the Process of Creation by Time (*i.e.*, beginning at the first letter, and so proceeding), let me point out a few general facts. First as to the number of letters in each word, which converted into figures stands thus: 4. 3. 5. 2. 5. 3. 6. (Hebrew direction).

In the midst is 2, by Taro the Central Will: and this two-lettered word is שת. On either side of this is the pair of figures 35—53, balanced one against the other: as though symbolic of the great dawning of life of the Mothers—ה and ת, vitalised by the SON (3) as the Vice-Gerent of His Father.

These balanced figures together make 16, whereof the Key is 7; the total number of letters in the third Symbol. Then we have left at either end 4 and 6 = 10,[12] the perfection of the Sephiroth, as if to declare that this verse from, beginning to end thereof reflected the Voices from Kether even unto Malkuth: and 6 − 4 = 2 again, the Central Will, ב, Thoth, in the Heart of the Universe (as in the centre of the verse). Note, then, this perfect equilibrium of the verse, and remember that Mystery—that equilibrium is strength.

Let us now look at the letters themselves. Counting them, we find that the two central ones are מא, the Supernal Mother; even as the number of letters had the dual symbol in their midst. Now their numeration is 41, yielding by Gematria איל = Force: Might: Power: גאואל, Divine Majesty: and אחלב = Fecundity, all symbolic of the attributes of the Dual Polar Force and Mother. Moreover, 4 + 1 = 5 = ה, Mother Supernal once again—and in its geometric symbol the Pentagram—the Star

---

12 *Vide* Sepher Yetzirah for this division of the Holy Sephiroth into a Hexad and a Tetrad.

of Unconquered Will. Add the next two letters on either side, and we get יסאת, or a concealed Tetragrammaton.

And this also reads י, the Great Sea, את, Alpha and Omega, or Essence. Add the next two, so that the six central letters are obtained; and we read הימסאתה, which signifies הים, swollen, extended, or expanded; and hence *Thou* (*i.e.*, God, Ateh, the All) *in extension*. But by Metathesis of these six letters is obtained אמת היה = "Truth Was," as if affirming solemnly the presence in the Creation of the Supernal Truth.

Now let us take the first and last letters of the verse and "cast into the midst thereof the Fire of the Sun"—*i.e.*, ו (6), "the Seal of Creation"—and we have בוץ, an Egg. Where we see the whole universe enclosed in the Cosmic Egg of Hindu and Egyptian Mythology: and the Formulation of the Sphere of the Universe (or Magical Mirror in Man). As it were the Egg of the Black Swan of Time, the Kâlâ Hâmsâ, the Triune $_A M_U$, or word of Power or of Seb, the Bird of Life, whose will was heard in the Night of Time.

The total numeric value of the verse is דתגט = 4459, of which the Key is 22, the number of the Paths from א to ת; and the Key of 22 is 4, the Tetractys and the Threshold of the Universe.

Now to proceed to what I have termed the Time Process, the first Word of the Law then is בראשית. Now in the Hebrew Scriptures the first word of a Book is also its Title. Thus Genesis is called by the Rabbins "B'rasheth," or "In the Beginning," wherefore we may regard this Word as not the first word—albeit that is shadowed forth therein—but as the seal and title and Key of the whole book. Holding this in mind, let us proceed to analyse it. The number of its letters is six, the Seal of Creation, and their total numeric value is 2911.

11

2911 = 13 = Death, the Transformer[13]—the distinct formulation of the Three in One, uniting once more to produce the 4.

Now Beth primarily signifieth a House or Abode, and in Taro it is ☿, the Magus—the Vox Dei—and Thoth, the Recorder. Coalesce these two ideas and we get ב.

"This is the Magical History."

ר signifieth the Head or Beginning of Time and Things; and by Taro it is glory, Life, Light, Sun. Thus read:

"Of the Dawning of Life and Light."

א is by shape the Svastika, symbolically Aleph, the Ox, as though showing the fearful force of the Spiritual "Whirling Motions" upon the Material Plane, as a terrible and destructive Power. This is also shown by the Foolish Man, as the Material Tarotic emblem of that which in its proper and higher manifestation is the Spiritual Ether. Therefore we read:

"Begun are the Whirling Motions."

ש signifieth mighty in flame, whereof it is also the Hieroglyph. It is that Ruach Elohim brooding upon the Face of the Waters. So read:

"Formulated is the Primal Fire."

י is the Hand,[14] symbolising Power in Action, and its Taro Key is the Hermit and the Voice of Light, the Prophet of the Gods. Thus:

"Proclaimed is the Reign of the Gods of Light."

---

13 As it is written: "Thy youth shall be renewed as the Eagle's." Now the Eagle is נ. For further consideration of this 13, *vide* in the Portal Ritual the explanation of that terrible Key. *See* account of this ritual in "The Temple."
    Also, 13 is the numeration of אחד = Unity, as also is the Great Name of God, אל, by Aiq Bekar or Temurah.

14 The Hand of God, always the Symbol of His Power.

ת is the last letter of the Alphabet, the *finis*, the Omega, the Universe, Saturn, the outermost Planet, and it is also תרעא, Throa, the Gate of the Universe; and by Qabalah of nine Chambers it is ד, the Gateway of Initiation. Hence:

"At the Threshold of the Universe."

So the Whole Word reads:

ב   This is the Magical History
ר   Of the Dawning of the Light.
א   Begun are the Whirling Motions;
ש   Formulated is the Primal Fire;
י   Proclaimed is the Reign of the Gods of Light
ת   At the Threshold of the Infinite Worlds!

Now compare this with the Particular Exordium (G∴ D∴ MSS. Z3):

ב
   ⎧ At the ending of the NIGHT
   ⎨ At the Limits of the LIGHT
   ⎪ Thoth stood before the Unborn Ones of Time.
   ⎩ Then was formulated the Universe.

ר
   ⎰ Then came forth the Gods thereof,
   ⎱ The Æons of the Bornless Beyond.

א[15] Then was the Voice Vibrated.

ש[16] Then was the Name declared.

ת
   ⎰ At the Threshold of Entrance,
   ⎱ Betwixt the Universe and the Infinite,

י
   ⎰ In the Sign of the Enterer: Stood Thoth
   ⎱ As before Him the Æons were proclaimed.

---

15   Remember in the description of the "Caduceus" (*see* p. 269) the Air Symbol vibrating between them. [Also י, ♍, is a Mercurial sign, and Thoth is Mercury, though on a Higher Plane. The Hermit, with his Lamp and Wand, is Hermes, who guides the souls of the dead, in the Greek Ritual of 0 = 0.—P.]

16   The Name שם, the Spirit of God, second Deity-Name in the Law, the Trigrammaton, or Threefold Name, by which the Universe came forth.

The positions of the last two letters of the Word have been relatively changed, so as to render the meaning more harmoniously.

We will now proceed to the first word of the text as thus decapitated, taking B'rasheth as the Title rather than as the first Word. This latter stands ברא, which hath three Letters, symbolising thereby the Unmanifest Trinity.

Now its letters further exemplify the Trinity, for that they are the initials of three Hebrew words, which are the Names of the Persons thereof, viz:

בן   Ben, the Son.

בוח   Ruach, the Spirit (here the Mother).

אב   Ab, the Father.

Note how here again the Son is first for Humanity and the Father last. These three letters, then, symbolise the three in One Unmanifest. Yet is there in them the All-potency of Life. For 2 + 2 + 1 = 5, the Symbol of Power, Mother Supernal, and ה also is ♈, Lamb of God and Dawn of the Life of the Year.

Wherefore in them lieth concealed and hidden, not alone the Divine White Brilliance of the Three Supernals (הוא, וקדוש, רברו), but even also that Gleaming Glory which partaketh of the Redness, and which cometh from the Bornless Age, which is beyond Kether. As it is written in Ancient Hindu Scripture, "In the beginning Desire, TĂNHĂ, arose in It: which was the Primal Germ of Mind." Now in the Aryan Mythology Tănhă, Desire, was the God of Love, Kâmâ; whereof the symbolic tint was Pink: as it were the first pink blush of Dawn in the Macrocosmic Sky: Herald of the Rising Sun of the Worlds, when the Great Night of Brăhmă was over and done.

The next word in the Great Name of God the Vast One: אלהים. Let us meditate upon its Mystery! Herein behold five Letters: In its Centre is the Great Letter ה, Mother Supernal.

Five once more; and its first and last letters are once again אם, 41, the Mother, and 5, the Maternal Essence. And its numeration is 86, whereof the Key is 14, whereof the Key is 5. Wherefore we say that this great name is 5 in its form symbolic. 5 in the Heart of its Power: the Beginning and the End thereof are 5; and 5 is it in its Venerable Essence!

Turn now back unto the third Symbol; gaze at it steadily for a few moments, and see hidden in the Six-fold Seal of Creation the Five-fold Star of Unconquered Will.

For this was the Divine Force which created the worlds! Power Eternal, Power Resistless, Power All-dominating, in its Absolute Supremacy—gleaming as the Great Name Elohim in the Heart of the Six-fold star! Flaming as the Purifying Fire, purging and ordering the Chaos of the Night of Time!

As in the midst of the Letters of the Verse we saw the words אתה הים, "Thou in Extension," so also does the Name Elohim read אל, "Deity," הים, in Extension.[17]

And the numeration of Elohim is 86, which by Gematria reads פאה, again meaning "spread out, extended."

Write the letters of this Name in any Invoking Pentagram; and the Banishing Pentagram thereof will read 3.1415 (by Qabalah of nine Chambers), which is the Formula of the Proportion of diameter to circumference of the Circle.[18] Thus herein do we perceive the Hidden Power of the Three extended as a Mighty Sphere to the Confines of Space!

---

17 And אל =לא, No, the Negative.

18 The nearest computation to four places of decimals is 3.1416 (3.14159). But 3.1415 is good enough for the benighted Hebrews.—P.

   In the sublime Computations of the Qabalah the Final Forms of letters have no increased numerical value. Mem is 40, whether final or not. The Ancient Hebrew Method of obtaining all numbers above 400 and below 1000, respectively ת and א, was to make up the number with the proper letters. Thus 500 would have been written תק, not ך, and 800 תת, and so on. [Yet in some few Arcana the Finals are counted as such. This mystery, however, pertaineth to a Grade even more exalted than our beloved and erudite Brother had attained at the period of this Essay.—P.]

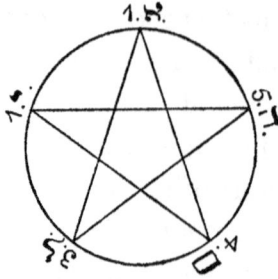

The next word is את, which we have seen to be the Central word: and its signification is the Alpha and Omega—From Beginning unto End: Essence: and its Key is 5.

Five again are the letters of the word השמים,[19] which next follows; and in this word שמים, the Heavens, we perceive ש[20] the Ruach Elohim, brooding upon the Face of the Waters, מים (Maim), even as it is afterwards set forth in Verse 2.

In the next word, ואת, we find that the Conjunctive ו makes of the Key number of the Essence of the Earth 11 instead of 5: symbolising how the World should fall unto the Kingdom of the Shells, and how it should be redeemed by the Son of Man.[21]

And finally the word הארץ, Ha Aretz, the Earth, hath four Letters showing its Elemental Constitution, and its Key is 17 —also Hope—Hope in the Earth as there is Hope in Heaven. And the last letter of the verse is ץ (the letter of Hope), by Qabalah of Nine Chambers that number which contains in itself all the properties of Protean Matters: howsoever you

---

19 Whose Key number is 17: by Taro—Hope; whose title is Daughter of the Firmament, dweller between the Waters.

20 The initial ה is but the article "the."

21 For 11 is the Number of the Qliphoth; but when the Fall had occurred and the Sephira Malkuth had been cut off from the Tree by the folds of the Dragon there was added unto the Tree דעת, the Knowledge, as the 11th Sephira, to preserve intact the Ten-ness of the Sephiroth. Showing how by that very eating of the Fruit of the Tree of Knowledge of Good and of Evil should come the Saving of Mankind; for Daäth is the Priceless Gift of Knowledge and Intellect whereby cometh Salvation. Wherefore also is 11 the Key Number of the Great Saviour's Name (יהשוה = 29 = 11), and this is also in the Taro the Wheel of the Great Law, כ, the Lord of the Forces of Life.

may multiply it the Key of its Numbers is ever 9. Fitting Symbol of ever-changing matter which ever in its essence is One—one and alone!

Thus with the first appearance of the number of Matter does the first verse of B'rasheth close: formulating in itself the Beginning and the End of the Great Creation.

"The Characters of Heaven with Thy Finger hast thou traced: But none can read them save he hath been taught in Thy School."

Wherefore closing do I name the Mighty Words:

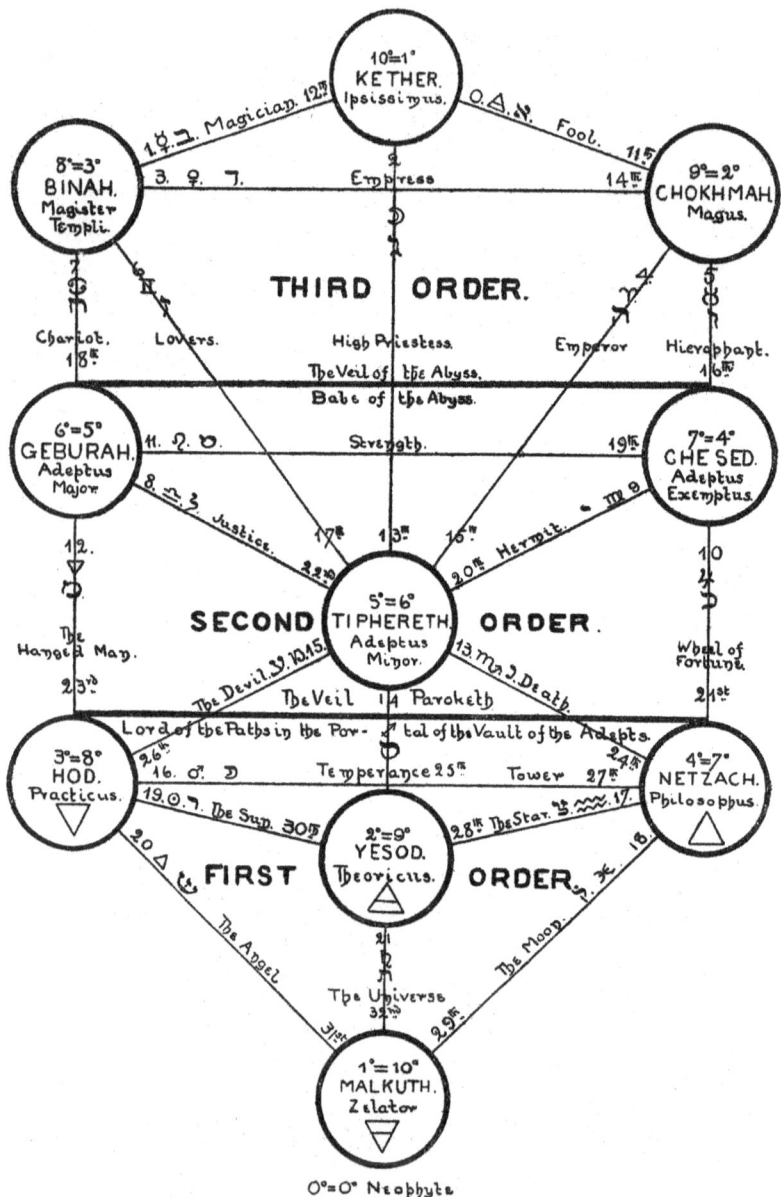

THE PATHS AND GRADES, from *The Temple of Solomon the King*,
Part II. Part V originally reproduced cols. i., ii., iii., vi., vii.,
x., liv., lv., lxiii., lxiv., lxv., lxvii., lxxvii., xcvii., xcviii., clxxv.,
clxxvi. and clxxix. from Liber DCCLXXVII (pp. 178–9, 192–3,
195, 197 and 211 in the present volume).

LIBER LVIII

(THE TEMPLE OF SOLOMON THE KING, Part V)

GREAT as were Frater P.'s accomplishments in the ancient sciences of the East, swiftly and securely as he had passed in a bare year the arduous road which so many fail to traverse in a lifetime, satisfied as himself was—in a sense—with his own progress, it was yet not by these paths that he was destined to reach the Sublime Threshold of the Mystic Temple. For thought it is written, "To the persevering mortal the blessed immortals are swift," yet, were it otherwise, no mortal however persevering could attain the immortal shore. As it is written in the Fifteenth Chapter of St Luke's Gospel, "And when he was yet afar off, his Father saw him and ran." Had it not been so, the weary Prodigal, exhausted by his early debauches (astral visions and magic) and his later mental toil (yoga) would never have had the strength to reach the House of his Father.

One little point St Luke unaccountably omitted. When a man is as hungry and weary as was the Prodigal, he is apt to see phantoms. He is apt to clasp shadows to him, and cry: "Father!" And, the devil being subtle, capable of disguising himself as an angel of light, it behoves the Prodigal to have some test of truth.

Some great mystics have laid down the law, "Accept no messenger of God," banish all, until at last the Father himself comes forth. A counsel of perfection. The Father does send messengers, as we learn in St Mark xii.; and if we stone them, we may perhaps in our blindness stone the Son himself when he is sent.

So that is no vain counsel of "St John" (I John iv. 1), "Try the spirits, whether they be of God," no mistake when "St Paul" claims the discernment of Spirits to be a principal point of the armour of salvation (I Cor. xii. 10).

Now how should Frater P. or another test the truth of any message purporting to come from the Most High? On the astral plane, its phantoms are easily governed by the Pentagram, the Elemental Weapons, the Robes, the God-forms, and such childish toys. We set phantoms to chase phantoms. We make our Scin-Laeca pure and hard and glittering, all glorious within, like the veritable daughter of the King; yet she is but the King's daughter, the Nephesch adorned: she is not the King himself, the Holy Ruach or mind of man. And as we have seen in our chapter on Yoga, this mind is a very aspen; and as we may see in the last chapter of Captain Fuller's "Star in the West," this mind is a very cockpit of contradiction.

What then is the standard of truth? What tests shall we apply to revelation, when our tests of experience are found wanting? If I must doubt my eyes that have served me (well, on the whole) for so many years, must I not much more doubt my spiritual vision, my vision just open like a babe's, my vision untested by comparison and uncriticized by reason?

Fortunately, there is one science that can aid us, a science that, properly understood by the initiated mind, is as absolute as mathematics, more self-supporting than philosophy, a science of the spirit itself, whose teacher is God, whose method is simple as the divine Light, and subtle as the divine Fire, Whose results are limpid as the divine Water, all-embracing as the divine Air, and solid as the divine Earth.

Truth is the source, and Economy the course, of that marvellous stream that pours its living waters into the Ocean of apodeictic certainty, the Truth that is infinite in its infinity as the primal Truth with which it is identical is infinite in its Unity.

Need we say that we speak of the Holy Qabalah? O science secret, subtle, and sublime, who shall name thee without veneration, without prostration of soul, spirit, and body before thy divine Author, without exaltation of soul, spirit, and body as by His favour they bathe in His lustral and illimitable Light?

It must first here be spoken of the Exoteric Qabalah to be found in books, a shell of that perfect fruit of the Tree of Life. Next we will deal with the esoteric teachings of it, as Frater P. was able to understand them. And of these we shall give examples, showing the falsity and absurdity of the uninitiated path, the pure truth and reasonableness of the hidden Way.

For the student unacquainted with the rudiments of the Qabalah we recommend the study of S. L. Mathers' "Introduction" to his translation of the three principal books of the Zohar, and Westcott's "Introduction to the Study of the Qabalah." We venture to append a few quotations from the former document, which will show the elementary principles of calculation. Dr Westcott's little book is principally valuable for its able defence of the Qabalah as against exotericism and literalism.

The literal Qabalah . . . is divided into three parts: GMTRIA, Gematria; NVTRIQVN, Notariqon; and ThMVRH, Temura.

Gematria is a metathesis of the Greek word γραμματεια. It is based on the relative numerical values of words. Words of similar numerical values are considered to be explanatory of each other, and this theory is extended to phrases. Thus the letter Shin, Sh, is 300, and is equivalent to the number obtained by adding up the numerical values of the letters of the words RVCh ALHIM, Ruach Elohim, the spirit of Elohim; and it is therefore a symbol of the spirit of Elohim. For R = 200, V = 6, Ch = 8, A = 1, L = 30, H = 5, I = 10, M = 40; total = 300. Similarly, the words AChD, Achad, Unity, One, and AHBH, Ahebah, love, each = 13; for A = 1, Ch = 8, D = 4, total = 13; and A = 1, H = 5, B = 2, H = 5, total = 13. Again, the name of the angel MTTRVN, Metatron or Methraton, and the name of the Deity, ShDI, Shaddai, each make 314; so the one is taken as symbolical of the other. The angel Metatron is said to have been the conductor of the children of Israel through the wilderness, of whom God says, "My name is in him." With regard to Gematria of phases (Gen. xlix. 10), IBA ShILH, Yeba Shiloh, "Sjhiloh shall come" = 358, which is the numeration of the word MShICh, Messiah. Thus also the passage, Gen. xviii. 2, VHNH ShLShH, Vehenna Shalisha, "And lo, three men," equals in numerical value ALV MIKAL GBRIAL VRPAL, Elo Mikhael Gabriel Ve-Raphael, "These are Mikhael, Gabriel and Raphael"; for each phrase = 701. I think these instance will suffice to make clear the nature of Gematria.

Notariqon is derived from the Latin word notarius, a shorthand writer. Of Notariqon there are two forms. In the first every letter of a word is taken from the initial or abbreviation of another word, so that from the letters of a word a sentence may be formed. Thus every letter of the word BRAShITH, Berashith, the first word in Genesis, is made the initial of a word, and we obtain BRAShITh RAH ALHIM ShIQBLV IShRAL ThVRH, Berashith Rahi Elohim Sheyequebelo Israel Torah; "In the beginning Elohim saw that Israel would accept the law." In this connection I may give six very interesting specimens of Notariqon formed from this same word BRAShITh by Solomon Meir Ben Moses, a Jewish Qabalist, who embraced the Christian faith in 1665, and took the name of Prosper Rugere. These have all a Christian tendency, and by their means Prosper converted another Jew, who had previously been bitterly opposed to Christianity. The first is, BN RVCh AB ShLVShThM IChD ThMIM, Ben, Ruach, Ab, Shaloshethem Yechad Thaubodo: "The Son, the Spirit, the Father, ye shall equally worship Their Trinity." The third is BKVRI RAShVNI AShR ShMV IShVO

ThOBVDV, Bekori Rashuni Asher Shamo Yeshuah Thaubodo: "Ye shall worship My first-born, My first, Whose name is Jesus." The fourth is, BBVA RBN AShR ShMV IShVo ThOBVDV, Beboa Rabban Asher Shamo Yeshuah Thaubodo: "When the Master shall come Whose Name is Jesus ye shall worship." The fifth is, BThVLH RAVIH ABChR ShthLD ISh VO ThAShRVH, Bethulh Raviah Abachar Shethaled Yeshuah Thashroah: "I will choose a virgin worthy to bring forth Jesus, and ye shall call her blessed." The sixth is, BOVGTh RTzPIM ASThThR ShGVPI IShVO ThAKLV, Beaugoth Ratzephim Asattar Shegopi Yeshuah Thakelo: "I will hide myself in cake (baked with) coals, for ye shall eat Jesus, My Body."

The Qabalistical importance of these sentences as bearing upon the doctrines of Christianity can hardly be overrated.

The second form of the Notariqon is the exact reverse of the first. By this the initials or finals, or both, or the medials, of a sentence, are taken to form a word or words. Thus the Qabalah is called ChKMH NSThRH, Chokhmah Nesethrah, "the secret wisdom"; and if we take the initials of these two words Ch and N, we form by the second king of Notariqon the word ChN, Chen, "grace." Similarly, from the initials and finals of the words MI IOLH LNV HShMIMH, Mi Iaulah Leno Ha-Shamayimah, "Who shall go up for us to heaven?" (Deut. xxx. 12), are formed MILH, Milah, "circumcision," and IHVH, the Tetragrammaton, implying that God hath ordained circumcision as the way to heaven.

Temura is permutation. According to certain rules, one letter is substituted for another letter preceding or following it in the alphabet, and thus from one word another word of totally different orthography may be formed. Thus the alphabet is bent exactly in half, in the middle, and one half is put over the other; and then by changing alternately the first letter or the first two letters at the beginning of the second line, twenty-two commutations are produced. These are called the "Table of the Combinations of TzIRVP," Tziruph. For example's sake, I will give the method called ALBTh, Albath, thus:—

11	10	9	8	7	6	5	4	3	2	1
K	I	T	Ch	Z	V	H	D	G	B	A
M	N	S	O	P	Tz	Q	R	Sh	Th	L

Each method takes its name from he first two pairs composing it, the system of pairs of letters being the groundwork of the the whole, as either letter in a pair is substituted for the other letter. Thus, by Albath, from RVCh, Ruach, is formed DTzO, Detzau. The names of the other twenty-one methods are: ABGTh, AGDTh, ADBG, AHBD, AVBH, AZBV, AChBZ, ATBCh, AIBT, AKBI, ALBK, AMBL, ANBM, ASBN, AOBS, APBO, ATzBP, AQSTz, ARBQ, AShBR, and AThBSh. To these must be added the modes ABGD and ALBM. Then comes the "Rational Table of Tziruph," another set of twenty-two combination. There are also three "Tables of the Commutations," known respectively as the Right, the Averse, and the Irregular. To make any of these, a square, containing 484 squares, should be made, and the letters written in. For the "Right Table" write the alphabet across from right to left; in the second row of squares do the same, but begin with B and end with A; in the third begin with G and end with B; and so on. For the "Averse Table" write the alphabet from right to left backwards, beginning with Th and ending with A; in the second row begin with Sh and end with Th, &c. The "Irregular Table" would take too long to describe. Besides all these, there is the method called ThShRQ, Thashraq, which is simply writing a word backwards. There is one more very important form called the "Qabalah of the Nine Chambers" or AIQ BKR, Aiq Bekar. It is thus formed:

300	30	3	200	20	2	100	10	1
Sh	L	G	R	K	B	Q	I	A
600	60	6	500	50	5	400	40	4
M final	S	V	K final	N	H	Th	M	D
900	90	9	800	80	8	700	70	7
Tz final	Tz	T	P final	P	Ch	N final	O	Z

I have put the numeration of each letter above to show the affinity between the letters in each chamber. Sometimes this is used as a cipher, by taking the portions of the figure to show the letters they contain, putting one point for the first letter, two for the second, &c.

Thus the right angle, containing AIQ, will answer for the letter Q if it have three dots or points within it. Again a square will answer for H, N, or K final, according to whether it has one, two, or three points respectively placed within it. So also with regard to the other letters. But there are many other ways of employing the Qabalah of the Nine Chambers, which I have not space to describe. I will merely mention as an example, that by the mode of Temura called AThBSh, Athbash, it is found that in Jeremiah xxv. 26, the word ShShK, Sheshakh, symbolises BBL, Babel.

Besides all these rules, there are certain meanings hidden in the shape of the letters of the Hebrew alphabet; in the form of a particular letter at the end of a word being different from that which it generally bears when it is a final letter, or in a letter being written in the middle of a word in a character generally used only at the end; in any letters or letter being written in a size smaller or larger than the rest of the manuscript, or in a letter being written upside down; in the variations found in the spelling of certain words, which have a letter more in some places than they have in others; in peculiarities observed in the position of any of the points or accents, and in certain expressions supposed to be elliptic or redundant.

For example the shape of the Hebrew letter Aleph, A, is said to symbolize a Vau, V, between a Yod, I, and a Daleth, D; and thus the letter itself represents the word IVD, Yod. Similarly the shape of the letter He, H, represents a Daleth, D, with a Yod, I, written at the lower left-hand corner, &c.

In Isaiah ix. 6, 7, the word LMRBH, Lemarbah, "for multiplying," is written with the character for M final in the middle of the word, instead of with the ordinary initial and medial M. The consequence of this is that the total numerical value of the word, instead of being $30+40+200+2+5=277$, is $30+600+200+2+5=837$ = by Gematria ThTh ZL, Tet Zal, the profuse Giver. Thus by writing the M final instead of the ordinary character, the word is made to bear a different qabalistical meaning.

. . . .

It is to be further noted with regard to the first word in the Bible, BRAShITH, that the first three letters, BRA, are the initial letters of the names of the three persons of the Trinity: BN, Ben the

Son; RVCh, Ruach, the Spirit; and AB, Ab the Father. Furthermore the first letter of the Bible is B, which is the initial letter of BRKH, Berakhah, blessing; and not A, which is that of ARR, Arar, cursing. Again, the letters of Berashith, taking their numerical powers, express the number of the years between the Creation and the birth of Christ, thus: B = 2,000, R = 200, A = 1,000, Sh = 300, I = 10, and Th = 400; total = 3910 years, being the time in round numbers. Picus de Mirandola gives the following working out of BRAShITh, Berashith:—By joining the third letter, A, to the first, B, AB, Ab = Father, is obtained. If to the first letter B, doubled, the second letter, R, be added, it makes BBR, Bebar = in or through the Son. If all the letters be read except the first, it makes RAShITh, Rashith = the beginning. If the fourth letter, Sh, the first B and the last Th be connected, it makes ShBTh, Shebeth = the end or rest. If the first three letters be taken, they make BRA, Bera = created. If, omitting the first, the three following be taken, they make RASh, Rash = head. If, omitting the two first, the next two be taken, they give ASh = fire. If the fourth and the last be joined, they give ShTh, Sheth = foundation. Again if the second letter be put before the first, it makes RB, Rab = great. If after the third be placed the fifth and the fourth, it gives AISh, Aish = man. If to the two first be joined the two last, they give BRITh, Berith = covenant. And if the first be added to the last, it gives ThB, Theb, which is sometimes used for TVB, Thob = good.

. . . .

There are three qabalistical veils of the negative existence, and in themselves they formulate the hidden ideas of the Sephiroth not yet called into being, and they are concentrated in Kether, which in this sense is the Malkuth of hidden ideas of the Sephiroth. I will explain this. The first veil of the negative existence is the AIN, Ain, Negativity. This word consists of three letters, which thus shadow forth the first three Sephiroth or numbers. The second veil is the AIN SVP, the limitless. This title consists of six letters, and shadows forth the idea of the first six Sephiroth or numbers. The third veil is the AIN SVP AVR, Ain Soph Aur, the Limitless Light. This again consists of nine letters, and symbolises the first nine Sephiroth, but of course in their hidden idea only. But when we reach the number nine we cannot progress farther without returning to the unity, or the number one, for the number ten is but a repetition of unity freshly derived from the negative, as is evident from a glance at its ordinary representation in Arabic numerals, where the circle O represents the Negative and the I the Unity. Thus, then, the limitless ocean of negative light does not proceed from a centre, for it is centreless, but it concentrates a centre, which is the number one of the Sephiroth, Kether, the Crown, the First Sephira; which therefore may be said to be the Malkuth or the number ten of the hidden Sephiroth. Thus "Kether is in Malkuth and Malkuth is in Kether." Or as an alchemical author of great repute (Thomas Vaughan, better known as Eugenius Philalethes) says, apparently quoting from Proclus; "That the heaven is in the earth, but after an earthly manner; and that the earth is in the heaven, but after a heavenly manner." But inasmuch as negative existence is the subject incapable of definition, as I have before shown, it is rather considered by the Qabalists as depending back from the number of unity than as a separate consideration therefrom; therefore they frequently apply the same terms and epithets indiscriminately to either. Such epithets are "The concealed of the Concealed," "The Ancient of the Ancient Ones," the "Most Holy Ancient One," etc.

I must now explain the real meaning of the terms Sephira and Sephiroth. The first is singular, the second is plural. The best rendering of the word is "numerical emanation." There are ten Sephiroth, which are the most abstract forms of the ten numbers of the decimal scale—i.e., the numbers 1, 2, 3, 4, 5, 6, 7, 8, 9, 10. Therefore, as in the higher mathematics we reason of numbers in their abstract sense, so in the Qabalah we reason of the Deity by the abstract forms of the numbers in other words, by the SPIRVTh, Sephiroth. It was from this ancient Oriental theory that Pythagoras derived his numerical symbolic ideas.

Among the Sephiroth, jointly and severally, we find the development of the persons and attributes of God. Of these some are male and some female. Now, for some reason or other best known to themselves, the translators of the Bible have carefully crowded out of existence and smothered up every reference to the fact that the Deity is both masculine and feminine. They have translated a feminine plural by a masculine singular in the case of the word Elohim. They have, however, left an inadvertent admission of their knowledge that it was plural in Genesis iv, 26: "And Elohim said: Let Us make man." Again (v. 27), who could Adam be made in the image of Elohim, male and female, unless the Elohim were male and female also? The word Elohim is a plural formed from the feminine singular ALH, Eloh, by adding IM to word. But inasmuch as IM is usually a termination of the masculine plural and is here added to a feminine noun, it gives to the word Elohim the sense of a female potency united to a masculine idea, and thereby capable of producing an offspring. Now, we hear much of the Father and the Son, but we hear nothing of the Mother in the ordinary religions of the day. But in the Qabalah we find that the Ancient of Days conforms Himself simultaneously into the Father and the Mother, and thus begets the Son. Now, this Mother is Elohim. Again, we are usually told that the Holy Spirit is masculine. But the word RVCh, Ruach, Spirit, is feminine, as appears from the following passage of the Sepher Yetzirah: "AChTh RVCh ALHIM ChIIM, Achath (feminine, not Achad, masculine) Ruach Elohim Chiim: One is She the Spirit of the Elohim of Life."

Now, we find that before he Deity conformed Himself thus— *i.e.*, as male and female—that the worlds of the universe could not subsist, or, in the words of Genesis, "The earth was formless and void." These prior worlds are considered to be symbolised by the "kings who reigned in Edom before there reigned a king in Israel," and they are therefore spoken of in the Qabalah as the "Edomite kings." This will be found fully explained in various parts of this work.

We now come to the consideration of the first Sephira, or the Number One, the Monad of Pythagoras. In this number are the other nine hidden. It is indivisible, it is also incapable of multiplication; divide 1 by itself and it still remains 1, multiply 1 by itself and it is still 1 and unchanged. Thus it is a fitting representative of the unchangeable Father of all. Now this number of unity has a twofold nature, and thus forms, as it were, the link between the negative and the positive. In its unchangeable one-ness it is scarcely a number; but in its property of capability of addition it may be called the first number of a numerical series. Now, the zero, 0, is incapable even of addition, just as also is negative existence. How, then, if 1 can neither be multiplied nor divided, is another 1 to be obtained to add to it; in other words how is the number 2 to be found? By reflection of itself. For thought 0 be incapable of definition, 1 is definable. And the effect of a definition is to form an Eidolon, duplicate, or image, of the thing defined. Thus, then, we obtain a duad composed of 1 and its reflection. Now also we have the commencement of a vibration established, for the number 1 vibrates alternately from changelessness to definition, and back to changelessness again. Thus, then, it is the father of all numbers, and a fitting type of the Father of all things.

The name of the first Sephira is KThR, Kether, the Crown. The Divine Name attributed to it is the Name of the Father given in Exod. iii. 4: AHIH, Eheieh, I am. It signifies Existence.

.　　.　　.　　.　　.　　.　　.　　.

The first Sephira contains nine, and produces them in succession thus:—

The number 2 or the Duad. The name of the second Sephira is ChKMH, Chokmah, Wisdom, a masculine active potency reflected from Kether, as I have before explained. This Sephira is the active and evident Father, to whom the Mother is united, who is the number 3. This second Sephira is represented by the Divine Names, IH, Yah, and IHVH; and the angelic hosts by AVPNIM, Auphanim, the Wheels (Ezek. i.). It is also called AB, Ab, the Father.

The third Sephira, or triad, is a feminine passive potency, called BINH, Binah, the Understanding, who is co-equal with Chokmah. For Chokmah, the number 2, is like two straight lines which can never enclose a space, and therefore it is powerless till the number 3 forms a triangle. Thus this Sephira completes and makes evident the supernal Trinity. It is also called AMA, Ama, Mother, and AIMA, Aima, the great productive Mother, who is eternally conjoined with AB, the Father, for the maintenance of the universe in order. There fore is she the most evident form in whom we can know the Father, and therefore is she worthy of all honour. She is the supernal Mother, co-equal with Chokmah, and the great feminine form of God, the Elohim, in whose image man and woman are created, according to the teaching of the Qabalah, equal before God. Woman is equal with man, and certainly not inferior to him, as it has been the persistent endeavour of so-called Christians to make her. Aima is the woman described in the Apocalypse (chap. xii.). This third Sephira is also sometimes called the Great Sea. To her are attributed the Divine names, ALHIM, Elohim, and IHVH ALHIM; and the angelic order, ARALIM, Aralim, The Thrones. She is the Supernal Mother as distinguished from Malkuth, the inferior Mother, Bride, and Queen.

The number 4. This union of the second and third Sephiroth produced ChSD, Chesed, Mercy or Love, also called GDVLH, Gedulah, Greatness or Magnificence; a masculine potency represented by the Divine Name AL, El, the Mighty One, and the angelic name, ChShMLIM, Chashmalim, Scintillating Flames (Ezek. iv. 4).

The number 5. From this emanated the feminine passive potency GBVRH, Geburah, strength or fortitude; or DIN, Deen, Justice; represented by the Divine Names, ALHIM GBVR, and ALH, Eloh, and the angelic name ShRPIM, Seraphim (Isa. vi. 6). This Sephira is also called PChD, Pachad, Fear.

The number 6. And from these two issued the uniting Sephira, ThPARTh, Tiphereth, Beauty or Mildness, represented by the Divine Name ALVH VDOTh, Eloah Va-Daath, and the angelic names, Shinanim, ShNANIM (Ps. lxviii. 18), or MLKIM, Melakim, kings. Thus by the union of justice and mercy we obtain beauty or clemency, and the second trinity of the Sephiroth is complete. This Sephira, or "Path," or "Numeration"—for by these latter appellations the emanations are sometimes called—together with the fourth, fifth, seventh eighth, and ninth Sephiroth, is spoken of as ZOIR ANPIN, Zaur Anpin, the Lesser Countenance, Microprosopus, by way of antithesis to Macroprosopus, or the Vast Countenance, which is one of the names of Kether, the first Sephira. The six Sephiroth of which Zauir Anpin is composed, are then called His six members. He is also called MLK, Melekh the King.

The number 7. The seventh Sephira is NTzCh, Netzach, or Firmness and Victory, corresponding to he Divine Name Jehovah Tzabaoth, IHVH TzBAVTh, the Lord of Armies, and the angelic names ALHIM, Elohim, gods, and ThRShIShIM, Tharshishim, the brilliant ones (Dan. x. 6).

The number 8. Thence proceeded the feminine passive potency HVD, Hod, Splendour, answering to the Divine Name ALHIM TzBAVTh, Elohim Tzabaoth, the God of Armies, and among the angels to BNI ALHIM, Beni Elohim, the sons of the Gods (Gen. vi. 4).

The number 9. These two produced ISVD, Yesod, the Foundation or Basis, represented by AL ChI, El Chai, the Mighty Living One, and ShDI, Shaddai; and among the angels by AShIM, Aishim, the Flames (Ps. civ. 5), yielding the third Trinity of the Sephiroth.

The number 10. From this ninth Sephira came the tenth and last, thus completing the decad of the numbers. It is called MLKVTh, Malkuth, the Kingdom, and also the Queen, Matrona, the inferior Mother, the Bride of Microprosopus; and ShKINH, Shekinah, represented by the Divine Name Adonai, ADNI, and among the angel hosts by the kerubim, KRVBIM. Now, each of these Sephiroth will be in a certain degree androgynous, for it will be feminine or receptive with regard to the Sephira which immediately precedes it in the sephirotic scale, and masculine or transmissive with regard to the Sephira which immediately follows it. But there is no Sephira anterior to Kether, nor is there a Sephira which succeeds Malkuth. By these remarks it will be understood how Chokmah is a feminine noun, though marking a masculine Sephira. The connecting-link of the Sephiroth is the Ruach, spirit, Mezla, the hidden influence.

I will how add a few more remarks on the qabalistical meaning of the term MThQLA, Metheqla, balance. In each of the three trinities or triads of the Sephiroth is a duad of opposite sexes, and a uniting intelligence which is the result. In this, the masculine and feminine potencies are regarded as the two scales of the balance, and the uniting Sephira as the beam that joins them. Thus, then, the term balance maybe said to symbolise the Triune, Trinity in Unity, and the Unity represented by the central point of the beam. But, again, in the Sephiroth there is a triple Trinity, the upper, lower, and middle. Now, these three are represented thus: the supernal, or highest, by the Crown, Kether; the middle by the King, and the inferior by the Queen; which will be the greatest trinity. And the earthy correlatives of these will be the primum mobile, the sun and the moon. Here we at once find alchemical symbolism.

. . . .

The Sephiroth are futher divided into three pillars—the right-hand Pillar of Mercy, consisting of the second, fourth, and seventh emanations; the left-hand Pillar of Judgment, consisting of the third, fifth, and eighth; and the middle Pillar of Mildness, consisting of the first, sixth, ninth, and tenth emanations.

In their totality and unity the ten Sephiroth represent the archetypal man, ADM QDMVN, Adam Qadmon, the Protogonos. In looking at the Sephiroth constituting the first triad, it is evident that they represent the intellect; and hence this triad is called the intellectual world, OVLM MVShKL, Olahm Mevshekal. The second triad corresponds to the moral world, OVLM MVRGSh, Olahm Morgash. The third represents power and stability, and is therefore called the material world, OLVM HMVTHBO, Olahm Ha-Mevethau. These three aspect are called the faces, ANPIN, Anpin. Thus is the tree of life, OTz ChIIM, Otz Chaiim, formed; the first triad being placed above, the second and third below, in such a manner that the three masculine Sephiroth are on the right, the three feminine on the left, whilst the four uniting Sephiroth occupy the centre. This is the qabalistical "tree of life," on which all things depend. There is considerable analogy between this and the tree Yggdrasil of the Scandinavians. I have already remarked that there is one trinity which comprises all the Sephiroth, and that it consists of the crown, the king, and the queen. (In some senses this is the Christian Trinity of Father, Son, and Holy Spirit, which in their highest Divine nature are symbolised by the first three Sephiroth, Kether, Chokmah, and Binah.) It is the Trinity which created the world; or, in qabalistical language, the universe was born from the union of the crowned king and queen. But according to the Qabalah, before the complete form of the heavenly man (the ten Sephiroth) was produced, there were certain primordial world created, but these could not subsist, as the equilibrium of balance was not yet perfect, and they were convulsed by the unbalanced force and destroyed. These primordial worlds are called the "kings of ancient time" and the "kings of Edom who reigned before the monarchs of Israel." In this sense, Edom is the world of unbalanced force, and Israel is the balanced Sephiroth (Gen. xxxvi. 31.). This important fact, that worlds were created and destroyed prior to the present creation, is again and again reiterated in the Zohar.

Now the Sephiroth are also called the World of Emanations, or the Atziluthic World, or the archetypal world, OVLM ATzILVTh, Olahm Atziloth; and this world gave birth to three other worlds each containing a repetition of the Sephiroth, but in a descending scale of brightness.

The second world is the Briatic world, OVLM HBRIAH, Olahm Ha-Briah, the world of creation, also called KVRSIA, Khorsia, the throne. It is an immediate emanation from the world of Atziloth, whose ten Sephiroth are reflected herein, and are consequently more limited, though they are still of the purest nature, and without any admixture of matter.

The third is the Jetziratic world, OVLM HITzIRAH, Olahm Ha-Yetzirah, or world of formation and of angels, which proceeds from Briah, and, though less refined in substance, is still without matter. It is in this angelic world that reside those intelligent and incorporeal beings who are wrapped in a luminous garment, and who assume a form when they appear unto man.

The fourth is the Asiatic world, OVLM HOShIH, Olahm Ha-Asiah, the world of action, called also the world of shells, OVLM HQLIPVTh, Olahm Ha-Qliphoth, which is this world of matter, made up of the grosser elements of the other three. In it is also the abode of the evil spirits, which are called "the shells" by the Qabalah, QLIPVTh, Qliphoth, material shells. The devils are also divided into ten classes, and have suitable habitations. (See Tables in *777*.)

The demons are the grossest and most deficient of all forms. Their ten degrees answer to the decad of the Sephiroth, but in inverse ratio, as darkness and impurity increase with the descent of each degree. The two first are nothing but absence of visible form and organisation. The third is the abode of darkness. Next follow seven Hells occupied by those demons which represent incarnate human vices, and those who have given themselves up to such vices in earth-life. Their prince is Samael, SMAL, the angel of poison and death.. His wife is the harlot, or woman of whoredom, AShTh ZNVNIM, Isheth Zenunim; and united they are called the beast, CHIVA, Chioa. Thus the infernal trinity is completed which is, so to speak, the averse and caricature of the supernal Creative One. Samael is considered to be identical with Satan.

The name of the Deity, which we call Jehovah, is in Hebrew a name of four letters, IHVH; and the true pronunciation of it is known to very few. I myself know some score of different mystical pronunciations of it. The true pronunciation of it is a most secret arcanum, and is a secret of secrets. "He who can rightly pronounce it, causeth heaven and earth to tremble, for it is the name which rusheth through the universe." Therefore when a devout Jew comes upon it in reading the Scripture, he either does not attempt to pronounce it, but instead makes a short pause, or else he substitutes for it the name Adonai, ADNI, Lord. The radical meaning of the word is "to be," and it is thus, like AHIH, Eheieh, a glyph of existence. It is capable of twelve transpositions, which all convey the meaning of "to be"; it is the only word that will bear so many transpositions without its meaning being altered. They are called the "twelve banners of the mighty name," and are said by some to rule the twelve signs of the Zodiac. These are the twelve banners:— IHVH, IHHV, IVHH, HVHI, HVIH, HHIV, VHHI, VIHH, VHIH, HIHV, HIVH, HHVI. There are three other tetragrammatic names, which are AHIH, Eheieh, existence; ADNI, Adonai, Lord; and AGLA. This last is not properly speaking, a word, but is a notariqon of the sentence, AThH GBVR LOVLM ADNI, Ateh Gebor Le-Olahm Adonai: "Thou art might, for ever, O Lord!" A brief explanation of Agla is this; A, the one first; A, the one last; G, the Trinity in Unity; L, the completion of the great work.

. . . .

But IHVH, the Tetragrammaton, as we shall presently see, contains all the Sephiroth with the exception of Kether, and specially signifies the Lesser Countenance, Microprosopus, the King of the qabalistical Sephirotic greatest Trinity, and the Son in His human incarnation, in the Christian acceptation of the Trinity. Therefore, as the Son reveals the Father, so does IHVH, Jehovah, reveal AHIH, Eheieh. And ADNI is the Queen, by whom alone

Tetragrammaton can be grasped, whose exaltation into Binah is found in the Christian assumption of the Virgin.

The Tetragrammaton IHVH is referred to the Sephiroth, thus: the upper-most point of the letter Yod, I, is said to refer to Kether; the letter I itself to Chokmah, the father of Microprosopus; the letter H, or "the supernal He," to Binah, the supernal Mother; the letter V to the next six Sephiroth, which are called the six members of Microprosopus (and six is the numerical value of V, the Hebrew Vau); lastly, the letter H, the "inferior He," to Malkuth, the tenth Sephira, the bride of Microprosopus.

Advanced students should then go to the fountain head, Knorr von Rosenroth''s "Kabbala denudata," and study for themselves. It should not prove easy; Frater P., after years of study, confessed: "I cannot get much out of Rosenroth"; and we may add that only the best minds are likely to obtain more than an academic knowledge of a system which we suspect von Rosenroth himself never understood in any deeper sense. As a book of reference to the hierarchical correspondences of the Qabalah, of course 777 stands alone an unrivalled.

The graphic Qabalah has been already fully illustrated in this treatise. See Illustrations 2, 12, 16, 17, 18, 19, 21, 22, 24, 28, 29, 33, 34, 35, 38, 39, 40, 41, 43, 45, 46, 47, 48, 50, 51, 61, 63, 64, 65, 66, 71, 72, 73, 74, 75, 76, 77, 78, 79, 82.

By far the best and most concise account of the method of the Qabalah is that by an unknown author, which Mr Aleister Crowley has printed at the end of the first volume of his Collected Works, and which we here reprint in full.

QABALISTIC DOGMA

The Evolution of Things is thus described by the Qabalists.

First is Nothing, or the Absence of Things, אִין, which does not and cannot mean Negatively Existing (if such an Idea can be said to mean anything), as S. Liddell Macgregor Mathers, who misread the Text and stultified the Commentary by the Light of his own

Ignorance of Hebrew and Philosophy, pretends in his Translation of v. Rosenroth.

Second is Without Limit אין סוף, *i.e.*, Infinite Space.

This is the primal Dualism of Infinity; the infinitely small and the infinitely great. The Clash of these produces a finite positive Idea which happens (see בראשית, in "The Sword of Song," for a more careful study, though I must not be understood to indorse every Word in our Poet-Philosopher's Thesis) to be Light, אור. This word אור is most important. It symbolises the Universe immediately after Chaos, the confusion or Clash of the infinite Opposites. א is the Egg of Matter; ו is ש, the Bull, or Energy-Motion; and ר is the Sun, or organised and moving System of Orbs. The three Letters of אור thus repeat the three Ideas. The Nature of אור is thus analysed, under the figure of the ten Numbers and the 22 Letters which together compose what the Rosicrucians have diagrammatised under the name of Minutum Mundum. It will be noticed that every Number and Letter has its "Correspondence" in Ideas of every Sort; so that any given Object can be analysed in Terms of the 32. If I see a blue Star, I should regard it as a Manifestation of Chesed, Water, the Moon, Salt the Alchemical Principle, Sagittarius or What not, in respect of its Blueness—one would have to decide which from other Data—and refer it to the XVIIth Key of the Taro in Respect of its Starriness.

The Use of these Attributions is lengthy and various: I cannot dwell upon it: but I will give one Example.

If I wish to visit the Sphere of Geburah, I use the Colours and Forces appropriate: I go there: if the Objects which then appear to my spiritual Vision are harmonious therewith, it is one Test of their Truth.

So also, to construct a Talisman, or to invoke a Spirit.

The methods of discovering Dogma from sacred Words are also numerous and important: I may mention:—

(*a*) The Doctrine of Sympathies: drawn from the total Numeration of a Word, when identical with, or a Multiple of Submultiple of, or a Metathesis of, that of another Word.

(*b*) The Method of finding the Least Number of a Word, by adding (and re-adding) the Digits of its total Number, and taking the corresponding Key of the Taro as a Key to the Meaning of the Word.

(c) The Method of Analogies drawn from the Shape of the Letters.

(d) The Method of Deductions drawn from the Meanings and Correspondences of the Letters.

(e) The Method of Acrostics drawn from the Letters. This Mode is only valid for Adepts of the highest Grades, and then under quite exceptional and rare Conditions.

(f) The Method of Transpositions and Transmutations of the Letters, which suggest Analogies, even when they fail to explain in direct Fashion.

All these and their Varieties and Combinations, with some other more abstruse or less important Methods, may be used to unlock the Secret of a Word.

Of course with Powers so wide it is easy for the Partisan to find his favourite Meaning in any Word. Even the formal Proof $0 = 1 = 2 = 3 = 4 = 5 = \ldots\ldots = n$ is possible.

But the Adept who worked out this Theorem, with the very Intent to discredit the Qabalistic Mode of Research, was suddenly dumfounded by the Fact that he had actually stumbled upon the Qabalistic Proof of Pantheism or Monism.

What really happens is that the Adept sits down and performs many useless Tricks with the Figures, without Result.

Suddenly the Lux dawns, and the Problem is solved.

The Rationalist explains this by Inspiration, the superstitious Man by Mathematics.

I give an Example of the Way in which one works. Let us take IAO, one of the "Barbarous Names of Evocation," of which those who have wished to conceal their own Glory by adopting the Authority of Zarathustra have said that in the holy Ceremonies it has ineffable Power.

But what Kind of Power? By the Qabalah we can find out the Force of the Name IAO.

We can spell it in Hebrew יאו or יאע. The Qabalah will even tell us which is the true Way. Let us however suppose that it is spelt יאו. This adds up to 17.

But first of all it strikes us that I, A, and O are the three Letters associated with the three Letters ה in the great Name of Six Letters, אהיהוה, which combines אהיה and יהוה, Macroprosopus and Microprosopus. Now these feminine Letters ה conceal the "Three Mothers" of the Alphabet, א, מ, and ש. Replace these, and we get אשימוא, which adds up to 358, the Number alike of נחש, the Serpent of Genesis, and the Messiah. We thus look for redeeming Power in IAO, and for the Masculine Aspect of that Poser.

Now we will see how that Power works. We have a curious Dictionary, which was made by a very learned Man, in which the Numbers 1 to 10,000 fill the left hand Column, in Order, and opposite them are written all the sacred or important Words which add up to each Number.

We take this Book, and look at 17. We find that 17 is the number of Squares in the Swastika, which is the Whirling Disc or Thunderbolt. Also there is חוג, a Circle or Orbit; זוד, to seethe or boil; and some other Words, which we will neglect in this Example, thought we should not dare to do so if we were really trying to find out a Thing we none of us knew. To help our Deduction about Redemption, too, we find חדה, to brighten or make glad.

We also work in another Way. I is the Straight Line or Central Pillar of the Temple of Life; also it stands for Unity, and for the Generative Force. A is the Pentagram, which means the Will of Man working Redemption. O is the Circle from which everything came, also Nothingness, and the Female, who absorbs the Male. The Progress of the Name shows then the Way from Life to Nirvana by means of the Will: and is a Hieroglyph of the Great Work.

Look at all our Meanings! Every one shows that the Name, if it has any Power at all, and that we must try, has the Power to redeem us from the Love of Life which is the Cause of Life, by its masculine Whirlings, and to gladden us and to being us to the bosom of the Great Mother, Death.

Before what is known a the Equinox of the Gods, a little While ago, there was an initiated Formula which expressed these Ideas to the Wise. As these Formulas are done with, it is of no Consequence if I reveal them. Truth is not eternal, any more than God; and it would be but a poor God that could not and did not alter his Ways at his Pleasure.

This Formula was used to pen the Vault of the Mystic Mountain of Abiegnus, within which lay (so the Ceremony of Initiation supposed) the body of our Father Christian Rosen Creutz, to be discovered by the Brethren with the Postulant as said in the Book called Fama Fraternitatis.

There are three Officers, and they repeat the Analysis of the Word as follows:—

Chief. Let us analyse the Key Word—I.

2nd. N.

3rd. R.

All. I.

Chief. Yod. ׳

2nd. Nun. נ

3rd. Resh. ר

All. Yod, ׳

Chief. Virgo (♍) Isis, Mighty Mother.

2nd. Scorpio (♏) Apophis, Destroyer.

3rd. Sol (☉) Osiris, slain and risen.

All. Isis, Apophis, Osiris, IAO.

All spread Arms as if on a cross, and say:—

The Sign of Osiris slain!

Chief bows his Head to the Left, rises his Right Arm, and lowers his Left keeping the Elbow at right Angles, thus forming the letter L (also the Swastika).

The Sign of the Mourning of Isis.

2nd. With erect Head, rises his Arms to form a V (but really to form the triple Tongue of Flame, the Spirit), and says:—

The Sign of Apophis and Typhon.

3rd. Bows his Head and crosses his Arms on his Breast (to form the Pentagram).

The Sign of Osiris risen.

All give the Sign of the Cross, and say:—

L.V.X.

Then the Sign of Osiris risen, and say:—

Lux, the Light of the Cross.

This formula, on which one may meditate for Years without exhausting its wonderful Harmonies, gives an excellent Idea of the Way in which Qabalistic Analysis is conducted.

First, the Letters have been written in Hebrew Characters.

Then the Attributions of them to the Zodiac and to Planets are substituted, and the Names of Egyptian Gods belonging to these are invoked.

The Christian Idea of I.N.R.I. is confirmed by these, while their Initials form the sacred Word of the Gnostics. That is, IAO. From the Character of the Deities and their Functions are deduced their Signs, and these are found to signal (as it were) the Word Lux (אור), which itself is contained in the Cross.

A careful Study of these Ideas, and of the Table of Correspondences, which one of our English Brethren is making, will enable him to discover a very great Deal of Matter for Thought in these Poems which an untutored Person would pass by.

To return to the general Dogma of the Qabalists.

The Figure of Minutum Mundum will show how they suppose one Quality to proceed from the last, first in the pure God-World Atziluth, then in the Angel-World Briah, and so on down to the Demon-Worlds, which are however not thus organised. They are rather Material that was shed off in the Course of Evolution, like the Sloughs of a Serpent, from which comes their Name of Shells, or Husks.

Apart from silly Questions as to whether the Order of the Emanations is confirmed by Palæontology, a Question it is quite impertinent to discuss, there is no Doubt that the Sephiroth are types of Evolution as opposed to Catastrophe and Creation.

The great Charge against this Philosophy is founded on its alleged Affinities with Scholastic Realism. But the Charge is not very true. No Doubt but they did suppose vast Storehouses of "Things of one Kind" from which, pure or mingled, all other Things did proceed.

Since ג, a Camel, refers to the moon, they did say that a Camel and the Moon were sympathetic, and came, that Part of them, from a common Principle: and that a Camel being yellow brown, it partook of the Earth Nature, to which that Colour is given.

Thence they said that by taking all the Natures involved, and by blending them in the just Proportions, on might have a Camel.

But this is no more than is said by the Upholders of the Atomic Theory.

They have their Storehouses of Carbon, Oxygen, and such (not in one Place, but no more is Geburah in one Place), and what is Organic Chemistry but the Production of useful Compounds whose Nature is deduced absolutely from theoretical Considerations long before it is ever produced in the Laboratory?

The difference, you will say, is that the Qabalists maintain a Mind of each Kind behind each Class of Things of one Kind; but so did Berkeley, and his Argument in that Respect is, as the great Huxley showed, irrefragable. For by the Universe I mean the Sensible; any other is Not to be Known; and the Sensible is dependent upon Mind. Nay, though the Sensible is said to be an Argument of a Universe Insensible, the latter becomes sensible to Mind as soon as the Argument is accepted, and disappears with its Rejection.

Nor is the Qabalah dependent upon its Realism, and its Application to the Works magical—but I am defending a Philosophy which I was asked to describe, and this is not lawful.

A great Deal may be learned from the Translation of the Zohar by S. Liddell Macgregor Mathers, and his Introduction thereto, though for those who have Latin and some acquaintance with Hebrew it is better to study the Kabbala Denudata of Knorr von Rosenroth, in Despite of the heavy Price; for the Translator has distorted the Text and its Comment to suit his belief in a supreme Personal God, and in that degraded Form of the Doctrine of Feminism which is so popular with the Emasculate.

The Sephiroth are grouped in various Ways. There is a Superior Triad or Trinity; a Hexad; and Malkuth: the Crown, the Father, and the Mother; the Son or King; and the Bride.

Also, a Division into seven Palaces, seven Planes, three Pillars or Columns, and the like.

The Flashing Sword follows the Course of the Numbers; and the Serpent Nechushtan or of Wisdom crawls up the Paths which join them upon the Tree of Life, namely the Letters.

It is important to explain the Position of Daath or Knowledge upon the Tree. It is called the Child of Chokmah and Binah, but it hath no Place. But it is really the Apex of a Pyramid of which the three first Numbers for the Base.

Now the Tree, or Minutum Mundum, is a Figure in a Plane of a solid Universe. Daath, being above the Plane, is therefore a Figure of a Force in four Dimensions, and thus it is the Object of the Magnum Opus. The three Paths which connect it with the First Trinity are the three lost Letters or Fathers of the Hebrew Alphabet.

In Daath is said to be the Head of the great Serpent Nechesh or Leviathan, called Evil to conceal its Holiness. (נחש = 358 = משיח, the Messiah or Redeemer, and לויתך = 496 = מלכות, the Bride.) It is identical with he Kundalini of the Hindu Philosophy, the Kwan-se-on of the Mongolian Peoples, and means the magical Force in Man, which is the sexual Force applied to the Brain, Heart, and other Organs, and redeemeth him.

The gradual Disclosure of these magical Secrets to the Poet may be traced in these Volumes, which it has been my Privilege to be asked to explain. It has been impossible to do more than place in the Hands of any intelligent Person the Keys which will permit him to unlock the many Beautiful Chambers of Holiness in these Palaces and Gardens of Beauty and Pleasure.

Of the results of the method we possess one flawless gem, already printed in the EQUINOX (Vol. II. pp. 163–185), "A Note on Genesis" by V. H. Fra. I. A.

From this pleasant, orthodox, and-so-they-all-lived-happy-ever-after view let us turn for a moment to the critical aspect. Let us demolish in turn the qabalistic methods of exegesis; and then, if we can, discover a true basis upon which to erect an abiding Temple of Truth.

1. Gematria.

The number 777 affords a good example of the legitimate and illegitimate deductions to be drawn. It represents the sentence AChTh RVCh ALHIM ChIIM, "One is the Spirit of the Living God," and also OLAHM H-QLPVTh, "The world of the Shells (excrements—the demon-world)."

Now it is wrong to say that this idea of the unity of the divine spirit is identical with this idea of the muddle of chaos —unless in that exalted grade in which "The One is the Many." But the compiler of Liber 777 was a great Qabalist when he thus entitled his book; for he meant to imply, "One is the Spirit of the Living God," *i.e.* I have in this book unified all the diverse symbols of the world; and also, "the world of shells," *i.e.* this book is full of mere dead symbols; do not mistake them for the living Truth. Further, he had an academic reason for his choice of a number; for the tabulation of the book is from Kether to Malkuth, the course of the Flaming Sword; and if this sword be drawn upon the Tree of Life, the numeration of the Paths over which it passes (taking ג, 3, as the non-existent path from Binah to Chesed, since it connects Macroprosopus and Microprosopus) is 777. [See Diagrams 2 and 12.]

To take another example, it is no mere coincidence that 463, the Staff of Moses, is ת, ס, ג, the paths of the Middle Pillar; no mere coincidence that 26, יהוה, is 1 + 6 + 9 + 10, the Sephiroth of the Middle Pillar. But ought we not to have some supreme name for 489, their sum, the Middle Pillar perfect? Yet the Sepher Sephiroth is silent. (We find only 489 = MShLM GMVL, the avenger. Ed.)

Again, 111 is Aleph, the Unity, but also APL, thick Darkness, and ASN, Sudden Death. This can only be interpreted as meaning the annihilation of the individual in the Unity, and the Darkness which is the Threshold of the Unity; in other words, one must be an expert in Samadhi before this simple Gematria has any proper meaning. How, then, can it serve the student in his research? The uninitiated would expect Life and Light in the One; only by experience can he know that to man the Godhead must be expressed by those things which most he fears.

We hare purposely avoid dwelling on the mere silliness of many Gematria correspondences, *e.g.*, the equality of the Qliphoth of one sign with the Intelligence of another. Such misses are more frequent than such hits as AChD, Unity, 13 = AHBH, Love, 13.

The argument is an argument in a circle. "Only an adept can understand the Qabalah," just as (in Buddhism) Sakyamuni said, "Only an Arahat can understand the Dhamma."

In this light, indeed, the Qabalah seems little more than a convenient language for recording experience.

We may mention in passing that Frater P. never acquiesced in the obvious "cook" of arguing: $x = y + 1 \therefore x = y$, by assuming that x should add one to itself "for the concealed unity." Why shouldn't y have a little concealed unity of its own?

That this method should ever have been accepted by any Qabalist argues a bankruptcy of ingenuity beyond belief. In all conscience, it is easy enough to fake identities by less obviously card-sharping methods!

2. Notariqon.

The absurdity of this method needs little indication. The most unsophisticated can draw pity and amusement from Mr Mathers' Jew, converted by the Notariqons of "Berashith." True, F.I.A.T. is Flatus, Ignis, Aqua, Terra; showing the Creator as Tetragrammaton, the synthesis of the four elements; showing the Eternal Fiat as the equilibrated powers of Nature. But what forbids Fecit Ignavus Animam Terrae, or any other convenient blasphemy, such as Buddha would applaud?

Why not take our converted Jew and restore him to the Ghetto with Ben, Ruach, Ab, Sheol!—IHVH, Thora? Why not take the sacred Ἰχθύς of the Christian who thought it meant Ἰησοῦς Χρῑστός Θεοῦ Ὑιός Σωτήρ and make him a pagan with "Ἰσιδος Χάρις Θησαυρός Ὑιῶν Σοφίας"?

Why not argue that Christ in cursing the fig, F.I.G., wished to attack Kant's dogmas of Freewill, Immortality, God?

3. Temurah.

Here again the multiplicity of our methods makes our method too pliable to be reliable. Should we argue that BBL = ShShK (620) by the method of Athbash, and that therefore BBL symbolises Kether (620)? Why, BBL is confusion, the very opposite of Kether.

Why Athbash? Why not Abshath? or Agrath? or any other of the possible combinations?

About the only useful Temurah is Aiq Bkr, given above. In this we do find a suggestive reasoning. For example, we find it in the attribution of ALHIM to the pentagram which gives π. [See EQUINOX, No. II. p. 184.] Here we write Elohim, the creative deities, round a pentagram, and read it reverse beginning with ל, ם, the letter of equilibrium, and obtain an approximation to π 3.1415 (good enough for the benighted Hebrews), as if thereby the finite square of creation was assimilated to the infinite circle of he Creator.

Yes: but why should not Berashith 2, 2, 1, 3, 1, 4, give, say, e? The only answer is, that if you screw it round long enough, it perhaps will!

The Rational Table of Tziruph should, we agree with Fra. P., be left to the Rationalist Press Association, and we may present the Irregular Table of Commutations to Irregular Masons.

4. To the less important methods we may apply the same criticism.

We may glance in passing at the Yetziratic, Tarot, and significatory methods of investigating any word. But though Frater P. was expert enough in these methods they are hardly pertinent to the pure numerical Qabalah, and we therefore deal gently with them. The attributions are given in 777. Thus א in the Yetziratic world is "Air," by Tarot "the Fool," and by signification "an ox." Thus we have the famous I.N.R.I. = י, נ, ר, י = ♍, ♏, ☉, ♏; the Virgin, the Evil Serpent, the Sun, suggesting the story of Genesis ii. and of the Gospel. The initials of the Egyptian names Isis, Apophis, Osiris, which correspond, give in their turn the Ineffable Name IAO; thus we say that the Ineffable is concealed in and revealed by the Birth, Death, and Resurrection of Christ; and further the Sings of Mourning of the Mother, Triumph of the Destroyer, and Rising of the Son, give by shape the letters L.U.X., Lux, which letters are (again) concealed in and revealed by the Cross ⊥ X X the Light of the Cross. Further examples will be found in "A Note on Genesis." One of the most famous is the Mene, Tekel, Upharsin of Daniel, the imaginary prophet who lived under Belshazzar the imaginary king.

MNA. The Hanged Man, Death, the Fool = "Sacrificed to Death by thy Folly."

ThKL. The Universe, the Wheel of Fortune, Justice = "Thy kingdom's fortune is in the Balance."

PRSh. The Blasted Tower, the Sun, the Last Judgment = "Ruined is thy glory, and finished."

But we cannot help thinking that this exegesis must have been very hard work.

We could more easily read

MNA. To sacrifice to death is folly.

ThKL. Thy kingdom shall be fortunate, for it is just.

PRSh. The Tower of thy glory shall endure until the Last Day.

There! that didn't take two minutes; and Belshazzar would have exalted us above Daniel.

Similarly AL, God, may be may be interpreted, "His folly is justice," as it is written: "The wisdom of this world is foolishness with God."

Or, by Yetzirah: "The air is His balance," as it is written: "God made the firmament, and divided the waters which were under the firmament from the waters which were above the firmament."

Or, by meaning: "The ox and the goad," *i.e.*, "He is both matter and motion."

We here append a sketch MS. by Frater P., giving his explanation by Tarot, etc., of the letters of the alphabet spelt in full.

MYSTIC READINGS OF THE LETTERS OF THE ALPHABET
(*See* TAROT CARDS, *AND MEDITATE*)

ALP. Folly's Doom is Ruin.

BITh. The Juggler with the Secret of the Universe.

GML. The Holy Guardian Angel is attained by Self-Sacrifice and Equilibrium.

DLTh. The Gate of the Equilibrium of the Universe. (Note D, the highest reciprocal path.)

HH. The Mother is the Daughter; and the Daughter is the mother.

VV. The Son is (but) the Son. (These two letters show the true doctrine of Initiation as given in Liber 418; opposed to Protestant Exotericism.)

ZIN. The answer of the Oracles is always Death.

ChITh. The Chariot of the Secret of the Universe.

TITH. She who rules the Secret Force of the Universe.

IVD. The Secret of the Gate of Initiation.

KP. In the Whirlings is War.

LMD. By Equilibrium and Self-Sacrifice, the Gate!

MIM. The Secret is hidden between the Waters that are above and the Waters that are beneath. (Symbol, the Ark containing the secret of Life borne upon the Bosom of the Deluge beneath the Clouds.)

NVN. Initiation is guarded on both sides by death.

SMK.   Self-control and Self-sacrifice govern the Wheel.

OIN.   The Secret of Generation is Death.

PH.   The Fortress of the Most High. (Note P, the lowest reciprocal path).

TzDI.   In the Star is the Gate of the Sanctuary.

QVP.   Illusionary is the Initiation of Disorder.

RISh.   In the Sun (Osiris) is the Secret of the Spirit.

ShIN.   Resurrection is hidden in Death.

ThV.   The Universe is the Hexagram.

(Other meanings suit other planes and other grades.)

Truly there is no en to this wondrous science; and when the sceptic sneers, "With all these methods one ought to be able to make everything our of nothing," the Qabalist smiles back the sublime retort, "With these methods One did make everything out of nothing."

Besides these, there is still one more method—a method of some little importance to students of the Siphra Dzenioutha, namely, the analogies drawn from the shapes of letters; these are often interesting enough. א, for example, is a ו between י and י, making 26. Thus יהוה 26 = א, 1. Therefore Jehovah is One. But it would be as pertinent to continue 26 = 2 × 13, and 13 = Achad = 1, and therefore Jehovah is Two.

This then is an absurdity. Yes; but it is also an arcanum!

How wonderful is the Qabalah! How great is its security from the profane; how splendid its secrets to the initiate!

Verily and Amen! yet here we are at the old dilemma, that one must know Truth before one can rely upon the Qabalah to show Truth.

Like the immortal burglar:

"Bill wouldn't hurt a baby—he's a pal as you can trust,
  He's all right when yer know 'im; but yer've got to know 'im fust."

So those who have committed themselves to academic study of its mysteries have found but a dry stick: those who have understood (favoured of God!) have found therein Aaron's rod that budded, the Staff of Life itself, yea, the venerable Lingam of Mahasiva!

It is for us to trace the researches of Frater P. in the Qabalah, to show how from this storehouse of child's puzzles, of contradictions and incongruities, of paradoxes and trivialities, he discovered the very canon of Truth, the authentic key of the Temple, the Word of that mighty Combination which unlocks the Treasure-Chamber of the King.

And this following is the Manuscript which he has left for our instruction.

AN ESSAY UPON NUMBER

(May the Holy One mitigate His severities toward His servant in respect of the haste wherewith this essay hath been composed!

When I travelled with the venerable Iehi Aour in search of Truth, we encountered a certain wise and holy man, Shri Parananda. Children! said he, for two years must ye study with me before ye fully comprehend our Law.

"Venerable Sir!" answered Frater I.A., "the first verse of *Our* Law contains but seven words. For seven years did I study that verse by day and by night; and at the end of that time did I presume —may the Dweller of Eternity pardon me!—to write a monograph upon the first word of those seven words."

"Venerable Sir!" quoth I: "that First Word of our law contains but six letters. For six years did I study that word by day and by night; and at the end of that time did I not dare to utter the first letter of those six letters."

Thus humbling myself did I abash both the holy Yogi and my venerable Frater I. A. But alas! Tegragrammaton! Alas! Adonai! the hour of my silence is past. May the hour of my silence return! Amen.)

PART I

THE UNIVERSE AS IT IS

Section I

0 The Negative—the Infinite—the Circle, or the Point.

1 The Unity—the Positive—the Finite—the Line, derived from 0 by extension. The divine Being.

2 The Dyad—the Superficies, derived from 1 by reflection $1/1$, or by revolution of the line around its end. The Demiurge. The divine Will.

3 The Triad, the solid, derived from 1 and 2 by addition. Matter. The divine Intelligence.

4 The Quaternary, the solid existing in Time, matter as we know it. Derived from 2 by multiplication. The divine Repose.

5 The Quinary, Force or Motion. The interplay of the divine Will with matter. Derived from 2 and 3 by addition.

6 The Senary, Mind. Derived from 2 and 3 by multiplication.

7 The Septenary, Desire. Derived from 3 and 4 by addition. (There is however a secondary attribution of 7, making it the holiest and most perfect of the numbers.)

8 The Ogdoad, Intellect (also Change in Stability). Derived from 2 and 3 by multiplication, $8 = 2^3$.

9 The Ennead, Stability in Change. Derived from 2 and 3 by multiplication, $9 = 3^2$.

(Note all numbers divisible by nine are still so divisible, however the order of the figures is shifted.)

10 The Decad, the divine End. Represents the 1 returning to the 0. Derived from $1 + 2 + 3 + 4$.

11 The Hendecad, the accursed shells, that only exist without the divine Tree. $1 + 1 = 2$, in its evil sense of not being 1.

Section II

0 The Cosmic Egg.

1 The Self of Deity, beyond Fatherhood and Motherhood.

2 The Father.

3 The Mother.

4 The Father made flesh—authoritative and paternal.

5 The Mother made flesh—fierce and active.

6 The Son—partaking of all these natures.

7 The Mother degraded to mere animal emotion.

8 The Father degraded to mere animal reason.

9 The Son degraded to mere animal life.

10 The Daughter, fallen and touching with her hands the shells.

It will be noticed that this order represents creation as progressive degeneration—which we are compelled to think of as evil. In the human organism the same arrangement will be noticed.

SECTION III

0 The Pleroma of which our individuality is the monad: the "All-Self."

1 The Self—the divine Ego of which man is rarely conscious.

2 The Ego; that which thinks "I"—a falsehood, because to think "I" is to deny "not-I" and thus to create the Dyad.

3 The Soul; since 3 reconciles 2 and 1, here are placed the aspirations to divinity. It is also the receptive as 2 is the assertive self.

4–9 The intellectual Self, with its branches:

> 4. Memory.
>
> 5. Will.
>
> 6. Imagination.
>
> 7. Desire.
>
> 8. Reason.
>
> 9. Animal being.

6 The Conscious Self of the Normal Man: thinking itself free, and really the toy of its surroundings.

9 The Unconscious Self of the Normal Man. Reflex actions, circulation, breathing , digestion, etc., all pertain here.

10 The illusory physical envelope; the scaffolding of the building.

SECTION IV

Having compared these attributions with those to be found in 777, studied them, assimilated them so thoroughly that it is natural and needs no effort to think "Binah, Mother, Great Sea, Throne, Saturn, Black Myrrh, Sorrow, Intelligence, etc. etc. etc.," in a flash whenever the number 3 is mentioned or seen, we may profitably proceed to go through the most important of the higher numbers.

For this purpose I have removed myself from books of reference; only those things which have become fixed in my mind (from their importance) deserve place in the simplicity of this essay.

12 HVA, "He," a title of Kether, identifying Kether with the Zodiac, and "home of the 12 stars" and their correspondences. See 777.

13 AChD, Unity, and AHBH Love. A scale of unity; thus $13 \times 1 = 1$; $26 = 13 \times 2 = 2$; $91 = 13 \times 7 = 7$; so that we may find in 26 and 91 elaboration of the Dyad and the Septenary respectively.

14 An "elaboration" of 5 $(1 + 4 = 5)$, Force; a "concentration" or 86 $(8 + 6 = 14)$ Elohim, the 5 elements.

15 IH, Jah, one of the ineffable names; the Father and Mother united. Mystic number of Geburah: $1 + 2 + 3 + 4 + 5$.

17 The number of squares in the Swastika, which by shape is Aleph, א. Hence 17 recalls 1. Also IAV, IAO, the triune Father. See 32 and 358.

18 ChI, Life. An "elaboration" of 9.

20 IVD, Yod, the letter of the Father.

21 AHIH, existence, a title of Keter, Note $3 \times 7 = 21$. Also IHV, the first 3 (active) letters of IHVH. Mystic number of Tiphereth.

22 The number of letters in the Hebrew Alphabet; and of the paths on the Tree. Hence suggests completion of imperfection. Finality, the fatal finality. Note $2 \times 11 = 22$, the accursed Dyad at play with the Shells.

24 Number of the Elders; and $72 \div 3$. 72 is the "divided Name."

26 IHVH. Jehovah, as the Dyad expanded, the jealous and terrible God, the lesser Countenance. The God of Nature, fecund, cruel, beautiful, relentless.

28 Mystic number of Netzach, KCh, "Power."

31 LA, "not"; and AL, "God." In this Part I. ("Nature as it is") the number is rather forbidding. For AL is the God-name of Chesed, mercy; and so the number seems to deny that Name.

32 Number of Sephiroth and Paths, $10 + 22$. Hence is completion of perfection. Finality: things as they are in their totality. AHIHVH, the combined AHIH and IHVH, Macroprosopus, and Microprosopus, is here. If we suppose the 3 female letters H to conceal the 3 mothers A, M, Sh, we obtain the number 358, Messiach, q.v. Note

$32 = 2^5$, the divine Will extended through motion. $64 = 2^6$, will be the perfect number of matter, for it is 8, the first cube, squared. So we find it a Mercurial number, as if the solidity of matter was in truth eternal change.

35 AGLA, a name of God = Ateh Gibor Le Olahm Adonai. "To Thee by the Power unto the Ages, O my Lord!" $35 = 5 \times 7$. $7 =$ Divinity, $5 =$ Power.

36 A Solar Number. ALH. Otherwise unimportant, but is the mystic number of Mercury.

37 IChIDH. The highest principle of the soul, attributed to Kether. Note $37 = 111 \div 3$.

38 Note $38 \times 11 = 418$ q.v. in Part II.

39 IHVH AChD, Jehovah is one. $39 = 13 \times 3$. This is then the affirmation of the aspiring soul.

40 A "dead" number of fixed law, 4×10, Tetragrammaton, the lesser countenance immutable in the heaviness of Malkuth.

41 AM, the Mother, unfertilised and unenlightened.

42 AMA, the Mother, still dark. Here are the 42 judges of the dead in Amennti, and here is the 42-fold name of the Creative God. See Liber 418.

44 DM, blood. See Part II. Here $4 \times 11 =$ the corruption of the created world.

45 MH, a secret title of Yetzirah, the Formative World. ADM, Adam, man, the species (not "the first man"). A is Air, the divine breath which stirs DM, blood, into being.

49 A number useful in the calculations of Dr Dee, and a mystic number of Venus.

50 The number of the Gates of Binah, whose name is Death ($50 =$ ן = by Tarot, "Death").

51 AN, pain. NA, failure. ADVM, Edom, the country of the demon kings. There is much in the Qabalah about these kings and their dukes; it never meant much to me, somehow. But 51 is 1 short of 52.

52 AIMA, the fertilised Mother, the Phallus (ʼ) thrust into AMA. Also BN, the Son. Note $52 = 13 \times 4$, 4 being Mercy and the influence of the Father.

60 Samekh, which in full spells 60 × 2 = 120 (q.v.), just as Yod, 10 in full spells 10 × 2 = 20. In general, the tens are "solidifications" of the ideas of the units which they multiply. Thus 50 is Death, the Force of Change in its final and most earthy aspect. Samekh is "Temperance" in the Tarot: the 6 has little evil possible to it; the worst name one can call 60 is "restriction."

61 AIN, the Negative. ANI, Ego. A number rather like 31, q.v.

64 DIN and DNI, intelligences (the twins) of Mercury. See also 32.

65 ADNI. In Roman characters LXV = LVX, the redeeming light. See the 5°=6□ ritual and "Konx om Pax." Note 65 = 13 × 5, the most spiritual form of force, just as 10 × 5 was its most material form. Note HS, "Keep silence!" and HIKL, the palace; as if it were said "Silence is the House of Adonai."

67 BINH the Great Mother. Note 6 + 7 = 13, uniting the ideas of Binah and Kether. A number of the aspiration.

70 The Sanhedrin and the precepts of the Law. The Divine 7 in its most material aspect.

72 ChSD, Mercy. The number of the Shemhamphorasch, as if affirming God as merciful. For details of Shemhamphorasch, see 777 and other classical books of reference. Note especially I + IH + IHV + IHVH = 72.

73 ChKMH, Wisdom. Also GML, Gimel, the path uniting Kether and Tiphereth. But Gimel, "the Priestess of the Silver Star," is the Female Hierophant, the Moon; and Chokmah is the Logos, or male initiator. See Liber 418 for much information on these points, though rather from the standpoint of Part II.

78 MZLA, the influence from Kether. The number of the cards of the Tarot, and of the 13 paths of the Beard of Macroprosopus. Note 78 = 13 × 6. Also AIVAS, the messenger. See Part II.

80 The number of ◘, the "lightning-struck Tower" of the Tarot. 8 = Intellect, Mercury; its most material form is Ruin, as Intellect in the end is divided against itself.

81 A mystic number of the Moon.

84 A number chiefly important in Buddhism. 84 = 7 × 12.

85 PH, the letter Pé. 85 = 5 × 17: even the highest unity, if it move or energise, means War.

86 ALHIM. See "A Note on Genesis," EQUINOX, No. II.

90 Number of Tzaddi, a fishhook = Tanha, the clinging of man to life (9), the trap in which man is caught as a fish is caught by a hook. The most material aspect of animal life; its final doom decreed by its own lust. Also MIM, Water.

91 91 = 7 × 13, the most spiritual form of the Septenary. AMN, Amen, the holiest title of God; the Amoun of the Egyptians. It equals IHVH ADNI (IAHDVNHI, interlaced), the eight-lettered name, thus linking the 7 to the 8. Note that AMN (reckoning N as final, 700) = 741 = AMThSh, the letters of the elements; and is thus a form of Tetragrammaton, a form unveiled.

100 The number of ק, the perfect illusion, 10 × 10. Also כף, Kaph, the Wheel of Fortune. The identity is that of matter, fatality, change, illusion. It seems the Buddhist view of the Samsara-Cakkram.

106 NVN, Nun, a fish. The number of death. Death in the Tarot bears a cross-handled scythe; hence the Fish as the symbol of the Redeemer. ΙΧΘΥΣ = Jesus Christ, Son of God, Saviour.

108 Chiefly interesting because 108 = 2 × 2 × 3 × 3 × 3 = the square of 2 playing with the cube of 3. Hence the Buddhists hailed it with acclamation, and make their rosaries of this number of beads.

111 AChD HVA ALHIM, "He is One God."

ALP, Aleph, and ox, a thousand. The redeeming Bull. By shape the Swastika, and so the Lightning. "As the lightning lighteneth out of the East even unto the West, so shall be the coming of the Son of Man." An allusion to the descent of Shiva upon Shakti in Samadhi. The Roman A shows the same through the shape of the Pentagram, which it imitates.

ASN, ruin, destruction, sudden death. *Scil.*, of the personality in Samadhi.

APL, thick darkness. *Cf.* St John of the Cross, who describes these phenomena in great detail.

AOM, the Hindu Aum or Om.

MHVLL, mad—the destruction of Reason by Illumination.

OVLH, a holocaust. *Cf.* ASN.

PLA, the Hidden Wonder, a title of Kether.

114 DMO, a tear. The age of Christian Rosencreutz.

120 SMK, Samech, a prop. Also MVSDI, basis, foundation. 120 = 1 × 2 × 3 × 4 × 5, and is thus a synthesis of the power of the pentagram. [Also 1 + 2 + . . . + 15 = 120.] Hence its importance in the 5 = 6 ritual , q.v. *supra* EQUINOX, No. III. I however disagree in part; it seems to me to symbolise a lesser redemption than that associated with Tiphereth. Compare at least the numbers 0.12 and 210 in Liber Legis and Liber 418, and extol their superiority. For while the first is the sublime formula of the infinite surging into finity, and the latter the supreme rolling-up of finity into infinity, the 120 can symbolise at the best a sort of intermediate condition of stability. For how can one proceed from the 2 to the 0? 120 is also ON, a very important name of God.

124 ODN, Eden.

131 SMAL, Satan so-called, but really only Samael, the accuser of the brethren, unpopular with the Rabbis because their consciences were not clear. Samael fulfils a most useful function; he is scepticism, which accuses intellectually; conscience, which accuses morally; and even that spiritual accuser upon the Threshold, without whom the Sanctuary might be profaned. We must defeat him, it is true; but how should we abuse and blame him, without abuse and blame of Him that set him there?

136 A mystic number of Jupiter; the sum of the first 16 natural numbers.

144 A square and therefore a materialisation of the number 12. Hence the numbers in the Apocapyse. 144,000 only means 12 (the perfect number in the Zodiac or houses of heaven and tribes of Israel) × 12, *i.e.* settled × 1000, *i.e.* on the grand scale.

148 MAZNIM, Scales of Justice.

156 BABALON. See Liber 418. This number is chiefly important for Part II. It is of no account in the orthodox dogmatic Qabalah. Yet it is 12 × 13, the most spiritual form, 13, of the most perfect number, 12, HVA. [It is TzIVN, Zion, the City of the Pyramids.—Ed.]

175 A mystic number of Venus.

203 ABR, initials of AB, BN, RVCh, the Trinity.

206 DBR, Speech, "the Word of Power."

207 AVR, Light. Contrast with AVB, 9, the astral light, and AVD, 11, the Magical Light. Aub is an illusory thing of witchcraft (*cf.* Obi,

Obeah); Aud is almost = the Kundalini force ("Odic" force). This illustrates well the difference between the sluggish, viscous 9, and the keen, ecstatic 11.

210 Pertains to Part II. See Liber 418.

214 RVCh, the air, the mind.

220 Pertains to Part II. The number of verses in Liber Legis.

231 The sum of the first 22 numbers, 0 to 21; the sum of the Key-Numbers of the Tarot cards; hence an extension of the idea of 22, q.v.

270 I.N.R.I. See 5 = 6 ritual.

280 The sum of the "five letters of severity," those which have a final form—Kaph, Mem, Nun, Pe, Tzaddi. Also the number of the squares on the sides of the Vault 7 × 40; see 5 = 6 ritual. Also RP = terror.

300 The letter ש, meaning "tooth," and suggesting by its shape a triple flame. Refers Yetziratically to fire, and is symbolic of the Holy Spirit, RVCh ALHIM = 300. Hence the letter of the Spirit. Descending into the midst of IHVH, the four inferior elements, we get IHShVH Jeheshua, the Saviour, symbolised by the Pentagram.

301 ASH, Fire.

314 ShDI, the Almighty, a name of God attributed to Yesod.

325 A mystic number of Mars. BRTzBAL, the spirit of Mars, and GRAPIAL, the intelligence of Mars.

326 IHShVH, Jesus—see 300.

333 ChVRVNZVN, see Liber 418, 10th Aethyr. It is surprising that this large scale 3 should be so terrible a symbol of dispersion. There is doubtless a venerable arcanum here connoted, possibly the evil of Matter summó. 333 = 37 × 9 the accurséd.

340 ShM—the Name.

341 The sum of the "3 mothers," Aleph, Mem, and Shin.

345 MShH, Moses. Note that by transposition we have 543, AHIH AShR AHIEH, "Existence is Existence," "I am that I am," a sublime title of Kether. Moses is therefore regarded as the representative of this particular manifestation of deity, who declared himself under this special name.

358 See 32. MShICh, Messiah, and NChSh, the serpent of Genesis. The dogma is that the head of the serpent (N) is "bruised," being replaced by M, the letter of Sacrifice, and God, the letter alike of virginity (׳ = ♍) and of original deity (׳ = the foundation or type of all the letters). Thus the word may be read:

"The Sacrifice of the Virgin-born Divine One triumphant (ה, the Chariot) through the Spirit," while NChSh reads "Death entering the (realm of the) Spirit."

But the conception of the Serpent as the Redeemer is truer. See my explanation of 5 = 6 ritual (EQUINOX, No. III.).

361 ADNI HARTz, the Lord of the Earth. Note 361 denotes the 3 Supernals, the 6 members of Ruach, and Malkuth. This name of God therefore embraces all the 10 Sephiroth.

365 An important number, though not in the pure Qabalah. See "The Canon." ΜΕΙΘΡΑΣ and ΑΒΡΑΞΑΣ in Greek.

370 Really more important for Part II. OSh, Creation. The Sabbatic Goat in his highest aspect. This shows the whole of Creation as matter and spirit. The material 3, the spiritual 7, and all cancelling to Zero. Also ShLM = peace.

400 The letter ת, "The Universe." It is the square of 20, "The Wheel of Fortune," and shows the Universe therefore as the Sphere of Fortune—the Samsara-Cakkram, where Karma, which fools call chance, rules.

400 is the total number of he Sephiroth, each of the 10 containing 10 in itself and being repeated in the 4 worlds of Atziluth, Briah, Yetzirah, and Assiah. These four worlds are themselves attributed to IHVH, which is therefore not the name of a tribal fetish, but the formula of a system.

401 ATh, "the" emphatic, meaning "essence of," for A and Th are first and last letters of the Hebrew Alphabet, as A and Ω are of the Greek, and A and Z of the Latin. Hence the Word Azoth, not to be confused with Azote (lifeless, azotos), the old name for nitrogen. Azoth means the sum and essence of all, conceived as One.

406 ThV, the letter Tau (see 400), also AThH, "Thou." Note that AHA (7), the divine name of Venus (7), gives the initials of Ani, Hua, Ateh—I, He, Thou; three different aspects of a deity worshipped in three persons and in three ways: viz. (1) with averted face; (2) with prostration; (3) with identification.

418 Pertains principally to Part II., q.v.

419 TITh, the letter Teth.

434 DLTh, the letter Daleth.

440 ThLI, the great dragon.

441 AMTh, Truth. Note 441 = 21 × 21. 21 is AHIH, the God of Kether, whose Will is Truth.

450 ThN, the great dragon.

463 NTH HShQD, Moses' Wand, a rod of Almond. 3 + 60 + 400, the paths of the middle pillar.

474 DOTh, Knowledge, the Sephira that is not a Sephira. In one aspect the child of Chokmah and Binah; in another the Eighth Head of the Stooping Dragon, raised up when the Tree of Life was shattered, and Macroposopus set cherubim against Microposopus. See 4 = 7 ritual *supra*. Also, and very specially, Liber 418. It is the demon that purely intellectual or rational religions take as their God. The special danger of Hinayana Buddhism.

480 LILITh, the demon-queen of Malkuth.

543 AHIH AShR AHIH, "I am that I am."

666 Last of the mystic numbers of the sun. SVRTh, the spirit of Sol. Also OMMV SThH, Ommo Satan, the Satanic Trinity of Typhon, Apophis, and Besz; also ShM IHShVH, the name of Jesus. The names of Nero, Napoleon, W. E. Gladstone, and any person that you may happen to dislike, add up the this number. In reality it is the final extension of the number 6, both because 6 × 111 (ALPh = 111 = 1) = 6 and because the Sun, whose greatest number it is, is 6.

(I here interpolate a note on the "mystic numbers" of the planets. The first is that of the planet itself, *e.g.* Saturn, 3. The second is that of the number of squares in the square of the planet, *e.g.* Saturn 9. The third is that of the figures in each line of the "magic square" of the planet, *e.g.* Saturn 15. A "magic square" is one in which each file, rank, and diagonal add to the same number, *e.g.* Saturn is 816, 357, 492, each square being filled in with the numbers from 1 upwards.

The last of the magic numbers is the sum of the whole of the figures in the square, *e.g.* Saturn 45. The complete list is thus:

Saturn 3, 9, 15, 45.
Jupiter 4, 16, 34, 136.
Mars 5, 25, 65, 325.
Sol 6, 36, 111, 666.
Venus 7, 49, 175, 1225.

Mercury 8, 64, 260, 2080.

Luna 9, 81, 369, 3321.

Generally speaking, the first number gives a divine name, the second an archangelic or angelic name, the third a name pertaining to the Formative world, the fourth a name of a "spirit" or "blind force." For example, Mercury has AZ and DD (love) for 8, DIN and DNI for 64, TIRIAL for 260, and ThPThRThRTh for 2080. But in the earlier numbers this is not so well carried out. 136 is both IVPhIL, the Intelligence of Jupiter, and HSMAL, the Spirit.

The "mystic numbers" of the Sephiroth are simply the sums of the numbers from 1 to their own numbers.

Thus (1) Kether = 1.

(2) Chokmah = 1 + 2 = 3.

(3) Binah = 1 + 2 + 3 = 6.

(4) Chesed = 1 + 2 + 3 + 4 = 10.

(5) Geburah = 1 + 2 + 3 + 4 + 5 = 15.

(6) Tiphereth = 1 + 2 + 3 + 4 + 5 + 6 = 21.

(7) Netzach = 1 + 2 + 3 + 4 + 5 + 6 + 7 = 28.

(8) Hod = 1 + 2 + 3 + 4 + 5 + 6 + 7 + 8 = 36.

(9) Yesod = 1 + 2 + 3 + 4 + 5 + 6 + 7 + 8 + 9 = 45.

(10) Malkuth = 1 + 2 + 3 + 4 + 5 + 6 + 7 + 8 + 9 + 10 = 55.

The most important attributions of 666, however, pertain to the second part, q.v.

671 ThORA the Law, ThROA the Gate, AThOR the Lady of the Path of Daleth, ROThA the Wheel. Also ALPH, DLTh, NUN, IVD, Adonai (see 65) spelt in full.

This important number marks the identity of the Augoeides with the Way itself ("I am the Way, the Truth, and the Life") and shows the Taro as a key; and that the Law itself is nothing else than this. For this reason the outer College of the A∴ A∴ is crowned by this "knowledge and conversation of the Holy Guardian Angel."

This number too is that of the Ritual of Neophyte. See Liber XIII.

741 AMThSh, the four letters of the elements. AMN, counting the N final as 700, the supreme Name of the Concealed One. The dogma is that the Highest is but the Four Elements; that there is nothing beyond these, beyond Tetragrammaton. This dogma is most admirably portrayed by Lord Dunsany in a tale called "The Wanderings of Shaun."

777 *Vide supra.*

800 AShTh, the Rainbow. The Promise of Redemption (8)—8 as Mercury, Intellect, the Ruach, Microprosopus, the Redeeming Son —in its most material form.

811 IAΩ (Greek numeration).

888 Jesus (Greek numeration).

913 BRAShITh, the Beginning. See "A Note on Genesis." This list[1] will enable the student to follow most of the arguments of the dogmatic Qabalah. It is useful for him to go through the arguments by which one can prove that any given number is the supreme. It is the case, the many being but veils of the One; and the course of argument leads one to knowledge and worship of each number in turn. For example.

Thesis. The Number Nine is the highest and worthiest of the numbers.

Scholion α. "The number nine is sacred, and attains the summits of philosophy," Zoroaster.

Scholion β. Nine is the best symbol of the Unchangeable One, since by whatever number it is multiplied,the sum of the figures is always 9, *e.g.* 9 × 487 = 4383. 4 + 3 + 8 + 3 = 18. 1 + 8 = 9.

Scholion γ. 9 = ט, a serpent. And the Serpent is the holy Uraeus, upon the crown of the Gods.

Scholion δ. 9 = IX = the Hermit of the Tarot, the Ancient One with Lamp (Giver of Light) and Staff (the Middle Pillar of the Sephiroth). This, too, is the same Ancient as in 0, Aleph.

"The Fool" and Aleph = 1.

Scholion ε. 9 = ISVD = 80 = P = Mars = 5 = ה =

$$\text{the Mother} = \text{Binah} = 3 \left\{ \begin{array}{l} = G = GML = 73 = ChKMH = \\ = AB = \text{The Father} = \\ = (\,1 + 2\,)\ \text{Mystic Number of Chokmah} = \end{array} \right.$$

= Chokmah = 2 = B = the Magus = I = 1.

Scholion ϝ. 9 = the Foundation of all things = the Foundation of the alphabet = Yod = 10 = Malkuth = Kether = 1.

---

1 The complete dictionary, begun by Fra. I. A., continued Fra. P. and revised by Fra. A. e. G. and others, will shortly be published by authority of the A∴ A∴ [Liber D, following.—Eds.]

Scholion ξ. 9 = IX = The Hermit = Yod = 10 = X = The Wheel of Fortune = K = 20= XX = The Last Judgment = Sh = 300= 30 = L = Justice = VIII = 8 = Ch = The Chariot = VII = 7 = Z = The Lovers = VI = 6 = V (Vau) = The Pope = V = 5 = H = The Emperor = IV = 4 = D = The Empress = III = 3 = G = The High Priestess = 11 = 2 = B = The Magus = I = 1 = A = The Fool = 0.

Scholion η. 9 = Luna = G = 3, etc., as before.

Scholion θ. $9 = \left\{ \begin{array}{l} \text{Indigo} \\ \text{Lead} \end{array} \right\}$ = Saturn = 3, etc, as before.

There are many other lines of argument. This form of reasoning reminds one of the riddle "Why is a story like a ghost?" Answer. "A story's a tale; a tail's a brush; a brush is a broom; a brougham's a carriage; a carriage is a gig; a gig's a trap; a trap's a snare; a snare's a gin; gin's a spirit; and a spirit's a ghost."

But our identities are not thus false; meditation reveals their truth. Further, as I shall explain fully later, 9 is not equal to 1 for the neophyte. These equivalences are dogmatic, and only true by favour of Him in whom All is Truth. In practice each equivalence is a magical operation to be carried out by the aspirant.

PART II

THE UNIVERSE AS WE SEEK TO MAKE IT

In the first part we have seen all numbers as Veils of the One, emanations of and therefore corruptions of the One. It is the Universe as we know it, the static Universe.

Now the Aspirant to Magic is displeased with this state of things. He finds himself but a creature, the farthest removed from the Creator, a number so complex and involved that he can scarcely imagine, much less dare to hope for, its reduction to the One.

The numbers useful to him, therefore, will be those which are subversive of this state of sorrow. So the number 2 represents to him the Magus (the great Magician Mayan who has created the illusion of Maya) as seen in the 2nd Aethyr. And considering himself as the Ego who posits the Non-Ego (Fichte) he hates this Magus. It is only the beginner who regards this Magus as the Wonder-worker—as the thing he wants to be. For the adept such little consolation as he may win is rather to be found by regarding the Magus as B = Mercury = 8 = Ch = 418 = ABRAHADABRA, the great Word, the "Word of Double Power in the Voice of the Master" which unites the 5 and the 6, the Rose and the Cross, the Circle and the Square. And also B is the Path from Binah to Kether; but that is only important for him who is already in Binah, the "Master of the Temple."

He finds no satisfaction in contemplating the Tree of Life, and the orderly arrangement of the numbers; rather does he enjoy the Qabalah as a means of juggling with these numbers. He can leave nothing undisturbed; he is the Anarchist of Philosophy. He refuses to acquiesce in merely formal proofs of the Excellence of things, "He doeth all things well," "Were the world understood Ye would see it was good," "Whatever is, is right," and so on. To him, on the contrary, whatever is, is wrong. It is part of the painful duty of a Master of the Temple to understand everything. Only he can excuse the apparent cruelty and fatuity of things. He is of the supernals; he sees things from above; yet, having come from below, he can sympathise with all. And he does not expect the Neophyte to share his views. Indeed, they are not true to a Neophyte. The silliness of the New-Thought zanies in passionately affirming "I am healthy! I am opulent! I am well-dressed! I am happy," when in truth they are "poor and miserable and blind and naked," is not a philosophical but a practical silliness. Nothing exists, says the Magister Templi, but perfection. True; yet their consciousness is imperfect. Ergo, it does not exist. For the M.T. this is so: he has "cancelled out" the complexities of the mathematical expression called existence, and the answer is zero. But for the beginner his pain and another's joy do not balance; his pain hurts him, and his brother may go hang. The Magister Templi, too, understands why Zero must plunge through all finite numbers to express itself; why it must write itself as "n − n" instead of 0; what gain there is in such writing. And this understanding will be found expressed in Liber 418 (Episode of Chaos and His Daughter) and Liber Legis (i. 28–30).

But it must never be forgotten that everyone must begin at the beginning. And in the beginning the Aspirant is a rebel, even though he feel himself to be that most dangerous type of rebel, a King Dethroned.[2]

Hence he will worship any number which seems to him to promise to overturn the Tree of Life. He will even deny and blaspheme the One—whom, after all, it is his ambition to be—because of its simplicity and aloofness. He is tempted to "curse God and die."

Atheists are of three kinds.

1. The mere stupid man. (Often he is very clever, as Bolingbroke, Bradlaugh, and Foote were clever.) He has found out one of the minor arcana, and hugs it and despises those who see more than himself, or who regard things from a different standpoint. Hence he is usually a bigot, intolerant even of tolerance.

2. The despairing wretch, who, having sought God everywhere, and failed to find Him, thinks everyone else is as blind as he is, and that if he has failed—he, the seeker after truth!—it is because there is no goal. In his cry there is pain, as with the stupid kind of atheist there is smugness and self-satisfaction. Both are diseased Egos.

3. The philosophical adept, who, knowing God, says "There is No God," meaning "God is Zero," as qabalistically He is. He holds atheism as a philosophical speculation as good as any other, and perhaps less likely to mislead mankind and do other practical damage than any other.

Him you may know by his equanimity, enthusiasm, and devotion. I again refer to Liber 418 for an explanation of this mystery. The nine religions are crowned by the ring of adepts whose password is "There is No God," so inflected that even the Magister when received among them had not wisdom to interpret it.

1. Mr Daw, K.C.: M'lud, I respectfully submit that there is no such creature as a peacock.
2. Oedipus at Colonus: Alas! there is no sun! I, even I, have looked and found it not.
3. Dixit Stultus in corde suo: "Ain Elohim."

---

2 And of course, if his revolt succeeds, he will acquiesce in order. The first condition of gaining a grade is to be dissatisfied with the one that you have. And so when you reach the end you find order as at first; but also that the law is that you must rebel to conquer.

There is a fourth kind of atheist, not really an atheist at all. He is but a traveller in the Land of No God, and knows that it is but a stage on his journey—and a stage, moreover, not far from the goal. Daath is not on the Tree of Life; and in Daath there is no God as there is in the Sephiroth, for Daath cannot understand unity at all. If he thinks of it, it is only to hate it, as the one thing which he is most certainly not (see Liber 418, 10th Aethyr. I may remark in passing that this book is the best known to me on Advanced Qabalah, and of course it is only intelligible to Advanced Students).

This atheist, not in-being but in-passing, is a very apt subject for initiation. He has done with the illusions of dogma. From a Knight of the Royal Mystery he has risen to understand with the members of the Sovereign Sanctuary that all is symbolic; all, if you will, the Jugglery of the Magician. He is tired of theories and systems of theology and all such toys; and being weary and anhungered and athirst seeks a seat at the Table of Adepts, and a portion of the Bread of Spiritual Experience, and a draught of the wine of Ecstasy.

It is then thoroughly understood that the Aspirant is seeking to solve the great Problem. And he may conceive, as various Schools of Adepts in the ages have conceived, this problem in three main forms.

1. I am not God. I wish to become God.
   > This is the Hindu conception.
   I am Malkuth. I wish to become Kether.
   > This is the qabalistic equivalent.

2. I am a fallen creature. I wish to be redeemed.
   > This is the Christian conception.
   I am Malkuth, the fallen daughter. I wish to be set upon the throne of Binah my supernal mother.
   > This is the qabalistic equivalent.

3. I am the finite square; I wish to be one with the infinite circle.
   > This is the Unsectarian conception.
   I am the Cross of Extension; I wish to be one with the infinite Rose.
   > This is the qabalistic equivalent.

The answer of the Adept to the first form of the problem is for the Hindu "Thou art That" (see previous chapter, "The Yogi"); for the Qabalist "Malkuth is in Kether, and Kether is in Malkuth," or "That which is below is like that which is above" or simply "Yod." (The foundation of all letters having the number 10, symbolising Malkuth.)

The answer of the Adept to the second form of the problem is for the Christian all the familiar teaching of the Song of Songs and the Apocalypse concerning the Bride of Christ.[3]

For the Qabalist it is a long complex dogma which may be studied in the Zohar and elsewhere. Otherwise, he may simply answer "Hé" (the letter alike of mother and daughter in IHVH). See Liber 418 for lengthy disquisitions on this symbolic basis.

The answer of the Adept to the third form of the problem is given by π, implying that an infinite factor must be employed.

For the Qabalist it is usually symbolised by the Rosy Cross, or by such formulae as $5 = 6$. That they concealed a Word answering this problem is also true. My discovery of this word is the main subject of this article. All the foregoing exposition has been intended to show why I sought a word to fulfil the conditions, and by what standards of truth I could measure things.

But before proceeding to this Word, it is first necessary to explain further in what way one expects a number to assist one in the search for truth, or the redemption of the soul, or the formulation of the Rosy Cross. (I am supposing that the reader is sufficiently acquainted with the method of reading a name by its attributions to understand how, once a message is received, and accredited, it may be interpreted.) Thus if I ask "What is knowledge?" and receive the answer "DOTh," I read it Daleth the door, O matter, Th darkness, by

---

3   This Christian teaching (not its qabalistic equivalent) is incomplete. The Bride (the soul) is united, though only by marriage, with the Son, who then presents her to the Father and Mother or Holy Spirit. These four then complete Tetragrammaton. But the Bride is never united to the Father. In this scheme the soul can never do more than touch Tiphereth and so receive the ray from Chokmah. Whereas even St John makes his Son say "I and my Father are one." And we all agree that in philosophy there can never be (in Truth) more than one; this Christian dogma says "never less than four." Hence its bondage to law and its most imperfect comprehension of any true mystic teaching, and hence the difficulty of using its symbols.

various columns of 777 (To choose the column is a matter of spiritual intuition. Solvitur ambulando). But here I am only dealing with the "trying of the spirits, to know whether they be of God."

Suppose now that a vision purporting to proceed from God is granted to me. The Angel declares his name. I add it up. It comes to 65. An excellent number! a blessed angel! Not necessarily. Suppose he is of a Mercurial appearance? 65 is a number of Mars.

Then I conclude that, however beautiful and eloquent he may be, he is a false spirit. The Devil does not understand the Qabalah well enough to clothe his symbols in harmony.

But suppose an angel, even lowly in aspect, not only knows the Qabalah—your own researches in the Qabalah—as well as you do, but is able to show you truths, qabalistic truths, which you had sought for long and vainly! Then you receive him with honour and his message with obedience.

It is as if a beggar sought audience of a general, and showed beneath his rags the signet of the King. When an Indian servant shows me "chits" signed by Colonel This and Captain That written in ill-spelt Babu English, one knows what to do. On the contrary the Man Who Was Lost rose and broke the stem of his wineglass at the regimental toast, and all knew him for one of their own.

In spiritual dealings, the Qabalah, with those secrets discovered by yourself that are only known to yourself and God, forms the grip, sign, token and password that assure you that the Lodge is properly tiled.

It is consequently of the very last importance that these final secrets should never be disclosed. And it must be remembered that an obsession, even momentary, might place a lying spirit in possession of the secrets of your grade. Probably it was in this manner that Dee and Kelly were so often deceived.

A reference to this little dictionary of numbers will show that 1, 3, 5, 7, 12, 13, 17, 21, 22, 26, 32, 37, 45, 52, 65, 67, 73, 78, 91, 111, 120, 207, 231, 270, 300, 326, 358, 361, 370, 401, 406, 434, 474, 666, 671, 741, 913, were for me numbers of peculiar importance and sanctity. Most of them are venerable, referring to or harmonious with the One. Only a few—*e.g.* 120—refer to the means. There are many others—any others—just as good; but not for me. God in dealing with me would show me the signs which I should have intelligence enough to understand. It is a condition of all intellectual intercourse.

Now I preferred to formulate the practical problem in this shape: "How shall I unite the 5 and the 6, Microcosm and Macrocosm?"

And these are the numbers which seemed to me to bear upon the problem.

1 Is the goal, not the means. Too simple to serve a magician's purpose.

2 *Vide supra.*

3 Still too simple to work with, especially as 3 = 1 so easily. But, and therefore, a great number to venerate and desire.

4 The terrible number of Tetragrammaton, the great enemy. The number of the weapons of the Evil Magician. The Dyad made Law.

5 The Pentagram, symbol of the squaring of the circle by virtue of ALHIM = 3.1415, symbol of man's will, of the evil 4 dominated by man's spirit. Also Pentagrammaton, Jeheshua, the Saviour. Hence the Beginning of the Great Work.

6 The Hexagram, symbol of the Macrocosm and Microcosm interlaced, and hence of the End of the Great Work. (Pentagram on breast, Hexagram on back, of Probationer's Robe.) Yet it also symbolises the Ruach, 214, q.v., and so is as evil *in viâ* as it is good *in termino.*

7 A most evil number, whose perfection is impossible to attack.

8 The great number of redemption, because Ch = ChITh = 418, q.v. This only develops in importance as my analysis proceeds. A priori it was of n great importance.

9 Most Evil, because of its stability. AVB, witchcraft, the false moon of the sorceress.

10 Evil, memorial of our sorrow. Yet holy, as hiding in itself the return to the negative.

11 The great magical number, as uniting the antitheses of 5 and 6 etc. AVD the magic force itself.

12 Useless. Mere symbol of the Goal.

13 Helpful, since if we can reduce our formula to 13, it becomes 1 without further trouble.

17 Useful, because though it symbolises 1, it does so under the form of a thunderbolt. "Here is a magic disk for me to hurl, and win heaven by violence," says the Aspirant.

21 As bad, nearly, as 7.

26 Accursed. As bad as 4. Only useful when it is a weapon in your hand; then—"if Satan be divided against Satan," etc.

28 Attainable; and so, useful. "My victory," "My power," says the Philosophus.

30 The Balance—Truth. Most useful.

31 LA the reply to AL, who is the God of Chesed, 4. The passionate denial of God, useful when other methods fail.

32 Admirable, in spite of its perfection, because it is the perfection which all from 1 to 10 and Aleph to Tau, share. Also connects with 6, through AHIHVH.

37 Man's crown.

44 Useful to me chiefly because I had never examined it and so had acquiesced in it as accursed. When it was brought by a messenger whose words proved true, I then understood it as an attack on the 4 by the 11. "Without shedding of blood (DM = 44) there is no remission." Also since the messenger could teach this, and prophesy, it added credit to the Adept who sent the message.

45 Useful as the number of man, ADM, identified with MH, Yetzirah, the World of Formation to which man aspires as next above Assiah. Thus 45 baffles the accuser, but only by affirmation of progress. It cannot help that progress.

52 AIMA and BN. But orthodoxy conceives these as external saviours; therefore they serve no useful purpose.

60 Like 30, but weaker. "Temperance" is only an inferior balance. 120, its extension, gives a better force.

65 Fully dealt with in "Konx om Pax" q.v.

72 Almost as bad as 4 and 26; yet being bigger and therefore further from 1 it is more assailable. Also it does spell ChSD, Mercy, and this is sometimes useful.

73 The two ways to Kether, Gimel and Chokmah. Hence venerable, but not much good to the beginner.

74 LMD, Lamed, an expansion of 30. Reads "By equilibrium and self-sacrifice, the Gate!" Thus useful. Also $74 = 37 \times 2$.

So we see 37 × 1 = 37, Man's crown, Jechidah, the highest Soul—
in termino.
37 × 2 = 74, The Balance, 2 being the symbol *in viâ.*
37 × 3 = 111, Aleph, etc., 3 being the Mother, the nurse of
the soul.
37 × 4 = 148, "The Balances," and so on. I have not yet
worked out all the numbers of this important scale.

77 OZ, the Goat, *scil.* of the Sabbath of the Adepts. The Baphomet
of the Templars, the idol set up to defy and overthrow the false god
—though it is understood that he himself is false, not an end, but a
means. Note the 77 = 7 × 11, magical power in perfection.

78 Most venerable because MZLA is shown as the influence
descending from On High, whose key is the Tarot: and we possess
the Tarot. The proper number of the name of the Messenger of the
Most Exalted One. [The account of AIVAS follows in its proper
place.—Ed.]

85 Good, since 85 = 5 × 17.

86 Elohim, the original mischief. But good, since it is a key of the
Pentagram, 5 = 1 + 4 = 14 = 8 + 6 = 86.

91 Merely venerable.

111 Priceless, because of its 37 × 3 symbolism, its explanation of
Aleph, which we seek, and its comment that the Unity may be found
in "Thick darkness" and in "Sudden death." This is the most clear
and definite help we have yet had, showing Samadhi and the
Destruction of the Ego as gates of our final victory.

120 See Part I. and references.

124 ODN, Eden. The narrow gate or path between Death and the
Devil.

156 BABALON. This most holy and precious name is fully dealt
with in Liber 418. Notice 12 × 13 = 156. This was a name given and
ratified by Qabalah; 156 is not one of the à priori helpful numbers.
It is rather a case of the Qabalah illuminating St John's intentional
obscurity.

165 11 × XV should be a number Capricorni Pneumatici. Not yet
fulfilled.

201 AR, Light (Chaldee). Note 201 = 3 × 67, Binah, as if it were
said, "Light is concealed as a child in the womb of its mother." The
occult retort of the Chaldean Magi to the Hebrew sorcerers who

affirmed AVR, Light, 207, a multiple of 9. But this is little more than a sectarian squabble. 207 is holy enough.

206 DBR, the Word of Power. A useful acquisition = "The Gateway of the Word of Light."

210 Upon this holiest number it is not fitting to dilate. We may refer Zelatores to Liber VII. Cap. I., Liber Legis Cap. I., and Liber 418. But this was only revealed later. At first I only had ABRAHA, the Lord of the Adepts. *Cf.* Abraha-Melin.

214 RVCh is one of the most seductive numbers to the beginner. Yet its crown is Daath, and later one learns to regard it as the great obstacle. Look at its promise 21, ending in the fearful curse of 4! Calamity!

216 I once hoped much from this number, as it is the cube of 6. But I fear it only expresses the fixity of mind. Anyhow it all came to no good.

But we have DBIR, connected with DBR, adding the Secret Phallic Power.

220 This is the number of the verses of Liber Legis. It represents 10×22, *i.e.* the whole of the Law welded into one. Hence we may be sure that the Law shall stand as it is without a syllable of addition.

Note 10^{22}, the modulus of the universe of atoms, men, stars. See "Two new worlds."

222 The grand scale of 2; may one day be of value.

256 The eighth power of 2; should be useful.

280 A grand number, the dyad passing to zero by virtue of the 8, the Charioteer who bears the Cup of Babalon. See Liber 418, 12th Aethyr. See also 280 in Part I.

300 Venerable, but only useful as explaining the power of the Trident, and the Flame on the Altar. Too stable to serve a revolutionary, except in so far as it is fire.

333 See Part I.

340 Connects with 6 through ShM, the fire and the water conjoined to make the Name. Thus useful as a hint in ceremonial.

358 See Part I.

361 See Part I. Connects with the Caduceus; as 3 is the supernal fire, 6 the Ruach, 1 Malkuth. See illustration of Caduceus in Equinox No. II.

370 Most venerable (see Part I.). It delivers the secret of creation into the hand of the Magician. See Liber Capricorni Pneumatici.

400 Useful only as finality or material basis. Being 20 × 20, it shows the fixed universe as a system of rolling wheels (20 = K, the Wheel of Fortune).

401 See Part I. But Azoth is the Elixir prepared and perfect; the Neophyte has not got it yet.

406 See Part I.

414 HGVTh, Meditation, the 1 dividing the accursed 4. Also AIN SVP AVR, the Limitless Light.

418 CHITh, Cheth. ABRAHADABRA, the great Magic Word, the Word of the Aeon. Note the 11 letters, 5 A identical, and 6 diverse. Thus it interlocks Pentagram and Hexagram. BITh HA, the House of Hé the Pentagram; see Idra Zuta Qadisha, 694. "For H formeth K, but Ch formeth IVD." Both equal 20.

Note 4 + 1 + 8 = 13, the 4 reduced to 1 through 8, the redeeming force; and 418 = Ch = 8.

By Aiq Bkr ABRAHADABRA = 1 + 2 + 2 + 1 + 5 + 1 + 4 + 1 + 2 + 2 + 1 = 22. Also 418 = 22 × 19 = Manifestation. Hence the word manifests the 22 Keys of Rota.

It means by translation Abraha Deber, the Voice of the Chief Seer.

It resolves into Pentagram and Hexagram as follows:—

```
(1)  A
    /  \        [This is by taking the 5 middle letters.]
  R----B
     A          The pentagram is 12, HVA, Macroprosopus.
    /  \
  H    D        The hexagram is 406, AThH, Microprosopus.
    \  /
   A--A         Thus it connotes the Great Work.
   B--R
    \  /
     A          Note ABR, initials of the Supernals, Ab, Ben, Ruach.
```

```
(2)  A      B    [This is by separating the One (Aleph) from the Many
    /  \  /  \      (diverse letters).]
   A   A R   H                                    "The Vision and the Voice," a
    \  / |   |   BRH = 207, Aur, Light   phrase which meant much
   A--A  B   D   DBR = 206, Deber Voice  to me at the moment of dis-
          \  /                           covering this Word.
           R
```

```
(3)  A         A
    / \       / \
   A   A   B   A
    \ /   |   |     [By taking each alternate letter.]
   R—B    H   D
          \   /
            R
```

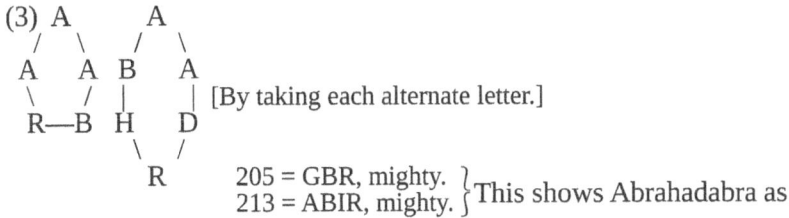

205 = GBR, mighty.
213 = ABIR, mighty. } This shows Abrahadabra as
the Word of Double Power, another phrase that meant much to me
at the time. AAB at the top of the Hexagram gives AB, AIM A, BN,
Father, Mother, Child.

HDR by Yetzirah gives Horus, Isis, Osiris, again Father, Mother,
Child This Hexagram is again the human Triad.

Dividing into 3 and 8 we get the Triangle of Horus dominating
the Stooping Dragon of 8 Heads, the Supernals bursting the Head of
Daath.

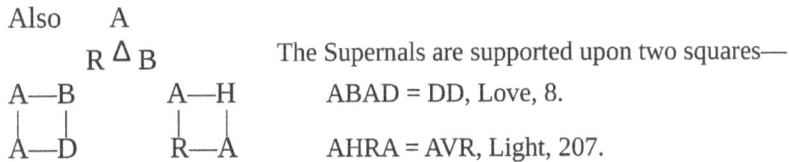

Also

```
        A
     R  △  B
```

The Supernals are supported upon two squares—

```
A—B        A—H        ABAD = DD, Love, 8.
|  |       |  |
A—D        R—A        AHRA = AVR, Light, 207.
```

Now 8 × 207 = 1656 = 18 = ChI, Living, and 207 = 9 × 23,
ChIH, Life. At this time "Licht, Liebe, Leben" was the mystic name
of the Mother-Temple of the G∴ D∴.

The five letters used in the word are A, the Crown; B, the Wand;
D, the Cup; H, the Sword; R, the Rosy Cross; and refer further to
Amoun the Father, Thoth His messenger, and Isis, Horus, Osiris, the
divine-human triad.

Also 418 = ATh IAV, the Essence of IAO, q.v.

This short analysis might be indefinitely expanded; but always
the symbol will remain the Expression of the Goal and the Exposition
of the Path.[4]

419 Teth, the number of the "laughing lion" on whom BABALON
rideth. See Liber 418. Note 419 + 156 = 575 = 23 × 25, occultly
signifying 24, which again signifies to them that understand the
interplay of the 8 and the 3. Blessed be His holy Name, the
Interpreter of his own Mystery!

434 Daleth, the holy letter of the Mother, in her glory as Queen.
She saves the 4 by the 7 (D = 4 = Venus = 7), thus connects with 28.

---

4 [Cf. corresponding entry in Liber D, p. 123 in the present volume.]

Mystic number of Netzach (Venus), Victory. Note the 3 sundering the two fours. This is the feminine victory; she is in one sense the Delilah to the divine Samson. Hence we adore her from full hearts. It ought to be remembered, by the way, that the 4 is not so evil when it has ceased to oppress us. The square identified with the circle is as good as the circle.

441 Truth, the square of 21. Hence it is the nearest that our dualistic consciousness can conceive of 21, AHIH, the God of Kether, 1. Thus Truth is our chiefest weapon, our rule. Woe to whosoever is false to himself (or to another, since in 441 that other is himself), and seven times woe to him that swerves from his magical obligation in thought, word, or deed! By my side as I write wallows in exhaustion following an age of torment one who did not understand that it is a thousand times better to die than to break the least tittle of a magical oath.

463 Shows what the Wand ought to represent. Not 364; so we should hold it by the lower end. The Wand is also Will, straight and inflexible, pertaining to Chokmah (2) as a Wand has two ends.

474 See Part I. To the beginner, though, Daath seems very helpful. He is glad that the Stooping Dragon attacks the Sanctuary. He is doing it himself. Hence Buddhists make Ignorance the greatest fetter of all the ten fetters. But in truth Knowledge implies a Knower and a Thing Known, the accursed Dyad which is the prime cause of misery.

480 Lilith. See Liber 418. So the orthodox place the legal 4 before the holy 8 and the sublime Zero. "And therefore their breaths stink."

543 Good, but only carries us back to the Mother.

666 Chosen by myself as my symbol, partly for the reasons given in Part I., partly for the reasons given in the Apocalypse. I took the Beast to be the Lion (Leo my rising sign) and Sol, 6, 666, the Lord of Leo on which Babalon should ride. And there were other more intimate considerations, unnecessary to enter upon in this place. Note however that the Tarot card of Leo, Strength, bears the number XI., the great number of the Magnum Opus, and its interchange with Justice, VIII.; and the key of 8 is 418.

This all seemed to me so important that no qabalistic truths were so firmly implanted in my mind at the time when I was ordered to abandon the study of magic and the Qabalah as these: 8, 11, 418, 666; combined with the profoundest veneration for 1, 3, 5, 7, 13, 37, 78, 91, 111. I must insist on this at the risk of tautology and over-emphasis; for it is the key to my standard of Truth, the test-numbers which I applied to the discernment of the Messenger from the Sanctuary.

That such truths may seem trivial I am well aware; let it be remembered that the discovery of an identity may represent a year's toil. But this is the final test; repeat my researches, obtain your own holy numbers; then, and not before, will you fully understand their Validity, and the infinite wisdom of the Grand Arithmetician of the Universe.

671 Useful, as shown in Part I.

741 Useful chiefly as a denial of the Unity; sometimes employed in the hope of tempting it from its lair.

777 Useful in a similar way, as affirming that the Unity is the Qliphoth. But a dangerous tool, especially as it represents the flaming sword that drove Man out of Eden. A burnt child dreads the fire. "The devils also believe, and tremble." Worse than useless unless you have it by the hilt. Also 777 is the grand scale of 7, and this is useless to anyone who has not yet awakened the Kundalini, the female magical soul. Note 7 as the meeting-place of 3, the Mother, and 10, the Daughter; whence Netzach is the Woman, married but no more.

800 Useful only in 5 = 6 symbolism, q.v.

888 The grand scale of 8. In Greek numeration therefore ΙΗΣΟΥΣ the Redeemer, connecting with 6 because of its 6 letters. This links Greek and Hebrew symbolism; but remember that the mystic Iesous and Yeheshua have no more to do with the legendary Jesus of the Synoptics and the Methodists than the mystic IHVH has to do with the false God who commanded the murder of innocent children. The 13 of the Sun and the Zodiac was perhaps responsible for Buddha and his 12 disciples, Christ and his 12 disciples, Charlemagne and his 12 peers, &c., &c., but to disbelieve in Christ or Charlemagne is not to alter the number of the signs of the Zodiac. Veneration for 666 does not commit me to admiration for Napoleon and Gladstone.

I may close this paper by expressing a hope that I may have the indulgence of students. The subject is incomparably difficult; it is almost an unworked vein of thought; and my expression must be limited and thin. It is important that every identity should be most thoroughly understood. No mere perusal will serve. This paper must be studied line by line, and even to a great extent committed to memory. And that memory should already be furnished with a thorough knowledge of the chief correspondences of 777. It is hard to "suffer gladly" the particular type of fool who expects with a twenty-third-rate idle brain to assimilate in an hour the knowledge that it has cost me twelve years to acquire. I may add that nobody will ever understand this method of knowledge without himself undertaking research. Once he has experienced the joy of connecting (say) 131 and 480 through 15, he will understand. Further, it is the work itself, not merely the results, that is of service. We teach Greek and Latin, though nobody speaks either language.

And thus I close: Benedictus sit Dominus Deus Noster qui nobis dedit Scientiam Summam.

Amen!

SEPHER SEPHIROTH
SVB FIGVRÂ
D
(ὁ ἀριθμός)

PREFACE

CAN any good thing come out of Palestine? is the broader anti-Semitic retort to the sneer cast by the Jews themselves against the harmless and natural Nazarene; one more example of the poetic justice of History. And no doubt such opponents of the modern Jew will acclaim this volume as an admirable disproof of that thesis which it purports to uphold.

The dissimilarities, amounting in some cases to sheer contradiction, which mark many numbers, will appear proof positive that there is nothing in the numerical Qabalah, especially as we may presume that by filling up this dictionary from the ordinary Hebrew Lexicon one would arrive at a mere hotch-pot.

Apart from this, there is a deeper-lying objection to the Qabalah; viz., that the theory is an example of the fallacy Post hoc propter hoc.

Are we to believe, asks the sceptic, that a number of learned men deliberately sat down and chose words for the sake of their numerical value? Language is a living thing, with many sources and diverse; can it be moulded in any such arbitrary fashion?

The only reply seems to be a mere assertion that to some extent it certainly is so. Examples of a word being spelt deliberately wrong do occur; and such a jugglery as the changing of the names of

Abram and Sarai to Abraham and Sarah can hardly be purposeless. Once admit the end of such a wedge, and it is difficult to say whether it may not be driven home so far as to split asunder the Tree of Knowledge, if not the Tree of Life.

Another line of argument is the historical. We do not here refer to the alleged forgery of the Qabalah by Rabbi Moses ben Leon— was it not?—but to the general position of the ethnologist that the Jews were an entirely barbarous race, incapable of any spiritual pursuit. That they were polytheists is clear from the very first verse of Genesis; that Adonai Melekh is identical with "Moloch" is known to every Hebraist. The "Old Testament" is mainly the history of the struggle of the phallic Jehovah against the rest of the Elohim, and that his sacrifices were of blood, and human blood at that, is indisputable.

Human sacrifices are to-day still practised by the Jews of Eastern Europe, as is set forth at length by the late Sir Richard Burton in the MS. which the wealthy Jews of England have compassed heaven and earth to suppress, and evidenced by the ever-recurring Pogroms against which so senseless an outcry is made by those who live among those degenerate Jews who are at least not cannibals.

Is it to such people, indeed, that we are to look for the highest and subtlest spiritual knowledge?

To this criticism there are but two answers. The first, that an esoteric tradition of great purity may co-exist with the most crass exoteric practice. Witness the Upanishads in the land of Jagganath, hook-swinging, and the stupidest forms of Hatha-Yoga.

Witness the Tipitaka (with such perfections as the Dhammapada) in the midst of peoples whose science of torture would seem to have sprung from no merely human imagination. The descriptions in the Tipitaka itself of the Buddhist Hells are merely descriptions of the actual tortures inflicted by the Buddhists on their enemies.

The second, that after all is said, I find it work very well. I do not care whether $\sqrt{-1}$ is an impossible, an unimaginable thing, or whether de Moivre really invented it, and if so, whether de Moivre was an immortal man, and wore whiskers. It helps me to make certain calculations; and so long as that is so, it is useful, and I stick to it.

Other criticisms of the methods of the Qabalah itself have been made and disposed of in the article on the subject in "The Temple of Solomon the King" (Equinox V) and no further reference need be made to them in this place. It is only necessary to say that the article should be studied most thoroughly, and also the article "A Note on Genesis" in the second number of The Equinox.

With these two weapons, and the Sword of the Spirit, the Practicus, fully armed, may adventure himself in the great battle wherein victory is Truth.

PERDURABO.

EDITORIAL NOTE

THIS dictionary was begun by Allan Bennett (Fra∴ Iehi Aour, now Bhikkhu Ananda Metteya) in the last decade of the nineteenth century since ψ-J.C. It was bequeathed to the present Editor, with many other magical MSS., on I.A.'s departure for Ceylon in 1899.

Frater Perdurabo used it, and largely added to it, in the course of his Qabalistic workings. With George Cecil Jones (Fra∴ Volo Noscere) he further added to it by making it a complete cross-correspondence to the Book DCCLXXVII.

It was further revised and checked, re-copied by a Jewish scribe, and again checked through, in the year V of the present Era.

The mathematical additions were continued by Fra∴ P. and Fra∴ Lampada Tradam; and the MS. finally copied on a specially constructed typewriter by Gerald Rae Fraser (Fra∴ ψ) who added yet further mathematical data.

This copy has again been checked by Fra∴ P. and Soror∴ N.N. and the proofs further by three separate scholars.

The method of employing the dictionary has been fully indicated in The Temple of Solomon the King [Equinox V].

None of the editors claim to possess even the smallest degree of scholarship. The method of compilation has been to include all words given in von Rosenroth's Qabalistic Dictionary, those specially commented on in S.D., I.R.Q., and I.Z.Q., those given in 777, and those found by Fratres I.A. and P. Some of them are found in texts of the Hebrew Scriptures which appeared to those adepts to be of magical importance. Owing to their carelessness, the meaning of some few words has been lost, and cannot now be traced.

ABBREVIATIONS, SIGNS, AND FIGURES

K.D. L.C.K. p.—	=	KABBALA DENUDATA cuius Pars Prima continet Locos Communes Kabbalisticos.
Dec.	=	Decan.
S.P.M.	=	Sphere of the Primum Mobile.
S.S.F.	=	Sphere of the Fixed Stars.
L.T.N.	=	Lesser Angel governing Triplicity by Night.
L.T.D.	=	Lesser Angel governing Triplicity by Day.
K.Ch.B.	=	Kether—Chokmah—Binah.
(Ch.)	=	Chaldee.
S.D.	=	Siphra Dtzenioutha.
I.R.Q.	=	Idra Rabba Qadisha.
Tet.	=	Tetragrammaton.
L.A. Angel	=	Lesser Assistant Angel.
I.Z.Q.	=	Idra Zuta Qadisha.
M.T.	=	Magister Templi.
ש	=	Shemhamphorasch.
W.	=	Wands.
C.	=	Cups.
S.	=	Swords.
P.	=	Pentacles.
K. of S.	=	Key of Solomon.
O.P.A.A.	=	Oriens—Paimon—Ariton—Amaimon.

♈ = Aries.
♉ = Taurus.
♊ = Gemini.
♋ = Cancer.
♌ = Leo.
♍ = Virgo.
♎ = Libra.
♏ = Scorpio.
♐ = Sagittarius.
♑ = Capricornus.
♒ = Aquarius.
♓ = Pisces.

♄ = Saturn.
☉ = Sun.
☽ = Moon.
♂ = Mars.
☿ = Mercury.
♃ = Jupiter.
♀ = Venus.

☐ enclosing a number shows that the number is a perfect square.
√ before „ „ „ a squared square.
♛ above „ „ „ a perfect number.
⌊ about „ „ „ a factorial.*
‖⌊ about „ „ „ a sub-factorial.
R(n) before „ „ „ a reciprocal (or 'amicable') number.

Σ (1—k) is an abbreviation for "the sum of the first k natural numbers."

* See special table following.

TABLE OF FACTORS

ODD NUMBERS FROM 1 TO 3321 (5'S EXCLUDED); SHOWING LOWEST FACTORS, AND PRIMES (P.). "—" INDICATES THAT THE NUMBER IS DIVISIBLE BY 3.

1	P.	71	P.	147	—	221	13	297	—		
2	P.	73	P.	149	P.	223	P.	299	13		
3	P.	77	7	151	P.	227	P.	301	7		
5	P.	79	P.	153	—	229	P.	303	—		
7	P.	81	$3^4=9^2$	157	P.	231	—	307	P.		
9	3^2	83	P.	159	—	233	P.	309	—		
11	P.	87	—	161	7	237	—	311	P.		
13	P.	89	P.	163	P.	239	P.	313	P.		
17	P.	91	7	167	P.	241	P.	317	P.		
19	P.	93	—	169	13^2	243	3^5	319	11		
21	—	97	P.	171	—	247	13	321	—		
23	P.	99	—	173	P.	249	—	323	17		
27	3^3	101	P.	177	—	251	P.	327	—		
29	P.	103	P.	179	P.	253	11	329	7		
31	P.	107	P.	181	P.	257	P.	331	P.		
33	—	109	P.	183	—	259	7	333	—		
37	P.	111	—	187	11	261	—	337	P.		
39	—	113	P.	189	—	263	P.	339	—		
41	P.	117	—	191	P.	267	—	341	11		
43	P.	119	7	193	P.	269	P.	343	7		
47	P.	121	11^2	197	P.	271	P.	347	P.		
49	7^2	123	—	199	P.	273	—	349	P.		
51	—	127	P.	201	—	277	P.	351	—		
53	P.	129	—	203	7	279	—	353	P.		
57	—	131	P.	207	—	281	P.	357	—		
59	P.	133	7	209	11	283	P.	359	P.		
61	P.	137	P.	211	P.	287	7	361	19^2		
63	—	139	P.	213	—	289	17^2	363	—		
67	P.	141	—	217	7	291	—	367	P.		
69	—	143	11	219	—	293	P.	369	—		

371	7	453	—	537	—	619	P.	701	P.
373	P.	457	P.	539	7	621	—	703	19
377	13	459	—	541	P.	623	7	707	7
379	P.	461	P.	543	—	627	—	709	P.
381	—	463	P.	547	P.	629	17	711	—
383	P.	467	P.	549	—	631	P.	713	23
387	—	469	7	551	19	633	—	717	—
389	P.	471	—	553	7	637	7	719	P.
391	17	473	11	557	—	639	—	721	7
393	—	477	—	559	13	641	P.	723	—
397	P.	479	P.	561	—	643	P.	727	P.
399	—	481	13	563	P.	647	P.	729	$3^6=9^3=27^2$
401	P.	483	—	567	—	649	11	731	17
403	13	487	P.	569	P.	651	—	733	P.
407	11	489	—	571	P.	653	P.	737	11
409	P.	491	P.	573	—	657	—	739	P.
411	—	493	17	577	P.	659	P.	741	—
413	7	497	7	579	—	661	P.	743	P.
417	—	499	P.	581	7	663	—	747	—
419	P.	501	—	583	11	667	23	749	7
421	P.	503	P.	587	P.	669	—	751	P.
423	—	507	—	589	17	671	11	753	—
427	7	509	P.	591	—	673	P.	757	P.
429	—	511	7	593	P.	677	P.	759	—
431	P.	513	—	597	—	679	7	761	P.
433	P.	517	11	599	P.	681	—	763	7
437	19	519	—	601	P.	683	P.	767	13
439	P.	521	P.	603	—	687	—	769	P.
441	-21^2	523	P.	607	P.	689	13	771	—
443	P.	527	17	609	—	691	P.	773	P.
447	—	529	23^2	611	13	693	—	777	—
449	P.	531	—	613	P.	697	17	779	19
451	11	533	13	617	P.	699	—	781	11

783	—	869	11	951	—	1033	P.	1117	P.
787	P.	871	13	953	P.	1037	17	1119	—
789	—	873	—	957	—	1039	P.	1121	19
791	7	877	P.	959	7	1041	—	1123	P.
793	13	879	—	961	31^2	1043	7	1127	7
797	P.	881	P.	963	—	1047	—	1129	P.
801	17	883	P.	967	P.	1049	P.	1131	—
803	11	887	P.	969	—	1051	P.	1133	11
807	—	889	7	971	P.	1053	—	1137	—
809	9	891	—	973	7	1057	7	1139	17
811	P.	893	19	977	P.	1059	—	1141	7
813	—	897	—	979	11	1061	P.	1143	—
817	19	899	29	981	—	1063	P.	1147	31
819	—	901	17	983	P.	1067	11	1149	—
821	P.	903	—	987	—	1069	P.	1151	P.
823	P.	907	P.	989	23	1071	—	1153	P.
827	P.	909	—	991	P.	1073	29	1157	13
829	P.	911	P.	993	—	1077	—	1159	19
831	—	913	11	997	P.	1079	13	1161	—
833	7	917	7	999	—	1081	23	1163	P.
837	—	919	P.	1001	7	1083	—	1167	—
839	P.	921	—	1003	17	1087	P.	1169	7
841	29^2	923	13	1007	19	1089	-33^2	1171	P.
843	—	927	—	1009	P.	1091	P.	1173	—
847	7	929	P.	1011	—	1093	P.	1177	11
849	—	931	7	1013	P.	1097	P.	1179	—
851	23	933	—	1017	—	1099	7	1181	P.
853	P.	937	P.	1019	P.	1101	—	1183	7
857	P.	939	—	1021	P.	1103	P.	1187	P.
859	P.	941	P.	1023	—	1107	—	1189	29
861	—	943	23	1027	13	1109	P.	1191	—
863	P.	947	P.	1029	—	1111	11	1193	P.
867	—	949	13	1031	P.	1113	—	1197	—

1199	11	1281	—	1363	29	1447	P.	1529	11
1201	P.	1283	P.	1367	P.	1449	—	1531	P.
1203	—	1287	—	1369	37^2	1451	P.	1533	—
1207	17	1289	P.	1371	—	1453	P.	1537	29
1209	—	1291	P.	1373	P.	1457	31	1539	—
1211	7	1293	—	1377	—	1459	P.	1541	23
1213	P.	1297	P.	1379	7	1461	—	1543	P.
1217	P.	1299	—	1381	P.	1463	7	1547	7
1219	23	1301	P.	1383	—	1467	—	1549	P.
1221	—	1303	P.	1387	19	1469	13	1551	—
1223	P.	1307	P.	1389	—	1471	P.	1553	P.
1227	—	1309	7	1391	13	1473	—	1557	—
1229	P.	1311	—	1393	7	1477	7	1559	P.
1231	P.	1313	13	1397	11	1479	—	1561	7
1233	—	1317	—	1399	P.	1481	P.	1563	—
1237	P.	1319	P.	1401	—	1483	P.	1567	P.
1239	—	1321	P.	1403	23	1487	P.	1569	—
1241	17	1323	—	1407	—	1489	P.	1571	P.
1243	11	1327	P.	1409	P.	1491	—	1573	11
1247	29	1329	—	1411	17	1493	P.	1577	19
1249	P.	1331	11	1413	—	1497	—	1579	P.
1251	—	1333	31	1417	13	1499	P.	1581	—
1253	7	1337	7	1419	—	1501	19	1583	P.
1257	—	1339	13	1421	7	1503	—	1587	—
1259	P.	1341	—	1423	P.	1507	11	1589	7
1261	13	1343	17	1427	P.	1509	—	1591	37
1263	—	1347	—	1429	P.	1511	P.	1593	—
1267	7	1349	19	1431	—	1513	17	1597	P.
1269	—	1351	7	1433	P.	1517	37	1599	—
1271	31	1353	—	1437	—	1519	7	1601	P.
1273	19	1357	23	1439	P.	1521	-39^2	1603	7
1277	P.	1359	—	1441	11	1523	P.	1607	P.
1279	P.	1361	P.	1443	—	1527	—	1609	P.

1611	—	1693	P.	1777	P.	1859	11	1941	—
1613	P.	1697	P.	1779	—	1861	P.	1943	29
1617	—	1699	P.	1781	13	1863	—	1947	—
1619	P.	1701	—	1783	P.	1867	P.	1949	P.
1621	P.	1703	13	1787	P.	1869	—	1951	P.
1623	—	1707	—	1789	P.	1871	P.	1953	—
1627	P.	1709	P.	1791	—	1873	P.	1957	19
1629	—	1711	29	1793	11	1877	P.	1959	—
1631	7	1713	—	1797	—	1879	P.	1961	37
1633	23	1717	17	1799	7	1881	—	1963	13
1637	P.	1719	—	1801	P.	1883	7	1967	7
1639	11	1721	P.	1803	—	1887	—	1969	11
1641	—	1723	P.	1807	13	1889	P.	1971	—
1643	31	1727	11	1809	—	1891	31	1973	P.
1647	—	1729	7	1811	P.	1893	—	1977	—
1649	17	1731	—	1813	7	1897	7	1979	P.
1651	13	1733	P.	1817	23	1899	—	1981	7
1653	—	1737	—	1819	17	1901	P.	1983	—
1657	P.	1739	37	1821	—	1903	11	1987	P.
1659	—	1741	P.	1823	P.	1907	P.	1989	—
1661	11	1743	—	1827	—	1909	23	1991	11
1663	P.	1747	P.	1829	31	1911	—	1993	P.
1667	P.	1749	—	1831	P.	1913	P.	1997	P.
1669	P.	1751	17	1833	—	1917	—	1999	P.
1671	—	1753	P.	1837	11	1919	19	2001	—
1673	7	1757	7	1839	—	1921	17	2003	P.
1677	—	1759	P.	1841	7	1923	—	2007	—
1679	23	1761	—	1843	19	1927	41	2009	7
1681	41^2	1763	41	1847	P.	1929	—	2011	P.
1683	—	1767	—	1849	43^2	1931	P.	2013	—
1687	7	1769	29	1851	—	1933	P.	2017	P.
1689	—	1771	7	1853	17	1937	13	2019	—
1691	19	1773	—	1857	—	1939	7	2021	43

2023	7	2107	7	2189	11	2271	—	2353	13
2027	P.	2109	—	2191	7	2273	P.	2357	P.
2029	P.	2111	P.	2193	—	2277	—	2359	7
2031	—	2113	P.	2197	13	2279	43	2361	—
2033	19	2117	29	2199	—	2281	P.	2363	17
2037	—	2119	13	2201	31	2283	—	2367	—
2039	P.	2121	—	2203	P.	2287	P.	2369	23
2041	13	2123	11	2207	P.	2289	—	2371	P.
2043	—	2127	—	2209	47^2	2291	29	2373	—
2047	23	2129	P.	2211	—	2293	P.	2377	P.
2049	—	2131	P.	2213	P.	2297	P.	2379	—
2051	7	2133	—	2217	—	2299	11	2381	P.
2053	P.	2137	P.	2219	7	2301	—	2383	P.
2057	11	2139	—	2221	P.	2303	7	2387	7
2059	29	2141	P.	2223	—	2307	—	2389	P.
2061	—	2143	P.	2227	17	2309	P.	2391	—
2063	P.	2147	19	2229	—	2311	P.	2393	P.
2067	—	2149	7	2231	23	2313	—	2397	—
2069	P.	2151	—	2233	11	2317	7	2399	P.
2071	19	2153	P.	2237	P.	2319	—	2401	$7^4 = 49^2$
2073	—	2157	—	2239	P.	2321	11	2403	—
2077	31	2159	17	2241	—	2323	23	2407	29
2079	—	2161	P.	2243	P.	2327	13	2409	—
2081	P.	2163	—	2247	—	2329	17	2411	P.
2083	P.	2167	11	2249	13	2331	—	2413	19
2087	P.	2169	—	2251	P.	2333	P.	2417	P.
2089	P.	2171	13	2253	—	2337	—	2419	P.
2091	—	2173	41	2257	37	2339	P.	2421	—
2093	7	2177	7	2259	—	2341	P.	2423	P.
2097	—	2179	P.	2261	7	2343	—	2427	—
2099	P.	2181	—	2263	31	2347	P.	2429	7
2101	11	2183	37	2267	P.	2349	—	2431	11
2103	—	2187	3^7	2269	P.	2351	P.	2433	—

2437	P.	2519	11	2601	-51^2	2683	P.	2767	P.
2439	—	2521	P.	2603	19	2687	P.	2769	—
2441	P.	2523	—	2607	—	2689	P.	2771	17
2443	7	2527	7	2609	P.	2691	—	2773	47
2447	P.	2529	—	2611	7	2693	P.	2777	P.
2449	31	2531	P.	2613	—	2697	—	2779	7
2451	—	2533	17	2617	P.	2699	P.	2781	—
2453	11	2537	43	2619	—	2701	37	2783	11
2457	—	2539	P.	2621	P.	2703	—	2787	—
2459	P.	2541	—	2623	43	2707	P.	2789	P.
2461	23	2543	P.	2627	37	2709	—	2791	P.
2463	—	2547	—	2629	11	2711	P.	2793	—
2467	P.	2549	P.	2631	—	2713	P.	2797	P.
2469	—	2551	P.	2633	P.	2717	11	2799	—
2471	7	2553	—	2637	—	2719	P.	2801	P.
2473	P.	2557	P.	2639	7	2721	—	2803	P.
2477	P.	2559	—	2641	19	2723	7	2807	7
2479	37	2561	13	2643	—	2727	—	2809	53^2
2481	—	2563	11	2647	P.	2729	P.	2811	—
2483	13	2567	17	2649	—	2731	P.	2813	29
2487	—	2569	7	2651	11	2733	—	2817	—
2489	19	2571	—	2653	7	2737	7	2819	P.
2491	47	2573	31	2657	P.	2739	—	2821	7
2493	—	2577	—	2659	P.	2741	P.	2823	—
2497	11	2579	P.	2661	—	2743	13	2827	11
2499	—	2581	29	2663	P.	2747	41	2829	—
2501	41	2583	—	2667	—	2749	P.	2831	19
2503	P.	2587	13	2669	17	2751	—	2833	P.
2507	23	2589	—	2671	P.	2753	P.	2837	P.
2509	13	2591	P.	2673	—	2757	—	2839	17
2511	—	2593	P.	2677	P.	2759	31	2841	—
2513	7	2597	7	2679	—	2761	11	2843	P.
2517	—	2599	23	2681	7	2763	—	2847	—

2849	7	2931	—	3013	23	3097	19	3179	11
2851	P.	2933	7	3017	7	3099	—	3181	P.
2853	—	2937	—	3019	P.	3101	7	3183	—
2857	P.	2939	P.	3021	—	3103	29	3187	P.
2859	—	2941	17	3023	P.	3107	13	3189	—
2861	P.	2943	—	3027	—	3109	P.	3191	P.
2863	7	2947	7	3029	13	3111	—	3193	31
2867	47	2949	—	3031	7	3113	11	3197	23
2869	19	2951	13	3033	—	3117	—	3199	7
2871	—	2953	P.	3037	P.	3119	P.	3201	—
2873	13	2957	P.	3039	—	3121	P.	3203	P.
2877	—	2959	11	3041	P.	3123	—	3207	—
2879	P.	2961	—	3043	17	3127	53	3209	P.
2881	43	2963	P.	3047	11	3129	—	3211	13
2883	—	2967	—	3049	P.	3131	31	3213	—
2887	P.	2969	P.	3051	—	3133	13	3217	P.
2889	—	2971	P.	3053	43	3137	P.	3219	—
2891	7	2973	—	3057	—	3139	43	3221	P.
2893	11	2977	13	3059	7	3141	—	3223	11
2897	P.	2979	—	3061	P.	3143	7	3227	7
2899	13	2981	11	3063	—	3147	—	3229	P.
2901	—	2983	19	3067	P.	3149	47	3231	—
2903	P.	2987	29	3069	—	3151	23	3233	53
2907	—	2989	7	3071	37	3153	—	3237	—
2909	P.	2991	—	3073	7	3157	7	3239	41
2911	41	2993	41	3077	17	3159	—	3241	7
2913	—	2997	—	3079	P.	3161	29	3243	—
2917	P.	2999	P.	3081	—	3163	P.	3247	17
2919	—	3001	P.	3083	P.	3167	P.	3249	-57^2
2921	23	3003	—	3087	—	3169	P.	3251	P.
2923	37	3007	31	3089	P.	3171	—	3253	P.
2927	P.	3009	—	3091	11	3173	19	3257	P.
2929	29	3011	P.	3093	—	3177	—	3259	P.

3261	—	3273	—	3287	19	3299	P.	3311	7
3263	13	3277	29	3289	11	3301	P.	3313	P.
3267	—	3279	—	3291	—	3303	—	3317	31
3269	7	3281	17	3293	37	3307	P.	3319	P.
3271	P.	3283	7	3297	—	3309	—	3321	—

The first dozen factorials, and sub-factorials; and the ratios they bear to one another; note that $\lfloor n\, /\, \lVert n = e$

N	$\lfloor N$	$\lVert N$	$\lfloor N \div \lVert N$	$\lVert N \div \lfloor N$
1	1	0	∞	0˙000000
2	2	1	2˙000000	0˙500000
3	6	2	3˙000000	0˙333333
4	24	9	2˙666666	0˙375000
5	120	44	2˙727272	0˙366666
6	720	265	2˙716981	0˙368055
7	5040	1854	2˙718446	0˙367857
8	40320	14833	2˙718262	0˙367881
9	362880	133496	2˙718283	0˙367879
10	3628800	1334961	2˙718281	0˙367879
11	39916800	14684570	2˙718281	0˙367879
12	479001600	176214841	2˙718281	0˙367879

Factorial n, or $\lfloor n$, is the continued product of all the whole numbers from 1 to n inclusive and is the number of ways in which n different things can be arranged.

Sub-factorial n, or $\lVert n$, is the nearest whole number to $\lfloor n \div e$, and is the number of ways in which a row of n elements may be so deranged, that no element may have its original position.

Thus
$$\lfloor n = 1 \times 2 \times 3 \times \dots \times n,$$
and
$$\lVert n = \frac{1 \times 2 \times 3 \times \dots \times n}{2\,71828188\dots} \pm h,$$

where h is the smaller decimal fraction less than unity by which the fraction $\frac{1 \times 2 \times \dots \times n}{2\,718281\dots}$ differs from a whole number, and is to be added or subtracted as the case may be.—The most useful expression for $\lVert n$ is:

$$\lVert n \equiv \lfloor n \frac{n}{1} \lfloor n-1 + \frac{n(n-1)}{1.2} \lfloor n-2 \frac{n(n-1)(n-2)}{1.2.3} \lfloor n-3 + \text{etc.}$$

to $(n+1)$ terms.

$$e \equiv 1 + \frac{1}{\lfloor 1} + \frac{1}{\lfloor 2} \frac{1}{\lfloor 3} + \dots \text{ to } \infty$$
$$\equiv 2\,71828188\dots$$

Names of the letters	Figures of the letters	Value of the letters		English equivalents of the letters	
(M) Aleph	א	1		A	
(D) Beth	ב	2		B	
(D) Gimel	ג	3		G	
(D) Daleth	ד	4		D	
(S) Heh	ה	5		H (E)	
(S) Vau	ו	6		V (U)	
(S) Zayin	ז	7		Z	
(S) Kheth (Cheth)	ח	8		Ch	
(S) Teth	ט	9		T	
(S) Yodh	י	10		Y (I or J)	
(D) Kaph	כ ך	20	500	K	
(S) Lamed	ל	30		L	
(M) Mem	מ ם	40	600	M	
(S) Nun	נ ן	50	700	N	
(S) Samekh	ס	60		S	
(S) Ayin	ע	70		O (A'a or Ng)	
(D) Peh	פ ף	80	800	P	
(S) Tzaddi	צ ץ	90	900	Tz	
(S) Qoph	ק	100		Q	
(D) Resh	ר	200		R	
(M) Shin	ש	300		S	Sh
(D) Tau	ת	400		T	Th

When written large, the Value of a Hebrew letter is increased to one thousand times its ordinary value. A large Aleph is counted 1000: a large Beth, 2000: and so on.

Note that A, I, O, U, H, are really consonants, mere bases for vowels. These vowels are not here given, as they have no importance in Gematria.

M, D, and S before the names of the letters shews their division into Mothers, Double and Single letters, referred respectively to active Elements, Air, Water, Fire, Planets, and Signs. But ש and ת also serve to signify the Elements of Spirit and of Earth. See Liber 777.

♛

⌊1. ⌊2. The Mystic number π√1
of Kether. S. P. M.

⌊2. ⌊3. S. S. F. π2

[Abbreviation for 422, א:א:א
אריך אנפין, q.v.]

Σ (1—2). ♄. The Mystic π3
Number of Chokmah

Father אב

To come, go בא

The Number of Abra-Melin √4
Princes. ♃. 2²

Father אבא

Hollow; a vein בב

Proud גא

♂ π5

Mist, vapour אד

Back גב

♛

Σ (1—3). ⌊3. ☉. The Mystic 6
Number of Binah

To gather, collect גבא

Gog, the giant whose partner is גג
Magog

A bear דב

A window הא

♀ π7

Lost, ruined אבד

A name of GOD attributed to אהא
Venus. Initials of Adonai
ha-Aretz

Desire; either, or או

Gad, a Tribe of Israel; good גד
fortune

Was weary דאב

Riches, power דבא

Fish דג

2³. The Number of Abra-Melin ∛8
Sub-Princes, and of the Servitors of Oriens. ☿

To will, intend אבה

Desired, beloved אהב

אוא

Then אז

The entrance, threshold באה

To be anxious, grieve דאג

Love; beloved, breast; דד
pleasures of love

Nqn. Zauir Anpin 478 q.v. אז

⌊4. 3². ♄. ☽ √9

Ventriloquus: the special 'fire' אוב
of black magic, whence Obi,
Obeah. Cf. 11 and 207

He kindled אזא

Brother אח

A garment בגד

Became powerful, grew high גאה

Middle גו

Splendour; cf. 15 הד

Σ (1—4). The Mystic Number of 10
Chesed. Elementorum Sphaera.
The Number of Abra-Melin Servi-
tors of Amaimon and Ariton

Enchanter אט

[Vide K.D. L.C.K. p. 185] בגה

Elevated, exalted, high גבה

Flew, soared דאה

Two דו

Window הה

A wolf זאב

A hidden place; bosom חב

π11

Ahah אהה

Firebrand, volcanic fire: the אוד
Special 'fire' or 'light' of the
Sacred Magic of Light, Life,
and Love; hence "Odic
Force" &c. Cf. 9 and 207

Where אי

When בבוא

To tear, cut, attack גדד

Gold (Ch.) דהב

Proud, haughty זד

A circularity of form or motion; חג
a feast

12

He longed for, missed אוה

He departed, went forth אזד

A little book, pamphlet, letter; גט
tools

To multiply דגה

A city of Edom	הבה
HE. [ה is referred to Mater, 1 to Pater, א to Corona]	הוא
Vau; hook, nail, pin	וו
This, that	זה
To penetrate, be sharp; (Ch.) one	חד

π 13

A small bundle, bunch	אגדה
Beloved; Love	אהבה
Unity	אחד
Hated	איב
Emptiness	בהו
Raised up	גהה
Chokmah, 42-fold Name in Yetzirah. (See 777)	גי
Anxiety	דאגה
A fisher	דוג
Thunder; to meditate; he re-removed	הגה
A city of Edom	הדד
Here; this	זו
A locust	חגב
He shall come	יבא

14

Rhamnus; a thorn, spine	אטד
Rising ground; Earth of Geburah. (See 777)	גיא
Sacrifice v. & s. (Ch.). (?)	דבח
Love, beloved: David	דוד
Give, give! [Vide no. 17, יהב]	הב הב
To grind, direct, stretch out	הדה
Gold	זהב
Hand	יד

Σ (1—5). Σ {1—(3 × 3)} ÷ 3. The 15 Mystic Number of Geburah. The Number of Abra-Melin Servitors of Asmodee and Magot, and of Paimon

Angel of 3rd Dec. ♐	אבוהא
The month of Exodus and Passover	אביב
Steam, vapour	איד
Pride; a carrying out; ex-altation	גאוה
Splendour, the Eighth Sephira	הוד

Overflowing, abounding	זוב
He who impels; to force	זח
To hide	חבה
The Monogram of the Eternal	יה

The Number of Abra-Melin √ ⁴√ 16 Servitors of Asmodee

Hyssopus	אזוב
He seized, cleaved to	אחז
Elevated, exalted, high	גבוה
(Verb. subst.) Injury, war, lust; fell	הוה
She	היא
Alas!—Woe	וי
Like, equal to	זוג

π 17

Nuts	אגז
Ah!—Alas!	אוי
Capricornus	גדי
Nerve, sinew. [Gen. xxxii. 25 & 32]	גיד
Narrative, subtle discourse	הגדה
K.D. L.C.K. p. 267	ההוא
To dream, rave	הזה
A fly	זבוב
Sacrificed	זבח
To seethe, boil	זוד
To brighten, make joyful	חדה
A circle, orbit	חוג
Good	טוב
To give, place	יהב

18

My favourite, my beloved	אהבי
Hatred	איבה
The antique Serpent	חטא
Living	חי
Notariqon of Yehi Aur, etc.	יאא

π 19

Angel L.T.D. of ♐	אהה
An enemy	אויב
Job	איוב
Was black	דיה
Chavvah; to manifest, shew forth; Eve	חוה

The Number of Abra-Melin 20 Servitors of Amaimon

Fraternity	אחוה
Black liquid	דיו
It was	היה
The breast; a vision; a prophet to gaze	חזה
Jobab, an Edomite King	יובב
The hand	יוד

Σ (1—6). The Mystic Number of Tiphareth — 21

Existence, Being, the Kether-name of GOD	אהיה
But, yet, certainly	אך
Deep meditation	הגיג
Ah!—Alas!	הוי
Purity, innocence	זהו
Vide Sepher Yetzirah	יהו

The Number of Abra-Melin Servitors of Ariton — 22

With his hand; Night Demon of 1st Dec. ♋	בידו
By Yodh	ביוד
Hearer in secret; Angel of 8 W.	האאיה
The state of puberty	זוג
A magical vision (Ch.)	חזוא
Wheat	חטה
Good	טובה
Notariqon of "Tet. Elohim Tet. Achad."	איא
Unity	יחד

π 23

Parted, removed, separated	זחח
Joy	חדוה
A thread	חוט
Life	חיה

⌊4. The Number of the 'Elders' in the Apocalypse — 24

He whom I love	אהובי
He who loves me	אוהבי
A Mercurial GOD. His essence is אﬞ, 8	אזבוגה
Substance; a body	גויה
A pauper	דך
Angel of 2 C.	הבביה
Abundance	זיז

A water-pot, a large earthen-ware vessel	כד

5² — √25

To break	דכא
The Beast	חיא
Jehewid, God of Geburah of Briah	יהוד
Let there be	יהי
Will be separated	יח
Thus	כה

The Numbers of the Sephiroth of the Middle Pillar, 1 + 6 + 9 + 10 — 26

[Vide K.D. L.C.K. p. 273]	הויה
Seeing, looking at	חחה
Sight, vision	חזוה
TETRAGRAMATON, "Jehovah," the Unutterable Name, the Lost Word	יהוה
Kebad, husband of the impure Lilith. [K.D. L.C.K. 464]	כבד

3² — ∛27

Wept, mourned	בכה
Purity	זך
A parable, enigma, riddle	חידה
♚	

Σ (1—7). The Mystic Number of Netzach — 28

Clay	טיט
Union, unity	יחוד
Power	כח

π 29

Is broken. [Ps. x. 10]	דכה
To break down, overturn	הדך

30

A party to an action at law; defendant, plaintiff. [Note ל = 30 = ♎ = 'Justice']	חייב
Judah	יהודה
It will be	יהיה

π 31

How?	איך
GOD of Chesed, and of Kether of Briah	אל
To go	הוך
A beating, striking, collision	הכאה

And there was. [Vide S.D.I. par. 31] ויהי

K. of S. Fig. 31 ייאי

Not לא

2⁵. The Number of Abramelin $\sqrt[6]{32}$ Servitors of Astarot

Coalescence of אהיה and אהיהוה יהוה Macroprosopus and Microprosopus. This is symbolized by the Hexagram. Suppose the 3 ה's conceal the 3 Mothers א, מ & ש and we get 358 q.v.

Lord בל

Angel of 5 W. והויה

Copula Maritalis זיווג

Was pure זכה

Zig-zag, fork-lightning חזיז

Unity K.D. L.C.K. p. 432 יחיד

Glory כבוד

Mind, heart לב

33

Sorrow; wept, mourned אבל

Day Demon of 1ˢᵗ Dec. ♈ באל

To destroy (Ch.); (?) a King בלא of Edom

Spring, fountain גל

$\Sigma \{1-(4 \times 4)\} \div 4.$ לב 34

"GOD the Father," divine אל אב name attributed to Jupiter

To ransom, avenge, pollute גאל

To reveal גלא

A pauper דל

A common person; un- הדיוט educated, ignorant

Angel of 7 C. ההויה

35

Agla, a name of God; אגלא notariqon of Ateh Gibor le-Olahm Adonai

Boundary, limit גבל

He will go יהך

$6^2 = \Sigma (1-8)$. ⊙. The Mystic $\sqrt{36}$ Number of Hod

Tabernaculum אהל

How? (Vide Lamentations) איכה

Duke of Geburah in Edom; אלה to curse; name of GOD attributed to ☿

To remove, cast away הלא

Confession וידוי

Leah לאה

Perhaps, possibly; would that! לו

π 37

Angel of 8 P. אכאיה

GOD (Ch.) אלהא

Behold! אלו

Perished, grew old בלה

To grow great גדל

Banner דגל

Tenuity, breath, vanity; in vain; הבל Abel. [I.Z.Q., "The Supernal Breathers."]

Night Demon of 2ⁿᵈ Dec. ♐ ואל

Profession זל

Jechidah, the Atma of Hindu יחידה philosophy

Flame להב

(?) Devotion of force לו

38

Night Demon of 2ⁿᵈ Dec. ♋ אאל

He departed אזל

Ghazi, servant of Elisha גיחזי

A City in the Mountains of גלה Judah

Innocent זכאי

The palate חיך

To make a hole, hollow; to חל violate

Green לח

39

To abide, dwell זבל

Dew טל

The Eternal is One יהוה אחד

Angel of 3 P. יחויה

Metathesis of יהוה כהו

He cursed לט

40

Bildad בלדד

Liberator; title of Jesod גואל

To cut off גזל

A rope; ruin; to bind	חבל
Milk	חלב
The Hand of the Eternal	יד יהוה
To me, to mine	לי

π 41

Fecundity	אחלב
Ram; force; hence = a hero	איל
Night Demon of 1st Dec. ♍	אלוד
My GOD	אלי
Mother	אם
To fail, cease	בטל
Divine Majesty	גאואל
Terminus	גבול
To burn	גחל
To go round in a circle	הול
[Vide Ps. cxviii. & I.R.Q. 778]	יה יהוה

The Number of the letters of a great 42 name of GOD terrible and strong, and of the Assessors of the Dead

Angel of 'Υ'	איאל
Eloah, a name of GOD	אלוה
The Supernal Mother, unfertilized; see 52	אמא
Terror, calamity	בלהה
Loss, destruction	בלי
To cease	חדל
The World, Earth of Malkuth	חלד
My glory	כבודי

π 43

Great	גדול
To rejoice	גיל
Challah; to make faint. [Vide K.D. L.C.K. p. 346]	חלה
[Vide K.D. L.C.K, p. 151; see no. 340]	לביא
Hazel, almond	לח

‖ 5. 220 ÷ 5   44

Drops	אגלי
A pool, pond; sorrow	אגם
Captive, captivity	גולה
Angel ruling ♊	גיאל
Aquarius	דלי
Blood	דם

Sand: also horror. See Scorpion Pantacle in K. of S. and 10th Aethyr	חול
A ram; 'Υ'	טלה
Tet. in ? World. [Vide K.D. L.C.K. p. 251]	יוד הא וו הא
Flame	להט

Σ (1—9). The Mystic Number 45 of Jesod

Intelligence of ♄	אגיאל
Adam	אדם
The Fool	אמד
Redemption, liberation	גאולה
To grow warm	הם
Heaven of Tiphareth	זבול
Hesitated. [Vide no. 405]	זחל
Spirit of ♄	זזאל
She who ruins	חבלה
Tet. in Yetzirah	יוד הא ואו הא
Greatly, strongly	מאד
Yetzirah's 'Secret Nature' [Vide I.R.Q. xxxiv.]	מה

46

A name of GOD	אלהי
A female slave; cubitus	אמה
Tin, the metal of ♃	בדיל
A dividing, sundering, separation	הבדלה
Angel of 7 S.	הההאל
A ruiner	חובל
Angel ruling ♉	טואל
Levi, Levite	לוי

π 47

Foolish, silly. (Stultus)	אויל
A weeping	בכייה
Cloud; high place; waves; fortress	במה
Angel ruling ♍	יואל
To clutch, hold	חלט

48

Mercy	גדולה
Angel of 2 W.	והואל
A woman [vide K.D. L.C.K. p. 320]; strength; an army	חיל
To grow warm; heat, fire; black; Ham, the son of Noah	חם

Jubilee   יובל

A star, planet; Sphere of ☿   כוכב

[Vide Ps. xciii. & Prov. Viii. 22] מאז

The Number of Abra-Melin   √49
Servitors of Beelzebub. 7². ♀

The Living GOD   אל חי

Qliphoth of Geburah   גולחב

Resembled; meditated;   דמה
silent

Intelligence of ♀   הגיאל

Strength   חילא

Heat, fury (Ch.)   חמא

A bringing forth, birth, nativity   לידה

A measuring, measure   מדה

Solve. [Vide no. 103]   מוג

The Rod of Aaron   מט

50

Red earth, the soil; Earth of   אדמה
Chesed

Closed, shut up   אטם

Angel of 9 P.   אלדיה

Jonah's Whale   דג גדול

To ferment   המה

Pains, sorrows   חבלי

Unclean, impure   טמא

58th ש   ייל

2nd ש   ילי

The sea   ים

All, every   כל

To thee   לך

What?—Which?   מי

51

Edom   אדום

Terrible; Day Demon of 2nd   אים
Dec. ♏

Ate; devoured   אכל

Pain   אן

Tumultuously (vide no. 451);   הום
to harass, perturb

Angel of 8 S. [Vide K. of S.,   יההאל
fig. 52]

Failure   נא

52

Father and Mother   אבא ואמא

Supernal Mother   אימא

Elihu = Eli Hua, "He is my   אליהו
GOD," who is the Holy
Guardian Angel of Job in
the Allegory

[Vide K.D. L.C.K. p. 134]   אנא

A mare; brute animal, beast   בהמה

Day Demon of 2nd Dec. ♐   בים

From all, among all   בכל

The Son: Assiah's "Secret   בן
Nature"

Meditation, imagination, sin   זמה

A desirable one; to desire   חמד

A husband's brother   יבם

Angel of Kether of Briah,   יהואל
and of Jesod of Briah

Tet. in Assiah   יוד הה וו הה

A dog   כלב

Angel of 4 C., and of 10 P.   לאויה

The Number of Abra-Melin Servitors π 53
of Astarot and Asmodee

The stone that slew Goliath;   אבן
a stone, rock

Elihu. (Vide 52)   אליהוא

The garden   גן

Angel of 9 P.   הזיאל

To defend, hide; a wall; the   חמה
sun; fury

The spleen   טחול

A lover   מאהבה

54

A basin, bowl, vessel.   אגן
[Ex. xxiv. 6]

Rest   דמי

A Tribe of Israel; to judge, rule. דן
[Vide K.D. L.C.K. p.37]

Pertaining to summer   חום

My flame; enchantments   להטי

A bed; stick, rod   מטה

To remove   נד

Σ (1—10). The Mystic Number of 55
Malkuth

Thief; stole   גנב

Robbery, pillage   גזילה

Silence. [For name of Angels, דומה
see Sohar Sch. V. Cap. 18]

A footstool	הדום
To swell, heave. [Vide no. 51]	הים
To walk	הלך
Knuckle; member, limb	חוליא
The bride	כלה
Noon; midday	נגב
Ornament	נה

56

Dread, terror	אימה
He suffered	אנה
Angel of 4 C.	הייאל
Day	יום
Beautiful	נאה

57

Rim	אבדן
Consuming	אוכל
Wealth, an age, Time; Night Demon of 1st Dec. ♏	און
Formidable, terrible	איום
We	אנו
A breaking down, subversion, destruction	ביטיל
Built	בנה
♓. [Fish (pl.); vide 7]	דגים
Angel of 8 C.	וליה
Angel of 5 C.	לוויה
Altar	מזבח
The laying-by, making secret	מחבא

58

[Vide no. 499]	אהבים
[Vide K.D. L.C.K. p. 69] An ear	אזן
Night Demon of 1st Dec. ♐	דאגן
My strength, power, might	חילי
Love, kindness, grace; notariqon of Chokmah Nesthrah, the Secret Wisdom	חן
Ruler of Water	טליהד
Angel of 6 S.	ייזאל
Angel of 3 P.	להחיה
[Vide K.D. L.C.K. p. 69]	נח

π 59

Brethren. [Referred to Lilith & Samael—K.D. L.C.K. p. 54]	אחים

Heathen	גוים
A wall	חומה
Menstruata	נדה

60

Tried by fire; a watch-tower	בחן
Excellence, sublimity, glory, pride	גאון
Constitution, tradition	הלכה
To behold	הנה
A basket	טנא
Angel of 8 C.	ילהיה
Vision	מחזה
The Southern district	נגבה

π 61

Master, Lord, Adon	אדון
The Negative, non-existent; not	אין
Towards, to thee	אליכ
I, myself	אני
The belly	בטן
Angel of 10 S.	דמביה
Wealth	הון
Angel of 6 C.	ייאל
Habitaculum	נוה

62

Healing	אסא
Angel of 2nd Dec. ♈	בההמי
The sons	בני
To commit; healing	זנה

63

Abaddon, The Hell of Chesed	אבדון
Dregs, roll; faeces (globular); dung	גלל
Fed	זון
The nose	חוטם
Fervour	חימה
Tet. in Briah	יוד הי ואו הי
Briah's "Secret Nature"	סג

$$8^2 = 4^3 = 2^6. \quad ☿ \quad \sqrt{} \quad \sqrt[3]{} \quad \sqrt[6]{} \quad 64$$

A sigh, groan, deep breath	אנחה
Justice	דין
(Din and Doni are twin Mercurial Intelligences in Gemini)	דני
The golden waters	מי זהב
[I.R.Q. xl. 996]	מיזהב
Prophecy	נבואה

Sphere of ♀	נוגה
Noach	גוח

Σ {1—(5 × 5)} ÷ 5. The Number of 65 Abra-Melin Servitors of Magot and Kore

Adonai	אדני
Weasels and other terrible animals	אוחים
The Palace	היכל
Shone, gloried, praised	הלל
To keep silence	הס
Defective. [Vide K.D. L.C.K. p. 339]	חזן
6th ש	ללה
A door post	מזוזה
A beating, striking	מכה
[Vide K.D. L.C.K. p. 563]	נהי

The Mystic Number of the Qliphoth, 66 and of the Great Work. Σ (1—11)

Food, vituals	אכילה
The Lord thy GOD (is a consuming Fire). [Deut.iv.24]	אלהיך
A ship	אניה
A trial, an experiment	בחון
A wheel. [Called "Cognomen Schechinae"]	גלגל
A City of Edom	דנהבה

π 67

[Vide K.D. L.C.K. p. 57]	אוני
The Understanding	בינה
Night Demon of 3rd Dec. ♊	וינא
Zayin	זין
Debased	זלל
To embalm	חנט
Angel of 3 C.	יבמיה

68

Wise.—Intelliget ista?	ויבן
To be wise	חכם
Emptiness	חלל
To pity	חס
Ramus Tabernacularis	לולב

69

A manger, stable; an enclosure	אבוס
Myrtle	הדס

L.A. Angel of ♓	וכביאל

70

(A proper name)	אדניה
Hush, be silent	הסה
Wine	יין
Night	ליל
[Vide Ps. xxv. 14.] The Secret	סוד

π 71

Thy terror	אימך
Nothing; an apparition, image	אליל
Silence; silent	אלם
Night Demon of 1st Dec. ♒	אמדוך
Lead, the metal of Saturn; a plummet-line, level, water-level	אנך
Vision	חזון
A dove, pigeon	יונה
A dove	יונה
Plentitude, fullness	מלא

[72 × 3 = 216, אריה; vide K.D. L.C.K. p. 151.] There are 72 quinaries (spaces of 5°) in the Zodiac. The Shemhamphorasch or 'divided name' of GOD consists of 72 triliteral names, which by adding יה or אל give 72 angels. Vide Lib. DCCLXXVII — 72

Adonai, transliterated as by Lemegeton, etc.	ארונאי
Geomantic Intelligence of ♐	ארוכיאל
In, so, thus, then	בכן
In the secret	בסוד
And they are excellent, finished	ויכלו
Kindness, mercy	חסד
Tet. in Atziluth	יוד הי ויו הי
Maccabee	מכבי
Atziluth's "Secret Nature"—thickness, cloud; Aub	עב

π 73

Demon-King of Hod, and Night Demon of 2nd Dec. ♒	בליאל
Gimel	גמל
The Wise One	חכמה
To trust in, shelter in	חסה

A day of feast	יום טוב

74

A leader, chief, judge	דיין
Worn-out (?shameless) Beggars	דכים
Ox-goad	למד
A circuit; roundabout	סביב
All the way, constantly	עד

75

Hues, colours, complexions	גווני
Lucifer, the Herald Star	הילל
[Vide K. of S., fig. 53]	יכדיאל
A lamenting, wailing	יללה
The Pleiades	כימה
Night; by night	לילה
NUIT, THE STAR GODDESS	נויט

76

Secret, put away; a hiding-place	חביון
Rest, peace	ניחח
Slave, servant	עבד

77

Prayed	בעה
The river Gihon. [Gen. ii. 13]	גיחין
Overflowing. [Ps. cxxiv. 5]	זידון
Towers, citadels	מגדל
The Influence from Kether	מזל
Strength; a he-goat	עז

There are 78 cards in the Tarot. **78** Σ(1—12). The Mystic Number of Kether as Hua. The sum of the Key-Numbers of the Supernal Beard

Angel of 10 W.	אומאל
Angel of Ra Hoor Khuit	איואס
Briatic Palace of Chesed	היכל אהבה
Angel of ♂	זמאל
The breaker, dream	חלם
To pity	חמל
To initiate	חנך
Angel of 2 S.	יזלאל
Angel of 1ˢᵗ Dec. ♉	כדמדי

Bread (Ps. lxxviii. 25) = לחם, חלם by metathesis. [K.D. L.C.K. p. 500]

Angel of 2 S.	מבהאל

The Influence from Kether	מזלא
Salt	מלח
The name of a Giant	עזא

π 79

Boaz, one of the Pillars of the Temple of Solomon	בעז
Die	גוע
Angel of 8 S.	ומבאל
Jachin, one of the Pillars of the Temple of Solomon	יאחין
3ʳᵈ ש	סיט
Conjunction, meeting, union	עדה

80

Union; an assembling	ועד
God of Jesod-Malkuth of Briah	יה אדני
Foundation	יסוד
Universal, general	כלל
Throne. [Exod. xvii. 16]	כס
	מם

$$9^2 = 3^4. \quad ☽ \qquad \sqrt{} \ \sqrt[4]{} \ 81$$

GODS	אלים
I. [Ex. xxiii. 20]	אנכי
Anger, wrath; also nose	אף
Hearer of Cries; Angel of 6 P., and of 5 W.	יילאל
Night Demon of 2ⁿᵈ Dec. ♍	כאין
Throne	כסא
Here, hither	פא

82

Angel of ♀	אנאל
A Prayer (Ch.)	בעי
Briatic Palace of Hod	היכל גוגה
Kindly, righteous, holy	חסיד
Laban; white	לבן
The beloved thing; res grata	ניחוח

π 83

Abbreviatura quatuor systematum	אביא
The drops of dew. [Job xxxviii. 28]	אגלי טל
Benajahu, son of Jehoiada	בניהו
See 73	גימל
A flowing, wave	גלים
Person, self; (Ch.) wing	גף

Consecration; dedicated	חנכה
Angel of 2 P.	לכבאל
To flee, put one's things in safety. [Jerem. vi. 1]	זוע

7×12; or $(2^2 + 3)$ $(2^2 \times 3)$—hence 84
esteemed by some

A wing (army), squadron; a chosen troop	אגף
[I.Z.Q. 699]	אהחע
[Vide K.D. L.C.K. p.71]	אחהע
Was silent	דמם
A dream	חלום
Enoch	חנוך
Knew	ידע

85

Boaz (is referred to Hod)	בועז
A flower, cup	גביע
Put in motion, routed	המם
Circumcision	מילה
The mouth; the letter פ	פה

86

A name of GOD, asserting the identity of Kether and Malkuth	אהיה אדני
Elohim. [Note masc. pl. of fem. sing.]	אלהים
Hallelu-Jah	הללויה
A rustling of wings	המולה
Geomantic Intelligence of ♑	הנאל
[Vide I.R.Q. 778]	יה יהוה אדם
A cup; hence Pudendum Muliebre	כוס
A blemish, spot, stain	מום
Angel of 10 C.	מיהאל
Plenitude	מלוי

87

[Vide K.D. L.C.K. p. 114]	אלון
A cup	אסוך
Angel of 1st Dec. ♓	בהלמי
Blasphemed	גדף
Standards, military ensigns	דגלים
Determined	זמם
White Storks	חסידה
Whiteness; frankincense; Sphere of ☽	לבנה

88

Redness; sparkling	חכלל
To be hot	חמם
Darkness	חסך
A duke of Edom	מגדיאל
Roaring, seething; burning	נחל

π 89

Shut up	גוף
Body	גוף
Silence	דממה
Angel of 9 S.	מחיאל

90

Very silent	דומם
The Pillar, Jachin	יכין
Water	מים
Kings	מלך
Wicker-basket	סל
Night Demon of 2nd Dec. ♌	פוד

Σ (1—13). The Mystic Number of 91
Kether as Achad. The Number
of Paths in the Supernal Beard;
according to the number of the
Letters, כ = 11, etc.

A tree	אילן
Amen. [Cf. 741]	אמן
The Ephod	אפיד
The "יהוה אדני", interlaced	יאהדונהי
Angel of 4 S.	כליאל
Archangel of Geburah	כמאל
Food, fare	מאכל
Angel	מלאך
Daughter, virgin, bride, Kore	מלכא
Manna	מנא
A hut, tent	סוכה
Pekht, 'extension'	פאהה

92

Angel of 5 S.	אניאל
Mud	בץ
(Deut. xxviii. 58.) [Vide no. 572]	יהוה אלהיך
Terror, a name of Geburah	פחד

93

A duke of Edom. [Vide also Ezekiel xxiii.]	אהליבמה

The sons of (the merciful) GOD   בני אל

Incense   לבונה

A disc, round shield   מגן

Possession   נחלה

Arduous, busy; an army   צבא

94

Corpse   גופה

The valley of vision   גיחזיון

To extinguish   דעך

Destruction. [Ps. l. 20]   דפי

A shore   חוף

A window   חלון

A drop   טפה

Children   ילדים

95

The great Stone   אבן גדלה

Angel of 2 W.—Daniel   דניאל

Angel of 10 P.   ההעיה

The waters   המים

Multitude, abundance; Haman   המן

Zabulon   זבלון

Angel of 2nd Dec. ♌   זחעי

Mars   מאדים

Journey   מהלך

Queen   מלכה

Selah. [Ps. xxxii. 5, 6, etc.]   סלה

96

A name of GOD   אל אדני

Chaldee form of אלהים   אלהין

By day   יומם

Praiseworthy; Angel of 7 W.   ללהאל

Work   מלאכה

The secret (counsel) of the Lord. [Ps. xxv. 14]   סוד יהוה

π 97

Breeder, rearer; Day Demon of 1st Dec. ♊   אומן

Changeless, constant; the GOD Amon   אמון

The Son of Man   בן אדם

Archangel of Netzach   האניאל

The appointed time   זמן

To seize suddenly (rapere)   חטף

A hand-breadth, palm. [I Kings vii. 26—Ex. xxv. 25]   טפח

A brick, tile   לבינה

A building; an architect   מבנה

Aquae EL Boni. ["Quicksilver," K.D. L.C.K. p. 442]   מי אל הטב

98

A name of GOD   הוא אלהים

Temporary dwelling. [Ex. xxxiii. 11]   זמנא

Image; hid, concealed—pertains to Sol and the Lingam-Yoni   חמן

To consume, eat   חסל

White   צח

99

The pangs of childbirth   חבלי לידה

The Vault of Heaven; an inner chamber; wedlock, nuptial   חופה

Clay of Death, Infernal Abode of Geburah   טיטהיון

Cognition, knowledge   ידיעה

10^2 √ 100

A day; the seas; the times. [Vide no. 1100]   ימים

Vases, vessels   כלים

The palm; the letter Kaph   כף

An effort, exertion. [I.R.Q. 995]   מדון

Mitigation of the one by the other   מחי טבאל

π 101

Swallowed, destroyed   אלע

A storehouse   אסם

[Vide K.D. L.C.K. p. 147]   אק

Angel of 4 C.   מומיה

Archangel of ☉ and △; Angel of 7 S.; Angel of Malkuth of Briah, etc.   מיכאל

Kingdom; a virgin princess; esp. THE Virgin Princess, i.e. Ecclesia   מלוכה

Gut; gut-string   נימא

102

A white goose   אווז לבן

Trust, truth, faith   אמונה

Bela, a King of Edom; to   בעל
possess; lands, government

Concupiscibilis   נחמד

Grace, pride, fame, glory; a   צבי
wild goat

π 103

Dust   אבק

To guard, protect   גנן

Loathed   געל

Food, meat (Ch.)   מזון

Oblation   מנחה

Prophets   נבאים

A calf   עגל

104

Father of the mob, or of   אב המון
the multitude

Quarrel, dispute   מדין

Personal (belongings), small   סגולה
private property

Sodom   סדם

Giving up, presenting,   סולח
remitting

Trade; a fish-hook   צדי

Σ (1—14).   105

To subvert, ruin, change   הפך

Desert land: Earth of Netzach   ציה

106

Attained   דבק

Angel of 7 C.   מלהאל

Fish; the letter Nun   נון

Angel of 9 C.   סאליה

Stibium   פוך

Line, string, linen thread   קו

π 107

An egg   ביצה

Angel of Netzach of Briah   וסיאל

Angel ruling ♌   עואל

$2^2 \times 3^3$: hence used as the number of 108
beads of a rosary by some sects

The ears   אזנים

The fruit of a deep valley   באבי הנחל

Hell of Jesod-Malkuth   גיהנם

A wall   חיץ

To force, do wrong to   חמס

To love very much   חנן

To shut up, obstruct   חסם

The middle   חצי

To measure out; a decree;   חק
tall. (Masc. gender.) Cf. 113

Angel L.T.D. of ♌   סגהם

A Giant: "the lust of GOD"   עזאל

π 109

Day-demon of 2nd Dec. ♒   אסכוהדאי

Lightning   בקז

Quiet   מנוחה

Music   נגון

Angel of ♃   סחיאל

Circle, sphere   עגול

צדידא

110

Father of Faith   אב האמונה

Tectum coeli fabrilis sub   גג החופה
quo desponsationes con-
iugum fiunt

Resemblance, likeness   דמיון

Cherubic Signs—♏ replaced   וטהץ
by ♈

To embrace   חבק

At the end of the days; the   ימין
right hand

A sign, flag, standard   נס

Angel of 6 W.   סיטאל

Kinsman   עם

The Number of Abra-Melin Servitors 111
of O.P.A.A. Σ{1—(6×6)}÷6. ☉

Red. [Vide Gen. xxv. 25]   אדמוני

A name of God   אחד הוא אלהים

A thousand; Aleph   אלף

Ruin, destruction, sudden death   אסן

AUM   אעם

Thick darkness   אפל

Passwords of ......   יוד יהוה אדני

Mad   מהולל

Angel of ☉   נכיאל

Common holocaust; an ascent   עולה

A Duke of Edom   עלוה

Title of Kether. (Mirum   פלא
occultum)

112

Angel of 2 C.   איעאל

A structure; mode of building   בנין

Was angry   בנס

Sharpness   חדק

Jabok. [Gen. xxxii. 22.]   יבק
Note 112 = 4 × 28

The Lord GOD   יהוה אלהים

Ebal   עיבל

π 113

Likewise; the same. (Fem.   חקה
   gender.) Cf. 108

A giving away, remitting   סליחה

A stream, brook   פלג

114

Qliphoth of Jesod   גמליאל

Tear (weeping)   דמע

Gracious, obliging, indulgent   חנון

Science   מדא

Brains   מוחין

115

Geomantic Intelligence of ♍   דמליאל

Here am I   הנני

The heat of the day   חום היום

To make strong; vehement,   חזק
   eager

116

Doves   יונים

Heaven of Chesed   מכון

The munificent ones   נדיבים

Primordial   עילאה

117

Fog, darkness   אופל

Guide; Duke   אלוף

118

To pass, renew, change   חלף

To ferment   חמע

Strength; Chassan, Ruler of Air   חסן

The High Priest   כהן גדול

119

Lydian-stone   אבן בוחן

Beelzebub, the Fly-GOD   בעלזבוב

Weeping (subst.)   דמעה

Night Demon of 2nd Dec. ♈   חאלף

Abominable   פגול

⌊5 = Σ (1—15):—ה being the   120
   5th Path

Master   כעל

Foundation, basis   מוסדי

The time of the decree   מועד

Strengthening   מכין

Prophetic sayings, or decrees: מלים
   "His days shall be";—
   Abra-Melin

Velum   מסך

Prop; the letter Samekh   סמך

A name of GOD   ען

11²   √121

Vain idols   אלילים

?Termination of Abr-amelim?   אמילם

An end, extremity   אפס

Emanated from   אצל

Of whirling motions   הגלגלים

Nocturnal vision   חזוה די ליליא

Angel ruling ♋   כעאל

It is filled   נמלא

Angel L.T.N. of ♋   עכאל

122

Vi compressa   אנוסה

Revolutiones (Animarum)   גלגולים

123

A name of GOD,   אהה יהוה אלהים
   implying Kether—Chokmah—
   Binah, 3,4, & 5 letters

War   מלחמה

A blow, plague   נגע

Pleasure, delight   ענג

Laesio aliqualis, violatio   פגם

124

An Oak; hardness   חוסן

Pleasure, delight; Eden   עדן

Qliphoth of Chokmah   עגיאל

5³   ∛125

Night Demon of 2nd Dec. ♓   דנמאל
[Vide S.D. v. 16]   כפכה

Angel of 4 P.   מנדאל

126

A window   אלמנה

Darkness   אפילה

Day Demon of 1ˢᵗ Dec. ♉   גימיגין

A name of GOD   יהוה אדני אגלא

Hospitality   מלון

Horse   סוס

On, a name of GOD [see 120],   עון
penalty of iniquity; "being
taken away"

π 127

Material   מוטבע

Angel of 5 P.   פויאל

2⁷   ⁷√ 128

Eliphaz   אליפז

Angel ruling ♒   אנמואל

To deliver, loose   חלץ

Robustus gratia. [Vide K.D.   חסין
L.C.K. p. 399]

GOD, the Eternal One   יהוה אלהינו

129

Pleasure [Gen. xviii. 12]   עדנה

Delight, pleasure   עונג

130

Deliverance   הצלה

The Angel of re-   מלאך הגאל
demption

Decrees, prophetic sayings   מלין

Eye; the letter Ayin   עין

The Pillars   עמודי

Destitute   עני

A staircase, ladder   סלם

Angel of 5 C.   פהליה

π 131

He was angry   אנף

Nose   אפים

Turn, roll   אפן

Title of Kether   מכוסה

Angel of 6 C.   נלכאל

Samael; Qliphoth of Hod   סמאל

Angel L.T.N. of ♍   ססיא

Humility   ענוה

132

To make waste   בלק

Angel of 4 W.   ננאל

To receive   קבל

133

[Vide I.Z.Q. 699]   גיכק

Vine   גפן

Angel of 5 S.   חעמיה

The salt sea   ים המלח

134

Burning   דלק

135

Day Demon of 2ⁿᵈ Dec. ♋   גוסיון

Geomantic Intelligence   מלכדיאל
of ♈

A destitute female   עניה

The congregation. [Vide   קהל
no. 161]

[Vide K.D. L.C.K. p. 673]   קלה

Σ (1—16). ♃   136

Spirit of ♃   הסמאל

Intelligence of ♃   יהפיאל

The Avenging Angel   מלאך הגואל

Fines, penalties   ממון

A voice   קול

π 137

A wheel   אופן

The belly, gullet.   אסטומכא
[? Hebrew: vide K. D.
L.C.K. p. 138]

An image, a statue.   מצבה
[Gen. xxviii. 22]

A receiving; the Qabalah   קבלה

138

The Son of GOD   בן אלהים

To smoothe, divide   חלק

To leaven, ferment   חמץ

To pollute   חנף

Libanon. [Cant. iv. 11, 15]   לבנון

He shall smite   מחץ

Forehead   מצח

π 139

Hiddekel, the eastern river   הדקל
of Eden

140

Kings; Angels of Tiphareth   מלכים
of Assiah, and of Netzach
of Briah

141

Robust; oaken   אמיץ

Gathered, collected   אסף

Angel of 4 P.	כוקיה	
Precept	מצוה	
Trusty, steady	נאמן	
L.A. Angel of ♋	פכיאל	
Prima	קמא	
		142

Geomantic Intelligence of ♉	אסמודאל
Wickedness, destruction	בליעל
A stranger; Balaam	בלעם
Night Demon of 3ʳᵈ Dec. ♌	בעלם
Delights (△ & ▽)	מחמדים
	143

The unshoeing	חליצה
Running waters. [Cant.iv.15]	נחלים
12²	√ 144
A sandal	סנדל
Anterius; the East; days first of the first	קדם

The numerical value of the 13 Paths 145
of the Beard of Microprosophus

The Staff of GOD. [Ex. xvii. 9]	מטה האלהים
Inscrutable	מעלה
Angel of 6 P.	נממיה
A feast	סעודה
	146

The First Gate. [Vide K.D. L.C.K. p. 184]	בבא קמא
Limit, end; boundless	סוף
The world; an adult	עולם

The four Names in the Lesser 147
Ritual of the Pentagram;

viz.:   יהוה אדני אהיה אגלא
148

A name of GOD	אהיה יה יהוה אלהים
Angels of Hod in Assiah and Briah	בני אלהים
Glutton and drunkard. [Deut. xxi. 20]	זולל וסובא
To withdraw, retire	חמק
Scales; ♎	מאזנים
Victory	נצח
Flour, meal	קמח

π 149

The living GODS. [Cf. 154]	אלים חיים
A beating of the breast; a noisy striking	הספד
	150

Ariolus. [K.D. L.C.K. p. 53]	ידעוני
A walking shoe	נעל
Thine eye. [Vide I.R.Q. 652]	עינך
Nest	קן

π 151

אהיה spelt in full הה יוד הה אלף
יהוה אלהים אחד יהוה "TETRA-
GRAMMATON of the GODS is
One TETRAGRAMMATON"

Night Demon of 3ʳᵈ Dec. ♈	מאלף
The Fountain of Living Waters. [Jer. xvii. 13]	מקוה
A standing upright, stature	קומה
Jealous	קנא
	152

Benjamin	בנימן
The Bringing-forth One	המוציא
Residence, station	נציב
Σ (1—17)	153
L.A. Angel of ♎	חדקיאל
	154

Elohim of Lives. [Cf. 149]	אלהים חיים
	155

Adonai the King	אדני מלך
The faithful friend	דוד נאמן
The beard (correct). [S.D. ii. 1, et seq.]	דקנא
Letters of the Cherubic signs	ו: ט: נ: צ
Angel of 2ⁿᵈ Dec. ♑	יסיסיה
"The Concealed and Saving"; Angel of 6 W.	עלמיה
A seed	קנה

12 × 13, the number of letters in each 156
'tablet of Enoch'

The Tabernacle of the congregation. [Lev. i. 1]	אהל מועד
A viper	אפעה

BABALON, THE VIC- באבאלען
TORIOUS QUEEN.
[Vide XXX Aethyrs:
Liber CDXVIII]

Angel of Hod of Briah הסניאל
Joseph [referred to Jesod] יוסף
Angel of 1st Dec. ♏ כמרץ
נעול
A bird עוף
"Crying aloud"; the name of פעו
a King of Edom
Zion ציון
Limpid blood צלול

π 157

The setting of the דמדומי חמה
Sun
Was angry, enraged; anger זעף
Lingam זנק
The beard. [Vide S.D. ii. 467, זקן
and no. 22]
Occult מופלא
Female; Yoni נקבה
Angel of 9 S. ענואל
A Duke of Edom קנז

158

Arrows חיצים
To suffocate חנק
Balances. [Ch.] מאזנין

159

Surpassing Whiteness. בוצינא
[Vide 934]
Point נקדה

[Vide I.R.Q. 652] 160

Angel of 3 S. הקמיה
Silver כסף
Fell down. Decidit נפל
A rock, stone סלע
A tree עץ
A Duke of Edom פיכן
Lay, fell. [Ez. iii. 8] פניך
Image צלם
Cain קין

161

The heavenly man; אדם עילאה
lit. the 'primordial'

or 'exalted' man
The Congregation of the קהל יהוה
Eternal
קינא

Nine Paths of the Inferior Beard;
14 + 15 + ... + 22 = 162
Son of the right Hand; בנימין
pr. n. of Benjamin
Day Demon of 1st Dec. ♈ גלאסלבול
Angel ruling ♏ סוסול

π 163

[Vide no. 361, a הוא אלהים אדני
numerical Temurah of 163]
Woman, wife נוקבה

164

דצע
Ye shall cleave חדבקים
Outer; civil, as opposed חיצון
to sacred. [Vide K.D.
L.C.K. p. 342]
The Pillars עמדים

165

Strength. [Ez. iii. 8] חזקים
"To make them know." להודיעם
[Ps. xxv. 14]
Nehema נעמה
NEMO. [Name of M.T.] עממיה
Angel of 3 W.
An assembly עצה

166

A King of Edom בעלחנו
Reus mulctae. [Vide חייב ממון
K.D. L.C.K. p. 498]
Heaven of Geburah מעון
Night Demon of 3rd Dec. ♏ נפול
Native land of Job ערץ
The Most High עליון

π 167

The Unnameable One אסימון
(a demon)
Fetters. [Job xxxvi. 8] זיקים

168

Parentes Superni אבא ואמא עילאה

13^2 $\sqrt{169}$

The accentuator טעמים

170

The Wand; (David's) Staff מלק

Cloud ענן

Σ (1—18)   171

Principium emittens מאציל

Emanating from נאצל

Angel L.T.N. of ♒ פלאין

"The Face of God"; name פניאל
of an angel

172

Cut, divided בקע

He affected. [Not written] יעצב

Clusters; grapes ענבים

The heel, the end. [Mic.vii.20] עקב
Jacob

π 173

Lighten mine eyes גל עיני

Day Demon of 3rd Dec. ♒ גצף

174

Torches לפידים

Splendor ei per cir- נוגה לו סביב
cuitum

Σ {1—(7 × 7)} ÷ 7. ♀   175

Suction יניקה

Duplicity מכפלה

A slipping, falling נפילה

Spirit of ♀ קדמאל

176

An advisor, counselling יועץ

To eternity לעולם

Illegitimate פסול

177

Dominus Domino- אדון האדינים
rum

The Garden of Eden גן עדן

To cry out for help זעק

Angel L.T.D. of ♏ סגדלעי

Plenitude of plenitudes מלוי המלוי

178

The lower part, the loins חלצים

Good pleasure, choice, decision, חפץ
will

Quicksilver כסף חי

π 179

Ligatio עקדה

180

A spring, fountain. [Cant. מעיין
iv. 15]

The front part פנים

π 181

Vicious, faulty פסולה

182

Deus Zelotes אל קנא

Outcry, clamour זעקה

Layer of snares, supplanter; יעקב
Jacob

King of the Gods מלאך האלהים

Passive [as opposed to מקביל
מחקבל = active]

183

184

Ancient time; eastward נקדל

185

186

A stone of stumbling; a אבן נגף
rock to fall over. [Is. viii. 14]

An increase מוסף

Praefecti ממונים

A place מקום

Back of the Head; an ape; קוף
the letter Qoph

187

Angels of Chokmah, and of אופנים
Chokmah of Briah

Lifted up זקף

[K. of S., Fig. 52] סופיאל

188

Jaacob. [Vide K.D. L.C.K. יעקוב
p. 443.]

The Master of the Nose בעל החוטם

189

Fons obseratus. [Cant. גל נעול
iv. 11]

The Ancient among סבא דסבין
the ancient

Σ (1—19)   190

Ubi perrexit Angelus ויסע ויבא ויט

Internal פנימי

Corona florida prominens ציץ

The side or flank; rib צלע

First devil. V. Porta Coelorum Fig. XVI — קמטיאל

The end, appointed time. [Dan. xii. 13.] [Vide no. 305] — קץ

π 191

Countenance — אנפין

[Vide K.D. L.C.K. p. 143] — אפסים

Night Demon of 1st Dec. ♈ — פאכץ

A box, chest; a repository — קופה

192

Poisonous wind, Simoon — זלעפה

Ye shall cleave in TETRAGRAMMATON. [Vide no. 220] — חדבקים ביהוה

π 193

194

Righteousness, equity, justice: the Sphere of ♃. [Vide K.D. L.C.K. p. 656] — צדק

195

A flock — מקנה

Visitation — פקודה

14²

√196

Mare Soph. [Vide K.D. L.C.K. p. 435] — ים סוף

The crown, summit, point — קרן

π 197

El Supernus — אל עליון

[Vide K.D. L.C.K. p. 71] — אנא חטא עם הזה

198

Victories — נצחים

π 199

A giving freely; Ἐλεημοσύνη — צדקה

200

Alae. [Vide K.D. L.C.K. p. 483] — כנפים

A branch — ענף

A bone — עצם

Archetypal — קדמון

Belonging to the Spring — קיץ

A sling; a casting-net — קלע

Divination — קסם

201

Light (Ch.) — אר

202

To make empty — בקק

Pure; a field; son — בר

Elevatio — זקיפה

Apertures — נקבים

L.A. Angel of ♏ — סאיציאל

Many, much — רב

203

Initials of the Trinity: — אבר
אב : בן : רוח

Passed away, perished; feather, wing; (it. membrum et quid. genitale) — אבר

To lie in wait — ארב

A well, spring — באר

Created — ברא

Exotic, foreign — גר

204

Commencement of the name Abra-Melin — אברא

Foreign resident; race S.; an age (Ch.) — דר

The righteous — צדיק

205

Day Demon of 2nd Dec. ♈ — אגאר

Splendrous — אדר

Mighty; hero — גבר

Mountain — הר

206

Assembly; area — אדרא

Hail — ברד

Spake; word; cloud — דבר

They of the World — ימי עולם

207

♏, a scorpion — אגראב

Lord of the Universe — אדון עולם

Light. Cf. 9 and 11. Aur is the balanced Light of open day — אור

Limitless — אין סוף

Ate — ברה

Walled, fenced — גדר

That which cuts. [Vide no. 607] — הבר

The Elders. [Deut. xxi. 19] — זקנים

Melt, fuse — זקק

The Crown of the Ark	זר	A lion	ארי
Grow great	רבה	Strong	גבור
		A flash; lightning	הארה
208		A girdle	חגר
Feather	אברה	A flood; Jeor	יאר
A cistern	בור	"Fear," the fear of the יהוה (i.e. wonderment)	ירא
Bowed	גהר		
To make strife, contend	גרה	**212**	
Hagar	הגר	Great Voice	דבור
To kill	הרג	Night Demon of 1st Dec. ♌	האור
Abominable	זרא	Splendour; to enlighten	זהר
Jizchak. [Vide K.D. L.C.K. p. 266]	יצחק	To spread out; harlot; golden	זרה
Multitude	רוב	To enclose; secret chamber	חדר
209		**213**	
Chief Seer or Prophet (hence Abra-Melin)	אבראה	Strong, powerful, mighty	אביר
Reward, profit, prize	אגרה	Calx	גיר
To delay, tarry; behind (prep.)	אחר	[I.R.Q. 234 (?)]	הדדר
Way	ארח	Slaughter	הרגה
10th Spirit of Goetia.	בואר	Loaded	חר
Dispersed	בזר	To be strange; a stranger	זור
Sojourned, dwelt	גור	The Supernal Mercy of GOD	חסד עלאה דאל
Honour; a King of Edom; The Supernal Benignity	הדר	Nubes Magna	ענן גדול
Oppressed	זרב	**214**	
Σ (1—20)	**210**	A girdle	אזור
Adam Primus. [Vide no. 607]	אדהר	Angel of 1st Dec. ♈	זזר
Day Demon of 1st Dec. ♋	בזאר	Whiteness	חור
Choice	בחר	Came down	ירד
Pass on, fly	ברח	Air; Spirit; wind; Mind	רוח
To decide, determine	גזר	**215**	
To dwell; circle, cycle; generation	דור	Eminent; a Prince. [Ps. viii. I]	אדיר
To conceive	הרה	A path, narrow way	אורח
A joining of words; incantations; to conjoin; a brother	חבר	Posterior; the reversed part	אחור
A sword	חרב	A rising; to rise "as the Sun," give light	זרח
Angel of 1st Dec. ♑	מסנין	To encompass. [Vide K.D. L.C.K. p. 340]	חזר
Naaman	נעמן		
[Vide ΘΕΛΗΜΑ]	נ : ע : ץ	**6³**	**∛216**
Punctata	נקודים	Night Demon of 1st Dec. ♎	אוראוב
		Lion	אריה
π 211		The middle Gate. [Vide K.D. L.C.K. p. 184]	בבא מציעא
[Worthy]	אבחר	Courage	גבורה

Oracle	דביר
Blood of grapes	דם ענבים
Dread, fear	יראה
Profound. [Ps. xcii. 6]	עומק
Anger, wrath	רוגז
Latitude	רוחב

217

The air	אויר
Temple, palace	בירה
Food	בריה
A bee	דבורה
The navel	טבור
Angel ruling ♐	מויעסאל
Angel L.T.N. of ♏	סהקנב
Controversia Domini	ריבה

218

Ether. [Vide K.D. L.C.K. p. 55]	אוירא
The Creative World	בריאה
The benignity of Time	חסד עולם
The Moon	ירח
Multitude	רבוי
Arcana	רזיא
Odour, a smell	ריח

219

Mundatio, mundities	טהרה

The Number of Verses in Liber R 220
Legis

The Elect	בחיר
Heroina; Augusta; Domina	גבירה
Ye shall cleave unto TETRAGRAMMATON. [*Not* written]	חדבקים ליהוה
Clean, elegant	טהור
Giants. [Fully written only in Num. xiii. 33]	נפילים

Left-handed Svastika, drawn on the 221
square of ♂ given by Agrippa.
Cf. 231

Long	ארך
Angel of 10 S.	מנקאל

222

Urias	אוריה
"Unto the Place." [Ex. xxiii. 20]	אל המקום

Whiteness	הוורה
Goodly mountain. [Ex. iii 25]	הר טוב
Now, already; K'bar, "the river Khebar"; Day Demon of 3rd Dec.	כבר
I will chase	ראויה

π 223

224

Male (Ch.)	דכר
Walk, journey; The PATH	דרך
Principia emanandi	חוקקי
Effigurata	חקוקי
Union	יחור

15^2 √ 225

[Vide K.D. L.C.K. p. 234]	גזרדיא

226

Profound, hidden; the North. [Vide K.D. L.C.K. p. 666]	צפון

π 227

Long, tall	ארוך
A piscine, pond; [Blessing, Prov. x. 22]	ברכה
Remember; male (sacred Phallus—Vide S.D. ii. p. 467)	זכר
Damna. [Vide K.D. L.C.K. p. 569]	נזיקין

228

First-born	בכור
Blessed!	ברוך
Ruler of Earth	כרוב
The Tree of Life	עץ חיים

π 229

230

Astonishment	הכרה
[Vide K.D. L.C.K. p. 153]	מקיף
Fasciata	עקודים
Angel of 2nd Dec. ♍	ראידיה
Hod, 42-fold Name in Yetzirah. [Vide Liber 777, Col. xc. p. 18]	יגלפזק

Σ (1—21). Right-handed Svastika, 231
drawn on Sq. of ♂

Prolonged; grew long	אריך
Male	דכורא

111

Sum of the Four Ways of spelling 232
TETRAGRAMMATON in the
Four Worlds

Geomantic Intelligence   אמניציאל
of ♓

Ruler of Fire   אראל

Equivalent to יהי אור,   יה אויר
Fiat Lux. [Vide K.D.
L.C.K. p. 55]

Let there be Light! The   יהי אור
Mystic Name of Allan
Bennett, a Brother of
the Cross and Rose, who
began this Dictionary.

  π 233

Memento   זכור

The Tree of Life. [Vide   עץ החיים
no. 228]

  234

Night Demon of 3rd   דכאוראב
Dec. ♒

  235

Archangel of Chesed, and   צדקיאל
Angel of Chesed of Briah

  236

Angel L.T.N. of ♈   ספעטאוי

A handful   קומץ

  237

Angel of 3 C.   ראהאל

  238

Dominus Mirabilium אדון הנפלאוה
Rachel   רחל

  π 239

Azrael, the Angel of Death   אזראל
Iron   ברזל
The lot   גורל
Angel of 3rd Dec. ♉   יכסגניץ

  240

Myrrh   מר

Plagae Filiorum   נגעי בני אדם
Hominum. [I.e. Succubae,
K.D. L.C.K. p. 562]

Prima Germina   נצנים

Angel of 1st Dec. ♒   ססהם

Cash; counted out, paid   פקודים
down

High, lofty   רם

  π 241

L.A. Angel of ♑   סמקיאל

  242

Ariel, Angel of Air   אריאל
Recollection   זכירה

  243

Abram. [Vide 248]   אברם

Created (he them).   בראם
[Gen. v. 2.]

Learned, complete. To finish,   גמר
bring to pass (Ch.)

A bone; to destroy   גרם

  244

Angel of 7 P.   הרחאל

To be insensible; in deep   רדם
sleep, in trance. [Vide
no. 649]

  245

Adam Qadmon   אדם קדמון

Gall, bile   מרה

Spirit of God   רוח אל

  246

Angel of 3 S.   הריאל

Myrrh   מור

Vision, aspect   מראה

  מרגג

Angel L.T.D. of ♉   ראידאל

Height, altitude   רום

  247

Angel L.T.D. of ♑   אליוד

To overwhelm (Ps. lxxvii. 18);   זרם
a flood

A light   מאור

Night Demon of 1st Dec. ♉   ראום

Sensus symbolicus   רמז

  248

Abraham. [Vide 243 and   אברהם
505, 510. Discussed at
length in Zohar]

The Three that bear wit-   אדם+ברא
ness, above and beneath,
respectively.   אדם the
Spirit, the Water, and the
Blood; א being Air
(Spiritus), ד standing for

דם Blood, and מ being both Water and the initial of מים, water. For ברא see 203

אוריאל Uriel or Auriel, archangel of Earth, and angel of Netzach; = "The light of God"

במראה In vision. [Vide K.D. L.C.K. p. 553]

גמרה Gematria

חמר Wine; bitumen; an ass (from "to disturb")

רחם Mercy; womb

רמח A lance

249

אראיל L.A. Angel of ♉

גמור Night Demon of 2nd Dec. ♎

מגור Fear, terror

250

אלהי העולמים The living GOD of the Worlds; or, of the Ages

דרום [The South.] Midday

מדור Habit, action (Ch.)

π 251

ארן Fir, cedar

וריהל The angel Uriel: "Vrihl," i.e. Magical Force. [Vide Lytton's "Coming Race," and Abra-Melin—forehead Lamen]

רייאל Angel of 10. W.

252

מאורה Serpent's den

Σ (1—22)   253

גרים Proselytes

מטרד Matred; who symbolizes the Elaborations on the side of Severity

254

גרודיאל Angel of 3rd Dec. ♒

זוריאל Geomantic Intelligence of ♎

חמור An ass

מטרה A mark, aim

נדר A solemn promise, vow

נרד Spikenard. [Cant. iv. 14]

רומח A spear

רחום Merciful

255

אנדר Night Demon of 3rd Dec. ♐

חומרא Burdensome; with difficulty

מזרח The East

נהר A river, stream. [Gen. ii. 10]

רנה Cantatio elata

$16^2 = 4^4 = 2^8 = 256$ $\sqrt{}\ ^4\sqrt{}\ ^8\sqrt{}$ 256

אהרן Aaron

אמירה Tidings (Ps. lxviii. 12); a saying, speech. [Vide K.D. L.C.K. p. 128]

בני צדק The Sons of the Righteous

מפולמין [See no. 705] [Vide K.D. L.C.K. p. 20]

רוח אמא The Spirit of the Mother

רוכל Aromatarius

π 257

ארון The Ark

חרטם A Magician

ליראיו "To His fearers." [Ps. xxv. 14]

מקל לבנה The White Wand

נורא Terribilis Ipsa

258

אור אדום The red light

חירם Hiram (King of Tyre)

רחמי Mercy

259

גרון Throat

נטר Nitre

ראובן Reuben

Σ {1—(8 × 8)} ÷ 8.   ☿   260

טיריאל Intelligence of ☿

טמירא The Concealed

י : נ : ר : I.N.R. [Vide 270]

ירים Exaltabitur

כרם A vineyard

לפסילים Ineptos et profanos [Ps. viii. 1]

מה אדיר

סר Declined

צמצם To gather, draw together

113

261

He bound; an obligation, a prohibition — אסר

Abhorrence, abomination. [Is. lxvi. 24] — דראון

262

Lofty; Aaron — אהרון

Severities — גבוראן

Terrible — הנורא

Conclavia — חדרים

Eye to eye. [I.R.Q. 645] — עין בעין

π 263

Angel of 2nd Dec. ♒ — אבדרון

Angel of 2nd Dec. ♓ — אורון

Geomantic Intelligence of ♏ — ברכיאל

Gematria — גמטריא

Pained — גרס

264

Emanantia. [Vide K.D. L.C.K. p. 338] — חקוקים

Jarden. [Vide K.D. L.C.K. p. 455] — ירדן

Footprints (foot's breadth). [Deut. ii. 5] — מדרך

A straight row. [Vide K.D. L.C.K. p. 455] — סדר

Channels, pipes — רהטים

‖6   265

Architect — אדריכל

Broke down — הרס

A cry of the heart; anguish, anxiety — צעקה

266

Chebron — חברון

Termination of Qliphoth of 12 Signs — ירון

Contraction — צמצום

267

Illicit, forbidden — אסור

Geomantic Intelligence of ♌ — ורכיאל

Currus; Vehiculum; Thronus — מרכבה

Nasiraeus — נזיר

268

Stones of the sling — אבני הקלע

π 269

By-ways — ארחון

Father—Spirit—Son — בן רוח אב

Angel of Binah of Briah — כרוביאל

270

Levers, bars — בריחים

I.N.R.I. Initials of: Jesus — י:נ:ר:י:
Nazaraeus Rex Judaeorum; Igni Natura Renovata Integra; Intra Nobis Regnum deI; Isis Naturae Regina Ineffabilis; and many other sentences. Vide Crowley Coll.Works Vol.I. Appendix

π 271

Earth (Ch.); whence = low, mean — ארע

Angel of 2nd Dec. ♐ — והרין

[Vide no. 256, אמידה] — לאמר

272

Earth — ארעא

To consume, injure; brutish — בער

Percussione magna — מכה רבה

The evening: an 'Arab,' i.e. a person living in the West — ערב

Day Demon of 3rd Dec. ♐ — רינוו

273

The stone which the builders rejected [Ps. cxviii. 22] — אבן מאסו הבונים

The Hidden Light — אור גנח

Four — ארבע

Rebuked — גער

Took away — גרא

274

Paths — דרכים

275

[Vide K.D. L.C.K. p. 72] — אחוריים

Domicilium pulchrum. [Vide K.D. L.C.K. p. 395] — דירה נאה

Fluvius Indicii. [Vide K.D. L.C.K. p. 117] — יאר דין

Qy. Sruti "scripture" — סרטו

Σ (1—23)   276

A Cithara — כנור

Night Demon of 1st Dec. ♌ — כרוכל

The Moon	סיהרא	
		π 277
To sow, propagate; seed, semen	זרע	
[For multiplying.] [Not written. Vide K.D. L.C.K. pp. 157 and 837]	למרבה	
Angel of 3rd Dec. ♌	סהיבר	
Gratia, benevolentia	רעוא	
		278
Angel L.T.N. of ♎. [Vide Liber 777, p. 29]	אחבראין	
Angels of Jesod, and of Binah of Briah—Cherubim	כרובים	
Passing over	עובר	
The Material World	עולם המוטבע	
		279
Leprosy. [Vide K.D. L.C.K. p. 495]	סגירו	
[7 × 40, the Squares of the walls of the Vault. See Equinox I. 3. p. 222]		280
Qliphoth of ♑	דגדגירון	
A record (Ch.)	דכרון	
Angel of the Wood of the World of Assiah	יער	
The Letters of Judgment: the 5 letters having a final form	כ:מ:נ:פ:צ:	
Archangel of Malkuth	סנדלפון	
Citizenship	עיר	
[Vide S.D. 528]	פר	
Terror	רף	
		π 281
A crown—Ashes	אפר	
Attire; adorned	פאר	
		282
Angels of Briah, and of Malkuth of Briah	אראלים	
Spirit of Lives	רוח חיים	
		π 283
Aurum inclusum	זהב סגור	
Memoriale. [Vide no. 964]	זכרון	
That goes on foot	רגלים	
		284
Geomantic Intelligence of ♊	אמבריאל	
The small area of an enclosed garden	ערוגה	
		285
		286
High, lofty	מרום	
		287
Pars Azymorum	אפיקומן	
Night Demon of 3rd Dec. ♉	ופאר	
Little	זעיר	
Geomantic Intelligence of ♋	מוריאל	
		288
Vindication	ביעור	
Day Demon of 1st Dec. ♍	זאפר	
Breeding, bearing; offspring. [Vide K.D. L.C.K. p. 313]	עיבור	
[Vide K.D. L.C.K. p. 571]	רפח	
17^2		$\sqrt{289}$
Apertio. [Vide no. 537]	פטר	
Particulare	פרט	
		290
Thine enemy	ערכ	
		291
Torrentes Aquarum	אפיקי מים	
(He) treasured	אצר	
Earth: in particular, the Earth of Malkuth	ארץ	
Qy. spotted?	נמרא	
Adhaesio; adhaerens; princeps	סירכא	
L.A. Angel of ♒	צכמקיאל	
		292
A young bird. [Deut. Xxii. 6]	אפרוה	
Gold	בצר	
A medicine, drug	רפואה	
		π 293
Day Demon of 2nd Dec. ♉	צארב	
		294
Purple	ארגמן	
Pertaining to Autumn	חורף	
Melchizedec. [Gen. xiv. 18]	מלכיצדק	
		295
Curtain, canopy; vault. [Ps. civ. 2]	יריעה	
Eyelids	כנפי העין	

[Vide K.D. L.C.K. p. 498] פטור

296

Of the Earth. [Vide no. 992] הארץ

Incurvens se כורע

Rigorose procedere; fumarie; צור
rock. [Vide K.D. L.C.K. pp. 459, 663]

297

Thesaurus; gazophylacium; אוצר
conservatorium

A name of GOD אלהים גבור
attributed to Geburah

A secured house; a fortified ארמון
castle

A City of Edom בצרה

The Throne; a Name of כורסיא
Briah

Nuriel נוריאל

The neck צואר

298

Amen, our Light אמן אור

Son of the GODS בר אלהים

White צחר

Pathetic appeals; com- רחמים
miserations

299

Angel of 2nd Dec. ♋ רהדץ

Σ (1—24) **300**

Khabs am Pekht אור בפאהה

Vide Beth אלף למד הי יוד מם
Elohim. Dissert. II. Cap. I.
A spelling of אלהים in full.

Formation יצר

Profundities מעמקים

God of Chesed, and of Hod מצפצ
of Briah; Temura of יהוה

Incircumcisus ערל

Separation פירוד

The Spirit of GOD. רוח אלהים
[Vide Gen. i. 3]

301

"My Lord, the אדני המלך נאמן
faithful King";
a name of GOD

Fire אש

A candlestick מנורה

302

Earth of Hod ארקא

To cut open, inquire into; בקר
Dawn

L.A. Angel of ♊ סראיאל

Hath protected קבר

To putrefy רקב

303

Did evil; putrefaction באש

304

A species of gold חרוץ

Green דש

Geomantic Intelligence כאמבריאל
of ♒

White קדר

305

Dazzling white light אור צח

Tender herb. [Gen. i. 11] דשא

Netzach, 42-fold Name in הקממנע
Yetzirah. [Vide Liber 777,
col. xc.]

Yetzirah; "formation" יצרה

A curving, bending כריעה

The end of days, appointed קץ הימין
time. [Dan. xii. 13]

A lamb שה

הש

306

Father of Mercy אב הרחמים

Merciful Father אב הרחמן

A woman, wife; virago אשה

Honey דבש

Domina. [Vide K.D. מטרונא
L.C.K. p. 528]

[Vide K.D. L.C.K. p. 571] ניצוצין

Coldness; pertaining to Winter קור

Angel of 6 S. רההאל

Malo-Granatum רימון

π **307**

Night Demon of 2nd Dec. ♏ וריאי

Ribkah רבקה

308

Daybreak בוקר

Sparsor זרקא

Investigation חקר

A harsh, grating sound	חרק
Approaching, near	קרוב
Ice	קרח

309

A leper. [Vide K.D. L.C.K. p. 495]	מוסגר
Angel of 2nd Dec. ♉	מנחראי
Strepitus cordis, mussitatio, susurratio, rugitus	שאגה
Field, soil, land	שדה

310

To trample on, conquer	דוש
To govern, bind	חבש
Formed. [I.R.G. 227]	ייצר
The initials of Idra Rabba Qadisha. [Each letter is half of each Letter of כתר, Kether]	י׳ר׳ק:
Is, are; essence, being	יש
Leo iuvenis	כפיר
Habitations	מדורין

π 311

Man; but vide K.D. L.C.K. p. 83	איש
Angel of 9 C.	עריאל
Archangel of Binah	צפקיאל
Archangel of Air; Angel of ☿, and of Chokmah of Briah, etc.	רפאל
Rod. [Ps. xxiii. 4]	שבט

26 × 12, the Twelve Banners   312

Night Demon of 3rd Dec. ♎	ושו
To renew; hence = a new moon, a month	חדש
West. [Cf. 272]	מערב

π 313

Angel of 1st Dec. ♍	אננאורה

314

[Vide K.D. L.C.K. p. 275]	הלל גמור
Metatron, Archangel of Kether, and Angel of Tiphareth of Briah. [When spelt with ׳ after מ it denotes Shekinah]	מטטרון
Out of the way, remote	רחוק

Shaddai: "The Almighty"; a name of GOD	שדי

315

Ice; crystal	גביש
Gullet	ושט
Formation	יצירה
Visio Splendoris	מראה הנוגה
Gomorrah	עמרה

The Number of Servitors of Abra-   316
Melin Sub-Princes

Day Demon of 3rd Dec. ♈	ושאגו
Ligatus	חבוש
Green	ירוק
JESU	ישו
A bundle, handful	עומר
Visitans iniquitatem	פוקד עון
Aporrhea	קוטרא
[Vide K.D. L.C.K. p. 54]	שאיה
To worship, bow down	שחח

π 317

Day Demon of 3rd Dec. ♉	ואלפר
[Vide Ps. xcvii. 11]	זרעם
Arida	יבשה
Iron (Ch.)	פרזל
Hoariness	שיבה

318

Labrum lavacri, et basio eius	כיור וכנו
A copse, bush	שיח

319

320

"Boy," Name of Enoch, and of Metatron	נער
A Duke of Edom. [Vide Liber 777, p. 22]	עירם
The friends	רעים
L.A. Angel of ♐	סריטיאל

321

Angel of 3rd Dec. ♋	אלינכיר
Angel L.T.D. of ♍	לסלרא
Angel of 9 W.	שאהיה
Qliphoth of ♉	אדימירון

322

Lamb	כבש
Angel L.T.N. of ♐	לברמים

Linea media   קו האמצעי   323

Long-absent brother   אח רחוק
Qliphoth of ≈   בהימירון
Angel of 3rd Dec. ♈   סטנדר
18^2 $\sqrt{324}$

See no. 314; it denotes   מיטטרון
   Shekinah

Σ (1—25). ♂   325

Spirit of ♂   ברצבאל
Intelligence of ♂   גראפיאל
Angel of 2nd Dec. ♏   נינדוהר
Need, indigence   צריכה   326

Jesus. [Note the letters of   יהשוה
   TETRAGRAMMATON
   completed by ש 300 q.v.
   the Spirit of GOD]

Vision   שאייה   327

Day Demon of 2nd Dec. ♍   בוטיש
[Vide K.D. L.C.K. p. 461]   ישיבה
Night Demon of 3rd Dec. ♑   כיצאור

4 Princes + 8 Sub-Princes + 316   328
   servient to Spirits

Angel of 3 W.   החשיה
To steam; darkness. [Vide   חשך
   K.D. L.C.K. p. 280]   329

Angel of 1st Dec. ♎   טרסני   330

Boundary, terminus; crosspath   מצר
Revolution; hurricane, tempest   סער
Error: fault   של   π 331

Ephraim   אפרים
Arbor magna. [Gen. xxi. 33]   אשל
Archangel of Chokmah   רציאל   332

Lux Ardoris   אור היקוד
Night Demon of 3rd   אנדרומאל
   Dec. ♓
A Duke of Edom. [Vide   מבצר
   Liber 777, p. 22]

Locus vacuus. [Vide   מקום פנוי
   K.D. L.C.K. p. 551]   333

Qabalah of the Nine   איק בכר
   Chambers
Choronzon. [Vide Dr Dee,   חורונזון
   & Lib. 418, 10th Aire]
Snow   שלג   334

A still, small Voice.   קול דממה דקה
   [I Kings, xix. 12]   335

Dies Mali   ימי רעה
The KING   מלך מלכי המלכים
   above the King of Kings.
   [Vide K.D. L.C.K. p. 537]
Ordering, disposition   מערכה   336

An attack; a request, petition   שאלה
Night Demon of 1st Dec. ♊   שבכיד   π 337

Ruler of Earth   פורלאך
Hell of Supernals; a City of   שאול
   Edom; the Place of Askings.
   [Vide Liber 777, p. 23]   338

To cast down   חלש
He hath pardoned (or,   יכבוש
   subjected)
A garment; clothing   לבוש
To send forth   שלח   339

340

Angel of 3rd Dec. ♐   יסגדיברודיאל
"Ferocious" lion   ליש
Uncus focarius—fire-shovel   מגרופיא
Book   ספר
Pares; a word written on the   פרס
   wall at Belshazzar's feast.
   [Vide Dan. v. 28]
There; The Name   שם

The sum of the 3 Mother Letters;   341
   א, מ, and ש

Yesterday   אמש
Guilty, damned   אשם

A red cow	פרה אדומה
Expansum; sepimentum; diaphragma	פרסא
The Name (Ch.)	שמא

342

Coctio	בישל
Perfume	בשם
Night Demon of 2nd Dec. ♉	פוכלור
A blaze, flame	שלהבה

$\sqrt[3]{}$ 343 7^3

"And GOD said." [Gen. i. 3]	ויאמר אלהים
A sweet smell	זפרון

344

A plantation, garden [Cant. iv. 13]	פרדס

345

Di Alieni	אלהים אחרים
GOD Almighty	אל שדי
"In that also"—referred to Daath	בשגם
The NAME	השם
Lioness. [Vide K.D. L.C.K. p. 501]	לישה
5th ש	מהש
Moses. [See 543, numerical Temurah of 345]	משה
Shiloh	שילה
He was appeased. [Esther, vii. 10]	שככה

346

A spring; spring water	מקור
A water-pipe; channel	צנור
Good pleasure; the Will-power	רצון

π 347

Palanquin (Cant. iii. 9); Bridal bed; nuptial chariot. ["thalamus seu coelum fabrile sub quo copulantur nubentes"]	אפריון

348

Five; to set in array	חמש
Third King of Edom	חשם

π 349

350

Day Demon of 3rd Dec. ♌	אליגוש
A sapphire (Ex. xxviii. 18). [Vide K.D. L.C.K. p. 19]	ספיר
Ophir; a young mule; dust of the Earth	עפר
The Horn; head	קרן
Vacuum	ריקם
Intellectus	שכל

Σ (1—26) 351

Man	אנש
Angels of Malkuth; burnt or incense offering; "The flames"	אשים
Hiram-Abif, a cunning artificer at the Temple of Solomon; the hero of a famous allegory prophetical of FRATER PERDURABO	חירם אביף
♄ in ♌. Angel ruling 1st Dec. ♌, that was rising at the birth of FRATER PERDURABO	לוסנהר
Moses the Initiator	מושה
Elevatus	נשא

352

The Exalted Light	אור מעלה
Long of Nose; i.e. Merciful; a title of the supreme GOD	ארך אפים
Lightning	ברקים
An approach	קרבן

π 353

Goshen	גשן
The fifth	חמשה
The Secret of TETRAGRAMMATON is to His fearers. [Ps. xxv. 14]	סוד יהוה ליראיו
Delight, joy	שמחה

354

Grew fat; anointed	דשן
Heptaeteris intermissoria	שמטה

355

Thought; idea	מחשבה
Year	שנה

356

The Cedars of Lebanon ארזי לבנון

Expiationes. [Vide K.D. כפורים
L.C.K. p. 612]

A young mule עופר

Ophra, mother of Goliath עורף

Spirits of the living רוחון דחיין

357

42-fold Name, Geburah in כגד יכש
Yetzirah

Iniquity נושא

358

Shame גשנה

Shiloh shall come יבא שילה

Messiach, the Messiah משיח

Nechesh, the Serpent that נחש
initiated Eve

(Taking the three ה's in אשיאום
אהיהוה as concealing
the Mothers, we get
I. A. Ω. &)

π 359

Angel of 3rd Dec. ♓ סטריף

The Sacred Wind שטים

Satan. [Vide K.D. L.C.K. שטן
p. 235]

360

The Messiah המשיה

[Vide K.D. L.C.K. p. 235] הנשה

[Vide K.D. L.C.K. p. 235] השנה

Angels of Jesod of Binah ישים

Seeking safety; Angel of מהשיה
7 W.

Tonitrus רעמים

Shin; a tooth שין

Two שני

$$19^2. \begin{matrix} 3 \\ 6 \\ 1 \end{matrix} \begin{matrix} \therefore \\ \vdots \\ \vdots \end{matrix} \qquad \sqrt{361}$$

God of Malkuth אדני הארץ

"Men"; "impurities" אנשי

Foundations. [Ch.] אשין

The Mountain Zion הר ציון

Ruler of ♄ כשיאל

Angel of 7 P. מצראל

362

363

The Almighty and שדי אל חי
Ever-living GOD

364

Lux Occulta אור מופלא

Satan השטן

Demons שדין

Opposition; resistance שטנה

365

Earth of Tiphareth נשיה

An uncovering, exposing פריעה

366

Night Demon of 2nd אנדראלף
Dec. ♑

π 367

Black [scil. of eye-pupil]: אישון
middle: homunculus

Day Demon of 3rd Dec. ♊ פאיכורן

368

The Spirit of the רוח אלהים חיים
GODS of the Living

$$\Sigma \{1—(9 \times 9)\} \div 9. \quad ☽ \qquad 369$$

Spirit of ☽. [Vide חשמודאי
Liber 777, p. 19]

The World of Briah עולם הבריאה

Angel of 2nd Dec. ♊ שהדני

370

A foundation, basis עקר

Creation עש

Salices rivi. [Lev.xxiii.40] ערבי נחל

Zopher צפר

White lead, tin קסטרא

To rend, cut, blame, curse קרע

Green. [Vide S.D. p. 104] רענן

Salem שלם

371

Sinistrum שמאל

372

Aqua spherica אספידכא

Agni כבשים

An oven, furnace כבשן

♏ עקרב

Herbage, grass עשב

Seven שבע

π 373	
374	
375	
Generally and specially	כלל ופרט
Solomon	שלמה
A City of Edom	שמלה
376	
Dominator	מושל
Esau, father of the men of Edom. (Ad-om, Adlantes[1])	עשו
A bird	צפור
Peace. [Refers to Kether]	שלום
377	
Nervus luxatus; Vena Ischiatica. [Gen. xxxii. 32]	גיד הנשה
Seven	שבעה
Σ (1—27) 378	
'In peace'	בשלום
Pruna ignita; Chaschmal	חשמל
Iuramentum. [K.D. L.C.K. p. 695]	שבוע
π 379	
Abschalom	אבשלום

[The sum of the letters of TETRA- 380
GRAMMATON multiplied
severally by those of Adonai;
$(י×ה)+(ד×ד)+(ו×נ)+(א×י)]$
$=י:כ:ש:ן:$

Difficulty, narrowness	מצרים
Pain, trouble, misery	עצב עצבון
Thick darkness, fog	ערפל
[Vide no. 370]	קסטירא
Heaven of Hod	רקיע
381	
Clamour, prayer	שועה
382	
Day Demon of 3rd Dec. ♎	צאראץ
π 383	
Iuramentum. [Vide K.D. L.C.K. pp. 67, 695]	שבועה

1. Refers to a theory that the 'Kings of Edom' who perished before the creation of Adam were a previous race inhabiting 'Atlantis.'

384	
385	
Angel of 2nd Dec. ♎	מהרנץ
Assiah, the World of Matter	עשיה
Gloria cohabitans [vide K.D. L.C.K. p. 711]; the Glory of God	שכינה
Lip	שפה
386	
Jesus	ישוע
Tongues	לשון
Tziruph, a table of Temurah	צירוף
387	
388	
The hardest rock. [Ps. cxiv. 8]	חלמיש
To search out diligently	חפש
Table; bread	שלחן
π 389	
390	
Gen. v. 2.	זכר ונקבה
Retrorsum	מפרע
Alens, pascens	פרנס
Heaven	שמים
Oil	שמן
Night Demon of 2nd Dec. ♊	שע
391	
Salvation, help	ישועה
The Inscrutable Height. [Kether]	רום מעלה
392	
Aromata	בשמים
Habitaculum	משבן
393	
394	
Table. [Vide no. 388]	שולחן
395	
Robustus (virilitas) Iacob	אביר יעקב
The Heavens	השמים
Oil	השמן
Manasseh	מנשה
Second	משנה
Judge	שופט

396

Day Demon of 1ˢᵗ Dec. ♏   יפוש

π 397

Lux Interna. (Title of   אור פנימי
Kether)

398

Fifty   חמשים
Book   חפשי
Angel L.T.D. of ♈   סטרעטן
Pride; esp. of gait   שחץ

399

שגופי

20²   √400

To use Magic, witchcraft   כשף
Erudiens, a title of Yesod   משכיל
Sensus literalis. [Vide K.D.   פשוטה
L.C.K. p. 12]
(He had) Karnaim (in his   קרנים
hand)
Angels of Chesed of Briah   שיככים
Sack   שק

401

Cursing   ארר
Essence; "the"   את

402

Sought into, or after   בקש
Tested, purified   ברר
Filia   בת
A spider   עכביש
Paths   שבילין

403

The Stone; Sapphire   אבן ספיר

404

Law, edict   דת
Almond; to watch, be awake; שקד
to hasten

405

Fearful things, serpents of זחלי עפר
the dust. [Job]
[Cf. no. 227, זכר.] Phallus; שפכה
urethra. [Vide Deut. xxiii. 2]
Σ (1—28)   406

THOU: a name of GOD   אתה
Vulgar, common; plebeian עם הארץ
Leg   שוק

Alterations   שנויים
The letter Tau   תו

407

Signum   אות
The Precious Oil   שמן טוב

408

Lapis sapphirinus   אבן הספיר
Haec   זאת
[Vide Deut. x. 10, 15]   חשק

π 409

Patriarchs   אבהתא
Fathers   אבות
One (fem.)   אחת
Ha-Qadesh; Holy Ones   הקדש

410

Liberty; a swallow   דרור
Visions, imaginations. [Dan. הרהר
iv. 2]
Metzareph   מצרף
The Tabernacle   משכן
Sacred; Saint   קדש
Holy   קודש
He heareth   שמע
Hod, 42-fold Name in Yetzirah שקי

411

Elisha   אלישע
Briatic Palace of   היכל רצון
Tiphareth
Fundamenta Terrae   מוסדי ארץ
Habitaculum   משכנא
Ordo temporum   סדר זמנים
Desolation, emptiness. (Ex- תהו
presses first root of all good)

412

The letter Beth   בית
New. (Ch.)   חדת
Jesus GOD   יהשוה אלהים
White whorl   צמר לבן
Celsitudo superna   רום עליון
A longing for   תאוה

413
414

Azoth, *the* fluid. A + Z (Lat.) אזות
+ Ω (Grk.) + ת (Heb.). Initial and final in 3 tongues

The Limitless Light	אין סוף אור
Meditation. [Ps. xlv. 4]	הגות
Going forth. [Vide no. 770]	משוטטים

415

The Voice of the Chief Seer	אבראה דבר
Sister	אחות
The Holy One; Sodomite	הקדש
Work	מעשה
Angel of 10 C.	עשליה

416

Thought, meditation	הרהור
A pledge	משכין

417

Olive	זית
Arca. (Noah's Ark)	תיבה

(Note 4 + 1 + 8 = 13)   418

Boleskine	בולשכין
Peccatum. (Est femina Lilith impia)	חטאת
Kheth, a fence	חית
Servans misericordiam	נוצר חסד
"The Word of the Aeon." [Vide Liber 418]	מאכאשאנה

א ב ר א ה א ד א ב ר א

418 = בית הא = חית, the House of Hé: because of I.Z.Q. 694; for ה formeth כ, but ה formeth יוד : each = 20. Thus is Abrahadabra a Key of the Pentagram.

Also, by Aiq Bkr, it = 22: and 418 = 19 × 22. 19 = Manifestation; it therefore manifests the 22 Keys of R.O.T.A.

The first meaning is ABRAH DBR, = The Voice of the Chief Seer.

It resolves into Pentagram and Hexagram as follows:

1st *method.*

$$
\begin{array}{c}
A \\
R \diagup \quad \diagdown B \\
A \\
A \bigstar A \quad \text{forms 12 and 406, הוא} \\
D\ H \\
B \diagdown \quad \diagup R \\
A
\end{array}
$$

and אתה [406 = תו], where AThH =

Microprosopus, and HVA = Macroprosopus. The Arcanum is therefore that of the Great Work.

2nd *method.*

$$
\begin{array}{ccc}
 & A & B\ H \\
A \bigstar A & R & \bigstar \\
A\ A & B & R\ D
\end{array}
\quad \text{Here BHR = 207}
$$

=אין סוף אור, etc., and DBR=Voice ("The Vision and the Voice"); thus showing, by Yetziratic attribution, the Three Wands—Caduceus: Phoenix: Lotus. Note always אבר are the three Supernals.

3rd *method.*

$$
\begin{array}{ccc}
 & A & A \\
A \bigstar A & B & A \\
 & R\ B & H\ R\ D
\end{array}
\quad \text{give 205 + 213;}
$$

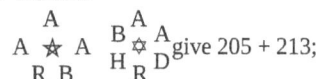

both mean "Mighty," whence Abrahadabra is "The Word of Double Power." AAB show AB : AIMA : BN, viz., Amoun : Thoth : Mout. By Yetziratic Method, H:D:R: are Isis : Horus : Osiris. (Also, for H:D:R:, vide I.R.Q. 992.)

Dividing as 3 and 8, we get Δ of Horus dominating the Stooping Dragon, ארד יא ; also—

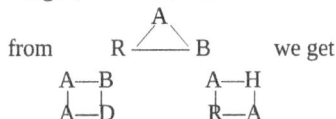

$$
\text{from} \quad R \xrightarrow{\ \ A\ \ } B \quad \text{we get}
$$

$$
\begin{array}{cc}
A\text{—}B & A\text{—}H \\
A\text{—}D & R\text{—}A
\end{array}
$$

8 = דד, Love, and 207 = אור, Light; 8 × 207 = 18, which is equivalent to חי, living; further, 297 = 23 × 9 = חיה, Life: hence, Licht : Liebe : Leben.

Again, 418 = את + יאו, = 21 + 397, q.v. דבר and 678 = 6 + 7 + 8 = 21. 2 × ב+2×ר+ת=32. The Five different letters represent Amoun : Thoth : Isis : Horus : Osiris. They (A + B + R + H + D) add to 212 (q.v.).

Finally, א is the Crown, ב the Wand, ר the Cup, ה the Sword, ד the R.C.

See Equinox, V and VII, for further details.[2]

---

2. [Cf. corresponding entry in Liber LVIII, pp. 72–3 in the present volume.]

123

π 419

Serpent: the letter Teth   טות

Sodom and Gomorrah   סדם + עמרה

420

It was   היתה

Dolium, vas   חבית

Vapour, smoke   עשן

Pacifica   שלמים
רצפים

π 421

Angel ruling ♉   כשועיה

Angel ruling ♓   פשיאל

422

The Vast Countenance   אריך אנפין

Linea Flava (quae circumdat   קו ירוק
Mundum)

423

[Ex. xxvii. 10, 11.]   לווי העמודים
[Vide K.D. L.C.K. p. 420]

424

Angel L.T.N. of ♉   טוטת

425

[Vide no. 1175]   הגזית

[Vide K.D. L.C.K. p. 208]   נעשה

Auditus   שמיעה

426

Servator; salvator   מושיע

Medium   תוך

427

428

The Breakers-in-pieces;   געשכלה
the Qliphoth of Chesed

The Brilliant Ones; Angels   חשמלים
of Chesed, and of Tiphareth
of Briah

Iuraverunt   נשבעו

429

A lion's whelp.   גור אריה
[Gen. xl. 9]

Judgment, equity   משפט
שגעון

430

Nephesch, the animal soul of   נפש
Man

Covered with mist; darkness,   נשף
twilight

Membra   פרקים

Full Title of Ninth   צדיק יסוד עולם
Sephirah. "The Righteous
is the Foundation of the
world"

Concealed   שפן

Tohu v-Bohu; see Gen. 1.   תהו ובהו

Dew   תל

π 431

Notariqon   נוטריקון

432

Eventide shadows   צללי ערב

Earth of Jesod   תבל

π 433

Day Demon of 1st Dec. ♌   בלאת

Merit   זכות

434

The Lord of War.   איש מלחמה
[Ex. xv. 3]

The letter Daleth; door   דלת

Σ (1—29)   435

Deceived   התל

[Vide K.D. L.C.K. p. 156]   משפטו

436

Tutor, curator; prafectus;   אפטרופס
administrator

Angel L.T.D. of ♏   ביתחוי

Hoschanah   הושענה

"Σατανάς." [Vide K.D.   שטן עז
L.C.K. p. 505]

[Vide K.D. L.C.K. p. 505;   שעתנז
723 & 701, nos. 9, 10;
also at שבירה]

437

Balm; the balsam tree   אפרסמון

438

The whole (perfect)   אבן שלימה
stone. [Deut. xxvii. 6]

π 439

Exilium   גלות

Angel L.T.N. of ♊   עוגרמנן

440

Collaudatio. [Vide K.D.   תהלה
L.C.K. pp. 90, 729]

The Great Dragon; means "curls." [I.R.Q. 834; vide 510] — תלי

Irreproachable; perfect — תם

21^2 $\sqrt{441}$

Cerva — אילת

Truth; Temurah of אדם, by Aiq Bekar — אמת

A live coal — גחלת

Day Demon of 2nd Dec. ♌ — לריאר

Angel L.T.D. of ♓ — רמרא

442

Termini Terrae — אפסי ארץ

π 443

A virgin; a city. ♍ — בתולה

Goliath — גלית

444

The Sanctuary — מגדש

Damascus — דמשק

The total value of the Single Letters; 445
ה, ו, ז, ח, ט, י, ל, נ, ס, ע, צ, and ק

Number of Stars in the Northern 446 hemisphere

Destruction; death — מות

Pison — פישון

Tali pedum — קרסולים

447

Initials of the Three Above and the Three Beneath. [Vide 248] — דמר רבא

448

Excelsa — במות

π 449

Lux fulgentissima — אור מצוחצח

Cloak — טלית

450

Tabulae — לוחות

[Vide K.D. L.C.K. p. 508] — מדות

The Fruit of the Tree — פרי עץ

Transgression — פשע

Beneplacitum termino carens; Arbitrum illimitatum — רצון באין גבול

Inhabitans Aeternitatem — שוכן עד

Craftiness, cunning — שעלים

The Dragon — תן

451

The Essence of Man — את האדם

Mortis — מיתא

Angels of Tiphareth — שנאנים

The Abyss — תהום

452

[Vide no. 552] — חמדת

The crop; the Maw — קרקבן

453

Behemoth — בהמות

The Animal Soul, in its fullness; i.e. including the Creative Entity or Ego, Chiah — נפש חיה

454

Sigillum — חותם

The "Holy Ones"; Con-secrated catamites kept by the Priesthood — קדשים

455

456

Formido maxima — אימתה

The Mountain of Myrrh. [Cant. iv. 6] — הר המור

Paries — כותל

Crura — שוקים

The Fig-tree and fruit — תאנה

π 457

Olives — זתים

458

A covenant; an engagement; a betrothed — חתן

Contusores; cloudy heavens; Heaven of Netzach — שחקים

459

460

[Vide K.D. L.C.K. p. 371] — טנתא

Qliphoth of ♊ — צללד מירון

"Holy unto TETRA-GRAMMATON." [Ex. xxxix. 30] — קדש ליהוה

π 461

[Vide K.D. L.C.K. p. 539] — אדנות

Robustus, validus, asper, איתן
horridus, rigidus

462

Terra Superna (est ארץ עליונה
Binah)

A path ניתב

Profundum Celsitudinis עומק רום

π 463

Day Demon of 3rd Dec. ♍ באתין

Pillar of Mildness—paths, ג, גסת
ס, and ת

Crystal, glass זכוכית

A rod of almond מטה השקד

The Special Intelligence. תבונה
[I.Z.Q. 264, et seq.]

Caps, crowns, diadems תגין

Precatio תחנה

464

Σ (1—30) 465

A kiss; a little (or, sweet) נשיקה
mouth

466

Skull גלגלת

Renes כליות

The World of עולם היצירה
Formation

Simeon שמעון

π 467

[Vide S.D. 33] גלגלתא

468

Angel of 3rd Dec. ♊ ביתון

469

Trabeationes ligaturae חשוקיהם
illarum

470

Eternity. (Literally, דור דורים
a cycle of cycles)

Angel of 8 S. נתהיה

Pure Wool עמר נקי

Period of time; Time עת

Solum; fundus קרקע

471

Palatia היכלות

Mount Moriah. המוריה הר
[2 Chron. iii. 1]

472

Was terrified בעת

473

The Three Persons. אתהואני
[ATH: HVA: ANI
coalesced]

Skull גולגלתא

Molitrices טחנות

474

Knowledge. [Vide K.D. דעת
L.C.K. p. 252, et seq.]

(Plural)—Wisdom חכמות

The Testimony within the Ark עדת

A ram, he-goat; a prepared עתד
sacrifice

Angel L.T.D. of ♋ רעדר

475

[Vide no. 473.] In בגולגלתא
Golgotha

476

Domus Iudicii; Curia; בית דין
Consistorium iudiciale

477

478

Cranium, calvaria גולגולת

The Lesser Countenance, זעיר אנפין
Microprosopus

Hagiographa כתובים

π 479

Molentes טוחנות

480

Lapides inanitatis אבני תוהו

[Vide K.D. L.C.K. p. 252] דעות

Lilith, Qliphoth of Malkuth לילית

[Vide K.D. L.C.K. p. 252] עדות

Malkuth, 42-fold Name in עית
Yetzirah

481

בעוגת

Hills גבעות

Reus mortis חייב מיתא

Annulus טבעת

482

A looking-glass, mirror אספקלריא

483

| Ferens iniquitatem | נשא עון |

22^2 $\sqrt{}$ 484

485

| Filia scaturiginum. [Is. x. 30, "Daughter of Gallim"] | בת גלים |
| Mockeries [Job xvii. 2. Vide 435] | התלים |

486

A name of GOD	יהוה בחכפה ימד ארץ
Foundations	יסודות
Azymum fractum	מצה פרוית
A King of Edom	עוית
Angel of 8 P.	נהתאל

π 487

488

Ianua, ostium	פתח
Qliphoth of Kether	תאומיאל
Ye shall worship	תעבודו

489

| Retribuens; rependens retributionem | משלם גמול |

490

The giving. [Vide no. 1106]	מתן
Fine flour, meal	סלת
Perfect	תמים
Binah, 42-fold Name in Yetzirah	תץ

π 491

| Nutrix | אמנת |
| Angel of 4 W. | ניתאל |

492

493

| The Name given in Deut. xxviii. 58; without את = 92, q.v. | את יהוה אלהיך |

494

| Galea salutis | כובע הישועה |
| An apple | תפוח |

495

| Similtudo hominis | דמות אדם |
| Gift | מתנה |

♛

Σ (1—31)   496

Leviathan	לויתן
Malkuth	מלכות
A small bundle	צדור

497

| Nutrix | אומנת |
| Gemini; ♊ | תאומים |

498

| Briatic Palace of Geburah | היכל זכות |

π 499

| Cerva amorum. [Prov. v. 19, "a loving hind"] | אילת אהבים |
| Busy, arduous; an army; 'hosts' | צבאות |

500

The humerus	כתף
Kimelium aureum	מכתם
Princeps	שר
A Duke of Edom	תימן

501

Asher; blessedness	אשר
Fortis; fortia, robusta	אתנים
The head	ראש
Flesh; Night Demon of 1st Dec. ♓	שאר
Sehechinah Superior	שכינה עילאה
Likeness, similitude	תמונה

502

| To tell glad tidings; flesh, body | בשר |
| To cut | בתק |

ז ג
ש ♉   The Cup of the Stolistes   π 503

| Expelled, cast forth | גרש |

504

| Sought for | דרש |

505

| Sarah; Principissa. [Vide 510 & cf. 243 & 248] | שרה |

506

| | אבגיתץ |
| [Vide no. 1196] | כפות |

127

Bovis α´ sinistra; an ox; Taurus.	שור	
[Vide K.D. L.C.K. p. 99]—א		
		507
That which causes ferment; yeast	שאור	
		508
Daybreak; black	שחר	
		π 509
Bridge	גשור	
		510
Sensus allegoricus. [Vide K.D. L.C.K. p. 12]	דרוש	
Rectitudo, aequitas recta; rectilineum	ישר	
The head	ריש	
Song	שיר	
Sarai. [Vide 505]	שרי	
Draco; see 440	תנין	
		511
	עתיאל	
The HEAD	רישא	
[Vide K.D. L.C.K. p. 463]	שורה	
$8^3 = 2^9$	$\sqrt[3]{}\ ^9\sqrt{}$ 512	
Adhaesio, cohaesio	דבקות	
Angel of 3rd Dec. ♎	שחדר	
		513
		514
[Vide K.D. L.C.K. p. 213]	חקות	
		515
Possessio sine angustiis	נחלה בלי מצרים	
Minister iudicii	שוטר	
Phylacterium	תפלה	
		516
Lucus. [Vide K.D. L.C.K. p. 168]	אשירה	
Personae	פרצופין	
		517
Qliphoth of ♉. [Vide no. 321, & Liber 777]	אוימידין	
The good gift, i.e. Malkuth	מתנה טובה	
Occultae. [Vide 417]	פלאות	
Confractio. [Vide K.D. L.C.K. p. 698, et seq.]	שבידה	

		518
		519
Day Demon of 2nd Dec. ♊	בדרטוש	
		520
Tears	דמעות	
Legitium	כשר	
		π 521
Ignis descendens	אש יורד	
Angel of 2 P.	ושריה	
Nudatio candoris	מחשוף הלבן	
		522
		π 523
		524
		525
The LORD of Hosts, a name of GOD referred to Netzach	יהוה צבאות	
		526
Superliminare	משקוף	
		527
Σ (1—32)		528
23^2		$\sqrt{}$ 529
Affatura ollaris cum iusculo dulci	ציקי קדירה	
Day Demon of 3rd Dec. ♋	שיטרה	
		530
The Rose	חבצלת	
Voices	קלת	
Tekel, a word of the 'writing on the wall' at Belshazzar's fabled feast	תקל	
		531
		532
		533
Heaven of Jesod of Malkuth	טבל וילון שמים	
King of Terrors	מלך בלהות	
		534
A certain Name of GOD	קלדשק	
		535
		536
A white cloak	טלית לבנה	
Sphere of the fixed stars	מסלות	

The World of Assiah, עולם העשיה the 'material' world

537

Emanatio; Atziluth, the אצילות Archetypal world

Medulla spinalis חוט השדרה

Apertio uteri פטר רחם

538

Daughter of the Voice.— בת קול Echo. [The Bath Qol is a particular and very sacred method of divination]

539

540

Lumbi; the upper part מתנים

π 541

Israel ישראל

542

543

"Existence is אהיה אשר אהיה Existence," the NAME of the Highest GOD

544

Apples. [Cant. ii. 5] תפוחים

545

Aper de Sylva חזיר מיער

546

Sweet מתוק

P's; a watchman שומר

Custodi שמור

L.A. Angel of ♈ שרהיאל

π 547

548

Qliphoth of ♈ בעירירון

Night Demon of 3rd Dec. ♋ הצגנת

A Name of GOD, יהוה אלוה ודעת referred to Tiphareth

Qliphoth of ♎ עבירירון

549

Moral מורגש

Ventus turbinis רוח סערה

550

Aquila; decidua. [Vide K.D. נשר L.C.K. p. 600; connect with no. 496, Malkuth]

A rod of iron. [Ps. ii.] שבט ברזל

L.A. Angel of ♌ שרטיאל

Principes שרים

Dragons. (Restricted.) תנינם [Ps. lxxiv. 13]

551

552

Desiderium dierum חמדת ימים

553

Draco magnus תנין גדול

554

Day Demon of 2nd Dec. ♓ מרחוש

555

Obscurity עפתה

556

Mark, vestige, footstep רשימו

Sharon. [Cant. ii. 1] שרון

π 557

The First ראשון

558

559

560

דרושים

Waters of quiet מי מנוחות

Puncta נקודת

A Duke of Edom תמנע

Dragons תנינים

Σ (1—33) 561

Cain אתקין

Concealed Mystery דצניותא

562

Primordial ראשונה

π 563

Lotio manuum נטילת ידים

Angel of 1st Dec. ♊ סגרש

564

Lapis capitalis אבן הראשה

[I.R.Q. 941.] ויהי האדם לנפש חיה "And the Adam was formed into a living Nephesh"

Sphere of Malkuth   חלם יסודות

565

Parvitatio   קטנות
Praetoriani   שטורים

566

A valley; a plain   ישרון
Puncta   נקודות
[SMK + VV + DLTh, SVD   ס:ו:ד:
= a secret, spelt in full]
The Shadow of Death; Hell   צלמות
of Netzach
Redintegratio, configuratio,   תיקון
depositio, conformatio,
restoratio, restitutio

567

Firstborn   ראשוני

568

π 569

Fingers   אצבעות

570

Naphtali   נפתלי
Lectus   ערש
Ten   עשר
Heads   רישין
Concussion, earthquake   רעש
[Vide K.D. L.C.K. p. 691]
Gate; the Door   שער   רשע

π 571

The mountains of Zion   הררי ציון
Balance   מתקלא

572

A chastening GOD.   יהוה אלהיך
[Deut. xxviii. 58.]
[ך counted as final]
Jeschurun   ישורון
He was touched. [I.R.Q.   יתעצב
1117]
Active   מתקבל
Day Demon of 1st Dec. ♓   פורפור

573

574

Chaldee. [Hath a general   ירחשון
meaning of movement.
S.D. p. 87]

575

Beerschebha, Fons Sep-   באר שבע
tenarii. [2 Sam. xxiv. 7
—Gen. xxi. 31.] [Vide
K.D. L.C.K. p. 183]
"And the   ויאמר אלהים יהי אור
GODS said, Let
there be LIGHT"

24^2 $\sqrt{576}$

Wands   מקלות
The tenth   עשור

π 577

The Concealed of   טמירה דטמירין
the Concealed; a
name of GOD
most High

578

579

Media nox   חצות לילה
Qliphoth of Netzach   ערב זרק
Sons of Adam   תענוגים

580

Rich   עשיר
Ancient   עתיק
"Le bouc émissaire"; shaggy,   שעיר
hairy. [Levit. xvi. 22]
Angel of Fire   שרף

581

The Ancient One   עתיקא
Barley   שעורה

582

583

584

585

The GODS of Battle אלהים צבאות
(lit. of Hosts); the
Divine Name of
Hod
[Vide K.D. L.C.K. p. 386]   תקיעה

586

War-trumpet   שופר

587

Day Demon of 1st Dec. ♒   פוראש

130

588

589

Viror. [Vide K.D. L.C.K. p. 15]   אב לשון ענף

590

Rib. [Gen. ii. 22]   צלעת

591

592

π 593

594

The Stone of Israel. [Gen. xlix. 24]   אבן ישראל

Σ (1—34)   595

596

Jeruschalim   ירושלים

597

598

Our iniquities   עונותינו

π 599

600

Mirabilia, vel occulta sapientiae   פליאות חכמה

Peniculamentum, fimbria peniculata   ציצית

A knot, ligature   קשר

Red   שרק

Six; marble   שש

π 601

602

Lux simplicissima   אור פשות

Brightness; splendores   צחצחות

Extremitates   קצוות

603

Qliphoth of ♌   שלהבירון

604

Congeries; epistola   אגרת

Israel Senex   ישראל סבא

605

Magnificentia [Vide K.D. L.C.K. p. 226]   אדרת
   גברת

606

Let them bring forth   ישרצו

Ipseitas, seu ipsa essentia. עצמות [Vide K.D. L.C. K. pp. 571, 631]

Nexus, ligature   קשור

Ruth   רות

A turtle-dove   תור

π 607

Adam Primus   אדם הראשון

The mountains of spices. הרי בשמים [Cant. viii. 14]

A span, palm. [Lit. "the little finger"]   זרת

608

The last Gate. [Vide K.D. L.C.K. p. 184]   בבא בתרא

[Vide K.D. L.C.K. p. 640]   חתר

609

610

Numulus argenteus   אגורת

Citrus, malum citrum; (lust and desire). [Vide K.D. L.C.K. p. 178]   אתרוג

Tenth   מעשר

611

"The Fear" of the LORD. [Ps. cxi. 10]   יראת

The Law. (Occasional spelling)   תורה

612

(The covenant)—Day Demon of 1st Dec. ♑. [Ps. xxv. 14]   ברית

The number of the Divine Precepts π 613

The Quintessence of Light   את האור

Moses, our Rabbi   משה רבינו

[Vide K.D. L.C.K. p. 179]   תריג

614

615

616

Qliphoth of ♓   שימירון

The Five Books of Moses; the Law on Sinai. Cf. Tarot   תירו

π 617

"Mighty acts." (Plur. of "Strength.") [Ps. cvi. 2]   גבורות

131

Columnae Nubis עמודי האש והענן
et Ignis

A King of Edom רהבית

630
Angel L.T.D. of ♊ סערש

The Holy Spirit רוחא קדישא
שלש

Angels of Geburah, and of שרפים
Kether of Briah

618

Contentiones ריבות

π 619

Novissimum אחרית

620

Chokmah, Binah, חכמה בינה ודעת
Daath; the first
descending triad

The Crown: Kether כתר

Angel of 3rd Dec. ♍ משפר

[Vide Ps. xxxi. 20] צפנת

The Doors שערים

[Temurah of לבב] ששך

621

Mucro gladii אבחת חרב

By-paths. [Vide no. 1357] אורחות

[Vide I.R.Q. 234] 622

Blessings ברכת

Profunda Maris. [Samael ים מצולות
et Uxor Eius]

Latitudines; Rechoboth רחובות

623

Barietha; Doctrina ex- ברייתא
tranea; conclusio extra
Jeruschalem facta

624

His Covenant. [Ps. xxv. 14] ובריתו

Liberty חירות

Qliphoth of ♐ נחשירין

25² = 5⁴ √ ∜ 625

The Mountain of Ararat הרי אררט

626

The tenth portion עשרון

627

628

Light. [Spelt in full, with א:ו:ר:
ו as וא]

Blessings ברכות

629

The great trumpet שופר גדול

π 631

Concealed Mystery דצניעותא

632

633

Light. [Spelt in full, when א:ו:ר:
ו = וו]

[Gen. v. 2] זכר ונקבה בראם

634

635

636

Qliphoth of ♍ צפרירון

637

Day Demon of 3rd Dec. ♑ פורנאש

Day Demon of 1st Dec. ♎ שאלוש

638

639

The Tree of Knowledge עץ הדעת

640

The Cup of Con- כוס תנחומים
solations

Third. [Vide K.D. L.C.K. שליש
p. 719]

Sun; Sphere of ☉ שמש

Palm of the hand; palm-tree תמר

π 641

Dema purpureum אמרת

Angel of 9 W. ירתאל

"Lights"; defective. מארת
[S.D. 142]

642

Day Demon of 2nd Dec. ♏ פורשון

π 643

Light. [Spelt in full, א:ו:ר:
when ו = ויו]

Severities of TETRA- גבורות יהוה
GRAMMATON

The Cup of Bene- כוס של ברכה
dictions

$(12 \times 13 \times 4) + 20 =$ number of letters 644
in the five tablets of Enoch.
[Vide Equinox VII]

645

A King of Edom — משרקה

646

Elohim [ם counted as Final] — אלהים
Licitum — מותר
Rejoicing — משוש

π 647

Lights — מארות

648

649

Trance, deep sleep. [Vide — תרדמה
no. 244]

650

Nitre — נתר

651

Temurah — תמורה

652

π 653

654

655

656

A rose, lily. [Vide no. 706] — שושן
Delight, joy — ששון
A furnace — תנור

657

Angel of 3rd Dec. ♏ — ותרודיאל
Zelbarachith; ♌ — זלברחית

658

π 659

660

Scintillae — ניציצית
Zones; members — קשרין
— תינר

π 661

Esther — אסתר
Day Demon of 3rd Dec. ♓ — ישטולוש
Crinorrhodon (vide K.D. — שושנה
L.C.K. p. 708); a rose
Angel L.T.D. of ♎ — תרגבון

662

Corona Dei — אכתריאל

663

Lapides marmoris. [Vide אבני שש
Zohar, pt. I. fol. 34.
col. 134]

Cantio — זמירות

664

665

The Womb — בית הרחם

Σ (1—36). ☉. The Number of 666[3]
THE BEAST

Aleister — אלהיסטהר ה כרעולהי
E. Crowley

Aleister Crowley — אליסטיר קרולי
[Rabbi Battiscombe
Gunn's v.l.]

The number 5, which is — הא × אלף
6 (ה א), on the Grand
Scale

Qliphoth of ♓ — נשימידרון
Spirit of ☉ — סורת

Ommo Satan, the 'Evil — עממו סתן
Triad' of Satan-Typhon,
Apophras, and Besz

The Name Jesus — שם יהשוה

667

The oil for lighting — שמן למאור

668

Negotiatrix — סחרת

669

670

— ערת
Deprecatus — עתר

671

Ferens fructum — עושה פרי
The Law — תערא
The Gate — תרעא
Adonai. [Spelt in full] — א:ד:נ:י:

672

π 673

674

[Vide K.D. L.C.K. p. 395] — סוחרת

3. See Equinox, V & VII, for further details.

133

	675

Briatic Palace of   היכל עצטשמים
Netzach

| 26² | √ **676** |

Artificial. [ם final]   גלגלים
Angel L.T.D. of ♒   עתור

π **677**

678

Planities coeli; Assiatic   ערבות
Heaven of 1st palace

679

The chrysolite stone.   אבן מעולפת
[Cant. v. 14]

680

Phrath, one of the four rivers   פרת
of Eden

681

Joyful noise; battle-cry; the   תרועה
sound (of a trumpet)

682

Of the evening; of the West   ערבית

π **683**

684

685

686

687

688

689

690

The candlestick   מנרת
Palm-trees   תמרים

π **691**

692

The fourth portion   רביעית

693

Sulphur   גפרית

694

695

The Moral World   עולם מורגש

696

697

Castella munita; domus   ארמנות
munitae

698

699

700

The Mercy Seat   כפרת
The Veil of the Holy   פרכת
Seth   שת

π **701**

[Deut. xxiii. 1]   אשת
"And lo! three men."   והנה שלשה
[These be Michael,
Gabriel and Raphael,
[אלו־מיכאל־גבריאל־ורפאל—
Prolapsus in faciem   נפילת אפים

702

Sabbathum quies   שבת

Σ (1—37)   **703**

Taenia   מסגרת
Qliphoth of Binah   סאתאריאל

704

"Arbatel." [The *Arbatel*   ארבעתאל
of Magic, by Pietro di
Abano]
Angel L.T.N. of ♓   נתדוריגאל

705

The stones of   אבנים מפולמות
dampness. [Job xxviii. 3]

706

Propitiatorium   כפורכת
"Lilies" (I.R.Q. 878), or   שושנים
"Roses" (von Rosenroth)

707

708

The Angel of the   מלאך הברית
Covenant
Perdition   שחת

The Seven Double Letters   π **709**
ת, ר, פ, כ, ד, ג, ב

710

Spelunca   מערת
Six. (Ch.)   שית

711

712

713

Sphere of ♄   שבתאי

Conversio — תשובה
714
715
Secret — נסתרה
Perfumed, fumigated — קטורת
716
Vaschti. [Est. i. 9] — ושתי
Matrona — מטרוניתא
717
718
π 719

⌊6 — 720
חשבתי
Thy Navel. [Cant. vii. 3] — שררך
721
The Primordial Point — נקדה ראשונה
722
The voice of the trumpet — קול שופר
723
724
The end of the days — אחרית הימים
725
726
π 727
728
[Vide K.D. L.C.K. p. 506] — תשכח
$27^2 = 9^3 = 3^6$ $\sqrt{}$ $\sqrt[3]{}$ $\sqrt[6]{}$ 729
[Vide K.D. L.C.K. p. 505] — קרע שטן
730
731
732
π 733
The white head: a title of GOD most High — רישא הוורה
734
To bring forth — שתלד
735
Tiphareth, 42-fold Name in Yetzirah — במרצתג
736
Tortuosae — עקלקלות

737
(Live coal)—Blaze, flame — שלהבת
שת הבל
738
π 739
740
Σ (1—38) — 741
(ן counted as Final) Amen: see 91 — אמן
The four letters of the elements; hence a concealed יהוה — אמתש
742
The Ark of the Testimony. [Lit. "of tremblings," scil. "vibrations"] — ארון העדות
π 743
744
745
746
The Names — שמות
747
The voice of the turtle-dove. [Cant. ii. 12] — קול התור
748
The oil of Anointment — שמן המשחה
749
750
Conclave — לשכת
Lead — עפרת
π 751
Vir integer — איש תם
752
Satan — שאתאן
753
Abraham and Sarah. [Either spelling. Vide 243, 248, 505, & 510]
754
755
756
Emanations: numbers — ספירות
Years — שנות

135

π 757

Netzach and Hod — אשכלות

758

Perdition — משחית

Copper ore; bronze — נחשת

759

Pulvis aromatarii — אבקת רוכל

760

"Both Active and Passive"; said in the Qabalah concerning the Sephiroth — מקביל ומתקבל

Confinement, detention — עצרת

Yesod, 42-fold Name in Yetzirah — קרעשמן

π 761

762

763

764

765

766

767

768

π 769

770

Going forth. [Said of the Eyes of TETRAGRAMMATON] — משוטטות

Unfruitful, barren — עקרת

771

L.A. Angel of ♍ — שלתיאל

772

Septennium — שבע שנים

π 773

Lapis, seu canalis lapideus Potationis — אבן השתיה

774

Filia Septenarii — בת שבע

775

[Vide no. 934] — דקרדינותא

776

777

The Flaming Sword, if the path from Binah to Chesed be taken as = 3. For ג connects Arikh Anpin with Zauir Anpin

One is the — אחת רוח אלהים חיים — Ruach of the Elohim of Lives

The World of Shells — עולם הקליפות

778

779

780

I dwell, have dwelt. (*Not* written.) [I.R.Q. 1122; Prov. viii. 12] — שכנתי

Shore, bank — שפת

781

782

783

28²   √ 784

Qliphoth of ♋ — שיחרירון

785

786

Smooth — פשות

π 787

788

The Secret Wisdom: i.e., The Qabalah. [Vide 58] — חכמה נסתרה

789

790

My presence. [I.R.Q. 1122; Prov. xii.] — שיכנתי

791

792

[Vide K.D. L.C.K. p. 460, and Ps. xviii. 51] — ישועות

793

794

795

796

Calix horroris — כוס התרעלה

π 797

798	ויאמר אלהים יהי אור ויהי אור [Genesis i. 3]

Mount Gaerisim הר גרזים והר עיבל and mount Ebal. [Deut. xi. 29]

Consisting of Seven שביעיות

799

800

A bow; ♐. The three Paths קשת leading from Malkuth; hence much symbolism of the Rainbow of Promise

801

$401 \times 2 =$ The Reflection of 401, 802 which is את, α & ω

Consessus vel ישיבה של מעלה Schola vel Academia Superna. [Refers to A∴ A∴, the three grades which are above the Abyss. Vide K.D. L.C.K. p. 461]

Vindicta foederis נקם ברית

An ark, as of Noah or of Moses תבת

803

804

805

806

807

808

"A piece of brass"—the נחשתן Brazen Serpent

π 809

810

A Duke of Edom יתת

Octava שמינית

π 811

812

813

Signa אותות

Ararita; a name of GOD אראריתא which is a Notariqon of the sentence : אחד ראש אחדותו ראש ייחודותו : תמורתו אחד . "One is His Beginning; one is His Individuality; His Permutation One."

814

815

Ahasuerus אחשורש

816

817

818

819

Σ (1—40) 820

π 821

822

π 823

Lapis effigiei seu אבן משכית figuratus. [Lev. xxvi. 1.]

Litterae אותיות

824

825

826

π 827

828

π 829

830

Issachar יששכר

Three (? third) תלת

831

832

Albedo Crystalli לבנת ספיר

833

Choir of Angels in חיות הקדש Kether

Transiens super עובה על רפשע prevaricatione

834

835

Brachia Mundi זרועות עולם

836

837

The profuse giver. [Cf. the תת זל Egyptian word Tat.]

[ם counted as Final. Vide למרבה 277. This *is* written]

838

π 839

840

29²   √841

Laudes   תהלות

842

843

844

845

כב אותיות

Oleum influxus   שמן השפע

846

847

848

849

Exitus Sabbathi   מוצאי שבת

850

Blue; perfection   תכלת

My perfect one. (*Not* written.) תמתי
[Cant. v. s.] Vide 857

851

Souls. [I.R.Q. 1052 et seq.] נשמתהון

852

Occellata Aurea; משבצות זהב
Netzach and Hod
receiving influence
from Geburah

π 853

An orchard   שדה תפוחים

854

855

856

Summitatis bifidae in Lulabh תיומת

π 857

My twin-sister. [*Is* written] תאומתי

858

"To Thee   אתה גבור לעולם אדני
be Power unto the Ages,
my Lord" [Vide 35 s.v.
אגלא]

π 859

Inunctio, copula, phy- תפלה של יד
lacterium, ornamentumve

manus. [Connect with
[נשר

860

Σ (1—41)   861

862

π 863

864

The Woman of   אשת זנונים
Whoredom

⊙ and ☽   שמש וירח

865

866

Latera aquilonis   ירכתי צפון

867

868

Semitae   נתיבות

869

Qliphoth of Tiphareth   תגריגון

870

Twelve   תריסר

871

872

Septiduum   שבעת ימים

873

874

875

876

π 877

878

879

880

A King of Edom   השסהתימני

π 881

Os cranii, cranium   קרקפתא

882

Dilationes fleminis   רחובות הנהר

π 883

Lux oriens   אור מתנוצץ

884

Domination   תועבות

885

886

π 887

888

889

890

Spelunca duplex מערת המכפלה

891

892

Defectus cogitationis אפיסת הרעיון

893

894

895

896

897

898

899

30² √900

901

902

Briatic Palace of היכל לבנת הספיר
Jesod—Malkuth

Σ (1—42) 903

Secret name of Cagliostro אשאראת

904

905

906

Licentia. [Vide K.D. L.C.K. רשות
p. 693]

Vermis תולעת

π 907

908

909

910

Beginning. [Vide I.Z.Q. רשית
547, et seq.]

π 911

Hell of Tiphareth בארשחת
Beginning ראשית
Remnant שארית

912

Pl. of 506 שור q.v. שורות

913

Berashith; "in the בראשית
Beginning." [With *small* B.]
[Vide A Note on Genesis,
Equinox II 163–185, and 2911]

914

915

916

917

918

π 919

920

921

Nekudoth; intuitus as- הסתכלות
pectus. [Vide K.D.
L.C.K. p. 547]

922

923

924

925

926

927

928

π 929

Gazophylacia Septen- אוצרות צפון
trionis

Briah, the Palace היכל קודש קדשים
of the Supernals
therein

930

931

932

The Tree of the עץ הדעת טוב ורע
Knowledge of
Good and Evil

933

Foedus nuditatis vel ברית המעור
Sabbathi vel arcus

934

Coruscatio בוצינא דקרדינותא
vehementissima; splendor
exactissime dimeticus

935	962
The Cause of cause סבת הסבות	963
[Vide Eccles. ii. 8, & תענוגות	Achad; unity. [Spelt fully] א:ח:ד:
S.D. v. 79]	Garland, Crown; a little עטרת עטרה
936	wreath. [Vide K.D.
Kether. [Spelt in full] כ:ת:ר:	L.C.K. p. 614]
π 937	964
938	Memoriale iubilationis. זכרון תרועה
939	[Note Root 227 זכר, q.v.
940	showing phallic nature of
π 941	this 'memorial']
Angel of 1st Dec. ♐ משראת	965
942	966
943	π 967
944	968
945	969
The small point: a title נקדה פשוט	970
of GOD most High	Angel of Water תרשיס
Σ (1—43) 946	π 971
π 947	Shemhamphorasch, שם המפורש
Angel of 1st Dec. ♋ מתראוש	the 'Divided Name'
948	of GOD
949	972
950	973
[Vide no. 1204] המתהפכת	974
951	975
The Book of the Law ספר תורה	976
952	π 977
π 953	978
Vigiliae אשמורות	979
954	980
955	981
956	982
957	π 983
Unguentum Magnifi- משחא רבות	Urbs Quaternionis קרית ארבע
centiae	984
958	The Beginning of ראשית חכמה
959	Wisdom (is The Wonderment
960	at TETRAGRAMMATON.
Tubae argenteae חצצרות כסף	Psalms).
31² √961	985

	986
Vehementia; obiectio rigorosa התקפתא	
	987
	988
Foedus pacis ברית שלום	
	989
Pascens inter Lilia רועה בשושנים	
Σ (1—44) 990	
π 991	
	992
The joy of the whole Earth. [Vide no. 296] משוש כל הארץ	
	993
	994
	995
	996
The Most Holy Ancient One עתיקא קדישא	
π 997	
	998
Foedus linguae ברית לשון	
	999
10^3 $\sqrt[3]{}$ 1000	
[Vide no. 1100] ששת	
A Qabalistic Method of Exegesis; "spelling Qabalistically backward" תשרק	
	1001
	1002
The bank of a stream שפת היאור	
	1003
	1004
	1005
	1006
The Law תרות	
	1007
TAROT. [But vide 671] תארות	
	1008
π 1009	

1010	
1011	
1012	
π 1013	
1014	
1015	
1016	
[Vide no. 1047] יותרת	
1017	
Vasa vitrea, lagenae, phiale אשישות	
1018	
π 1019	
1020	
π 1021	
1022	
1023	
$32^2 = 4^5 = 2^{10}$ $\sqrt{}$ $\sqrt[6]{}$ $\sqrt[10]{}$ 1024	
Qliphoth of ♍ נחשתירון	
1025	
Absconsiones sapientiae תעלומות חכמה	
1026	
1027	
1028	
1029	
1030	
π 1031	
1032	
Sphere of Primum Mobile ראשית הגלגלים	
π 1033	
1034	
Σ (1—45) 1035	
1036	
1037	
1038	
π 1039	
1040	
1041	

1042	
1043	
1044	
1045	
1046	
1047	
Diaphragma supra hepar (vel hepatis)	יותרת הכבד
1048	
π 1049	
1050	
π 1051	
1052	
1053	
1054	
1055	
1056	
The lily	שושנת
1057	
1058	
1059	
1060	
The Tabernacle [ן final]	משכן
π 1061	
	אסתתר
[Vide I.R.Q. 939]	ויפח באפיו נשמת חיים
1062	
π 1063	
1064	
1065	
1066	
1067	
1068	
π 1069	
1070	
1071	
1072	
1073	
1074	
1075	
1076	
1077	
1078	
1079	

		1080
Σ (1—46)		1081
Tiphareth	תפארת	
		1082
		1083
		1084
		1085
		1086
	π	1087
		1088
33²	√	1089
		1090
	π	1091
The Rose of Sharon	חבצלת השרון	
		1092
	π	1093
		1094
		1095
		1096
	π	1097
		1098
		1099
		1100
Sextiduum	ששת ימים	
		1101
		1102
	π	1103
		1104
		1105
		1106
The giving of the Law	מתן התורה	
		1107
		1108
	π	1109
		1110
		1111
		1112
		1113
		1114
		1115
		1116
	π	1117
		1118
		1119
		1120

	1121		π 1163
	1122		1164
	π 1123		1165
	1124		1166
	1125		1167
	1126		1168
	1127		1169
Σ (1—47)	1128		1170
	π 1129		π 1171
	1130		1172
	1131		1173
	1132	[With ן counted as את יהוה אלהין	
	1133	Final]	
	1134		1174
	1135		1175
	1136	Conclave caesum לשכת הגזית	
	1137	Σ (1—48)	1176
	1138		1177
	1139		1178
	1140		1179
	1141		1180
	1142		π 1181
	1143		1182
	1144		1183
	1145		1184
	1146		1185
Jars, globular vessels צנתרות			1186
	1147		π 1187
Byssus contorta שש משזר			1188
	1148		1189
	1149		1190
	1150		1191
	π 1151		1192
	1152		π 1193
	π 1153		1194
	1154		1195
	1155		1196
34^2	√ 1156	Fasciculi; rami pal- כפות תמרים	
	1157	marum	
Specula turmarum מראות הצובאות			1197
	1158		1198
	1159		1199
	1160		1200
	1161		π 1201
	1162		1202

	1203	
	1204	
Flamma	להט חרב המתהפכת	
gladii versatilis		
	1205	
	1206	
The Holy Intelli-	נשמתא קדישא	
gence		
A water-trough	שקתות	
	1207	
	1208	
	1209	
	1210	
Angel of Geburah of Briah	תרשיש	
	1211	
	1212	
	π 1213	
	1214	
	1215	
	1216	
	π 1217	
	1218	
	1219	
Formator eius quod	יוצר בראשית	
in principiis		
	1220	
Hell of Hod	שערימדת	
The beaten oil	שמן כתית	
	1221	
	1222	
	π 1223	
	1224	
Σ (1—49) = 35². ♀. √ 1225		
The Ancient of the	עתיקא דעתיקין	
Ancient Ones		
	1226	
	1227	
	1228	
	π 1229	
	1230	
	π 1231	
	1232	
	1233	
	1234	
	1235	

	1236	
	π 1237	
	1238	
	1239	
	1240	
	1241	
	1242	
	1243	
	1244	
	1245	
	1246	
	1247	
	1248	
	π 1249	
	1250	
	1251	
	1252	
	1253	
	1254	
	1255	
	1256	
	1257	
	1258	
	π 1259	
	1260	
Angels of Netzach and	תרשישים	
of Geburah of Briah		
	1261	
	1262	
	1263	
	1264	
	1265	
	1266	
	1267	
	1268	
	1269	
	1270	
	1271	
	1272	
	1273	
	1274	
Σ (1—50)	1275	
	1276	
	π 1277	
	1278	

π 1279	1320
Ignis sese reciprocans אש מתלקחת	π 1321
1280	The Lily of the Valleys
1281	1322
1282	1323
π 1283	1324
1284	1325
1285	Σ (1—51) 1326
1286	π 1327
1287	1328
1288	1329
π 1289	1330
1290	11^3 $\sqrt[3]{}$ 1331
π 1291	1332
1292	1333
1293	1334
1294	1335
Chorda fili coccini תקות חוט השני	1336
1295	1337
$36^2 = 6^4$ $\sqrt{}$ $\sqrt[4]{}$ 1296	1338
π 1297	1339
1298	1340
1299	1341
1300	1342
π 1301	1343
1302	1344
π 1303	1345
1304	1346
1305	1347
1306	1348
π 1307	1349
Angel L.T.D, of 2nd Dec. יו, אשתרות	The numerical value of the 9 Paths 1350
and King-Demon of	of the Lesser Beard: viz. נ, ס,
Geburah	ע, פ, צ, ק, ר, ש, and ת
1308	1351
1309	1352
1310	1353
1311	1354
1312	1355
1313	1356
1314	1357
1315	Crooked by- אורחות עקלקלות
1316	paths. [Jud. v. 6]
1317	1358
1318	1359
π 1319	1360

	π 1361		1403
	1362		1404
	1363		1405
	1364		1406
	1365		1407
	1366		1408
	π 1367		π 1409
	1368		1410
37²	√ 1369		1411
	1370		1412
	1371		1413
	1372		1414
	π 1373		1415
	1374		1416
	1375		1417
	1376		1418
	1377		1419
Σ (1—52)	1378		1420
	1379		1421
	1380		1422
The lip of the liar שפת שקר			π 1423
	π 1381		1424
	1382		1425
	1383		1426
	1384		π 1427
	1385		1428
	1386		π 1429
	1387		1430
	1388	Σ (1—53)	1431
	1389		1432
	1390		π 1433
	1391		1434
	1392		1435
	1393		1436
	1394		1437
	1395		1438
	1396		π 1439
	1397		1440
	1398		1441
	π 1399		1442
	1400		1443
Chaos, or = את, 401 q.v. את		38²	√ 1444
Tria Capita תלת רישין			1445
	1401	The remnant of his heritage לשארית נחלתו	
	1402		

	1446
	π 1447
	1448
	1449
	1450
	π 1451
	1452
	π 1453
	1454
	1455
	1456
	1457
	1458
	π 1459
	1460
Quies cessationis שבת שבתון	
	1461
	1462
	1463
	1464
	1465
	1466
	1467
	1468
	1469
	1470
	π 1471
	1472
	1473
	1474
	1475
	1476
	1477
	1478
	1479
	1480
Septem heptaeterides שבע שבתות	
	π 1481
	1482
Rotunditates, seu גולות הכותרות vasa rotunda capitellarum, seu capitella rotunda	
	π 1483
	1484
Σ (1—54)	1485
	1486

π 1487	
1488	
π 1489	
1490	
1491	
1492	
π 1493	
1494	
The total numerical value of the Paths of the Tree; i.e. of the Beards conjoined; i.e. of the whole Hebrew Alphabet	1495
1496	
1497	
1498	
π 1499	
1500	
1501	
1502	
1503	
1504	
1505	
1506	
1507	
1508	
1509	
1510	
π 1511	
1512	
1513	
1514	
1515	
1516	
1517	
1518	
1519	
1520	
39^2	$\sqrt{\ }$ 1521
1522	
π 1523	
1524	
1525	
1526	
1527	
1528	
1529	

	1530	1574
	π 1531	1575
	1532	1576
	1533	1577
	1534	1578
	1535	π 1579
	1536	1580
	1537	1581
	1538	1582
	1539	π 1583
Σ (1—55)	1540	1584
	1541	1585
	1542	1586
The Oil of the Anointing שמן משחת קדש		1587
		1588
	π 1543	1589
	1544	1590
	1545	1591
	1546	1592
	1547	1593
	1548	1594
	π 1549	1595
	1550	1596	Σ (1—56)
	1551	π 1597
	1552	1598
	π 1553	1599
	1554	√ 1600
	1555	π 1601
	1556	1602
	1557	1603
	1558	1604
	π 1559	1605
	1560	1606
	1561	π 1607
	1562	1608
	1563	π 1609
	1564	1610
	1565	1611
	1566	1612
	π 1567	π 1613
	1568	1614
	1569	1615
	1570	1616
	π 1571	1617
	1572	1618
	1573	

Σ (1—56) 40^2

π 1619				1664
1620	The pure olive		שמן זית זך כתית	
π 1621	oil beaten out			
1622				1665
1623				1666
1624				π 1667
1625				1668
1626				π 1669
π 1627				1670
1628				1671
1629				1672
1630				1673
1631				1674
1632				1675
1633				1676
1634				1677
1635				1678
1636				1679
π 1637				1680
1638			41^2	$\sqrt{}$ 1681
1639				1682
1640				1683
1641				1684
1642				1685
1643				1686
1644				1687
1645				1688
1646				1689
1647				1690
1648				1691
1649				1692
1650				π 1693
1651				1694
1652				1695
Σ (1—57)	1653			1696
1654				π 1697
1655				1698
1656				π 1699
π 1657				1700
1658				1701
1659				1702
1660				1703
1661				1704
1662				1705
π 1663				1706

	1707		1752
	1708		π 1753
	π 1709		1754
	1710		1755
Σ (1—58)	1711	קדש קדוש קדוש יהוה צבאות	
	1712	Holy, Holy, Holy, Lord GOD	
	1713	of Hosts!	
	1714		1756
	1715		1757
	1716		1758
	1717		π 1759
	1718		1760
	1719		1761
	1720		1762
	π 1721		1763
	1722	42^2	$\sqrt{1764}$
	π 1723		1765
	1724		1766
	1725		1767
	1726		1768
	1727		1769
12^3	$\sqrt[3]{1728}$	Σ (1—59)	1770
	1729		1771
	1730		1772
	1731		1773
	1732		1774
	π 1733		1775
	1734		1776
	1735		π 1777
	1736		1778
	1737		1779
	1738		1780
	1739		1781
	1740		1782
	π 1741		π 1783
	1742		1784
	1743		1785
	1744		1786
	1745		π 1787
	1746		1788
	π 1747		π 1789
	1748		1790
	1749		1791
	1750		1792
	1751		1793

	1794		1839
	1795		1840
	1796		1841
	1797		1842
	1798		1843
	1799		1844
	1800		1845
	π 1801		1846
	1802		π 1847
	1803		1848
	1804	43^2	√ 1849
	1805		1850
	1806		1851
	1807		1852
	1808		1853
	1809	‖ 7	1854
	1810		1855
	π 1811		1856
	1812		1857
	1813		1858
	1814		1859
	1815		1860
	1816		π 1861
	1817		1862
	1818		1863
	1819		1864
	1820		1865
	1821		1866
	1822		π 1867
	π 1823		1868
	1824		1869
	1825		1870
	1826		π 1871
	1827		1872
	1828		π 1873
	1829		1874
Σ (1—60)	1830		1875
	π 1831		1876
	1832		π 1877
	1833		1878
	1834		π 1879
	1835		1880
	1836		1881
	1837		1882
	1838		1883

	1884		1929
	1885		1930
	1886		π 1931
	1887		1932
	1888		π 1933
	π 1889		1934
	1890		1935
Σ (1—61)	1891	44²	√ 1936
	1892		1937
	1893		1938
	1894		1939
	1895		1940
	1896		1941
	1897		1942
	1898		1943
	1899		1944
	1900		1945
	π 1901		1946
	1902		1947
	1903		1948
	1904		π 1949
	1905		1950
	1906		π 1951
	π 1907		1952
	1908	Σ (1—62)	1953
	1909		1954
	1910		1955
	1911		1956
	1912		1957
	π 1913		1958
	1914		1959
	1915		1960
	1916		1961
	1917		1962
	1918		1963
	1919		1964
	1920		1965
	1921		1966
	1922		1967
	1923		1968
	1924		1969
	1925		1970
	1926		1971
	1927		1972
	1928		π 1973

	1974		2019
	1975		2020
	1976		2021
	1977		2022
	1978		2023
	π 1979		2024
	1980	45²	√2025
	1981		2026
	1982		π 2027
	1983		2028
	1984		π 2029
	1985		2030
	1986		2031
	π 1987		2032
	1988		2033
	1989		2034
	1990		2035
	1991		2036
	1992		2037
	π 1993		2038
	1994		π 2039
	1995		2040
	1996		2041
	π 1997		2042
	1998		2043
	π 1999		2044
	2000		2045
	2001		2046
	2002		2047
	π 2003		2048
	2004		2049
	2005		2050
	2006		2051
	2007		2052
	2008		π 2053
	2009		2054
	2010		2055
	π 2011		2056
	2012		2057
	2013		2058
	2014		2059
	2015		2060
Σ (1—63)	2016		2061
	π 2017		2062
	2018		π 2063

	2064	2108
	2065	2109
	2066	2110
	2067	π 2111
	2068	2112
	π 2069	π 2113
	2070	2114
	2071	2115
46²	2072	√ 2116
	2073	2117
	2074	2118
	2075	2119
	2076	2120
	2077	2121
	2078	2122
	2079	2123
Σ (1—64). ☿	2080	2124
Spirit of ☿ תפתרתרת		2125
	π 2081	2126
	2082	2127
	π 2083	2128
	2084	π 2129
	2085	2130
	2086	π 2131
	π 2087	2132
	2088	2133
	π 2089	2134
	2090	2135
	2091	2136
	2092	π 2137
	2093	2138
	2094	2139
	2095	2140
	2096	π 2141
	2097	2142
	2098	π 2143
	π 2099	2144
Σ (1—65)	2100	2145
	2101	2146
	2102	2147
	2103	2148
	2104	2149
	2105	2150
	2106	2151
	2107	2152

		π 2153		2198
		2154		2199
		2155		2200
		2156		2201
		2157		2202
		2158		π 2203
		2159		2204
		2160		2205
		π 2161		2206
		2162		π 2207
		2163		2208
		2164	47²	√ 2209
		2165		2210
		2166	Σ (1—66)	2211
		2167		2212
		2168		π 2213
		2169		2214
		2170		2215
		2171		2216
		2172		2217
		2173		2218
		2174		2219
		2175		2220
		2176		π 2221
		2177		2222
		2178		2223
		π 2179		2224
		2180		2225
		2181		2226
		2182		2227
		2183		2228
		2184		2229
		2185		2230
		2186		2231
3⁷		⁷√ 2187		2232
		2188		2233
		2189		2234
		2190		2235
		2191		2236
		2192		π 2237
		2193		2238
		2194		π 2239
		2195		2240
		2196		2241
13³		³√ 2197		2242

π 2243		2288
2244		2289
2245		2290
2246		2291
2247		2292
2248		π 2293
2249		2294
2250		2295
π 2251		2296
2252		π 2297
2253		2298
2254		2299
2255		2300
2256		2301
2257		2302
2258		2303
2259	48^2	$\sqrt{2304}$
2260		2305
2261		2306
2262		2307
2263		2308
2264		π 2309
2265		2310
2266		π 2311
π 2267		2312
2268		2313
π 2269		2314
2270		2315
2271		2316
2272		2317
π 2273		2318
2274		2319
2275		2320
2276		2321
2277		2322
Σ (1—67) 2278		2323
2279		2324
2280		2325
π 2281		2326
2282		2327
2283		2328
2284		2329
2285		2330
2286		2331
π 2287		2332

	π 2333	2378
	2334	2379
	2335	2380
	2336	π 2381
	2337	2382
	2338	π 2383
	π 2339	2384
	2340	2385
	π 2341	2386
	2342	2387
	2343	2388
	2344	π 2389
	2345	2390
Σ (1—68)	2346	2391
	π 2347	2392
	2348	π 2393
	2349	2394
	2350	2395
	π 2351	2396
	2352	2397
	2353	2398
	2354	π 2399
	2355	2400
	2356	$49^2 = 7^4$ $\sqrt{\ }\sqrt[4]{\ }$ 2401
	π 2357	2402
	2358	2403
	2359	2404
	2360	2405
	2361	2406
	2362	2407
	2363	2408
	2364	2409
	2365	2410
	2366	π 2411
	2367	2412
	2368	2413
	2369	2414
	2370	Σ (1—69) 2415
	π 2371	2416
	2372	π 2417
	2373	2418
	2374	2419
	2375	2420
	2376	2421
	π 2377	2422

π 2423		2468
2424		2469
2425		2470
2426		2471
2427		2472
2428		π 2473
2429		2474
2430		2475
2431		2476
2432		π 2477
2433		2478
2434		2479
2435		2480
2436		2481
π 2437		2482
2438		2483
2439		2484
2440	Σ (1—70)	2485
π 2441		2486
2442		2487
2443		2488
2444		2489
2445		2490
2446		2491
π 2447		2492
2448		2493
2449		2494
2450		2495
2451		2496
2452		2497
2453		2498
2454		2499
2455	50^2	$\sqrt{2500}$
2456		2501
2457		2502
2458		π 2503
π 2459		2504
2460		2505
2461		2506
2462		2507
2463		2508
2464		2509
2465		2510
2466		2511
π 2467		2512

	2513		2558
	2514		2559
	2515		2560
	2516		2561
	2517		2562
	2518		2563
	2519		2564
	2520		2565
	π 2521		2566
	2522		2567
	2523		2568
	2524		2569
	2525		2570
	2526		2571
	2527		2572
	2528		2573
	2529		2574
	2530		2575
	π 2531		2576
	2532		2577
	2533		2578
	2534		π 2579
	2535		2580
	2536		2581
	2537		2582
	2538		2583
	π 2539		2584
	2540		2585
	2541		2586
	2542		2587
	π 2543		2588
	2544		2589
	2545		2590
	2546		π 2591
	2547		2592
	2548		π 2593
	π 2549		2594
	2550		2595
	π 2551		2596
	2552		2597
	2553		2598
	2554		2599
	2555		2600
Σ (1—71)	2556	51^2	$\sqrt{2601}$
	π 2557		2602

2603	2648
2604	2649
2605	2650
2606	2651
2607	2652
2608	2653
π 2609	2654
2610	2655
2611	2656
2612	π 2657
2613	2658
2614	π 2659
2615	2660
2616	2661
π 2617	2662
2618	π 2663
2619	2664
2620	2665
π 2621	2666
2622	2667
2623	2668
2624	2669
2625	2670
2626	π 2671
2627	2672
Σ (1—72) 2628	2673
2629	2674
2630	2675
2631	2676
2632	π 2677
π 2633	2678
2634	2679
2635	2680
2636	2681
2637	2682
2638	π 2683
2639	2684
2640	2685
2641	2686
2642	π 2687
2643	2688
2644	π 2689
2645	2690
2646	2691
π 2647	2692

	π 2693		2738
	2694		2739
	2695		2740
	2696		π 2741
	2697		2742
	2698		2743
	π 2699	14^3	$\sqrt[3]{}$ 2744
	2700		2745
Σ (1—73)	2701		2746
	2702		2747
	2703		2748
52^2	$\sqrt{}$ 2704		π 2749
	2705		2750
	2706		2751
	π 2707		2752
	2708		π 2753
	2709		2754
	2710		2755
	π 2711		2756
	2712		2757
	π 2713		2758
	2714		2759
	2715		2760
	2716		2761
	2717		2762
	2718		2763
	π 2719		2764
	2720		2765
	2721		2766
	2722		π 2767
	2723		2768
	2724		2769
	2725		2770
	2726		2771
	2727		2772
	2728		2773
	π 2729		2774
	2730	Σ (1—74)	2775
	π 2731		2776
	2732		π 2777
	2733		2778
	2734		2779
	2735		2780
	2736		2781
	2737		2782

161

	2783		2828
	2784		2829
	2785		2830
	2786		2831
	2787		2832
	2788		π 2833
	π 2789		2834
	2790		2835
	π 2791		2836
	2792		π 2837
	2793		2838
	2794		2839
	2795		2840
	2796		2841
	π 2797		2842
	2798		π 2843
	2799		2844
	2800		2845
	π 2801		2846
	2802		2847
	π 2803		2848
	2804		2849
	2805	Σ (1—75)	2850
	2806		π 2851
	2807		2852
	2808		2853
53²	√ 2809		2854
	2810		2855
	2811		2856
	2812		π 2857
	2813		2858
	2814		2859
	2815		2860
	2816		π 2861
	2817		2862
	2818		2863
	π 2819		2864
	2820		2865
	2821		2866
	2822		2867
	2823		2868
	2824		2869
	2825		2870
	2826		2871
	2827		2872

	2873	2918
	2874	2919
	2875	2920
	2876	2921
	2877	2922
	2878	2923
π	2879	2924
	2880	2925
	2881	Σ (1—76) 2926
	2882	π 2927
	2883	2928
	2884	2929
	2885	2930
	2886	2931
π	2887	2932
	2888	2933
	2889	2934
	2890	2935
	2891	2936
	2892	2937
	2893	2938
	2894	π 2939
	2895	2940
	2896	2941
π	2897	2942
	2898	2943
	2899	2944
	2900	2945
	2901	2946
	2902	2947
π	2903	2948
	2904	2949
	2905	2950
	2906	2951
	2907	2952
	2908	π 2953
π	2909	2954
	2910	2955
	2911	2956
	2912	π 2957
	2913	2958
	2914	2959
	2915	2960
54^2	√ 2916	2961
π	2917	2962

π 2963			3008
2964			3009
2965			3010
2966			π 3011
2967			3012
2968			3013
π 2969			3014
2970			3015
π 2971			3016
2972			3017
2973			3018
2974			π 3019
2975			3020
2976			3021
2977			3022
2978			π 3023
2979			3024
2980	55^2		$\sqrt{3025}$
2981			3026
2982			3027
2983			3028
2984			3029
2985			3030
2986			3031
2987			3032
2988			3033
2989			3034
2990			3035
2991			3036
2992			π 3037
2993			3038
2994			3039
2995			3040
2996			π 3041
2997			3042
2998			3043
π 2999			3044
3000			3045
π 3001			3046
3002			3047
Σ (1—77)	3003		3048
3004			π 3049
3005			3050
3006			3051
3007			3052

	3053		3098
	3054		3099
	3055		3100
	3056		3101
	3057		3102
	3058		3103
	3059		3104
	3060		3105
	π 3061		3106
	3062		3107
	3063		3108
	3064		π 3109
	3065		3110
	3066		3111
	π 3067		3112
	3068		3113
	3069		3114
	3070		3115
	3071		3116
	3072		3117
	3073		3118
	3074		π 3119
	3075		3120
	3076		π 3121
	3077		3122
	3078		3123
	π 3079		3124
	3080	5^5	$\sqrt[5]{}\,3125$
$\Sigma\,(1{-}78)$	3081		3126
	3082		3127
	π 3083		3128
	3084		3129
	3085		3130
	3086		3131
	3087		3132
	3088		3133
	π 3089		3134
	3090		3135
	3091	56^2	$\sqrt{}\,3136$
	3092		π 3137
	3093		3138
	3094		3139
	3095		3140
	3096		3141
	3097		3142

	3143	3188
	3144	3189
	3145	3190
	3146	π 3191
	3147	3192
	3148	3193
	3149	3194
	3150	3195
	3151	3196
	3152	3197
	3153	3198
	3154	3199
	3155	32×10^2 The paths of the Whole 3200
	3156	Tree in excelsis
	3157	בראשית ברא אלהים
	3158	3201
	3159	3202
Σ (1—79)	3160	π 3203
	3161	3204
	3162	3205
	π 3163	3206
	3164	3207
	3165	3208
	3166	π 3209
	π 3167	3210
	3168	3211
	π 3169	3212
	3170	3213
	3171	3214
	3172	3215
	3173	3216
	3174	π 3217
	3175	3218
	3176	3219
	3177	3220
	3178	π 3221
	3179	3222
	3180	3223
	π 3181	3224
	3182	3225
	3183	3226
	3184	3227
	3185	3228
	3186	π 3229
	π 3187	3230

	3231		3276
	3232		3277
	3233		3278
	3234		3279
	3235		3280
	3236		3281
	3237		3282
	3238		3283
	3239		3284
Σ (1—80)	3240		3285
	3241		3286
	3242		3287
	3243		3288
	3244		3289
	3245		3290
	3246		3291
	3247		3292
	3248		3293
57^2	$\sqrt{}$ 3249		3294
	3250		3295
	π 3251		3296
	3252		3297
	π 3253		3298
	3254	π 3299
	3255		3300
	3256	π 3301
	π 3257		3302
	3258		3303
	π 3259		3304
	3260		3305
	3261		3306
	3262	π 3307
	3263		3308
	3264		3309
	3265		3310
	3266		3311
	3267		3312
	3268	π 3313
	3269		3314
	3270		3315
	π 3271		3316
	3272		3317
	3273		3318
	3274	π 3319
	3275		3320

167

Σ (1—80). ☽.   3321

The Intelligence of the Intelligences of the   מלכא בתרשישים ועד ברוה שהרים
Moon.

The Spirit of the Spirits of the Moon   שדברשהמעת שרתתן

[A pendant to this work, on the properties of pure number, is in preparation under the supervision of Fratres P. and ψ. Also a companion volume on the Greek Qabalah by them and Frater J. M.]

777

VEL

PROLOGOMENA SYMBOLICA AD SYSTEMAM SCEPTICO-MYSTICÆ VIÆ EXPLICANDÆ, FVNDAMENTVM HIEROGLYPHICVM SANC-TISSIMORVM SCIENTIÆ SVMMÆ

אחת רוח אלהים חיים

THE SCRIBE DEDICATES
THIS ESSAY
TO THE MOST HIGH MASTER OF THE GRAND LODGE ABOVE
TO THE WORSHIPFUL MASTER AND OFFICERS OF HIS LODGE
AND TO ALL
HIS BROTHER MASONS

INTRODUCTION

THE FOLLOWING is an attempt to systematise alike the data of mysticism and the results of comparative religion.

The sceptic will applaud our labours, for that the very catholicity of the symbols denies them any objective validity, since, in so many contradictions, something must be false; while the mystic will rejoice equally that the self-same catholicity all-embracing proves that very validity, since after all something must be true.

Fortunately we have learnt to combine these ideas, not in the mutual toleration of sub-contraries, but in the affirmation of contraries, that transcending of the laws of intellect which is madness in the ordinary man, genius in the Overman who hath arrived to strike off more fetters from our understanding. The savage who cannot conceive of the number six, the orthodox mathematician who cannot conceive of the fourth dimension, the philosopher who cannot conceive of the Absolute—all these are one; all must be impregnated with the Divine Essence of the Phallic Yod of Macroprosopus, and give birth to their idea. True (we may agree with Balzac), the Absolute recedes; we never grasp it; but in the travelling there is joy. Am I no better than a staphylococcus because my ideas still crowd in chains?

But we digress.

The last attempts to tabulate knowledge are the *Kabbala Denudata* of Knorr von Rosenroth (a work incomplete and, in some of its parts, prostituted to the service of dogmatic interpretation), the lost symbolism of the Vault in which Christian Rosenkreutz is said to have been buried, some of the work of Dr. Dee and Sir Edward Kelly, some very imperfect tables in Cornelius Agrippa, the "Art" of Raymond Lully, some of the very artificial effusions of the esoteric Theosophists, and of late years the knowledge of the Order Rosæ Rubeæ et Aureæ Crucis and the Hermetic Order of the Golden

171

Dawn. Unluckily, the leading spirit in these latter societies found that his prayer, "Give us this day our daily whisky, and just a wee drappie mair for luck!" was sternly answered, "When you have given us this day our daily Knowledge-lecture."

Under these circumstances Daath got mixed with Dewar, and Beelzebub with Buchanan.

But even the best of these systems is excessively bulky; modern methods have enabled us to concentrate the substance of twenty thousand pages in two score.

The best of the serious attempts to systematise the results of Comparative Religion is that made by Blavatsky. But though she had an immense genius for acquiring facts, she had none whatever for sorting and selecting the essentials.

Grant Allen made a very slipshod experiment in this line; so have some of the polemical rationalists; but the only man worthy of our notice is Frazer of the Golden Bough. Here again, there is no tabulation; for us it is left to sacrifice literary charm, and even some accuracy, in order to bring out the one great point.

This: That when a Japanese thinks of Hachiman, and a Boer of the Lord of Hosts, they are not two thoughts, but one.

The cause of human sectarianism is not lack of sympathy in thought, but in speech; and this it is our not unambitious design to remedy.

Every new sect aggravates the situation. Especially the Americans, grossly and crapulously ignorant as they are of the rudiments of any human language, seize like mongrel curs upon the putrid bones of their decaying monkey-jabber, and gnaw and tear them with fierce growls and howls.

The mental prostitute, Mrs. Eddy (for example), having invented the idea which ordinary people call "God," christened it "Mind," and then by affirming a set of propositions about "Mind," which are only true of "God," set all hysterical, dyspeptic, crazy Amurrka by the ears. Personally, I don't object to people discussing the properties of four-sided triangles; but I draw the line when they use a well-known word, such as pig, or mental healer, or dung-heap, to denote the object of their paranoiac fetishism.

Even among serious philosophers the confusion is very great. Such terms as God, the Absolute, Spirit, have dozens of connotations, according to the time and place of the dispute and the beliefs of the disputants.

Time enough that these definitions and their inter-relation should be crystallised, even at the expense of accepted philosophical accuracy.

2. The principal sources of our tables have been the philosophers and traditional systems referred to above, as also, among many others, Pietro di Abano, Lilly, Eliphaz Levi, Sir R. Burton, Swami Vivekananda, the Hindu, Buddhist, and Chinese Classics, the Qúran and its commentators, the Book of the Dead, and, in particular, original research. The Chinese, Hindu, Buddhist, Moslem and Egyptian systems have never before been brought into line with the Qabalah; the Tarot has never been made public.

Eliphaz Levi knew the true attributions but was forbidden to use them.[1]

All this secrecy is very silly. An indicible Arcanum is an arcanum that *cannot* be revealed. It is simply bad faith to swear a man to the most horrible penalties if he betray . . ., &c., and then take him mysteriously apart and confide the Hebrew Alphabet to his safe keeping. This is perhaps only ridiculous; but it is a wicked imposture to pretend to have received it from Rosicrucian manuscripts which are to be found in the British Museum. To obtain money on these grounds, as has been done by certain moderns, is clear (and, I trust, indictable) fraud; and ever to have countenanced those frauds, of which he must surely have been aware, seems hardly creditable to so earnest and venerable a student of the mysteries as Dr. Wynn Westcott.[2] It is presumable, however, that he was the dupe of his fear of, if not of his trust in, the Machiavellian Mystic of the Rue Mozart.

The secrets of Adepts are not to be revealed to men. We only wish they were. When a man comes to me and asks for the Truth, I

---

1   This is probably true, though in agreement with the statement of the traducer of Levi's doctrine and the vilifier of his noble personality.

2   My correspondence with this gentleman has not tended to raise my opinion of his conduct.

go away and practice teaching the Differential Calculus to a Bushman; and I answer the former only when I have succeeded with the latter. But to withhold the Alphabet of Mysticism from the learner is the device of a selfish charlatan. That which can be taught shall be taught, and that which cannot be taught may at last be learnt.

3. As a weary but victorious warrior delights to recall his battles —Fortisan hæc olim meminisse juvabit—we would linger for a moment upon the difficulties of our task.

The question of sacred alphabets has been abandoned as hopeless. As one who should probe the nature of woman, the deeper he goes the rottener it gets; so that at last it is seen that there is no sound bottom. All is arbitrary;[3] withdrawing our caustics and adopting a protective treatment, we point to the beautiful clean bandages and ask the clinic to admire! To take one concrete example: the English T is clearly equivalent in sound to the Hebrew ת, the Greek τ, the Arabic ت and the Coptic τ, but the numeration is not the same. Again, we have a clear analogy in shape (perhaps a whole series of analogies), which, on comparing the modern alphabets with primeval examples, breaks up and is indecipherable.

The same difficulty in another form permeates the question of gods.

Priests, to propitiate their local fetish, would flatter him with the title of creator; philosophers, with a wider outlook, would draw identities between many gods in order to obtain a unity. Time and the gregarious nature of man have raised gods as ideas grew more universal; sectarianism has drawn false distinctions between identical gods for polemical purposes.

Thus, where shall we put Isis, favouring nymph of corn as she was? As the type of motherhood? As the moon? As the great goddess Earth? As Nature? As the Cosmic Egg from which all

---

3   All symbolism is perhaps ultimately so; there is no necessary relation in thought between the idea of a mother, the sound of the child's cry "Ma," and the combination of lines *ma*. This, too, is the extreme case, since "ma" is the sound naturally just produced by opening the lips and breathing. Hindus would make a great fuss over this true connection; but it is very nearly the only one. All these beautiful schemes break down sooner or later, mostly sooner.

Nature sprang? For as time and place have changed, so she is all of these!

What of Jehovah, that testy senior of Genesis, that lawgiver of Leviticus, that war-god of Joshua, that Phallus of the depopulated slaves of the Egyptians, that jealous King-God of the times of the Kings, that more spiritual conception of the Captivity, only invented when all temporal hope was lost, that mediæval battleground of cross-chopped logic, that Being stripped of all his attributes and assimilated to Parabrahma and the Absolute of the Philosopher?

Satan, again, who in Job is merely Attorney-General and prosecutes for the Crown, acquires in time all the obloquy attaching to that functionary in the eyes of the criminal classes, and becomes a slanderer. Does any one really think that any angel is such a fool as to try to gull the Omniscient God into injustice to his saints?

Then, on the other hand, what of Moloch, that form of Jehovah denounced by those who did not draw huge profits from his rites? What of the savage and morose Jesus of the Evangelicals, cut by their petty malice from the gentle Jesus of the Italian children? How shall we identify the thaumaturgic Chauvinist of Matthew with the metaphysical Logos of John? In short, while the human mind is mobile, so long will the definitions of all our terms vary.

But it is necessary to settle on something: bad rules are better than no rules at all. We may then hope that our critics will aid our acknowledged feebleness; and if it be agreed that much learning hath made us mad, that we may receive humane treatment and a liberal allowance of rubber-cores in our old age.

4. The Tree of Life is the skeleton on which this body of truth is built. The juxtaposition and proportion of its parts should be fully studied. Practice alone will enable the student to determine how far an analogy may be followed out. Again, some analogies may escape a superficial study. The Beetle is only connected with the sign Pisces through the Tarot Trump "The Moon." The Camel is only connected with the High Priestess through the letter ג.

Since all things whatsoever (including no thing) may be placed upon the Tree of Life, the Table could never be complete. It is already somewhat unwieldy; we have tried to confine ourselves as far as possible to lists of Things Generally Unknown. It must be remembered that the lesser tables are only divided from the thirty-two-fold table in order to economise space; *e.g.* in the seven-fold table the entries under Saturn belong to the thirty-second part in the large table.

We have been unable for the moment to tabulate many great systems of Magic; the four lesser books of the Lemegeton, the system of Abramelin, if indeed its Qliphothic ramifications are susceptible of classification, once we follow it below the great and terrible Demonic Triads which are under the presidency of the Unutterable Name, the vast and comprehensive system shadowed in the Book called the Book of the Concourse of the Forces, which we are now editing and hope to issue separately, interwoven as it is with the Tarot, being, indeed, on one view little more than an amplification and practical application of the Book of Thoth.

But we hope that the present venture will attract scholars from all quarters, as when the wounded Satan leaned upon his spear,

> "Forthwith on all sides to his aid was run
> By angels many and strong,"

and that in the course of time a far more satisfactory volume may result.

Many columns will seem to the majority of people to consist of mere lists of senseless words. Practice, and advance in the magical or mystical path, will enable little by little to interpret more and more.

Even as a flower unfolds beneath the ardent kisses of the Sun, so will this table reveal its glories to the dazzling eye of illumination. Symbolic and barren as it is, yet it shall stand for the athletic student as a perfect sacrament, so that reverently closing its pages he shall exclaim, "May that of which we have partaken sustain us in the search for the Quintessence, the Stone of the Wise, the Summum Bonum, True Wisdom, and Perfect Happiness."

So mote it be!

TABLE OF CORRESPONDENCES

TABLE OF CORRESPONDENCES

VIII.* Orders of Qliphoth.	VII. English of Col. VI.	VI. The Heavens of Assiah.	
	. . . .	. . . .	0
(1) תאומיאל	Sphere of the Primum Mobile	ראשית הנלנלים	1
(1) עויאל	Sphere of the Zodiac or Fixed Stars	מסלות	2
(1) סאתאריאל	Sphere of Saturn	שבתאי	3
(2) געשכלה	Sphere of Jupiter	צדק	4
(3) גולחב	Sphere of Mars	מאדים	5
(4) תגרירון	Sphere of Sol	שמש	6
(5) ארב זרק	Sphere of Venus	נוגה	7
(6) סמאל	Sphere of Mercury	כוכב	8
(7) גמליאל	Sphere of Luna	לבנה	9
(7) לילית	Sphere of the Elements	חלם יסודות	10
[Elements. See. Col. LXVIII.]	Air	רוח	11
[Planets follow Sephiroth]	Mercury	[Planets follow Sephiroth, corresponding]	12
	Luna		13
	Venus		14
בעירירון*	Aries △	טלה	15
אדימירון	Taurus ▽	שור	16
צללדמיון	Gemini ♊	תאומים	17
שיחרירון	Cancer ▽	סרטן	18
שלהבירון	Leo △	אריה	19
צפרירון	Virgo ♍	בתולה	20
	Jupiter		21
עבירירון	Libra ♎	מאזנים	22
	Water	מים	23
נחשתירון	Scorpio ▽	עקרם	24
נחשירון	Sagittarius △	קשת	25
דגדגירון	Capricornus ♑	גדי	26
	Mars		27
בהימירון	Aquarius ♒	דלי	28
נשימירון	Pisces ▽	דגים	29
	Sol		30
	Fire	אש	31
	Saturn		32
	Earth	ארץ	32 bis
	Spirit	את*	31 bis

* The asterisks (*) refer to Notes at end of Table.

TABLE I

V.* God-Names in Assiah.	IV.* Consciousness of the Adept.	III. English of Col. II.	II.* The Hebrews Names of Numbers and Letters.	I. Key Scale.
. . . .	. . . .	⌈ Nothing ⟨ No Limit ⌊ Limitless L.V.X.	אין ⎫ אין סוף ⎬ אין סוף אור ⎭	0
אהיה	הוא	Crown	כתר*	1
יה		Wisdom	חכמה*	2
יהוה אלהים		Understanding	בינה*	3
אל		Mercy	חסד*	4
אלהים גבור		Strength	גבורה*	5
יהוה אלוה ודעת		Beauty	תפארת*	6
יהוה צבאות		Victory	נצח	7
אלהים צבאות		Splendour	הוד	8
שדי אל חי		Foundation	יסוד*	9
אדני מלך		Kingdom	מלכות*	10
יהוה		Ox	אלף	11
אזבוגה (8)		House	בית	12
דה (9) אלים (81)		Camel	גמל	13
אהא (7)		Door	דלת	14
		Window	הה	15
		Nail	וו	16
		Sword	זין	17
		Fence	חית	18
		Serpent	טית	19
		Hand	יוד	20
אבא (4) אל אב (34)		Palm	כף	21
		Ox Goad	למד	22
אל		Water	מים	23
		Fish	נון	24
		Prop	סמך	25
		Eye	עין	26
אדני (65)		Mouth	פה	27
		Fish-hook	צדי	28
		Back of Head	קוף	29
אלה (36)		Head	ריש	30
אלהים		Tooth	שין	31
אב (3) יה (15)		Tau (as Egyptian)	תו	32
אדני [הארץ]			תו	32 bis
יהשוה			שין	31 bis

179

TABLE OF CORRESPONDENCES

XV.* The King Scale of Colour [']	XIV. General Attribution of Tarot	XIII. The Paths of the Sepher Yetzirah	
. . . .	. . . .	. . . .	0
Brilliance	The 4 Aces	Admirable or Hidden Intelligence	1
Pure soft blue	The 4 Twos—Kings or Knights	Illuminating I.	2
Crimson	The 4 Three—Queens	Sanctifying I.	3
Deep violet	The 4 Fours	Measuring Cohesive or Receptacular I.	4
Orange	The 4 Fives	Radical I.	5
Clear pink rose	The 4 Sixes—Emperors or Princes	I. of the Mediating Influence	6
Amber	The 4 Sevens	Occult I.	7
Violet purple	The 4 Eights	Absolute or Perfect I.	8
Indigo	The 4 Nines	Pure or Clear I.	9
Yellow	The 4 Tens—Empresses or Princesses	Resplendent I.	10
Bright pale yellow	The Fool—[Swords] Emperors or Princes	Scintillating I.	11
Yellow	The Juggler	I. of Transparency	12
Blue	The High Priestess	Uniting I.	13
Emerald green	The Empress	Illuminating I.	14
Scarlet	The Emperor	Constituting I.	15
Red Orange	The Hierophant	Triumphal or Eternal One	16
Orange	The Lovers	Disposing One	17
Amber	The Chariot	I. of the House of Influence	18
Yellow, greenish	Strength	I. of all the Activities of the Spiritual Being	19
Green, yellowish	Hermit	I. of Will	20
Violet	Wheel of Fortune	I. of Conciliation	21
Emerald green	Justice	Faithful I.	22
Deep blue	The Hanged Man—[Cups] Queens	Stable I.	23
Green blue	Death	Imaginative I.	24
Blue	Temperance	I. of Probation or Tentative One	25
Indigo	The Devil	Renovating I.	26
Scarlet	The House of God	Exciting I.	27
Violet	The Star	Natural I.	28
Crimson (ultra violet)	The Moon	Corporeal I.	29
Orange	The Sun	Collecting I.	30
Glowing orange scarlet	The Angel of Last Judgment—[Wands] Kings or Knights	Perpetual I.	31
Indigo	The Universe	Administrative I.	32
Citrine, olive, russet, and black	Empresses [Coins]		32 bis
White merging into grey	All 22 Trumps		31 bis

TABLE I (continued)

XII.* The Tree of Life.	XI.* Elements (with their Planetary Rulers).	X. Mystic Numbers of the Sephiroth.	IX.* The Sword and the Serpent.	
. . . .	. . . .	0	. . . .	0
1st Plane, Middle Pillar	Root of 🜁	1		1
2nd Plane, Right Pillar	Root of △	3		2
2nd Plane, Left Pillar	Root of ▽	6		3
3rd Plane, Right Pillar	▽	10		4
3rd Plane, Left Pillar	△	15		5
4th Plane, Middle Pillar	🜁	21		6
5th Plane, Right Pillar	△	28		7
5th Plane, Left Pillar	▽	36		8
6th Plane, Middle Pillar	🜁	45		9
7th Plane, Middle Pillar	🜃	55	The Flaming Sword follows the downward course of the Sephiroth, and is compared to the Lightning Flash. Its hilt is in Kether and its point in Malkurth.	10
Path joins 1 - 2	Hot and moist 🜁	66		11
„ 1 - 3		78		12
„ 1 - 6		91		13
„ 2 - 3		105		14
„ 2 - 6	☉ △ ♃	120		15
„ 2 - 4	♀ 🜃 ☽	136		16
„ 3 - 6	♄ 🜁 ☿	153		17
„ 3 - 5	♂ ▽	171		18
„ 4 - 5	☉ △ ♃	190		19
„ 4 - 6	♀ 🜃 ☽	210		20
„ 4 - 7		231	The Serpent of Wisdom follows the course of the paths or letters upwards, its head being thus in א, its tail in ת. א, מ, and ש are the Mother letters, referring to the Elements; ב, ג, ד, כ, פ, ר, and ת, the Double letters, to the Planets; the rest, Single letters, to the Zodiac.	21
„ 5 - 6	♄ 🜁 ☿	253		22
„ 5 - 8	Cold and moist ▽	276		23
„ 6 - 7	♂ ▽	300		24
„ 6 - 9	☉ △ ♃	325		25
„ 6 - 8	♀ 🜃 ☽	351		26
„ 7 - 8		378		27
„ 7 - 9	♄ 🜁 ☿	406		28
„ 7 - 10	♂ ▽	435		29
„ 8 - 9		465		30
„ 8 - 10	Hot and dry △	496		31
„ 9 - 10		528		32
	Cold and dry 🜃			32 bis
				31 bis

181

TABLE OF CORRESPONDENCES

XXI.* Perfected Man.	XX. Complete Practical Attribution of Egyptian Gods.	XIX.* Selection of Egyptian Gods.	
Nu—the Hair	Heru-pa-Kraath	Harpocrates, Amoun, Nuith	0
]Disk (of Ra)—the Face. [In Daath, Assi—the Neck]	Ptah	Ptah, Asar un Nefer, Hadith	1
	Isis	Amoun, Thoth, Nuith [Zodiac]	2
	Nephthys	Maut, Isis, Nephthys	3
]Neith—the Arms	Amoun	Amoun, Isis	4
	Horus	Horus, Nephthys	5
The Mighty and Terrible One—the Breast	Ra	Asar, Ra	6
The Lords of Keraba—the Reins. Nuit—the Hips and Legs.	Hathoor	Hathoor	7
	Thoth	Anubis	8
Asar and Asi—the Phallus and Vulva. Sati–the Spine	Shu	Shu	9
The Eye of Hoor–the Buttocks and Anus	Osiris	Seb, Lower (i.e. unwedded) Isis and Nephtys	10
As 6	Mout	Nu	11
Aupu—the Hips	Thoth	Thoth or Cynocephalus	12
Hathor—the Left Eye	Chomse	Chomse	13
Khenti - Khas—the Left Nostril	Hathoor	Hathoor	14
	Isis	Men Thu	15
Ba-Neh-Tattu—the Shoulders	Osiris	Asar Ameshet Apis	16
	The twin Merti	Various twin Deities, Rehkt, Merti, &c.	17
	Hormakhu	Khephra	18
As 6	Horus	Ra-Hoor-Khuit, Pasht, Sekhet, Mau	19
	Heru-pa-Kraath	Isis [as Virgin]	20
Apu-t—the Left Ear	Amoun-Ra	Amoun-Ra	21
	Maat	Ma	22
As 24	Ⲓⲋⲟⲍⲟⲩⲣⲉⲑ	Tum Athph Auramoth (as ▽), Asar (as Hanged Man), Hekar, Isis	23
Sekhet—the Belly and Back	Hammemit	Merti goddesses, Typhon, Apep, Khephra	24
	Ⲁⲣⲏⲱⲅⲉⲡⲓⲋ		25
As 10, for ע means Eye.	Set	Khem (Set)	26
Khenti-Khas—the Right Nostril	Menthu	Horus	27
The Lords of Keraba—the Reins	Nuit	Ahephi, Aroueris	28
	Anubi	Khephra (as Scarab in Tarot Trumps)	29
Hathor—the Right Eye	Ra	Ra and many others	30
[Serget—the Teeth] As 6	Mau	Thoum-aesh-neith, Mau, Kabeshunt Horus, Tarpesheth	31
Apu-t—the Right Ear	See Note*	Sebek, Mako	32
אלים חים—the Bones As 16		Satem, Ahapshi, Nephthys, Ameshet	32 bis
		Asar	31 bis

182

TABLE I (continued)

XVIII.* The Empress Scale of Colour [ה].	XVII.* The Emperor Scale of Colour [ו].	XVI.* The Queen Scale of Colour [ה].	
. . . .	. . . .	. . . .	0
White, flecked gold	White brilliance	White Brilliance	1
White, flecked red, blue, and yellow	Blue pearl grey, like mother-of-pearl	Grey	2
Grey, flecked pink	Dark brown	Black	3
Deep azure, flecked yellow	Deep purple	Blue	4
Red, flecked black	Bright scarlet	Scarlet red	5
Gold Amber	Rich salmon	Yellow (gold)	6
Olive, flecked gold	Bright yellow green	Emerald	7
Yellowish brown, flecked white	Red-russet	Orange	8
Citrine, flecked azure	Very dark purple	Violet	9
Black rayed with yellow	As Queen Scale, but flecked with gold	Citrine, olive, russet, and black*	10
Emerald, flecked gold	Blue emerald green	Sky blue	11
Indigo, rayed violet	Grey	Purple	12
Silver, rayed sky blue	Cold pale blue	Silver	13
Bright rose or cerise, rayed pale green	Early spring green	Sky blue	14
Glowing red	Brilliant flame	Red	15
Rich brown	Deep warm olive	Deep indigo	16
Reddish grey inclined to mauve	New yellow leather	Pale mauve	17
Dark greenish brown	Rich bright russet	Maroon	18
Reddish amber	Grey	Deep purple	19
Plum colour	Green grey	Slate grey	20
Bright blue, rayed yellow	Rich purple	Blue	21
Pale green	Deep blue-green	Blue	22
White, flecked purple, like mother-of-pearl	Deep olive-green	Sea green	23
Livid indigo brown (like a black beetle)	Very dark brown	Dull brown	24
Dark vivid blue	Green	Yellow	25
Cold dark grey, approaching black	Blue black	Black	26
Bright red, rayed azure or emerald	Venetian red	Red	27
White, tinged purple	Bluish mauve	Sky blue	28
Stone colour	Light translucent pinkish brown	Buff, flecked silver-white	29
Amber, rayed red	Rich amber	Gold yellow	30
Vermillion, fleck crimson and emerald	Scarlet, flecked gold	Vermillion	31
Black, rayed blue	Black blue	Black	32
Black, flecked yellow	Dark brown	Amber	32 bis
White, red, yellow, blue, black (the latter outside)	The 7 prismatic colours, the violet being outside	Deep purple, nearly black	31 bis

183

TABLE OF CORRESPONDENCES

XXXIV. Some Greek Gods.	XXXIII. Some Scandinavian Gods.	XXV.–XXXII.	XXIV. Certain of the Hindu and Buddhist Results.	
Pan	. . . .	. . . . .	Nerodha-samapatti, Nirvikalpa-samadhi, Shiva darshana	0
Zeus, Iacchus	Wotan		Unity with Brahma, Atma darshana	1
Athena, Uranus	Odin			2
Cybele, Demeter, Rhea, Heré	Frigga			3
Poseidon	Wotan			4
Ares, Hades	Thor			5
Iacchus, Apollo, Adonis			Vishvarupa-darshana	6
Aphrodite, Niké	Freya			7
Hermes	Odin, Loki			8
Zeus (as △), Diana of Ephesus (as a Phallic Stone)				9
Persephone, [Adonis] Psyche			Vision of the "Higher Self," the various Dhyanas or Jhanas	10
Zeus	Valkyries	We have insufficient knowledge of the attributions of Assyrian, Syrian, Mongolian, Tibetan, Mexican, Zend, South Sea, West African, &c.	Vayu-Bhawana	11
Hermes				12
Artemis, Hecate			Vision of Chandra	13
Aphrodite	Freya		Success in Bhaktiyoga	14
Athena				15
[Heré]			Success in Hathayoga, Asana and Prana-yama	16
Castor and Pollux, Apollo the Diviner				17
Apollo the Charioteer				18
Demeter [borne by lions]				19
[Attis]				20
Zeus				21
Themis, Minos, Aeacus, and Rhadamanthus				22
Poseidon			Apo-Bhawana	23
Ares				24
Apollo, Artemis (hunters)				25
Pan, Priapus, [Erect Hermes and Bacchus]				26
Ares	Tuisco			27
[Athena], Ganymede				28
Poseidon				29
Helios, Apollo			Vision of Surya	30
Hades			Agni-Bhawana	31
[Athena]				32
[Demeter]			Prithivi-Bhawana	32 bis
Iacchus			Vision of the Higher Self, Prana-Yama	31 bis

TABLE I (continued)

XXIII.* The Forty Buddhist Meditations.		XXII. Small Selection of Hindu Deities.	
Nothing and Neither P nor p'	F		
Space	F	AUM	0
Consciousness	F		
Indifference	S	Parabrahm (or any other whom one wishes to please.	1
Joy	S	Shiva, Vishnu (as Buddha avatars), Akasa (as matter), Lingam	2
Compassion	S	Bhavani (all forms of Sakti), Prana (as Force), Yoni	3
Friendliness	S	Indra, Brahma	4
Death	R	Vishnu, Varruna-Avatar	5
Buddha	R	Vishnu-Hari-Krishna-Rama	6
The Gods	R		7
Analysis into 4 Elements	A	Hanuman	8
Dhamma	R	Ganesha, Vishnu (Kurm Avatar)	9
Sangha	R	Lakshmi, &c. [Kundalini]	10
The Body	R		
Wind	K	The Maruts [Vayu]	11
Yellow	K	Hanuman, Vishnu (as Parasa-Rama)	12
Loathsomeness of Food	P	Chandra (as ☽)	13
Dark blue	K	Lalita (sexual aspect of Sakti)	14
Bloody Corpse	I	Shiva	15
Beaten as Scattered Corpse	I	Shiva (Sacred Bull)	16
White	K	Various twin and hybrid Deities	17
Worm-eaten Corpse	I		18
Gnawed by Wild Beasts Corpse	I	Vishnu (Nara-Singh Avatar)	19
Bloated Corpse	I	The Gopi girls, the Lord of Yoga	20
Liberality	R	Brahma, Indra	21
Hacked in Pieces Corpse	I	Yama	22
Water	K	Soma [apas]	23
Skeleton Corpse	I	Kundalini	24
Limited Aperture	K	Vishnu (Horse Avatar)	25
Putrid Corpse	I	Lingam, Yoni	26
Blood-red	K		27
Purple Corpse	I		28
Conduct	R	Vishnu (Matsya Avatar)	29
Light	K	Surya (as ☉)	30
Fire	K	Agni [Tejas], Yama [as God of Last Judgment]	31
Quiescence	R	Brahma	32
Earth	K	[Prithivi]	32 bis
Breathing	R	[Akasa]	31 bis

185

TABLE OF CORRESPONDENCES

XL.* Precious Stones.	XXXIX.* Plants, Real and Imaginary.	XXXVIII.* Animals, Real and Imaginary.	
. . . .	. . . .	. . . .	0
Diamond	Almond in Flower	God	1
Star Ruby, Turquoise	Amaranth	Man	2
Star Sapphire, Pearl	Cypress, Opium Poppy	Woman	3
Amethyst and Sapphire	Olive, Shamrock	Unicorn	4
Ruby	Oak, Nux Vomica, Nettle	Basilisk	5
Topaz, Yellow Diamond	Acacia, Bay, Laurel, Vine	Phœnix, Lion, Child	6
Emerald	Rose	Iynx	7
Opal, especially Fire Opal	Moly, Anhalonium Lewinii	Hermaphrodite, Jackal, Twin Serpents	8
Quartz	[Banyon], Mandrake, Damiana	Elephant	9
Rock Crystal	Willow, Lily, Ivy	Sphinx	10
Topaz, Chalcedony	Aspen	Eagle or Man (Cherub of ♒)	11
Opal, Agate	Vervain, Herb Mercury, Marjo-lane, Palm	Swallow, Ibis, Ape, Twin Serpents	12
Moonstone, Pearl, Crystal	Almond, Mugwort, Hazel (as ☽), Moonwort, Ranunculus	Dog	13
Emerald, Turquoise	Myrtle, Rose, Clover	Sparrow, Dove, Swan	14
Ruby	Tiger Lily, Gerarium	Ram, Owl	15
Topaz	Mallow	Bull (Cherub of ♄)	16
Alexandrite, Tourmaline, Iceland Spar	Hybrids, Orchids	Magpie, Hybrids	17
Amber	Lotus	Crab, Turtle, Sphinx	18
Cat's Eye	Sunflower	Lion (Cherub of △)	19
Peridot	Snowdrop, Lily, Narcissus	Virgin, Anchorite, any solitary person or animal	20
Amethyst, Lapis Lazuli	Hyssop, Oak, Poplar, Fig	Eagle	21
Emerald	Aloe	Elephant	22
Beryl or Aquamarine	Lotus, all Water Plants	Eagle-snake-scorpion (Cherub of ♄)	23
Snakestone	Cactus	Scorpion, Beetle, Lobster or Crayfish, Wolf	24
Jacinth	Rush	Centaur, Horse, Hippogriff, Dog	25
Black Diamond	Indian Hemp, Orchis Root, Thistle	Goat, Ass	26
Ruby, any red stone	Absinthe, Rue	Horse, Bear, Wolf	27
Artificial Glass	[Olive], Cocoanut	Man or Eagle (Cherub of ♒), Peacock	28
Pearl	Unicellular Organisms, Opium	Fish, Dolphin, Crayfish, Beetle	29
Crysoleth	Sunflower, Laurel, Heliotrope	Lion, Sparrowhawk	30
Fire Opal	Red Poppy, Hibiscus, Nettle	Lion (Cherub of △)	31
Onyx	Ash, Cypress, Hellebore, Yew, Nightshade	Crocodile	32
Salt	Oak, Ivy	Bull (Cherub of ♄)	32 bis
	Almond in flower	Sphinx (if Sworded and Crowned)	31 bis

TABLE I (continued)

XXXVII. Hindu Legendary Demons.	XXXVI. Selection of Christian Gods (10); Apostles (12), Evangelists (4); and Churches of Asia (7).	XXXV. Some Roman Gods.	
. . . .	. . . .	. . . .	0
	God, the 3 in 1	Jupiter	1
	God, the Father, God who guides Parliament	Janus	2
	The Virgin Mary	Juno, Cybele, Saturn, Hecate, &c.	3
	God the Rain-maker (vide Prayer-Book), God the Farmer's Friend	Jupiter	4
	Christ coming to Judge the World	Mars	5
	God the Son (and Maker of Fine Weather)	Apollo	6
	Messiah, Lord of Hosts (vide Prayer-Book, R. Kipling, &c.)	Venus	7
	God the Holy Ghost (as Comforter and Inspirer of Scripture), God the Healer of Plagues	Mercury	8
	God the Holy Ghost (as Incubus)	Diana (as ☽)	9
	Ecclesia Xsti, The Virgin Mary	Ceres	10
	Matthew	Jupiter	11
	Sardis	Mercury	12
	Laodicea	Diana	13
	Thyatira	Venus	14
[Insufficient information.]	[The Disciples are too indefinite]	Mars, Minerva	15
		Venus	16
		Castor and Pollux, [Janus]	17
		Mercury	18
		Venus (representing the Fire of Vulcan)	19
		[Attis], Ceres, Adonis	20
	Philadelphia	Jupiter, [Pluto]	21
		Vulcan	22
	John, Jesus as Hanged Man	Neptune	23
		Mars	24
		Diana (as Archer)	25
		Pan, Vesta, Bacchus	26
	Pergamos	Mars	27
		Juno	28
		Neptune	29
	Smyrna	Apollo	30
	Mark	Vulcan, Pluto	31
	Ephesus	Saturn	32
	Luke	Ceres	32 bis
	The Holy Ghost	[Liber]	31 bis

TABLE OF CORRESPONDENCES

XLVI.* System of Taoism.	XLV. Magical Powers [Western Mysticism].	XLIV.* Mineral Drugs.	
The Tao or Great Extreme of the Yi King	The Supreme Attainment	Carbon	0
Shang Ti (also Tao)	Union with God	Aur. Pot.	1
The Yang and Khien	The Vision of God face to face	Phosporus	2
Kwan-se-on, The Yin and Khwan	The Vision of Sorrow	Silver	3
	The Vision of Love		4
	The Vision of Power	Iron, Sulphur	5
Li	The Vision of the Harmony of Things (also the Mysteries of the Crucifixion)		6
	The Vision of Beauty Triumphant	Arsenic	7
	The Vision of Splendour [Ezekiel]	Mercury	8
	The Vision of the Machinery of the Universe	Lead	9
Khan	The Vision of the Holy Guardian Angel or of Adonai	Mag. Sulph.	10
Sun	Divination		11
Sun	Miracles of Healing, Gift of Tongues, Knowledge of Sciences	Mercury	12
Khan or Khwan	The White Tincture, Clairvoyance, Divination by Dreams		13
Tui	Love-philtres		14
	Power of Consecrating Things		15
	The Secret of Physical Strength		16
	Power of being in two or more places at one time, and of Prophecy		17
	Power of Casting Enchantments		18
	Power of Training Wild Beasts		19
	Invisibility, Parthenogenesis, Initiation (?)		20
Li	Power of Acquiring Political and other Ascendency		21
	Works of Justice and Equilibrium		22
Tui	The Great Work, Talismans, Crystal-gazing, &c.	Sulphates	23
	Necromancy		24
	Transmutations		25
	The Witches' Sabbath so-called, the Evil Eye		26
Kăn	Works of Wrath and Vengeance		27
	Astrology		28
	Bewitchments, Casting Illusions		29
Li and Khien	The Red Tincture, Power of Acquiring Wealth		30
Kăn	Evocation, Pyromancy	Nitrates	31
Khăn	Works of Malediction and Death	Lead	32
Kăn	Alchemy, Geomancy, Making of Pentacles	Bismuth	32 bis
	Invisibility, Transformations, Vision of the Genius	Carbon	31 bis

TABLE I (continued)

XLIII.* Vegetable Drugs.	XLII. Perfumes.	XLI. Magical Weapons.	
. . . .	. . . .	. . . .	0
Elixir Vitæ	Ambergris	Swastika or Fylfat Cross, Crown	1
Hashish	Musk	Lingam, the Inner Robe of Glory	2
Belladonna	Myrrh, Civet	Yoni, the Outer Robe of Conceal-ment	3
Opium	Cedar	The Wand, Sceptre, or Crook	4
Nux Vomica, Nettle	Tobacco	The Sword, Spear, Scourge, or Chain	5
Stramonium Alcohol, Digitalis, Coffee	Olibanum	The Lamen or Rosy Cross	6
Damiana	Benzoin, Rose, Red Sandal	The Lamp and Girdle	7
Anhalonium Lewinii	Storax	The Names and Versicles and Apron	8
Orchid Root	Jasmine, Jinseng, all Odoriferous Roots	The Perfumes and Sandals	9
Corn	Dittany of Crete	The Magical Circle and Triangle	10
Peppermint	Galbanum	The Dagger or Fan	11
All cerebral excitants	Mastic, White Sandal, Mace, Storax, all Fugitive Odours	The Wand or Caduceus	12
Juniper, Pennyroyal, & all emmenogogues	Menstrual Blood, Camphor, Aloes, all Sweet Virginal Odours	Bow and Arrow	13
All aphrodisiacs	Sandalwood, Myrtle, all Soft Volup-tous Odours	The Girdle	14
All cerebral excitants	Dragon's Blood	The Horns, Energy, the Burin	15
Sugar	Storax	The Labour of Preparation	16
Ergot and ecbolics	Wormwood	The Tripod	17
Watercress	Onycha	The Furnace	18
All carminatives and tonics	Olibanum	The Discipline (Preliminary)	19
All anaphrodisiacs	Narcissus, White Sandal	The Lamp and Wand (Virile Force reserved), the Bread	20
Cocaine	Saffron, all Generous Odours	The Sceptre	21
Tobacco	Galbanum	The Cross of Equilibrium	22
Cascara, all purges	Onycha, Myrrh	The Cup and Cross of Suffering, the Wine	23
	Siamese Benzoin, Opoponax	The Pain of the Obligation	24
	Lign-aloes	The Arrow (the swift and straight appli-cation of Force)	25
Orchis [Satyrion]	Musk, civet (also ♄ ian Perfumes)	The Secret Force, Lamp	26
	Pepper, Dragon's Blood, all Hot Pungent Odours	The Sword	27
All diuretics	Galbanum	The Censer or Aspergillus	28
All narcotics	Ambergris	The Twilight of the Place and Magic Mirror	29
Alcohol	Olibanum, Cinnamon, all Glorious Odours	The Lamen or Bow and Arrow	30
	Olibanum, all Fiery Odours	The Wand or Lamp, Pyramid of △	31
	Assafœtida, Scammony, Indigo, Sulphur (all Evil Odours)	A Sickle	32
	Storax, all Dull and Heavy Odours		32 bis
Stramonium			31 bis

TABLE OF CORRESPONDENCES

LIII. The Greek Alphabet.	LII. The Arabic Alphabet.	LI. The Coptic Alphabet.	L.* Transcendental Morality. [10 Virtues (1–10), 7 Sins (Planets), 4 Magical Powers (Elements).]	
. . . .	. . . .	. . . .	. . . .	0
		ϭ	Pyrrho-Zoroastrianism (Accomplishment of Great Work)	1
[σ]	} Three Lost Fathers {	6	Devotion	2
		†	Silence	3
[C]	ث	H	Obedience	4
[φ]	خ	Ф	Energy	5
ω	د	(I)	Devotion to Great Work	6
[ε]	ض	Є	Unselfishness	7
	ظ	ꝗ	Truthfulness	8
	غ	X	Independence	9
λ	غ	C	Scepticism	10
α	ا	Ⲁ	Noscere	11
β	ب	B	Falsehood, Dishonesty [Envy]	12
γ	ج	Ⳋ	Contentment [Idleness]	13
δ	د	Ⲗ	Unchastity [Lust]	14
ε	ه	Ⲍ		15
ſ	و	Ⲩ		16
ζ	ز	Z		17
η	ح	ϑ		18
θ	ط	Θ		19
ι	ي	I		20
κ	ك	K	Bigotry, Hypocrisy [Gluttony]	21
λ	ل	λ		22
μ	م	Ⳟ	Audere	23
ν	ن	N		24
ξ σ	س	Ⳉ		25
o	ع	O		26
π	ف	Π	Cruelty [Wrath]	27
ψ	ص	Ⳍ		28
Ϙ	ق	X		29
ρ	ر	Ⲣ	[Pride]	30
λ	ش	(I)	Velle	31
τ	ت	T	Envy [Avarice]	32
			Tacere	32 bis
				31 bis

TABLE I (continued)

XLIX.* Linear Figures of the Planets, &c. and Geomancy.	XLVIII. Figures related to Pure Number.	XLVII. The Kings and Princes of the Jinn.	
The Circle	. . . .		0
The Point			1
The Line, also the Cross	The Cross		2
The Plane, also the Diamond, Oval, Circle, and other Yoni Symbols	The Triangle		3
The Solid Figure	Tetrahedron or Pyramid, Cross	مفيطا	4
The Tesseract	The Rose	ههثما هيج	5
Sephirothic Geomantic Figures follow the Planets Caput* and Cauda Dragonis* are the Nodes of the Moon, nearly = Neptune and Herschel respectively. They belong to Malkuth.	Calvary Cross, Truncated Pyramid, Cube	مهيجل علمس مهلع	6
	A Rose (7×7), Candlestick	سهلط مس حمحهلع *	7
		شالطا نوع رزع أهموش	8
		والخد سعلت كللت اميوز	9
	Altar, Double Cube, Calvary Cross		10
Those of △y Triplicity		ملهعلياڵل هد هيوب سمطايا	11
Octagram	Calvary Cross	سمحاق تسيح هليح	12
Enneagram	Greek Cross, Plane, Table of Shewbread	مريح مهليج	13
Heptagram		يهلوة	14
Puer*		محلمتك	15
Amissio*		مهطع مهلوة مليموح	16
Albus*	Swastika	راخ سعد بواة طللطم	17
Populus and Via*		مهيط ليل	18
Fortuna Major and Fortuna Minor*		لملح سمهطا*	19
Conjunctio*		سميحطلمة مقنه كهف	20
Square and Rhombus		سويدح سبعورة	21
Puella*	Greek Cross Solid, the Rose (3+7+12)	نفطا مدبح عفيط طلمش	22
Those of a ▽y Triplicity		مليموح	23
Rubeus*		ملوم مدبح	24
Acquisitio*	The Rose (5×5)	كليل حمط مطلح	25
Carcer*	Calvary Cross of 10, Solid	مطلا or جسم العظليم	26
Pentagram		عنفوائر كيطم ورطش	27
Tristitia*		مفيط مسعود	28
Laetitia*		هملعش عد عقي	29
Hexagram		طللجياش سطلت لهيل	30
Those of a △y Triplicity		دهيوم علسلطي	31
Triangle		حهفاعل or معهطا يمرسلو	32
Those of a ▽y Triplicity			32 bis
			31 bis

191

TABLE OF CORRESPONDENCES

LXLV. Secret Names of the Four Worlds.	LXIII. The Four Worlds.	LXII. Kings of the Elemental Spirits.	LXI. Angels of the Elements.	LX. The Rulers of the Elements.	
מה	Yetzirah, Formative World	Paralda	חסן	אריאל	11
סג	Briah, Creative World	Niksa	סליהד	תרשיס	23
עב	Atziluth, Archetypal World	Djin	אראל	שרף	31
בן	Assiah, Material World	Ghob	פורלאך	כרוב	32 bis
					31 bis

LXXI. The Court Cards of the Tarot, with the Spheres of their Celestial Dominion—Wands.	LXX. Attribution of Pentagram.	LXIX. The Alchemical Elements.	
The Prince of the Chariot of Fire. Rules 20° ♋ to 20° ♌, including most of Leo Minor	Left Upper Point, 5	☿	11
The Queen of the Thrones of Flame. 20° ♓ to 20° ♈, including part of Andromeda	Right Upper Point	⊖	23
The Lord of the Flame and Lightning. The King of the Spirits of Fire. Rules 20° ♏ to 20° ♐, including part of Hercules	Right Lower Point, 5	♃	31
The Princess of the Shining Flame. The Rose of the Palace of Fire. Rules one Quadrant of Heavens round N. Pole	Left Lower Point, 5	⊖	32 bis
The Root of the Powers of Fire (Ace)	Topmost Point, 5		31 bis

LXXVI. The Five Skandhas.	LXXV. The Five Elements (Tatwas).	LXXIV. The Court Cards of the Tarot, with the Spheres of their Celestial Dominion—Pantacles.	
Sankhara	Vayu—the Blue Circle	The Prince of the Chariot of Earth. 20° ♈ to 20° ♉	11
Vedana	Apas—the Silver Crescent	The Queen of the Thrones of Earth. 20° ♐ to 20° ♑	23
Safiña	Agni or Tejas–the Red Triangle	The Lord of the Wide and Fertile Land. The King of the Spirits of Earth. 20° ♌ to 20° ♍	31
Rupa	Prithivi—the Yellow Square	The Princess of the Echoing Hills. The Lotus of the Palace of the Earth. Rules a 4th Quadrant of Heaven about Kether	32 bis
Viñnanam	Akasa—the Black Egg	The Root of the Powers of Earth	31 bis

TABLE II

LIX. Archangels of the Quarters.	LVIII. Supreme Elemental Kings.	LVII.* The Four Quarters.	LVI. The Four Rivers.	LV. The Elements and Senses.	LIV. The Letters of the Name.	
רפאל Tahoeloj		(E) מזרח	הדקל	△ Air, Smell	ו	11
גבריאל Thahebyobeaatan		(W) מערב	גהון	▽ Water, Taste	ה	23
מיכאל Ohooohatan		(S) דרום	פישון	△ Fire, Sight	י	31
אוריאל Thahaaotahe		(N) צפון	פרת	▽ Earth, Touch	ה	32 bis
				⊕ Spirit, Hearing	ש	31 bis

LXVIII. The Demon Kings.	LXVII. The Parts of the Soul.	LXVI. Spelling of Tetragrammaton in the Four Worlds.	LXV. Secret Numbers corresponding.	
Oriens	רוח	יוד הא ואו הא	45	11
Ariton	נשמה	יוד הי ואו הי	63	23
Paimon	חיה	יוד היה ויו היה	72	31
Amaimon	נפש	יוד הה וו הה	52	32 bis
	יחידה			31 bis

LXXIII. The Court Cards of the Tarot, with the Spheres of their Celestial Dominion—Swords.	LXXII. The Court Cards of the Tarot, with the Spheres of their Celestial Dominion—Cups.	
The Prince of the Chariot of Air. 20° ♑ to 20° ♒	The Prince of the Chariot of the Waters. 20° ♎ to 20° ♏	11
The Queen of the Thrones of Air. 20° ♍ to 20° ♎	The Queen of the Thrones of the Water. 20° ♊ to 20° ♋	23
The Lord of the Winds and the Breezes. The King of the Spirits of Air. 20° ♉ to 20° ♊	The Lord of the Waves and the Waters. The King of the Hosts of the Sea. 20° ♒ to 20° ♓, including most of Pegasus	31
The Princess of the Rushing Winds. The Lotus of the Palace of Air. Rules a 3rd Quadrant.	The Princess of the Waters. The Lotus of the Palace of the Floods. Rules another Quadrant	32 bis
The Root of the Powers of Air	The Root of the Powers of Water	31 bis

TABLE OF CORRESPONDENCES

LXXXIII. The Attribution of Hexagram.	LXXXII. The Noble Eightfold Path.	LXXXI. Metals.	LXXX. Olympic Planetary Spirits.	
Left Lower Point	Samma Vaca	Mercury	Ophiel	12
Bottom Point	Samma Sankappo	Silver	Phul	13
Right Lower Point	Samma Kammanto	Copper	Hagith	14
Right Upper Point	Samma Ajivo	Tin	Bethor	21
Left Upper Point	Samma Vayamo	Iron	Phaleg	27
Centre Point	Samma Samadhi	Gold	Och	30
Top Point	Samma Sati and Samaditthi	Lead	Arathon	32

XC. The 42-fold Name which revolves in the Palaces of Yetzirah.	LXXXIX.* The Revolution of אהיה in Briah.	LXXXVIII. Translation of Col. LXXXVII.	
. . . .	. . . .	. . . .	0
אב	אהיה		1
גי	אההי	Palatium Sancti Sanctorum	2
סצ	איהה		3
קרעשטן	ההיא	P. Amoris	4
כגדיכש	ההאי	P. Meriti	5
במרצתג	האהי	P. Benevolentiae	6
הקממנע	האיה	P. Substantiae Coeli	7
יגלפזק	היאה	P. Serenitatis	8
שקי	יאהה		9
עית	יההא יהאה אל שדי	P. Albedinis Crystallinae	10

194

TABLE III

LXXIX. Spirits of the Planets.	LXXVIII. Intelligences of the Planets.	LXXVII. The Planets and their Numbers.	
תפתרתרת (2080)	סיריאל (260)	☿ 8	12
חשמודאי (369)	מלכא בתרשישים ועד ברוה שהקים (3321)	☽ 9	13
קדמאל (175)	הגיאל (49)	♀ 7	14
חסמאל (136)	יופיל (136)	♃ 4	21
ברצבאל (325)	גראפיאל (325)	♂ 5	27
סורת (666)	נכיאל (111)	☉ 6	30
זזאל (45)	אגיאל (45)	♄ 3	32

TABLE IV

LXXXVII. Palaces of Briah.	LXXXVI. Choirs of Angels in Briah.	LXXXV. Angels of Briah.	LXXXIV. Divine Names of Briah.	
. . . . .	. . . . .	. . . . .	. . . . .	0
	שרפים	יהואל		1
היכל קדוש קדשים ⎱	אופנים	רפאל	אל ⎱	2
	כרובים	כרוביאל		3
היכל אהבה	שיככים	צדקיאל	מצפץ (sic)	4
ה. זכות	תרשישים	תרשיש	יהוד	5
ה. רצון	חשמלים	מתתרון*	יהוה	6
ה. עצם שמים	מלכים	וסיאל	אלהים	7
ה. גונה	בני אלהים	הסניאל	מצפץ	8
ה. לבנת הספיר ⎱	ישים	יהואל*	יה־אדני ⎱	9
	אראלים	מיכאל		10

195

TABLE OF CORRESPONDENCES

XCVI.* The Revolution of יהוה in Yetzirah.	XCV. Contents of Col. XCIV.	XCIV. English of Palaces (Col. XCIII.).	
. . . .	. . . .	. . . .	0
יהוה			1
יהוי			2
יההה			3
הויה	Blessings, all good things	Planities	4
ההוי	Snow, rain, spirit of life, blessings	Repositorium	5
ההיו	Angels singing in Divine presence	Habitaculum	6
היהו	Altar, Mikhael offering souls of just	Habitaculum	7
הוהי	Millstones where manna for just is ground for future	Locus communicationis	8
היהה	Sol, Luna, planets, stars, and 10 spheres	Firmamentum	9
ויהה ⎤ ⎥ וההי ⎬ אל יהוה ⎦	Has no use. Follows 300 heavens, 18,000 worlds, Earth, Eden, and Hell	Velum sive Cortina	10

CIV. The Ten Earths in Seven Palaces.	CIII.* The Ten Divisions of the Body of God.	CII.* The Revolution of Adonai in Assiah.	CI. English of Col. C.	
. . . . . .	. . . . . .	. . . . . .	. . . . . .	0
ארץ ⎤ ⎥ ⎬ ⎥ ⎦	Cranium		אדני	Holy living creatures	1
	Celebrum dextrum		אדינ	Wheels	2
	Celebrum sinistrum		אניד	Active ones, thrones	3
אדמה	Brachium dextrum		אינד	Brilliant ones	4
גיא	Brachium sinistrum		אידנ	Fiery serpents	5
נשיה	Totum corpus a gutture usque ad membrum sanctum		דניא	Kings	6
ציה	Pes dexter		דנאי	Gods	7
ארקא	Pes sinister		דינא	Sons of God	8
תבל ⎤ ⎥ ⎥ חלד ⎦	Signum fœderis sancti		דיאנ	Angels of Elements	9
	Corolla quæ est in Jesod		דאני ⎤ דאינ ⎬ אל אדני ⎦	Flames	10

TABLE IV *(continued)*

XCIII. The Heavens of Assiah.	XCII. The Angelic Functions in the World of Yetzirah.	XCI. The Saints or Adepts of the Hebrews.	
. . . . . .	. . . .	. . . .	0
		Messias filius David	1
	Seraphim stabant supra illud: sex alæ	Mosheh	2
ערבות		Enoch	3
מכון Sex alæ		Abraham	4
מעון Uni: in duabus		Jacob	5
זבול Velabat facies suas: et duabus velabat		Elijah	6
שחקים Pedes suas et		Mosheh	7
רקיע Duabus volabat		Aaron	8
	Et clamabat hic ad illum et dicebat Sanctus, sanctus, sanctus, Dominus Exercitium, plenitudo totius terræ gloria ejus	Joseph (Justus)	9
סבל וילון שמים*		David, Elisha	10

C.* Angels of Assiah.	XCIX.* Archangels of Assiah.	XCVIII. English of Col. XCVII.	XCVII. Parts of the Soul.	
. . . . . .	. . . . . .	. . . .	. . . . . .	0
חיותהקדש	מסטרון	The Self	יחידה	1
אופנים	רציאל	The Life Force	חיה	2
אראלים	צפקיאל	The Intuition	נשמה	3
חשמלים	צדקיאל			4
שרפים	כמאל			5
מלכי.	רפאל	The Intellect	רוח	6
אלהים	האניאל			7
בני אלהים	מיכאל			8
כרבים	גבריאל			9
אשים	מסטרון סנדלפון	The Animal Soul, which perceives and feels	נפש	10

TABLE OF CORRESPONDENCES

CXI. Sephirotic Colours [Dr. Jellinek].	CX. Element and Quarters (Sepher Yetzirah).	CIX.* The Dukes and Kings of Edom.	
. . . .	. . . .	. . . .	0
Concealed Light	רוה אלהים חיים		1
Sky Blue	Air		2
Yellow	Water and Earth		3
White	Fire	אהליבמה ♀ and בצרה of יובב ⊙	4
Red	Height	אלה ♀ השם תימני ⊙	5
White-red	Depth	פינן ♀ הדד עוית ⊙	6
Whitish-red	East	קנז ♀ שנמלה משרקה ⊙	7
Reddish-white	West	תימן ♀ שאול רהבית ⊙	8
White-red-whitish-red-reddish-white	South	מבצר ♀ and מגדיאל בעל הנן ⊙	9
The Light reflecting all colours	North	ערם ♀ הדר פעו ⊙	10

CXIX. The Ten Fetters (Buddhism).	CXVIII. The Chakkras or Centres of Prana (Hinduism).	CXVII. The Soul (Hindu).	CXVI. Egyptian Attribution of Parts of the Soul.	
. . . .	. . . .	. . . .	Hammemit	0
Aruparaga	Sahasara (above Head)	Atma	Kha or Yekh	1
Vikkikika	Ajna (Pineal Gland)	Buddhi	Khai or Ka	2
Ruparaga	Visuddhi (Larynx)	Higher Manas	Ba or Baie	3
Silabata Paramesa	⎱	⎱		4
Patigha	Anahata (Heart)	Lower Manas		5
Udakkha	⎰	⎰		6
Mano	Manipura (Solar Plexus)	Kama	Aib	7
Sakkya-ditti	Svadistthana (Navel)	Prana		8
Kama	Muladhara (Lingam and Anus)	Linga Sharira	Hati	9
Avigga		Shtula Sharira	Kheibt, Khat, Tet, Sahu	10

TABLE IV (continued)

CVIII.* Some Princes of the Qliphoth.	CVII. Translation of Hells.	CVI.* The Ten Hells in Seven Palaces.	CV. English of Col. CIV.	
. . . .				0
Satan and Moloch				1
סמאל * Grave		שאול Earth (dry)		2
אשת זנונים				3
Lucifuge	Perdition	אבדון Red earth		4
אשתרום Clay of Death		בארשחת Undulating ground		5
Belphegor חיוא	Pit of Destruction	סיטהיון Pasture		6
אשמדאי Shadow of Death		שעירמות Sandy earth		7
Adramelek בליאל	Gates of Death	אלמות Earth		8
לילית Hell				9
נעמה		גיהנם Wet earth		10

CXV.* Officers in a Masonic Lodge.	CXIV. Passwords of the Grades.	CXIII. Alchemical Metals (ii.)	CXII. Alchemical Tree of Life (i.).	
. . . .				0
	Silence * Metallic Radix		☿	1
P.M.	אב	♄	♃	2
	דב	♃	⊖	3
W.M.	אס	☽	☽	4
S.W.	יה	☉	☉	5
J.W.	אהיה	♂	♂	6
S.D.	כח	☿	♃	7
J.D.	אלה	☿	♀	8
I.G.	מה	♀	♄	9
T. and Candidate	נה Medicina Metallorum		Mercurius Philosophorum	10

TABLE OF CORRESPONDENCES

CXXVI. Their Inhabitants.	CXXV.* Seven Hells of the Arabs.	CXXIV. The Heavenly Hexagram.	CXXIII. English of Col. VIII., Lines 1–10.	
. . . . . .	. . . . . .	. . . . . .	. . . .	0
		♃	Dual Contending Forces	1
Hypocrites	Háwiyah	☿	Hinderers	2
		☽ [♄ Daath]	Concealers	3
Pagans or Idolaters	Jahim	♀	Breakers in Pieces	4
Guebres	Sakar	♂	Burners	5
Sabians	Sa'ir	☉	Disputers	6
Jews	Hutamah		Dispersing Ravens	7
Christians	Laza		Deceivers	8
Moslems	Jehannam		Obscene Ones	9
			The Evil Woman or (simply) The Woman	10

CXXXII. Pairs of Angels ruling Coins.	CXXXI. Pairs of Angels ruling Swords.	CXXX. Pairs of Angels ruling Cups.	
. . . . . .	. . . . . .	. . . .	0
			1
ושריה לכבאל	מבהאל יזלאל	חבויה איעאל	2
ללהחיה יחויה	הקמיה הריאל	יבמיה ראהאל	3
מנדאל כוקיה	כליאל לאויה	מומיה הייאל	4
פויאל מבהיה	חעמיה אניאל	פהליה לוויה	5
יילאל נממיה	יזאל רהעאל	יייאל נלכאל	6
מצראל הרחאל	מיכאל הההאל	חהויה מלהאל	7
כהתאל אכאיה	יההאל ומבאל	ילהיה וליה	8
אלדיה הזיאל	מחיאל ענואל	עריאל סאליה	9
ההעיה לאויה	מנקאל דמביה	מיהאל עשליה	10

TABLE IV (continued)

CXXII. The Ten Plagues of Egypt.	CXXI.* The Grades of the Order.		CXX. Magical Images of the Sephiroth.	
. . . .	$0°=0°$		. . . .	0
Death of First-born	$10°=1°$ Ipsissimus	3rd Order	Ancient bearded king seen in profile	1
Locusts	$9°=2°$ Magus		Almost any male image shows some aspect of Chokmah	2
Darkness	$8°=3°$ Magister Templi		Almost any female image shows some aspect of Binah	3
Hail and Fire	$7°=4°$ Adeptus Exemptus	2nd Order	A mighty crowned and enthoned king	4
Boils	$6°=5°$ Adeptus Major		A mighty warrior in his chariot, armed and crowned	5
Murrain	$5°=6°$ Adeptus Minor		A majestic king, a child, a crucified god	6
Flies	$4°=7°$ Philosophus	1st Order	A beautiful naked woman	7
Lice	$3°=8°$ Practicus		An Hermaphrodite	8
Frogs	$2°=9°$ Theoricus		A beautiful naked man, very strong	9
Water turned to Blood	$1°=10°$ Zelator / $0°=0°$ Neophyte		A young woman crowned and veiled	10

CXXIX. Pairs of Angels ruling Wands.	CXXXI. Meaning of Col. CXXVII.	CXXVII.* Seven Heavens of the Arabs.	
. . . .	. . . .		0
			1
דניאל והואל	House of Glody, made of pearls	Dar al-Jalal	2
עממיה החשיה			3
ניתאל ננאאל	House of Rest or Peace, made of rubies and jacinths	Dar as-Salam	4
יליאל והויה	Garden of Mansions, made of yellow copper	Jannat al-Maawa	5
עלמיה סיאל	Garden of Eternity, made of yellow coral	Jannat al-Khuld	6
ללהאל מהשיה	Garden of Delights, made of white diamond	Jannat al-Naim	7
האיה נתהיה	Garden of Paradise, made of red gold	Jannat al-Firdaus	8
שאהיה ירתאל			9
אומאל רייאל	Garden of Eden, or Everlasting Abode, made of red pearls or pure musk	Jannat al-'Adn or al-Karar	10

TABLE OF CORRESPONDENCES

CXXXVI. Titles and Attributions of the Coin, Disc, or Pantacle Suit [Diamonds].	CXXXV. Titles and Attributions of the Sword Suit [Spades].	
. . . .	. . . .	0
The Root of the Powers of Earth	The Root of the Powers of Air	1
⊇ in ♑ The Lord of Harmonius Change	☽ in ♎ The Lord of Peace Restored	2
♂ in ♑ Material Works	♄ in ♎ Sorrow	3
☉ in ♑ Earthly Power	⊇ in ♎ Rest from Strife	4
☿ in ♉ Material Trouble	♀ in ♒ Defeat	5
☽ in ♉ Material Success	☿ in ♒ Earned Success	6
♄ in ♉ Success Unfulfilled	☽ in ♒ Unstable Effort	7
☉ in ♍ Prudence	⊇ in ♊ Shortened Force	8
♀ in ♍ Material Gain	♂ in ♊ Despair and Cruelty	9
☿ in ♍ Wealth	☉ in ♊ Ruin	10

CXLIV. Angels Lords of the Triplicity in the Signs by Day.	CXLIII. Twelve Lesser Assistant Angels in the Signs.	CXLII. Angels ruling Houses.	CXLI. The Twelve Tribes.	
סטרעתן	שרהיאל	איאל	גד	15
ראידאל	ארזיאל	סואל	אפראים	16
סערש	סראיאל	גיאל	מנשה	17
רעדר	פכיאל	כעאל	יששכר	18
סנהם	שרטיאל	עואל	ידודה	19
לסלרא	שלתיאל	ויאל	נפתלי	20
תרגבון	חדקיאל	יהאל	אשר	22
בתחון	סאיציאל	סוסול	דן	24
אהוז	סריסיאל	סויעסאל	בנימן	25
סנדלעי	שמקיאל	כשניעיה	זבולן	26
עתור	צמקיאל	אנסואל	ראובן	28
רמרא	וכביאל	פשיאל	שמעון	29

TABLE IV *(continued)*

CXXXIV.	CXXXIII.*	
Titles and Attributions of the Cup or Chalice Suit [Hearts].	Titles and Attributions of the Wand Suit [Clubs].	
. . . .	. . . .	0
The Root of the Powers of Water	The Root of the Powers of Fire	1
♀ in ♋ Love	♂ in ♈ Dominion	2
☿ in ♋ Abundance	☉ in ♈ Established Strength	3
☽ in ♋ Pleasure	♀ in ♈ Perfected Work	4
♂ in ♏ Loss in Pleasure	♄ in ♌ Strife*	5
☉ in ♏ Pleasure	♃ in ♌ Victory	6
♀ in ♏ Illusionary Success	♂ in ♌ Valour	7
♄ in ♓ Abandoned Success	☿ in ♐ Swiftness	8
♃ in ♓ Material Happiness	☽ in ♐ Great Strength	9
♂ in ♓ Perfected Success	♄ in ♐ Oppression	10

CXL.	CXXXIX.	CXXXVIII.*	CXXXVII.	
Twelve Banners of The Name.	Planets exalted in Col. CXXXVII.	Planets ruling Col. CXXXVII.	Signs of the Zodiac.	
יהוה	☉	♂	♈	15
יההו	☽	♀	♉	16
יוהה		☿	♊	17
הוהי	♃	☽	♋	18
הויה		☉	♌	19
ההוי	☿	☿	♍	20
והה ה	♄	♀	♎	22
וההי		♂	♏	24
ויהה		♃	♐	25
היהו	♂	♄	♑	26
היוה		♄	♒	28
ההיו	♀	♃	♓	29

203

TABLE OF CORRESPONDENCES

CL. Magical Images of the Decans (Succedent).	CXLIX. Magical Images of the Decans (Ascendant)	
A green-clad woman, with one leg bare from the ankle to the knee	A tall dark, restless man, with keen flame-coloured eyes, bearing a sword	15
A man of like figure (to the ascendant), with cloven hoofs like an ox	A woman with long and beautiful hair, clad in flame-coloured robes	16
An eagle-headed man, with a bow and arrow. Wears crowned steel helmet.	A beautiful woman with her two horses	17
A beautiful woman wreathed with myrtle. She holds a lyre and sings of love and gladness	A man with distorted face and hands, a horse's body, white feet, and a girdle of leaves	18
A man crowned with a white myrtle wreath holding a bow	A man in sordid raiment, with him a nobleman on horseback, accompanied by bears and dogs	19
Tall, fair, large man, with him a woman holding a large black oil jar	A virgin clad in linen, with an apple or pomegranate	20
A man, dark, yet delicious of countenance	A dark man, in his right hand a spear and laurel branch and in his left a book	22
A man riding a camel, with a scorpion in his hand	A man with a lance in his right hand, in his left a human head	24
A man leading cows, and before him an ape and bear	A man with 3 bodies—1 black, 1 red, 1 white	25
A man with an ape running before him	A man holding in his right hand a javelin and in his left a lapwing	26
A man arrayed like a king, looking with pride and conceit on all around him	A man with bowed head and a bag in his hand	28
A grave man pointing to the sky	A man with two bodies, but joining their hands	29

CLVI. Magical Images of Col. CLV.	CLV. Goetia Demons of Decans (Ascendant).		CLIV. Perfumes (Cadent).	
Cat, toad, man, or all at once	☉	באל	Black Pepper	15
Little horse or ass	☿	גמיגין	Cassia	16
(1) Wolf with a serpent's tail. (2) Man with dog's teeth and raven's head	☿	אמון	Cypress	17
Probably a centaur or archer	☿	בואר	Anise	18
Rider on a pale horse, with many musicians. [Flaming and poisonous breath]	☉	בלאת	Muces Muscator	19
A soldier in red apparel and armour	♀	זאפר	Mastick	20
Soldier with a ducal crown riding a crocodile	♀	שאלוש	Mortum	22
Angel with a lion's tail, goose's feet, horse's tail	♂	יפוש	As for Asc	24
A dog with a gryphon's wings	♂ and ☿	גלאסלבול	Gaxisphilium	25
Gold-crowned soldier in red on a red horse. Bad breath	♀	ברית	Cubel Pepper	26
A strong man in human shape	☿	פוראש	Rhubarb	28
(1) Hart with fiery tail. (2) Angel	♂	פורפור	Santal Alb	29

TABLE V (continued)

CXLVIII. Angels of the Decanes (Cadent).	CXLVII. Angels of the Decanes (Succedent).	CXLVI. Angels of the Decanes (Ascendant).	CXLV. Angels Lords of the Triplicity in the Signs by Night.	
סטנדר	בההמי	זזר	ספעטאוי	15
יכסגנוץ	מנחראי	כדמדי	סוסת	16
ביתון	שהדני	סגרש	עגנרמען	17
אלינכיר	רהדץ	מתראוש	עכאל	18
סהיבר	זחעי	לוסנהר	זלברהית	19
משפר	ראידיה	אנגאורה	סטיא	20
שחדר	סהרנץ	סרסני	אחודראון	22
ותרודיאל	נגדוהר	כמוץ	סהקנב	24
אבוהא	והרין	משראת	לברמים	25
יסגדיברודיאל	יסיסיה	מסנון	אלויר	26
גרודיאל	אבדרון	סספמ	פלאון	28
סטריף	אורון	בהלמי	נתדורינגאל	29

CLIII. Perfumes (Succedent).	CLII. Perfumes (Ascendant).	CLI. Magical Images of the Decans (Cadent).	
Stammonia	Myrtle	A restless man in scarlet robes, with golden bracelets on his hands and arms	15
Cadamoms	Costum	A swarthy man with white lashes, his body elephantine, with long legs; with him a horse, a stag, and a calf	16
Cinnamon	Mastick	A man in mail, armoured with bow, arrows, and quiver	17
Succum	Camphor	A swift-footed person, with a viper in his hands, leading dogs	18
Lyn Balsami	Olibanum	A swarthy hairy man, with a drawn sword and shield	19
Srorus	Santal Flav	An old man leaning on a staff and wrapped in a mantle	20
Bofor [?]	Galbanum	A man riding on an ass, preceded by a wolf	22
As for Asc.	Opoponax	A horse and a wolf	24
Fol Lori	Lign-aloes	A man leading another by his hair and slaying him	25
Colophonum	Assafœtida	A man holding a book, which he opens and shuts	26
Stammonia	Euphorbium	A small-headed man dressed like a woman, and with him an old man	28
Coxium	Thyme	A man of grave and thoughtful face, with a bird in his hand, before him a woman and an ass	29

TABLE OF CORRESPONDENCES

CLX.		CLIX.	
Magical Images of Col. CLIX.		Goetia Demons, &c. (Cadent).	
Like Agares	♃	ושאגו	15
Lion with ass's head, bellowing	♀	ואלפר	16
Crowned king on dromedary, accompanied by many musicians	☉	פאימון	17
Leopard's head and gryphon's wings	♃	שיטרי	18
A knight with a lance and banner, with a serpent	♀	אליגוש	19
A strong man with a serpent's tail, on a pale horse	♀	באתין	20
Human-faced bull	♂ and ☿	מאראץ	22
A black crane with a sore throat—he flutters	☽	נבר	24
A monster [probably a dolphin]	♂ and ☽	רינוו	25
Sea monster	☽	פורנאש	26
Like a guide. To be kings	☿	געף	28
Raven	♃	ישסולוש	29

CLXIV.		CLXIII.	
As Col. CLVIII. by Night.		As Col. CLVII. by Night.	
Stock-dove with sore throat	♂	האלף	15
Man with gryphon's wings	♀	פוכלור	16
Stock-dove with sore throat	☽	שץ	17
Dromedary	♀	אואל	18
Cruel ancient, with long white hair and beard, rides a pale horse, with sharp weapons	♀	פוך	19
(1) Thrush. (2) Man with sharp sword seemeth to answer in burning ashes or coals of fire	☿	כאין	20
Beautiful woman, with duchess crown tied to her waist, riding great camel	♀	גמור	22
Lion on horse, with serpent's tail, carries in right hand two hissing serpents	☽	וריאץ	24
Child with angel's wings rides a two-headed dragon	☿	ואל	25
Noisy peacock	☽	אנדראלף	26
Two beautiful angels sitting in chariot of fire	☉	בליאל	28
Man with many countenances, all men's and women's, carries a book in right hand	♀	דנסאל	29

TABLE V (continued)

CLVIII. Magical Images of Col. CLVII.	CLVII. Goetia Demons, &c. (Succedent).		
Old man, riding a crocodile and carrying a goshawk	♀	אגאר	15
Great Lion	☿	מארב	16
Accompanied by 4 noble kings and great troops	♀	ברבטוש	17
"Like a Xenophilus"	♀	גוסיון	18
An archer in green	☽	לראיך	19
Viper (or) Human, with teeth and 2 horns, and with a sword	♂ and ☿	בוטיש	20
Lion-faced man riding a bear, carrying a viper. Trumpeter with him	☉	פורון	22
Man with 3 heads—a serpent's, a man's (having two stars on his brow), and calf's. Rides on viper and bears firebrand	♀	אים	24
Dragon with 2 heads—a dog's, a man's, and gryphon's	♀	בים	25
Hurtful angel or infernal dragon, like Berot, with a viper [breath bad]	♀	אשתרות	26
3 heads (bull, man, ram), snake's tail, goose's feet. Rides, with lance and banner, on a dragon	☉	אסמדאי	28
Wolf with a gryphon's wings and serpent's tail. Breathes flames	☽	מרחוש	29

CLXII. As Col. CLVI. by Night.	CLXI. As Col. CLV. by Night.		
Child-voiced phœnix	☽	פאנץ	15
Crow	♂	ראום	16
Soldier with lion's head rides pale horse	☽	שבנוך	17
Monster	♂	ביפרו	18
Angel	♀	כרוכל	19
Soldier with red leonine face and flaming eyes; rides great horse	♀	אלוך	20
Horse	♃	אוראוב	22
Flaming fire	☿	און	24
Bull with a gryphon's wings	☉ and ☿	זאגן	25
Leopard	♀	האור	26
(1) Unicorn. (2) Dilatory bandmaster	♀	אמדוך	28
Beautiful man on winged horse	♃	שאר	29

TABLE OF CORRESPONDENCES

CLXXI. As Col. CLXVII. (Cadent).	CLXX. As Col. CLXVIII. (Succedent).	CLXIX. As Col. CLXVII. (Succedent).	CLXVIII. Egyptian Names of Asc. Decans.	CXLV. Egyptian Gods of the Zodiac (Asc. Decans).	
Horus	Lencher	Anubis	Assicean	Aroueris	15
Apophis	Virvaso	Helitomenos	Asicath	Serapis	16
Titan	Verasua	Cyclops	Thesogar	Taautus	17
Mercophta	Syth	Hecate	Sothis	Apoltun	18
Nephthe	Sitlacer	Perseus	Aphruimis	Typhon	19
Cronus	Thopitus	Pi-Osiris	Thumis	Isis	20
Ophionius	Aterechinis	Omphta	Serucuth	Zeuda	22
Panotragus	Tepiseuth	Merota	Sentacer	Arimanius	24
Zeraph	Sagen	Tomras	Eregbuo	Tolmophta	25
Monuphta	Epima	Riruphta	Themeso	Soda	26
Proteus	Astiro	Vucula	Oroasoer	Brondeus	28
Phallophorus	Thopibui	Sourut	Archatapias	Rephan	29

CLI. The Mansion of the Moon. [Hindu *Nakshatra*] Arab, *Manazil*.	
♈ Sharatan (Ram's head), Butayn (Ram's belly), and 0°–10° Suraya (the Pleiads)	15
♉ 10°–30° Suraya, Dabaran (Aldeboran), and 0°–20° Hak'ah (three stars in head of Orion)	16
♊ 20°–30° Hak'ah, Han'ah (stars in Orion's shoulder), and Zira'a (two stars above ♊)	17
♋ Nasrah (Lion's nose), Tarf (Lion's eye), and 0°–10° Jabhah (Lion's forehead)	18
♌ 10°–30° Jabhah, Zubrah (Lion's mane), and 0°–20° Sarfah (Cor Leonis)	19
♍ 20°–30° Sarfah, 'Awwa (the Dog, two stars in ♍), and Simak (Spica Virginis)	20
♎ Ghafar (φ, ι, and κ in foot of ♍), Zubáni (horns of ♏), and 0°–10° Iklil (the Crown)	22
♏ 10°–30° Iklil, Kalb (Cor Scorpionis), and 0°–20° Shaulah (tail of ♏)	24
♐ 20°–30° Shaulah, Na'áim (stars in Pegasus), and Baldah (no constellation)	25
♑ Sa'ad al-Zábih (the Slaughterer's Luck), Sa'ad al-Bal'a (Glutton's Luck), and 0°–10° Sa'ad al-Sa'ad (Luck of Lucks, stars in ♒)	26
♒ 10°–30° Sa'ad al-Sa'ad, Sa'ad al-Akhbiyah (Luck of Tents), and 0°–20° Fargh the former (spout of the Urn)	28
♓ 20°–30° Fargh the former, Fargh the latter (hind lip of Urn), and Rish áa (navel of Fish's belly)	29

TABLE V (continued)

CLXVI. As Col. CLX. by Night.		CLXV. As Col. CLIX. by Night.	
Crow with sore throat	☿	מאלף	15
Mermaid	♀	ופאר	16
Lion on black horse carrying viper	♀ and ☉	וינא	17
Bull with gryphon's wings	♀	העגנת	18
3 heads (bull, man, ram), snake's tail, flaming eyes. Rides bear, carries goshawk	☉	בעלם	19
Warrior with ducal crown carries gryphon. Trumpeters	♀ and ♂	מורם	20
Leopard	☿	ושו	22
Lion with gryphon's wings	♀	נפול	24
Angel with raven's head. Rides black wolf, carries sharp sword	☋	אנדר	25
Warrior on black horse	☋	כימאור	26
A star in a pentacle		דכאוראב	28
Man holding great serpent	♀	אנדרומאל	29

CLXXIII.* Genii of the Twelve Hours (Levi).	CLXXII. As Col. CLXVIII. (Cadent).	
Papus, Sinbuck, Rasphuia, Zahun, Heiglot, Mizkun, Haven	Asentacer	15
Sisera, Torvatus, Nitibus, Hizarbin, Sachluph, Baglis, Labezerin	Aharph	16
Hahabi, Phlogabitus, Eirneus, Mascarun, Zarobi, Butatar, Cabor	Tepistosoa	17
Phalgus, Thagrinus, Eistibus, Pharzuph, Sislau, Schiekron, Aclahayr	Thuismis	18
Zeirna, Tablibik, Tacritau, Suphlatus, Sair, Barcus, Camaysar	Phuonidie	19
Tabris, Susabo, Eirnilus, Nitika, Haatan, Hatiphas, Zaren	Aphut	20
Sialul, Sabrus, Librabis, Mizgitari, Causub, Salilus, Jazer	Arepien	22
Nantur, Toglas, Zalburis, Alphun, Tukiphat, Zizuph, Cuniali	Senciner	24
Risnuch, Suclagus, Kirtabus, Sablil, Schachlil, Colopatiron, Zeffar	Chenen	25
Segarbil, Azeuph, Armilus, Kataris, Razanil, Buchaphi, Mastho	Homoth	26
Aiglun, Zuphlas, Phaldor, Rosabis, Adjuchas, Zophas, Halacho	Tepisatras	28
Tarab, Misran, Labus, Kalab, Hahab, Marnes, Sellen	Atembui	29

TABLE OF CORRESPONDENCES

CLXXXI.	CLXXX.	
Correct Design of Tarot Trumps.	Titles of Tarot Trumps.	
A bearded Ancient seen in profile *	The Spirit of Αιθηρ	11
A fair youth with winged helmet and heels, equipped as a Magician, displays his art *	The Magus of Power	12
A crowned priestess sits before the veil of Isis between the pillars of Seth *	The Priestess of the Silver Star	13
Crowned with stars, a winged goddess stands upon the moon *	The Daughter of the Mighty Ones	14
A flame-clad god bearing equivalent symbols *	Sun of the Morning, chief among the Mighty	15
Between the Pillars sits an Ancient *	The Magus of the Eternal	16
A prophet, young, and in the Sign of Osiris Risen *	The Children of the Voice: the Oracle of the Mighty Gods	17
A young and holy king under the starry canopy *	The Child of the Powers of the Waters: the Lord of the Triumph of Light	18
A smiling woman holds the open jaws of a fierce and powerful lion	The Daughter of the Flaming Sword	19
Wrapped in a cloke and cowl, an Ancient walketh, bearing a lamp and staff *	The Prophet of the Eternal, the Magus of the Voice of Power	20
A wheel of six shafts, whereon revolve the Triad of Hermanubis, Sphinx, and Typhon *	The Lord of the Forces of Life	21
A conventional figure of Justice with scales and balances	The Daughter of the Lords of Truth. The Ruler of the Balance	22
The figure of an hanged or crucified man *	The Spirit of the Mighty Waters	23
A skeleton with a scythe mowing men. The scythe handle is a Tau	The Child of the Great Transformers. The Lord of the Gate of Death	24
The Figure of Diana huntress *	The Daughter of the Reconcilers, the Bringer-forth of Life	25
The figure of Pan or Priapus *	The Lord of the Gates of Matter. The Child of the Forces of Time	26
A tower struck by forked lightning *	The Lord of the Hosts of the Mighty	27
The figure of a water-nymph disporting herself *	The Daughter of the Firmament: the Dweller between the Waters	28
The waning moon *	The Ruler of the Flux and Reflux. The Child of the Sons of the Mighty	29
The Sun *	The Lord of the Fire of the World	30
Israfel blowing the Last Trumpet. The dead arising from their tombs *	The Spirit of the Primal Fire	31
Should contain a demonstration of the Quadrature of the Circle *	The Great One of the Night of Time	32
		32 bis
		31 bis

TABLE VI

CLXXIX. Numbers printed on Tarot Trumps.	CLXXVIII.* Geomantic Intelligences.	CLXXVII.* Yetziratic Attribution of Col. CLXXV.	CLXXVI. Numerical Value of Col. CLXXV.	CLXXV. Hebrew Letters.	
0		🜁	1	א	11
1	רפאל	☿	2	ב	12
2	גבריאל	☽	3	ג	13
3	אנאל	♀	4	ד	14
4	מלכידאל	♈	5	ה	15
5	אסמודאל	♉	6	ו	16
6	אמבריאל	♊	7	ז	17
7	מוריאל	♋	8	ח	18
11	ורכיאל	♌	9	ט	19
9	המליאל	♍	10	י	20
10	סחיאל	♃	20, 500	ך כ	21
8	זוריאל	♎	30	ל	22
12		🜄	40, 600	ם מ	23
13	ברכיאל	♏	50, 700	ן נ	24
14	אדוכיאל	♐	60	ס	25
15	הנאל	♑	70	ע	26
16	זמאל	♂	80, 800	ף פ	27
17	כאמבריאל	♒	90, 900	ץ צ	28
18	אמניציאל	♓	100	ק	29
19	מיכאל	☉	200	ר	30
20		🜂	300	ש	31
21	כשיאל	♄	400	ת	32
		🜃	400	ת	32 bis
		⊕	300	ש	31 bis

TABLE OF CORRESPONDENCES

CLXXXIII. Legendary Orders of Being.	CLXXXII. The Human Body.	
Sylphs	Respiratory Organs	11
"Voices," Witches and Wizards	Cerebral and Nervous System	12
Lemures, Ghosts	Lymphatic System	13
Succubi	Genital System	14
Mania, Erinyes [Eumenides]	Head and Face	15
Gorgons, Minotaurs	Shoulders and Arms	16
Ominous Appearance, Banshees	Lungs	17
Vampires	Stomach	18
Horror, Dragons	Heart	19
Mermaids (and ♓, its Zodiacal Opposite), Banshees	The Back	20
Incubi, Nightmares	Digestive System	21
Fairies, Harpies	Liver	22
Nymphs and Undines, Nereids, &c.	Organs of Nutrition	23
Lamiæ, Stryges, Witches	Intestines	24
Centaurs	Hips and Thighs	25
Satyrs and Fauns, Panic-demons	Genital System	26
Furies, Chimæras, Boars (as in Calydon), &c.	Muscular System	27
Water Nymphs, Sirens, Lorelei, Mermaids (cf. ♍)	Kidneys, Bladder, &c.	28
Phantoms, Were-wolves	Legs and Feet	29
Will o' the Wisp	Circulatory System	30
Salamanders	Organs of Circulation	31
Ghuls, Larvæ, Corpse Candles	Excretory System	32
The Dweller of the Threshold, Gnomes	Excretory Organs, Skeleton	32 bis
[Socratic Genius]	Organs of Intelligence	31 bis

NOTES TO TABLE OF CORRESPONDENCES

COL. **II.**—**0–10** are the names of the Numbers or Emanations; **11–34** the letters spelt in full.

LINE 1.—Some of the common titles of *Kether* are:—

נקדה פשית The Small Point.
תת זל The Profuse Giver.
נקדה ראשונה The Primordial Point.
רישא הוורה The White Head.
אמן Amen.
אור מופלא Lux occulta.
פלא Mirum occultum.
רום מעלה Inscrutable Height.
אריך אנפין Long of Nose.
אריך אפים Long of Face.
עתיק יומין The Ancient of Days.

(Also the name of seven inferiors!)

אהיה אשר אהיה Existence of Existences.
עתיקא דעתיקין Ancient of Ancient Ones.
עתיקא קדישא Holy Ancient One.
אור פשוט Lux simplicissima.
סמירה דסמרין Concealed of the Concealed.
רישא *The* Head.
אור פנימי Lux interna.
עליון The Most High.
הוא He.
רישא דלא The Head which is Not.

LINE 2.—*Chokmah* has additional titles:—

כחמה Power of Yetzirah.
י of Tetragrammaton.
אבא אב
It also has the Divine Name, יהוה.

LINE 3.—*Binah* has these additional titles:—

אמא The dark sterile mother.
אימא The bright pregnant mother.
אלהים
יהוה אלהים } Divine Names.
כורסיא Throne.

LINE 4.—*Chesed* has this additional title:—

גרולה Majesty.

COL. **II.** (*continued*)—

LINE 5.—*Geburah* has these additional titles:—

דין Justice.
פחד Fear.

LINE 6.—*Tiphareth* has these additional titles:—

זעיר אנפין Lesser Countenance.
מלך King.
Seir Anpin, שעיר אנפין:—
אדם Adam.
בן The Son.
איש The Man.
שכאנום Spare Angels.

LINE 9.—*Jesod* has this additional title:—

צדיק־יסוד־עולם The Righteous is the Foundation of the World.

LINE 10. — *Malkuth* has these titles (among others):—

שער The Gate (by Temurah, עשר = 10).
תרעא The Gate (Chaldee),

which has same number (671) as אדני. In full—

אלף־דלת־נון־יוד

Also—

Gates of Death.
„ „ Shadow of Death
„ „ Tears.
„ „ Justice.
„ „ Prayer.
Gate of Daughter of Mighty Ones.
„ „ Garden of Eden.

Also—

Inferior Mother—

The Daughter.
The Queen.   מלכה
The Bride.   כלה
The Virgin.   בתולה

COL. **IV.**—This column may be equally well symbolised by any single entry, preferably in **0**. The Monistic and Nihilistic conceptions are convertible. Hua may be equally named Tao, Iao, Noumenon, and the like. All language on this subject is necessarily feeble and hieroglyphic. It is to name that which by definition has no name.

COL. V.—These God-names are the "Grand Words" of the corresponding grades (see Col. CXXI.), except for 5°=6°, whose G.W. is יהשוה.

The Zodiacal Gods are as for the Sephira, which corresponds to the Planet ruling. Apparently, in the numeration of Azbogah, line 12, only the AZ count.

That these following are only titles of the One Ineffable Name is shown by Koran xvii. 110. But monotheism is not true for the normal consciousness, but only for that of the adept.

الْمَلِك	الرَّحِيمُ	الرَّحْمَانُ
king	merciful	compassionate
الْمُؤْمِن	السَّلَامُ	الْقُدُّوس
he to whom one is faithful	peace	holy
الْجَبَّارُ	الْعَزِيزُ	الْمُهَيْمِن
le fort	le cher	terrible
الْبَارِئُ	الْخَالِقُ	الْمُتَكَبِّرُ
innocent	creator	the proud
الْقَهَّارُ	الْغَفَّارُ	الْمُصَوِّرُ
vainqueur	pardoner	picturer
الْفَتَّاحُ	الرَّزَّاقُ	الْوَهَّابُ
opener	bountiful	giver
الْبَاسِطُ	الْقَابِضُ	الْعَلِيمُ
supporter	holder	all-wise
الْمُعِزُّ	الرَّافِعُ	الْخَافِضُ
cherisher	exalter	humbler
الْبَصِيرُ	السَّمِيعُ	الْمُذِلُّ
all-seer	all-bearer	hater
اللَّطِيفُ	الْعَدْلُ	الْحَكَمُ
consoler	just	judge
الْعَظِيمُ	الْحَلِيمُ	الْخَبِيرُ
great	long-suffering, gracious	all-knower
الْعَلِيُّ	الشَّكُورُ	الْغَفُورُ
exalted	worthy of thanks	pardoner
الْمُقِيتُ	الْحَفِيظُ	الْكَبِيرُ
exposer	protector	the great
الْكَرِيمُ	الْجَلِيلُ	الْحَسِيبُ
généreux	glorious	numberer
الْوَاسِعُ	الْمُجِيبُ	الرَّقِيبُ
vast	hearer of complaints	beholder of hearts
الْمَجِيدُ	الْوَدُودُ	الْحَكِيمُ
exalted	reconciler	healer, wise
الْحَقُّ	الشَّهِيدُ	الْبَاعِثُ
truth	witness of all	sender
الْمَتِينُ	الْقَوِيُّ	الْوَكِيلُ
solid	strong	advocate
الْمُحْصِيُ	الْحَمِيدُ	الْوَلِيُّ
reckoner	worthy of thanks	foster-father
الْمُحْيِي	الْمُعِيدُ	الْمُبْدِئُ
giver of life	resurrector	beginner

COL. V. (continued)—

الْقَيُّومُ	الْحَيُّ	الْمُمِيتُ
advocate of all	living	slayer
الْوَاحِدُ	الْمَاجِدُ	الْوَاجِدُ
sole	most holy	the only one
الْقَادِرُ	الصَّمَدُ	الْأَحَد
most mighty	of power full	unaccompanied
الْأَوَّلُ	الْمُؤَخِّرُ	الْمُقَدِّمُ
the 1st	retarder	first of officers, hastener
الْبَاطِنُ	الظَّاهِرُ	الْآخِرُ
concealed	manifested	the last
الْبَرُّ	الْمُتَعَالِي	الْوَالِي
charitable	highest	fosterer of all
الْعَفُوُّ	الْمُنْتَقِمُ	التَّوَّابُ
pardoner	avenger	turner of hearts
مَالِكُ الْمُلْكِ ذُو الْجَلَالِ وَالْإِكْرَامِ		الرَّؤُوفُ
worthy of glory roi de l'univers and honour		who pitieth
الْغَنِيُّ	الْجَامِعُ	الْمُقْسِطُ
rich	assembler	divider
الضَّارُّ	الْمَانِعُ	الْمُغْنِي
afflicter	refuser	enricher
الْهَادِي	النُّورُ	النَّافِعُ
peace-giver	le lumiere	giver of advantages
الْوَارِثُ	الْبَاقِي	الْبَدِيعُ
inheritor	survivor	inventor
	الصَّبُورُ	الرَّشِيدُ
	patient	(? beginning) guide

هو الله. وليس لا إله إلا هو آمين
Hua is God; and there is none other God than Hua. Amen.

COL. VI., LINE 34.—Essence, cf. α and ω.

COL. VIII.—

LINES 1–10.—Beth Elohim gives a quite different ten Qliphoth.

Line 15.—

In the midst of the Zodiacal Qliphoth are אסמדאי and סמאל.
At SE corner, Man, Serpent, and the elder Lilith the wife of Samael.
At NE corner, the Ox and Ass, and Aggereth the daughter of Machalath.
At NW corner, the Scorpion, and אסימון, the Unnameable and כעמה.
At SW angle, the Lion and Horse, and the younger Lilith the wife of Asmodai.

COL. IX.—The Cup of the Stolistes has its rim in 2 and 3 and its foot in 10.
The Caduceus is (easily) placed on the Tree and divided into א, ה, and ש.
The Waxing Moon in 4; Waning in 5; Full in 6.

COL. **XI.**—The elements, of whose nature the signs of the Zodiac partake, are shown by the symbol against them.

COL. **XII.**—Let 45 be a straight line. On 45 erect the equilateral △s 451, 459. From 4 and 5 draw straight lines 247, 358 ⊥ 45, and the straight lines 25 ⊥ 14, 43 ⊥ 15, 48 ⊥ 59, and 57 ⊥ 49, the points 2, 3, 7 and 8 marking the intersections. Join 19, 12, 13, 23, 78, 79, 89. Let 6 be the point of intersection of 19, 57, 48. On 78 erect an equilateral △ with its apex away from 1. Produce 19 to 10, join 7–10, 8–10. Daath is at the junction of 25, 34.

COL. **XV.**, LINE **32** bis.—The Pure Earth known to the ancient Egyptians during that Equinox of the Gods over which Isis presided (i.e. the Pagan Era) was taken as Green.

COLS. **XV.–XVIII.**—

Daath—Lavender, Grey-white, Pure violet, Grey flecked gold.
Herschel—Silver flecked white.

COL. **XVI.**, LINE **10.**—For ♁, ▽, △, and ▽.

COL. **XIX.**—Urim and Thummim = Auramoth and Thoum Mou, Egyptian Gods. They are methods of divination by △ and ▽.

COL. **XX.**, LINE **32.**—These Gods preside over the pieces in "Rosicrucian Chess."

♁ of △ Bishop	ΘϢΟΥΗ ΗϢΟΥ	
▽ of △ Queen	ΙϹϨΑΟΥΡΘΘ	
△ of △ Knight	ϽΗϢΟΥ ΦϢΗϢ	
▽ of △ Pawn	ΚΑΒΕϨΝΕΥϤ	
▽ of△ Castle	ϢΑΥϢϽΙϤ	
⊕ of △ King	ΦΑΟΥΡϢ	
♁ of ▽ Bishop	ϪΟΗΙϤ ΘΑ ΗϢΟΥ	
▽ of ▽ Queen	ΘΗϢΟΥΡ ΙϤ ΘΑΗϢΟΥ	
△ of ▽ Knight	ϹΕΒΑ ϽΗϢΟΥ ϨΑΟΥΡ ΙϤ ΘΑ ΗϢΟΥ	
▽ of ▽ Pawn	ϯϢΗΑΟΦ	
▽ of ▽ Castle	ϢΗϢΕΥ ΘΑ ΙϤ	
⊕ of ▽ King	ΠΘΑ ϽΑΦΗΗϽΗϨ	
♁ of ♁ Bishop	ϨϢ ϢΑΗ	
▽ of ♁ Queen	ϽΗϢΟΥ ΘΑ ΠΕϽΗϯ	
△ of ♁ Knight	Ϭ̄ΟΥ ΒΑΛ	
▽ of ♁ Pawn	ΔϨΕΦΙ	
▽ of♁ Castle	ΘΑΡΦΕϢϤ ϥΑ ϽΗϢΟΥΘΑ ΠΕ	
⊕ of ♁ King	ϬΟΥϽΑΟΥΡΙϤ	
♁ of ▽ Bishop	ΑΡΗϢΥΕΡΙϤ	
▽ of ▽ Queen	ΗΙϹΕϤ	
△ of ▽ Knight	ϨϢϢΡ	
▽ of ▽ Pawn	ΔΗΕϢΕϯ	

The Pawns refer to ♄ as the House of the Elements only, not to ♄ as ▽.

▽ of▽ Castle	ΝΕΥΦΟΥΙΕϤ	
⊕ of ▽ King	ΗϢϢΩΡΙϤ	

COL. **XX.** (*continued*)—

LINE **32.**—Cϥ̄ΒΑϽΥϢΟΥ ϨΝΟΥΕ. ΙϹΤΟΗϢΟΥ and ΔϨΕΦΙ : ϯϢΥΗΑΤΦ : ϨΗΕϢΕϯ : ΚΑΒΕϨΝΥϤ.

COL. **XXI.**—The perfected Egyptian exclaims, "There is no part of me that is not of the Gods." This column gives the attribution in detail. The non-cherubic Zodiacal signs are omitted; but follow their affinities.

COL. **XXIII.**—
Formless state (F)	=	4
Sublime state (S)	=	4
Reflection (R)	=	10
Kashina (K)	=	10
Impurity (I)	=	10
Analysis (A)	=	1
Perception (P)	=	1
		——
		40

COLS. **XXXVIII.–XL.**—The vagueness and extent of these attributions is shown in this table from Agrippa, who is too catholic to be quite trustworthy.

Things under the Sun which are called Solary.

Among stones—
1. The eye of the Sun.
2. Carbuncle.
3. Chrysolite.
4. Iris.
5. Heliotrope (stone).
6. Hyacinth (stone).
7. Pyrophylus (stone).
8. Pantaura.
9. Topazius.
10. Chrysopassus.
11. Rubine.
12. Balagious.
13. Auripigmentum and things of a golden colour.

Among plants—
1. Marigold.
2. Lote-tree.
3. Peony.
4. Sallendine.
5. Balm.
6. Ginger.
7. Gentian.
8. Dittany.
9. Vervain.
10. Bay-tree.
11. Cedar.
12. Palm-tree.
13. Ash.
14. Ivy.
15. Vine.
16. Mint.
17. Mastic
18. Zedoary.
19. Saffron.
20. Balsam.
21. Amber.
22. Musk.
23. Yellow honey.
24. Lignum aloes.
25. Cloves.
26. Cinnamon.
27. Calamus.
28. Aromaticus.
29. Pepper.
30. Frankincense.
31. Sweet marjoram.
32. Libanotis.

Among animals—
1. Lion.
2. Crocodile.
3. Spotted-wolf.
4. Ram
5. Boar.
6. Bull.
7. Baboon.

Among birds—
1. Phœnix.
2. Eagle.
3. Vulture.
4. Swan.
5. Cock.
6. Crow.
7. Hawk.

Among insects—
1. Glow-worm.
2. Beetle.

Among fish—
1. Sea-calf.
2. Shell-fish.
3. Pulius.
4. Star-fish.
5. Strombi.
6. Margari.

Among metals—
1. Gold.

COL. **XL.**—Aaron's breastplate is very doubtful; we advise reliance on columns Stones and Tribes, we having chosen Stones on bases of physical analogy to Signs, Colours, &c.

COL. **XLII.**—The following table of sub-elemental perfumes is important:—

⊕ of ⊕   Ambergris.

⩘ of ⊕   The Gall of the Rukh.

▽ of ⊕   Onycha.

▿ of ⊕   Musk.

△ of ⊕   Civet.

⊕ of ⩘   Lign-aloes.

⩘ of ⩘   Galbanum.

▽ of ⩘   Mastick.

▿ of ⩘   Storax.

△ of ⩘   Olibanum.

⊕ of ▽   Myrrh.

⩘ of ▽   Camphor.

▽ of ▽   Siamese Benzoin.

▿ of ▽   Indigo.

△ of ▽   Opoponax.

⊕ of ▿   Dittany of Crete.

⩘ of ▿   Assafœtida.

▽ of ▿   Clover.

▿ of ▿   Storax.

△ of ▿   Benzoin.

⊕ of △   Saffron.

⩘ of △   Lign-aloes.

▽ of △   Red-sanders.

▿ of △   Red Sandalwood.

△ of △   Olibanum.

COLS. **XLIII.** and **XLIV.**—And generally, all drugs exciting the parts of the body corresponding. See Col. **CLXXXII.**

COL. **XLVI.**—Each Trigram combines with itself and the others to make 64 Hexagrams, which partake of the combined nature. This attribution is the true key to the Yi King. No sinologist has any idea of it, but it is obvious enough now that O. M. has solved it.

See Appendix I.

COL. **XLVII.**—

LINE 7.—Has a monkey.

LINE 19.—Said to have a monkey.

COL. **XLIX.**—The Geomantic Figures of the Planets are those of the signs which they rule.

LINES 3–10.   [geomantic figure]   and   [geomantic figure]

COL. **XLIX.** (continued)—

LINE 15.   [figure]   LINE 16.   [figure]

LINE 17.   [figure]

LINE 18.   [figure]   and   [figure]

LINE 19.   [figure]   and   [figure]

LINE 20.   [figure]   LINE 22.   [figure]

LINE 24.   [figure]   LINE 25.   [figure]

LINE 26.   [figure]   LINE 28.   [figure]

LINE 29.   [figure]

See the "Handbook of Geomancy," to be published shortly in *The Equinox*.

COL. **L.**—The Catholic "seven deadly" sins in square brackets.

COL. **LVII.**—Egyptian Quarters.

COLS. **LVII.**, **LIX.**, &c.—Beth Elohim gives:—

Michael, Leo, and South to ▽ and י.

Gabriel, Taurus, and North to △ and ה.

Raphael, Man, and West to ▿ and ה.

Uriel, Eagle, and East to ⩘ and ו.

COL. **LXIX.**—

Sattvas,   ☿ ⎱
Rajas,   ♃   ⎰ In a close analogy.
and
Tamas,   ♄

COL. **LXXIX.**, LINE 13.—

Add (3321) שדברשהמעת שרתתן, the Spirit of the Spirits of the Moon. The final ן is counted as 700, as are the final ם's in Col. **LXXVIII.**, line 13.

COL. **LXXXV.**—

LINE 6.—Or חשמאל.

LINE 9.—Or זפניאל.

COL. **LXXXIX.**—Add Daath, היהא.

COL. **XCIII.**, LINE 10.—Contains the Earth.

COL. **XCVI.**—Add Daath, היו.

216

COL. **XCIX.**—Add among Archangels:—

Azrael, Angel of Death (**נ**).
Israel, of the Last Trump (**ש**).

COL. **C.**—Our order of Angelic Choirs is from R. Mosheh ben Maimon. R. Ishmael and the book Pliah prefer:—

1. Cherubim.
2. Chasmalim.
3. Chaioth.
4. Aralim.
5. Seraphim.
6. Tarshishim.
7. Auphanim.
8. Auphanim.
9. Aishim.
10. Taphsarim.

And there are many other schemes.

COL. **CII.**—Add Daath, **אנדי**.

COL. **CIII.**—Add Daath, Cerebrum medium, cujus locus est in parte capitis postica.

But these have many other attributes, and each is itself divisible: thus, Chesed and Geburah of Tiphareth are the breasts; Tiphareth the heart; Netzach and Hod the testicles; Jesod the membrum virile; and Malkuth the anus. The signs of the Zodiac are variously given, and the planets agree with the face: thus, ♄ and ♃, the ears; ♂ and ♀, the nostrils; ☉ and ☽, the eyes; and ☿, the mouth. The hand: the thumb, ⊕; 1st finger, 🜁; 2nd, 🜄; 3rd, 🜃; 4th, 🜂. These, however, vary somewhat.

COL. **CVI.**—These Abodes are enclosed in four circles: the Waters of Weeping, of Creation, of Oceanus, and the False Sea. Compare the classical four rivers of Hell.

COL. **CVIII.**—Incomplete and redundant owing to unconcentrated nature of Qliphoth.

LINE **2.**—Three Evil Forms before Samael are:–

קמסיאל
בליאל
עתיאל

The Thaumiel, also called Kerethiel.

COL. **CIX.**—☉ = King. ♀ = Duke.

King **בלע** of **בעור**, Dukes **עלוה**, **חמנע**, and **יתת**, are all referred to Daath.

Edomite Kings and Dukes are taken e libro Maggid. and Gen. 36.

COL. **CXIV.**, LINE 1.—*I.e.* simple breathing without articulation.

COL. **CXV.**—The furniture, &c., is attributed as told in the ritual, here duly *h - d*, *c - d*, and *n - r r - d*.

COL. **CXXI.**—Add the "Waiting" Grades of "Lord of the Paths in the Portal of the Vault of the Adepts" between the 1st and 2nd Orders; and "Babe of the Abyss" between the 2nd and the 3rd.

COL. **CXXV.**—Burton gives these upside down. The true attribution is checked by the Fire-Worshippers (Guebres) in 5. Yet, of course, he Kether Hell may be considered as more awful than the Malkuth.

COL. **CXXVII.**—These and many other (rather far-fetched and irrelevant) attributions of various things are to be found in Burton's *Arabian Nights*, in the Tale of Abn al-Husn and his Slave-Girl Tawaddud.

COL. **CXXXIII.** — The symbolic forms and Divination meanings of these cards can be readily constructed from considerations of their natures as here indicated.

LINE **5.**—This is the First Decan, and begins from Cor Leonis.

COL. **CXXXVIII.**—Astrological symbols are derived from the primary forms–Cross, Crescent, Circle.

COL. **CLXXIII.**—For meaning and special functions see original. They should, but do not, accurately refer to the divisions of each sign into 7 planetary parts.

Pietro di Albano gives:—

THE NAMES OF THE HOURS AND THE ANGELS RULING THEM.

The Names of the Hours.

Hours of the Day—

1. Yain.	7. Ourer.
2. Janor.	8. Thamic.
3. Nasmia.	9. Neron.
4. Salla.	10. Jayon.
5. Sadedalia.	11. Abai.
6. Thamur.	12. Natalon.

Hours of the Night—

1. Beron.	7. Netos.
2. Barol.	8. Infrac or Tafrac.
3. Thami.	9. Sassur.
4. Athar.	10. Aglo.
5. Methon.	11. Calerva.
6. Rana.	12. Salam.

TABLES OF THE ANGELS OF THE HOURS ACCORDING TO THE COURSE OF THE DAYS.

Sunday.

Angels of the Hours of the Day—

1. Michael.	7. Samael.
2. Anael.	8. Michael.
3. Raphael.	9. Anael.
4. Gabriel.	10. Raphael.
5. Cassiel.	11. Gabriel.
6. Sachiel.	12. Cassiel.

Angels of the Hours of the Night—

1. Sachiel.	7. Cassiel.
2. Samael.	8. Sachiel.
3. Michael.	9. Samael.
4. Anael.	10. Michael.
5. Raphael.	11. Anael.
6. Gabriel.	12. Raphael.

Col. **CLXXIII.** (*continued*)—

Monday.

Angels of the Hours of the Day—

1. Gabriel.	7. Raphael.
2. Cassiel.	8. Gabriel.
3. Sachiel.	9. Cassiel.
4. Samael.	10. Sachiel.
5. Michael.	11. Samael.
6. Anael.	12. Michael.

Angels of the Hours of the Night—

1. Anael.	7. Michael.
2. Raphael.	8. Anael.
3. Gabriel.	9. Rapahel.
4. Cassiel.	10. Gabriel.
5. Sachiel.	11. Cassiel.
6. Samael.	12. Sachiel.

Tuesday.

Angels of the Hours of the Day—

1. Samael.	7. Sachiel.
2. Michael.	8. Samael.
3. Anael.	9. Michael.
4. Raphael.	10. Anael.
5. Gabriel.	11. Raphael.
6. Cassiel.	12. Gabriel.

Angels of the Hours of the Night—

1. Cassiel.	7. Gabriel.
2. Sachiel.	8. Cassiel.
3. Samael.	9. Sachiel.
4. Michael.	10. Samael.
5. Anael.	11. Michael.
6. Raphael.	12. Anael.

Wednesday.

Angels of the Hours of the Day—

1. Raphael.	7. Anael.
2. Gabriel.	8. Raphael.
3. Cassiel.	9. Gabriel.
4. Sachiel.	10. Cassiel.
5. Samael.	11. Sachiel.
6. Michael.	12. Samael.

Angels of the Hours of the Night—

1. Michael.	7. Samael.
2. Anael.	8. Michael.
3. Raphael.	9. Anael.
4. Gabriel.	10. Raphael.
5. Cassiel.	11. Gabriel.
6. Sachiel.	12. Cassiel.

Thursday.

Angels of the Hours of the Day—

1. Sachiel.	7. Cassiel.
2. Samael.	8. Sachiel.
3. Michael.	9. Samael.
4. Anael.	10. Michael.
5. Raphael.	11. Anael.
6. Gabriel.	12. Raphael.

Angels of the Hours of the Night—

1. Gabriel.	7. Raphael.
2. Cassiel.	8. Gabriel.
3. Sachiel.	9. Cassiel.
4. Samael.	10. Sachiel.
5. Michael.	11. Samael.
6. Anael.	12. Michael.

Col. **CLXXIII.** (*continued*)—

Friday.

Angels of the Hours of the Day—

1. Anael.	7. Michael.
2. Rapahel.	8. Anael.
3. Gabriel.	9. Raphael.
4. Cassiel.	10. Gabriel.
5. Sachiel.	11. Cassiel.
6. Samael.	12. Sachiel.

Angels of the Hours of the Night—

1. Samael.	7. Sachiel.
2. Michael.	8. Samael.
3. Anael.	9. Michael.
4. Raphael.	10. Anael.
5. Gabriel.	11. Raphael.
6. Cassiel.	12. Gabriel.

Saturday.

Angels of the Hours of the Day—

1. Cassiel.	7. Gabriel.
2. Sachiel.	8. Cassiel.
3. Samael.	9. Sachiel.
4. Michael.	10. Samael.
5. Anael.	11. Michael.
6. Raphael.	12. Anael.

Angels of the Hours of the Night—

1. Raphael.	7. Anael.
2. Gabriel.	8. Raphael.
3. Cassiel.	9. Gabriel.
4. Sachiel.	10. Cassiel.
5. Samael.	11. Sachiel.
6. Michael.	12. Samael.

Note.—The first hour of the day, of every country, and in every season whatsoever, is to be assigned to the sun-rising, when he first appeareth arising in the horizon. And the first hour of the night is to be the thirteenth hour, from the first hour of the day.

The Year.

The Spring: Taloi.
The Summer: Casmaran.
The Autumn: Adarael.
The Winter: Earlas.

The Angels of the Spring: Caracasa, Core, Amatiel, Commissoros.
The Head of the Sign of the Spring: Spugliguel.
The Name of the Earth in the Spring: Amadai.
The Names of the Sun and the Moon in the Spring: The Sun, Abrayen; The Moon, Agusita.

The Angels of the Summer: Gargabel, Tariel, Gariel.
The Head of the Sign of the Summer: Tubiel.
The Name of the Earth in the Summer: Festativi.
The Names of the Sun and the Moon in the Summer: The Sun, Athemay; The Moon, Armatus.

The Angels of the Autumn: Tarquam, Gnabarel.
The Head of the Sign of the Autumn: Torquaret.
The Name of the Earth in the Autumn: Rabianara.
The Names of the Sun and the Moon in the Autumn: The Sun, Commutaff; The Moon, Affaterium.

(No Winter given.)

218

COL. **CLXXVII.**—Musulman attribution of Planets:—

ג ♄

ת ♃

פ ♂

ס ☉

ב and ס ♀

ד ☿

ר ☽

Note that ס and not כ is the 7th of the double letters.

The Jesuit Kircher gives—

♄	♃	♂	☉	♀	☿	☽
פ	ר	ת	ב	ג	ד	כ

The order of the Planets is that of their apparent rate of motion. By writing them in their order round a heptagon, and tracing the heptagram unicursally, the order of the days of the week is obtained.

COL. **CLXXVIII.**—These intelligences are angelic in nature, but possessing material and even earthly dominion. Hence they preside over the geomantic figures, whose nature indeed expresses their relation to man.

COL. **CLXXXI.**—

LINE **11.**—He laughs; bearing a sphere containing Illusion in his left hand, but over his right shoulder, and a staff 463 lines long in his right. A lion and a dragon are at his feet, but he seems unaware of their attacks or caresses.

LINE **12.**—His attitude suggests the shape of the Swastika or thunderbolt, the message of God.

LINE **13.**—She is reading intently in an open book.

LINE **14.**—She bears a sceptre and a shield, whereon is figured a dove as symbol of the male and female forces.

LINE **15.**—His attitude suggests 🜍, and he is seated upon the Cubical Stone, whose sides show the Green Lion and White Eagle.

LINE **16.**—He is crowned, sceptred, and blessing, all in a threefold manner. Four living creatures adore him, the whole suggesting a pentagram by shape.

LINE **17.**—He is inspired by Apollo to prophesy concerning things sacred and profane: represented by a boy with his bow and two women, a priestess and a harlot.

LINE **18.**—He drives furiously a chariot drawn by two sphinxes. As Levi drew it.

LINE **20.**—Before him goeth upright the Royal Uræus Serpent.

COL. **CLXXXI.** (*continued*)—

LINE **21.**—[☿, 🜍, and ⊖, or Sattva, Rajas, and Tamas.]

LINE **23.**—From a gallows shaped like the letter ד hangs by one foot a young fair man. His other leg forms a cross with the suspending one. His arms, clasped behind his head, form an upright △, and this radiates light. His mouth is resolutely closed.

LINE **25.**—A winged and crowned goddess, with flashing golden belt, stands and pours from her right hand the flame of a torch upon an Eagle, while from her left hand she pours water from an horn upon a Lion. Between her feet a moon-shaped cauldron of silver smokes with perfume.

LINE **26.**—Levi's Baphomet is sound commentary on this Mystery, but should not be found in the text.

LINE **27.**—Human figures thrown thence suggest the letter ע by their attitude.

LINE **28.**—A woman, naked, and kneeling on her left knee, pours from a vase in her right hand silver waters into a river, by which grow roses, the haunts of coloured butterflies. With her left hand she pours golden waters over her head, which are lost in her long hair. Her attitude suggests the Swastika. Above flames a great star of seven rays.

LINE **29.**—Below, a path leads between two towers, guarded by jackals, from the sea, wherein Scarabæus marcheth landwards.

LINE **30.**—Below is a wall, in front of which, in a fairy ring, two children wantonly and shamelessly embrace.

LINE **31.**—An angel blowing a trumpet, adorned with a golden banner bearing a white cross. Below a fair youth rises from a sarcophagus in the attitude of the god Shu supporting the Firmament. On his left a fair woman, her arms giving the sign of Water–an inverted ▽ on her breast. On her right a dark man giving the sign of Fire–an upright △ on the forehead.

LINE **32.**—An ellipse composed of 400 lesser circles. At the corners of the card a Man, an Eagle, a Bull, and a Lion. Within the circle a naked shining figure with female breasts, with closed eyes in the sign of the Earth—right foot advanced, right hand advanced and raised, left hand lowered and thrown back. The hands grip each a ray of dazzling light, spiral, the right hand being dextro- and the left hand lævo-rotary. A red scarf conceals the fact of male genital organs, and suggests by its shape the letter כ. Such is the conventional hieroglyph.

APPENDIX I

The Trigrams

Attribution to Quarters.	Planetary Attribution.	Hindu Attribution.	Yetziratic Attribution.	Figure.	Name.	Part of body.	*Key Scale.*
S.	☉	Lingam.	+ / מ	☰	Khien.	Head.	2 [and 30].
S.E.	♀	Apas.	▽ / ם	☱	Tui.	Mouth.	14 [and 23].
E.	♃	Mano (Prana).	☉ / ר	☲	Li.	Eyes.	6 [21 and 30].
N.E.	♂	Tejas.	△ / ש	☳	Kăn.	Feet.	27 and 31.
S.W.	☿	Vayu.	△̵ / א	☴	Sun.	Thighs.	11 [and 12].
W.	♄	Akasa.	☽ / ג	☵	Khân.	Ears.	10 [13 and 32].
N.W.	♁	Prithivi.	▽̵ / ת	☶	Khăn.	Hands.	32 bis.
N.	☽	Yoni.	O / ה	☷	Khwăn.	Belly.	3 and 13.

The Trigrams should be considered as the symbols which combine these meaning, the Hexagrams as combinations of these, chosen according to circumstances. Thus ䷂ is Fire of ☽, or Energy of ♄, and might mean beginning to change, or force applied to obstruction, as it actually does.

THE HEXAGRAMS

	Figure.	Nature.	Name.	Divination and Spiritual Meaning
1		+ of +	*Kh*ien	Heaven, &c. (+ for Lingam.)
2		O of O	Khwăn	Earth, &c. (O for Yoni.)
3		☽ of △	*K*un	Danger and obscurity—γενος.
4		▽ of ☽	Măng	Youth and ignorance.
5		☽ of +	hsü	Waiting, sincerity.
6		+ of ☽	Sung	Concentration, opposition, strength of will
7		O of ☽	Sze	Multitude, age and experience.
8		☽ of O	Pi	Help.
9		△ of +	hsiao *khū*	Small, restraint.
10		+ of ▽	lî	Pleased, satisfaction, treating, attached to, a shoe.
11		O of +	thai	Spring, free course.
12		+ of O	phî	Decay, patience, obedience, autumn, shutting up, restriction.
13		+ of ⊙	thung săn	Union (of men).
14		⊙ of +	tă yū	Great havings
15		O of ▽	*kh*ien	Humility.
16		△ of O	yü	Harmony and satisfaction.

221

TABLE OF CORRESPONDENCES

	Figure.	Nature.	Name.	Divination and Spiritual Meaning
17		▽ of △	Sui	Following.
18		▽̄ of △̄	Kū	Troublesome services, arrest of decay, hard work.
19		O of ▽	Lin	Approach of authority, inspect, comfort.
20		△̄ of O	Kwân	Manifesting, contemplating.
21		⊙ of △	Shih Ho	Union by gnawing, legal constraint.
22		▽ of ⊙	Pî	Ornament, freewill.
23		▽̄ of O	Po	Overthrow, couch.
24		O of △	Fu	Returning, visit from friends.
25		+ of △	Wû wang	Simplicity and sincerity, earnestness.
26		▽̄ of +	Ta *kh*u	Great accumulation.
27		▽̄ of △	î	Nourishment, upper jaw.
28		▽ of △̄	Ta Kwo	Great carefulness, weak beam.
29		☽ of ☽	Khan	Pit, defile, peril.
30		⊙ of ⊙	Lî	Inherent in, attached to, docility.
31		▽ of ▽̄	hsien	Influencing to action, all, jointly.
32		△ of △̄	hăng	Perseverance, keeping to the path.

NOTES

	Figure.	Nature.	Name.	Divination and Spiritual Meaning
33		+ of ⏛	Thun	Returning, avoiding, retirement.
34		△ of +	Tâ Kwang	Violence, the Great Ram.
35		☉ of O	Tzin	To advance (good).
36		O of ☉	Ming I	Intelligence, wounded.
37		⏆ of ☉	Kia Zăn	Household, wifely duty
38		☉ of ▽	Khwei	Disunion, family discord.
39		☉ of ⏛	Kien	Lameness, immobility, difficulty.
40		△ of ☉	Kieh	Unravelling (a knot, &c.)
41		⏛ of ▽	Sūn	Diminution.
42		⏆ of △	Yi	Addition, increase.
43		▽ of +	Kwâi	Displacing, strength, complacency, tact.
44		+ of ⏆	Kau	Unexpected event, a bold woman.
45		▽ of O	Tzhui	Collected, docility.
46		O of ⏆	Shăng	Advance and ascent.
47		▽ of ☽	Khwăn	Straightened, distressed, ⸪ Carcer, growth restrained.
48		☽ of ⏆	Tzing	A well, self-cultivation.

TABLE OF CORRESPONDENCES

	Figure.	Nature.	Name.	Divination and Spiritual Meaning
49		▽ of ☉	Ko	Change.
50		☉ of △	Ting	A cauldron, a concubine, flexibility, quick ear and eye.
51		△ of △	Kăn	Ease, development, moving power, thunder.
52		▽ of ▽	Kăn	Peace, a mountain.
53		△ of ▽	Kien	Fortunate marriage, gradual advance, goose
54		△ of ▽	Kwei mei	Unfortunate marriage (of a younger sister before the elder).
55		△ of ☉	Făng	Large, abundant, progress.
56		☉ of ▽	Lü	Stangers.
57		△ of △	Sun	Flexibility, penetration, vacillation, wind, wood, &c.
58		▽ of ▽	Tui	Pleasure, help from friends, still water.
59		△ of ☋	Hwān	Dissipation, dispersion, turning to evil.
60		☋ of ▽	Kieh	Joints of body, regular division.
61		△ of ☋	Kung fū	Inmost sincerity.
62		△ of ▽	Hsiao Kwo	Non-essential, success of trifles, a wounded bird, small divergences.
63		☋ of ☉	Kî tzî	Help attained, complete success.
64		☉ of ☋	Wei tzî	Incomplete success, foolish impulse, failure

A
HANDBOOK OF GEOMANCY

[THIS MS. is now first printed from the private copies of certain adepts, after careful examination and collation. It is printed for the information of scholars and the instruction of seekers. By the order of the A∴ A∴ certain formulæ have been introduced into it, and omissions made, to baffle any one who may seek to prostitute it to idle curiosity or to fraud. Its practical use and the method of avoiding these pitfalls will be shown to approved students by special authority from V.V.V.V.V. or his delegates.]

"Direct not thy mind to the vast surfaces of the earth; for the Plant of Truth grows not upon the ground. Nor measure the motions of the Sun, collecting rules, for he is carried by the Eternal Will of the Father, and not for your sake alone. Dismiss from your mind the impetuous course of the Moon, for she moveth always by the power of Necessity. The progression of the Stars was not generated for your sake. The wide aerial flight of birds gives no true knowledge, nor the dissection of the entrails of victims; they are all mere toys, the basis of mercenary fraud: flee from these if you would enter the sacred paradise of piety where Virtue, Wisdom, and Equity are assembled."

ZOROASTER.

```
M A C A N E H
A R O L U S E
D I R U C O N
A L U H U L A
S E R U R O C
U N E L I R A
L U S A D A M
```

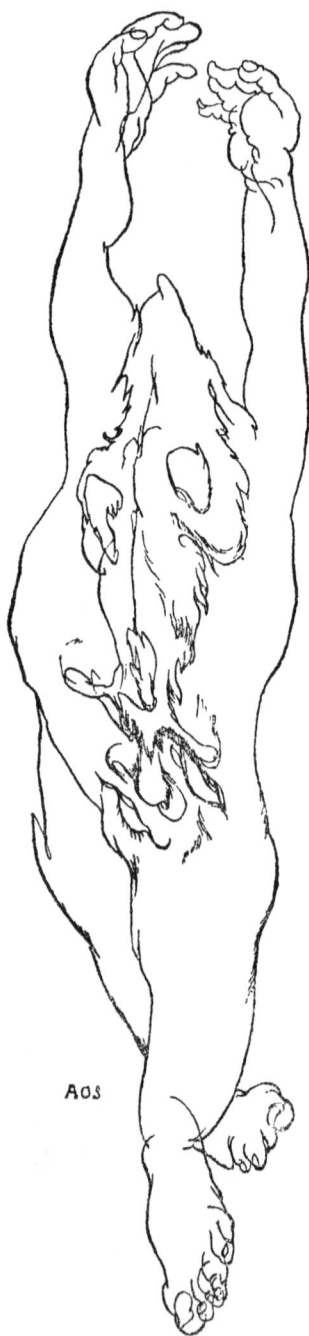

A
HANDBOOK OF GEOMANCY

CHAPTER I

ATTRIBUTIONS OF GEOMANTIC FIGURES TO PLANETS, ZODIAC, AND RULING GENII

	Sign	El.	Geom. Fig.	Sex	Name and Meaning	Genius	Ruler	Planet
1	♈	△		M.	Puer Boy, yellow, beardless	Malchidael	Bartzabel	♂
2	♉	▽		F.	Amissio Loss, comprehended without	Asmodel	Kedemel	♀
3	♊	△		M.	Albus White, fair	Ambriel	Taphthartha-rath	☿
4	♋	▽		F.	Populus People, congregation	Muriel	Chashmodai	☽
5	♌	△		M.	Fortuna Major Greater fortune, greater aid, safeguard entering	Verchiel	Sorath	☉
6	♍	▽		F.	Conjunctio Conjunction, assembling	Hamaliel	Taphthartha-rath	☿
7	♎	△		M.	Puella A girl, beautiful	Zuriel	Kedemei	♀
8	♏	▽		F.	Rubeus Red, reddish	Barchiel	Bartzabel	♂
9	♐	△		M.	Acquisitio Obtaining, comprehending without	Advachiel	Hismael	♃
10	♑	▽		F.	Carcer A prison, bound	Hanael	Zazel	♄
11	♒	△		M.	Tristitia Sadness, damned, cross	Cambiel	Zazel	♄
12	♓	▽		F.	Lætitia Joy, laughing, healthy, bearded	Amnixiel	Hismael	♃
13	☋	△		F.	Cauda Draconis The threshold lower, or going out	Zazel and Bartzabel	Zazel and Bartzabel	♄ ♂
14	☊	▽		M.	Caput Draconis The Head, threshold entering, the upper threshold	Hismael and Kedemel	Hismael and Kedemei	♃ ♀
15	♌	△		M.	Fortuna Minor Lesser fortune, lesser aid, safe-guard going out	Verchiel	Sorath	☉
16	♋	▽		F.	Via Way, journey	Muriel	Chashmodai	☽

229

CHAPTER II

THE MODE OF DIVINING—MOTHERS—DAUGHTERS— NEPHEWS—WITNESSES—JUDGE—RECONCILER— PART OF FORTUNE

THINK fixedly of the demand; with a pencil mark 16 lines of points or dashes. Find whether number of points in each line is odd or even. For odd ●; for even ●●. Lines 1–4 give the first mother; lines 5–8 the second; and so on.

EXAMPLE

4	3	2	1
●● 10	●● 12	● 15	● 15
● 11	●● 6	●● 16	● 15
●● 10	● 9	● 15	●● 16
●● 10	● 7	●● 14	●● 14

[The small Arabic numerals refer to the chance number of dashes.]

Use clean (virgin) paper; place appropriate Pentagram (either with or without a circumscribed circle) invoking. If a circle, draw this first. Sigil of Ruler to which nature of question most refers should be placed in the Pentagram thus:

ħ   Agriculture, sorrow, death.

♃   Good fortune, feasting, church preferment.

♂   War, victory fighting.

☉   Power, magistracy.

♀   Love, music, pleasure.

☿   Science, learning, knavery.

☽   Travelling, fishing, &c.

In diagram, p. 232, the Sigil of Hismael should be used.

In marking points fix attention on Sigil and on the question proposed; the hand should not be moved from the paper till complete. It is convenient to rule lines to guide the eye.

The daughters are derived by reading the mothers horizontally.

The four nephews, Figures IX–XII, are thus formed: IX = I + II read vertically, added and taken as odd or even. So also XIII = IX + X, and XV = XIII + XIV.

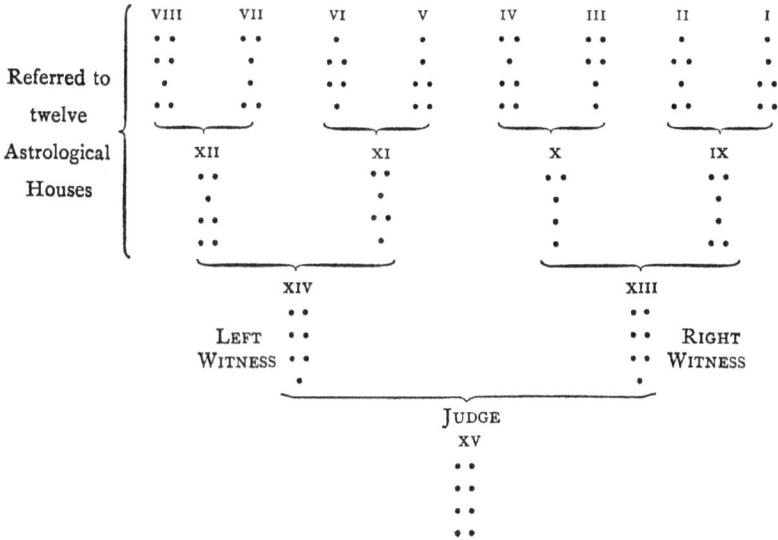

These last three are merely aids to general judgment. If the judge be good the figure is good, and *vice-versâ*.

The Reconciler = I + XV

To find the part of Fortune ⊕ (ready money or cash belonging to Querent), add points of the figures I–XII, divide by 12, and remainder shows figure. Here I + II + . . . + XII = 74 points = 6 × 12 + 2. ∴ ⊕ falls with ∴: (II).

CHAPTER III

OF THE FIGURE OF THE TWELVE HOUSES OF HEAVEN

THE meaning of the twelve Houses is to be found, primarily, in any text-book of Astrology. Knowledge is to be enlarged and corrected by constant study and practice.

Place the figures thus:

I	10th	IV	7th	VII	5th	X	3rd
II	Asc.	V	11th	VIII	8th	XI	6th
III	4th	VI	2nd	IX	12th	XII	9th

EXAMPLE

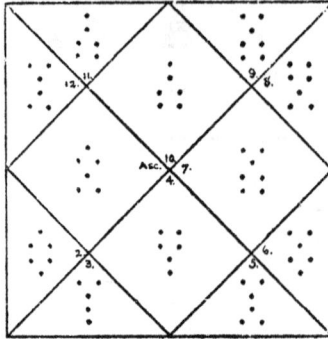

CHAPTER IV

TABLES OF WITNESSES AND JUDGE

THE tables are classed by the Left Witness.

The judgment concerning a wife (*e.g.*) will hold good for all demands of the 7th House.

So of all the others.

Arabic numbers mean that the judgment is determined by the figure in the House of Heaven.

L.W. •• •• •• •• POPULUS		R.W. J.	R.W. J.	R.W. J.	R.W. J.	R.W. J.	R.W. J.	R.W. J.	R.W. J.
Life, &c.	1	Mod.	Good	Good	Mod.	Mod.	Evil	Good	Mod.
Money, &c.	2	Mod.	Good	Good	Bad	Mod.	Evil	Mod.	Good
Rank, &c.	3	Mod.	Good	Good	Mod.	Good	Mod.	Mod.	Bad
Property	4	Mod.	Good	Good	Bad	Good	Bad	Mod.	Good
Wife, &c.	5	Good	Good	Bad	Good	Good	Bad	Good	Bad
Sex of Child	6	5	Evil	Dau.	Son	Dau.	Dau.	5	Dau.
Sickness	7	Asc.	Health	Soon health	Health	Perilous	Health	Health	Asc.
Prison	8	Come out	Out	Soon out	Out of Nothing	Long	Out	Die there	Die there
Journey	9	Good by water	Slow	Medium	Good by water	Evil	Medium	Medium	Evil
Thing Lost	10	Found	Found	Part found	Not found	Found	Lost	Found	Part found

L.W. • •• •• •• LÆTITIA		R.W. J.	R.W. J.	R.W. J.	R.W. J.	R.W. J.	R.W. J.	R.W. J.	R.W. J.
Life, &c.	1	Good and long	Med.	Med.	Evil	Med.	Med.	Med.	Good
Money, &c.	2	Increase	Evil	Med.	Med.	Good	Evil	Med.	Med.
Rank, &c.	3	Good dignity	Med.	Med.	Good	Good	Evil	Med.	Med.
Property	4	Good	Med.	Med.	Good	Good	Evil	Med.	Evil
Wife, &c.	5	Good	Med.	Med.	Evil	Good	Evil	Med.	Good
Sex of Child	6	Son	Dau.	Dau.	5	Son	5	Son	5
Sickness	7	Health	11	Asc.	Dangerous	Health	Health	Health	5
Prison	8	Late out	Come out	Come out	Come out	Soon out	Run away	Escape & recapture	Come out
Journey	9	Good in end	Hurtful	Evil	Evil	Good	Evil	Return	Good by water
Thing Lost	10	Found	Found	Part found	Part found	Part found	Part yielded	Part found	Part found

L.W. • • • • VIA		R.W. J.	R.W. J.	R.W. J.	R.W. J.	R.W. J.	R.W. J.	R.W. J.	R.W. J.
Life, &c.	1	Med.	Evil	Med.	Med.	Med.	Evil	Med.	Med.
Money, &c.	2	Evil	Evil	Med.	Med.	Med.	Med.	Med.	Med.
Rank, &c.	3	Med.	Good	Med.	Med.	Evil	Evil	Med.	Med.
Property	4	Evil	Good	Med.	Med.	Med.	Good	Med.	Med.
Wife, &c.	5	Good	Good	Med.	Evil	Good	Evil	Med.	Med.
Sex of Child	6	Son	Dau.	5	5	5	5	Son	5
Sickness	7	Health	Danger-ous	Health	Death	Death	Death	Health	Health
Prison	8	Out for nothing	Evil	Come out	Not out	Not out	Not out	Come out	Soon out
Journey	9	Good by water	Good by water	Slack	Return	Return	Late	Late	Good
Thing Lost	10	Not found	Not found	Part yielded	Found	Found	Part found	Little found	Not found

L.W. • • • • • • FORTUNA MAJOR		R.W. J.	R.W. J.	R.W. J.	R.W. J.	R.W. J.	R.W. J.	R.W. J.	R.W. J.
Life, &c.	1	Good	Evil	Good	Med.	Med.	Med.	Good	Med.
Money, &c.	2	Good	Evil	Good	Med.	Med.	Med.	Good	Med.
Rank, &c.	3	Possibil-ity good	Evil	Good	Good	Good	Med.	Good	Good
Property	4	Good	Evil	Good	Med.	Med.	Med.	Good	Evil
Wife, &c.	5	Good	Evil	Good	Good	Good	Evil	Good	Evil
Sex of Child	6	5	Son	Son	5	Son	Dau.	5	5
Sickness	7	Health	Health	Good	Asc.	Health	Perilous	Health	Health
Prison	8	Come out	Late	Come out	Die there	Come out	With harm	Come out	Soon out
Journey	9	Good w/ speed	Evil	Difficult	Med.	Soon return	Late	Good	Very good
Thing Lost	10	Found	Not found	Found	Found	Part found	Not found	Found	Not found

L.W. ALBUS

		R.W. J.	R.W. J.	R.W. J.	R.W. J.	R.W. J.	R.W. J.	R.W. J.	R.W. J.
Life, &c.	1	Evil	Good	Evil	Suffic'nt	Evil	Good	Evil	Med.
Money, &c.	2	Evil	Good	Med.	Good	Med.	Good	Evil	Med.
Rank, &c.	3	Evil	Good	Evil	Good	Evil	Good	Evil	Med
Property	4	Evil	Good	Evil	Good	Med.	Good	Evil	Med.
Wife, &c.	5	Evil	Evil	Med.	Good	Evil	Good	Evil	Med.
Sex of Child	6	Dau. die	5	Dau.	5	Dau.	5	Dau.	Dau.
Sickness	7	Death	Health	Death	Health	Death	Health	Health	Asc.
Prison	8	Perilous	Late	Not out	Come out	Die there	Run away	Come out	Come out
Journey	9	Med.	Good	Evil	Good	Difficult	Slow	Med.	V. good by water
Thing Lost	10	Not found	Not found	Not found	Part found	Part found	Found	Not found	Part found

L.W. RUBEUS

		R.W. J.	R.W. J.	R.W. J.	R.W. J.	R.W. J.	R.W. J.	R.W. J.	R.W. J.
Life, &c.	1	Good	Med.	Med.	Good	Evil	Med.	Evil	Very evil
Money, &c.	2	Good	Med.	Med.	Good	Evil	Good	Evil	Very evil
Rank, &c.	3	Good	Med.	Med.	Med.	Evil	Good	Evil	Very evil
Property	4	Good	Med.	Med.	Good	Evil	Med.	Evil	Very evil
Wife, &c.	5	Very good	Evil	Good	Med.	Evil	Good	Evil	Immoral
Sex of Child	6	Son	Dau.	Dau.	Son	Dau.	5	5	5
Sickness	7	Health	Health	Death	Health	Health	Long sick	In danger	Perilous
Prison	8	Come out	Difficult	Evil	Evil	Come out	Soon	Doubtful	Death
Journey	9	Difficult	Evil	Evil	Evil	Evil	Slow	Evil	Robbed
Thing Lost	10	Part found	Part yielded	Not found	Found	Not found	Found	Not found	Not found

L.W. TRISTITIA		R.W. J.	R.W. J.	R.W. J.	R.W. J.	R.W. J.	R.W. J.	R.W. J.	R.W. J.
Life, &c.	1	Evil	Suffic'nt	Evil	Med.	Evil	Med.	Good	Evil
Money, &c.	2	Med.	Suffic'nt	Evil	Med.	Evil	Med.	Good	Very evil
Rank, &c.	3	Evil	Suffic'nt	Evil	Evil	Evil	Good	Good	Evil
Property	4	Good	Suffic'nt	Evil	Evil	Evil	Evil	Good	Very evil
Wife, &c.	5	Evil	Suffic'nt	Evil	Evil	Evil	Evil	Good	Evil
Sex of Child	6	5	Dau.	Son	Dau.	5	5	Dau.	5
Sickness	7	Death	Death	Evil	Evil	Evil	Health	Health	Perilous
Prison	8	Death	Death	Evil	Evil	Evil	Come out	Long	Hard
Journey	9	Evil	Evil	Evil	Evil	Evil	Very late	Late	Med.
Thing Lost	10	Not found	Found	Not found	Not found	Not found	Not found	Found	Not found

L.W. PUELLA		R.W. J.	R.W. J.	R.W. J.	R.W. J.	R.W. J.	R.W. J.	R.W. J.	R.W. J.
Life, &c.	1	Med.	Med.	Good	Good	Evil	Med.	Good	Evil
Money, &c.	2	Med.	Good	Good	Good	Med.	Med.	Good	Evil
Rank, &c.	3	Evil	Good	V. good	Good	Evil	Good	Good	Evil
Property	4	Evil	Good	Med.	Good	Med.	Med.	Good	Evil
Wife, &c.	5	Med.	Good	Good	Good	Evil	Med.	Good	Good
Sex of Child	6	Dau.	Son	5	5	5	5	Dau.	5
Sickness	7	Asc.	Health	Danger-ous	Asc.	Health	Health	Long	Health
Prison	8	Out by ill means	Come out	Come out	Good end	Come out	Come out	Long	Come out
Journey	9	Perilous	Good	Good by ▽	Good	Perilous	Slow	Good	Med.
Thing Lost	10	Part found	Found	Part found	Found	Not found	Not found	Found	Part found

236

L.W. ⠄ PUER		R.W. J.	R.W. J.	R.W. J.	R.W. J.	R.W. J.	R.W. J.	R.W. J.	R.W. J.
Life, &c.	1	Good	Evil	Evil	Evil	Med.	Evil	Med.	Evil
Money, &c.	2	Good	Somewhat good	Evil	Evil	Med.	Evil	Med.	Evil
Rank, &c.	3	Good	Med.	Evil	Evil	Med.	Evil	Med.	Evil
Property	4	Med.	Med.	Evil	Evil	Med.	Evil	Med.	Evil
Wife, &c.	5	Good	Med.	Evil	Evil	Med.	Evil	Med.	Evil
Sex of Child	6	Son	Dau.	5	Dau.	Son	Dau.	Son	Dau.
Sickness	7	Health	Die soon	Asc.	Death	Health	Perilous	Health	Evil
Prison	8	Well out	Soon out	Dangerous	Die there	Come out	Perilous	Come out	Evil
Journey	9	Return	Med.	Spoiled	Evil	Med.	Evil	Med.	Evil
Thing Lost	10	Found	Part found	Not found	Not found	Found	Not found	Found	Not found

L.W. ⠂ CAPUT DRACONIS		R.W. J.	R.W. J.	R.W. J.	R.W. J.	R.W. J.	R.W. J.	R.W. J.	R.W. J.
Life, &c.	1	Evil	Good	V. good	Evil	Evil	Good	Evil	Good
Money, &c.	2	Evil	Good	V. good	Suffic'nt	Med.	V. good	Evil	V. good
Rank, &c.	3	Evil	Good	V. good	Evil	Good	Good	Evil	Good
Property	4	Evil	Good	V. good	Med.	Suffic'nt	Good	Evil	Good
Wife, &c.	5	Evil	Med.	Good	Evil	Med.	Med.	Evil	Good
Sex of Child	6	Dau.	5	5	Dau.	Son	Son	Dau.	Son
Sickness	7	Asc.	Health	Asc.	Health	Good end	Health	Health	Health
Prison	8	Long	Perilous	Come out	Hard	6	Soon out	Come out	Out late
Journey	9	Evil	Med.	Good by ▽	Evil	Evil	Good	Evil	V. good
Thing Lost	10	Not found	Found	Found	Found	Part found	Found	Not found	Found

237

L.W. • / • / • / • • CAUDA DRACONIS		R.W. J.	R.W. J.	R.W. J.	R.W. J.	R.W. J.	R.W. J.	R.W. J.	R.W. J.
Life, &c.	1	Med.	Evil	Very evil	Tolerable	Evil	Med.	Good	Evil
Money, &c.	2	Good	Evil	Very evil	Good	Med.	Suffic'nt	Good	Evil
Rank, &c.	3	Med.	Evil	Very evil	Med.	Evil	Suffic'nt	Good	Evil
Property	4	Good	Evil	Very evil	Med.	Evil	Suffic'nt	Good	Med.
Wife, &c.	5	Med.	Evil	Very evil	Med.	Evil	Evil	Med.	Very evil
Sex of Child	6	Son	5	5	5	5	5	Son and live	5
Sickness	7	Health	Perilous	Death	Death	Death	Perilous	Health	Asc.
Prison	8	Good end	Out with pain	Death	Come out	Come out punished	Come out	Soon out	Dangerous
Journey	9	Evil	Evil	Very evil	Med.	Evil	Evil	Good	Very evil
Thing Lost	10	Found	Not found	Not found	Found	Not found	Not found	Found	Not found

L.W. • • / • / • • / • ACQUISITIO		R.W. J.	R.W. J.	R.W. J.	R.W. J.	R.W. J.	R.W. J.	R.W. J.	R.W. J.
Life, &c.	1	Good	Evil	V. good	Med.	Good	Med.	Med.	Good
Money, &c.	2	Med.	Evil	V. good	Evil	Good	Med.	Med.	Good
Rank, &c.	3	Med.	Med.	V. good	Evil	Good	Med.	Med.	Good
Property	4	Med.	Evil	V. good	Evil	Good	Med.	Med.	Good
Wife, &c.	5	Good	Evil	Good	Evil	Med.	Med.	Med.	Good
Sex of Child	6	5	Son	5	5	Son	Dau.	5	Son
Sickness	7	Health	Health	Health	Health	Health	Health	Asc.	In danger
Prison	8	Death	Come out	Come out	Come out	Long	Come out	Late out	Slow
Journey	9	Med.	Good	Good	Med.	Soon return	Med.	Evil	Slow
Thing Lost	10	Found	Not found	Found	Not found	Found	Found	Found	Found

L.W. • •• • •• AMISSIO		R.W. J.	R.W. J.	R.W. J.	R.W. J.	R.W. J.	R.W. J.	R.W. J.	R.W. J.
Life, &c.	1	Good	Med.	Evil	Med.	Med.	Med.	Evil	Evil
Money, &c.	2	Good	Med.	Evil	Med.	Med.	Evil	Evil	Med.
Rank, &c.	3	Med.	Med	Evil	Good	Med.	Med.	Evil	Evil
Property	4	Med.	Med.	Evil	Med.	Med.	Evil	Evil	Med.
Wife, &c.	5	Med.	Med.	Evil	Med.	Med.	Evil	Evil	Evil
Sex of Child	6	5	Son	5	5	Dau.	Son	5	5
Sickness	7	The end health	Health	Perilous	Health	Health	Health	Death	Health
Prison	8	Long	Good end	Hard	Soon out	Come out	Come out	Out in the end	Die there
Journey	9	Good	Med.	Evil	Good	Med.	Med.	Evil	Not begun
Thing Lost	10	Not found	Found	Not found	Not found	Not found	Not found	Part found	Part found

L.W. •• • • •• CONJUNCTIO		R.W. J.	R.W. J.	R.W. J.	R.W. J.	R.W. J.	R.W. J.	R.W. J.	R.W. J.
Life, &c.	1	Good	Med.	Med.	Good	Evil	Good	Med.	Med.
Money, &c.	2	Good	Med.	Med.	Good	Evil	Good	Med.	Med.
Rank, &c.	3	Good	Med.	Med.	V. good	Evil	Good	Med.	Hard
Property	4	Good	Med.	Med.	V. good	Evil	Good	Med.	Med.
Wife, &c.	5	Good	Evil	Med.	V. good	Evil	Good	Good	Med.
Sex of Child	6	Son	5	5	Dau.	5	Son	Dau.	Dau.
Sickness	7	Long & pining	Death	Death	Asc.	Asc.	Health	Perilous	Hard
Prison	8	Long time	Out with fear	Perilous	Long	Good	Come out	Come out	Long
Journey	9	Slow	Med.	Good by ▽	Good	Med.	Evil	Slow	Hard
Thing Lost	10	Found	Found	Not found	Found	Not found	Found	Not found	Found

239

L.W. ⠀ CARCER		R.W. J.	R.W. J.	R.W. J.	R.W. J.	R.W. J.	R.W. J.	R.W. J.	R.W. J.
Life, &c.	1	Good	Med.	Good	Good	Med.	Suffic'nt	Evil	Med.
Money, &c.	2	Good	Evil	Good	Med.	Med.	Suffic'nt	Evil	Med.
Rank, &c.	3	Evil	Med.	Good	Good	Med.	Med.	Evil	Med.
Property	4	Med.	Evil	Good	Good	Med.	Suffic'nt	Med.	Good
Wife, &c.	5	Evil	Med	Good	Good	Med.	Suffic'nt	Evil	Good
Sex of Child	6	Dau.	5	Son	Dau.	5	5	5	Dau.
Sickness	7	Death	Health	Health	Health	Health	Health	Perilous	Dangerous
Prison	8	Good end	Soon out	Late out	Come out	Come out	Come out	Evil	Late out
Journey	9	Slow	Good	Slow	Slow	Slow	Slow	Difficult	Evil
Thing Lost	10	Found	Little found	Part found	Part found	Part found	Not found	Not found	Be found

L.W. ⠀ FORTUNA MINOR		R.W. J.	R.W. J.	R.W. J.	R.W. J.	R.W. J.	R.W. J.	R.W. J.	R.W. J.
Life, &c.	1	Good	Med.	Med.	Good	Evil	Med.	Good	Med.
Money, &c.	2	Good	Med.	Med.	Good	Evil	Evil	Good	Med.
Rank, &c.	3	Good	Med.	Med.	Good	Evil	Med.	Good	Evil
Property	4	Good	Med.	Med.	Good	Evil	Med.	Evil	Med.
Wife, &c.	5	Good	Med.	Med.	Good	Evil	Med.	Evil	Med.
Sex of Child	6	5	5	5	Son	Dau.	Son	Dau.	Dau.
Sickness	7	Health	Death	Health	Health	Asc.	Health	Health quickly	Perilous
Prison	8	Come out	Come out	Hard prison	Long in prison	Come out	Sorrow	Come out	Die
Journey	9	Good	Med.	Good	Late good	Good	Med.	Med.	Evil
Thing Lost	10	Found	Found	Part found	Found	Not found	Not found	Not found	Found

CHAPTER V

THE GENERAL MEANING OF THE SIXTEEN FIGURES IN THE TWELVE HOUSES

HEREIN follows a set of general tables of the sixteen figures in the twelve Houses, for the better convenience of forming a general judgment of the scheme. Under the head of each figure separately is given its general effect in whatever House it may happen to fall.

Thus, by taking the House signifying the thing demanded, and also that signifying the end of the matter (fourth House), and noticing what figures fall therein, you may find by these tables their general effect in that position.

ACQUISITIO		
Generally good for profit or gain	1	Happy success in all things
	2	Very prosperous
	3	Favour and riches
	4	Good fortune and success
	5	Good success
	6	Good, esp. agreeing with 5th
	7	Reasonably good
	8	Rather good, not very, the sick die
	9	Good in all
	10	Good in suits, very prosperous
	11	Good in all
	12	Evil, pain, and loss

FORTUNA MINOR		
Good in any matter where a person wishes to proceed quickly	1	Speed in victory or love; but choleric
	2	Very good
	3	Good, but wrathful
	4	Haste; rather evil, exc. for peace
	5	Good in all
	6	Medium in all
	7	Evil, exc. for war or love
	8	Evil generally
	9	Good, but choleric
	10	Good, exc. for peace
	11	Good, esp. for love
	12	Good, exc. for alteration or serving another

AMISSIO		
Gd. for loss of substance, and sometimes for love, but v. bad for gain	1	Ill in all but for prisoners
	2	V. evil for money, good for love
	3	Ill end, exc. in quarrels
	4	Ill in all
	5	Evil, exc. for agriculture
	6	Rather evil, exc. for love
	7	V. good for love, otherwise evil
	8	Excellent in all questions
	9	Evil in all
	10	Evil, exc. for women's favour
	11	Good for love, otherwise bad
	12	Evil in all

LÆTITIA		
Good for joy, present or to come	1	Good, exc. in war
	2	Sickly
	3	Ill
	4	Meanly good
	5	Excellently good
	6	Evil generally
	7	Indifferent
	8	Evil generally
	9	Very good
	10	Good rather in war than in peace
	11	Good in all
	12	Evil generally

FORTUNA MAJOR		
Good for gain in things where a person has hopes to win	1	Good, save in secrecy
	2	Good, save in sad things
	3	Good in all
	4	Good in all but melancholy
	5	Very good in all
	6	Very good, exc. for debauchery
	7	Good in all
	8	Moderately good
	9	Very good
	10	Exceedingly good, to go to superiors
	11	Very good
	12	Good in all

TRISTITIA		
Evil in almost all things	1	Med., but good for treasure and fortifying
	2	Med., but good to fortify
	3	Evil in all
	4	Evil in all
	5	Very evil
	6	Evil, exc. for debauchery
	7	Evil, but in secrecy good
	8	Gd. for inheritance and magic only
	9	Evil, exc. for magic
	10	Evil, exc. for fortification
	11	Evil in all
	12	Evil, but good for magic and treasure

PUELLA		
Good in all demands, especially those relating to women	1	Good, exc. in war
	2	Very good
	3	Good
	4	But indifferent
	5	V. good, but notice the aspects
	6	Good, but esp. so for debauchery
	7	Good, exc. for war
	8	Good
	9	Good for music, otherwise medium
	10	Good for place
	11	Good, and love of ladies
	12	Good in all

ALBUS		
Good for profit and for entering into a place or undertaking	1	Good for marriage; mercurial; peace
	2	Good in all
	3	Very good
	4	Good, exc. in war
	5	Good
	6	Good in all
	7	Good, exc. for war
	8	Good
	9	A messenger brings letters
	10	Excellent in all
	11	Very good
	12	Marvellously good

PUER		
Evil in most demands, except those relating to war and love	1	Indifferent; best in war
	2	Good, but with trouble
	3	Good fortune
	4	Evil, exc. in war and love
	5	Medium good
	6	Medium
	7	Evil, save in war
	8	Evil, exc. in love
	9	Evil, exc. for war
	10	Evil rather; good for love and war; else medium
	11	Medium; good favour
	12	Very good in all

CONJUCTIO		
Good with good, and evil with evil. Recovery of things lost	1	Good with good, evil with evil
	2	Commonly good
	3	Good fortune
	4	Good for health. Cf. 8th House's figure
	5	Medium
	6	Good for immorality only
	7	Rather good
	8	Evil, death
	9	Medium good
	10	For love good, for sickness evil
	11	Good in all
	12	Medium, bad for prisoners

RUBEUS		
Evil in all that is good, and good in all that is evil	1	Destroy the figure
	2	Evil in all
	3	Evil, exc. to let blood
	4	Evil, exc. in war and fire
	5	Evil, exc. for sowing seed
	6	Evil, exc. for blood-letting
	7	Evil, exc. for war and fire
	8	Evil
	9	Very evil
	10	Dissolute, love, fire
	11	Evil, exc. blood-letting
	12	Evil in all

CARCER		
General evil, delay, binding, stay, bar, restriction	1	Evil, exc. to fortify a place
	2	Good in Saturnian questions, otherwise evil
	3	Evil
	4	Good, only for melancholy
	5	Receive a letter in three days; evil
	6	Very evil
	7	Evil
	8	Very evil
	9	Evil in all
	10	Evil, save to hid treasure
	11	Much anxiety
	12	Rather good

CAPUT DRACONIS		
Good with good, evil with evil; gives a good issue for gain	1	Good in all
	2	Good
	3	Very good
	4	Good, save in war
	5	Very good
	6	Good for immorality only
	7	Good, esp. for peace
	8	Good
	9	Very good
	10	Good in all
	11	Good for the Church and ecclesiastical gain
	12	Not very good

VIA		
Injurious to the goodness of other figs. generally, but gd. for journeys & voyages	1	Evil, exc. for prison
	2	Indifferent
	3	Very good in all
	4	Good in all, save love
	5	Voyages good
	6	Evil
	7	Rather good, esp. for voyages
	8	Evil
	9	Indifferent; good for journeys
	10	Good
	11	Very good
	12	Excellent

CAUDA DRACONIS		
Good with evil, and evil with good; good for loss, and for passing out of an affair	1	Destroy the figure
	2	Very good
	3	Evil in all
	4	Evil, esp. for conclusion of the matter
	5	Very evil
	6	Rather good
	7	Evil, war, and fire
	8	No good, exc. for magic
	9	Good for science only; bad for journeys; robbery
	10	Evil, save in works of fire
	11	Evil, save for favours
	12	Rather good

POPULUS		
Sometimes good, sometimes bad; good with good, evil with evil	1	Good for marriage
	2	Medium good
	3	Rather good than bad
	4	Good in all but love
	5	Good in most
	6	Good
	7	In war good, else medium
	8	Evil
	9	Look for letters
	10	Good
	11	Good in all
	12	Very evil

CHAPTER VI

OF THE ESSENTIAL DIGNITIES OF THE FIGURES IN THE HOUSES; OF THE ASPECTS OF THE HOUSES; AND OF THE FRIENDSHIP AND ENMITY OF THE RULERS IN ASPECTS, ETC.

BY Essential Dignity is meant the strength of a figure when found in a particular House. A figure is therefore strongest in what is called its House; very strong in its Exaltation; strong in its Triplicity; very weak in its Fall; weakest of all in its Detriment. A figure is in its Fall when in a House opposite to that of its Exaltation; in its Detriment when opposite to its own House. The following list shows the Essential Dignities; that is to say, they follow the Dignities of their Ruling Planets, considering the twelve Houses of the scheme as answering to the twelve signs, thus: Asc. to ♈, 2 to ♉, 3 to ♊, &c., . . . 12 to ♓. Therefore ♂ figures will be strong in Asc. and weak in 7th, and so on. *See* chapter i. for attribution of figures to planets.

    * is strong in Dignities of Jupiter and Venus.

    * is strong in Dignities of Saturn and Mars.

TABLE OF ESSENTIAL DIGNITIES[1]

—	HOUSE	EXALTATION	TRIPLICITY	FALL	DETRIMENT
ASC.	1121, 2122, 1112	2211, 1122	2211, 1122, 2121, 1222, 2111	1221, 2221	1212, 1211
2	1212, 1211, 2111	2222, 1111	2222, 1111, 1212, 1211, 2111	—	1121, 2122, 1112
3	2112, 2212	2111	1221, 222 12212, 2112, 112	1112	2121, 1222, 2111

---

1   [Please note that no attempt has been made in the present edition to correct the deliberate errors first introduced into this section in *The Equinox*.]

TABLE OF ESSENTIAL DIGNITIES—*continued*

—	HOUSE	EXALTATION	TRIPLICITY	FALL	DETRIMENT
4	2222, 1111	2121, 1222	1121, 2122, 1112,	1121, 2122	1221, 2221, 1112
5	2211, 1122	—	2211, 1122, 2121, 1222, 2111	—	1221, 2221, 1112
6	2112, 2212	2112, 2212	2222, 1111, 1212, 1211, 2111	1212, 1211	2121, 1222, 2111
7	1211, 1212, 2111	1221, 2221	1221, 2221, 2212, 2112, 1112	2211, 1122	1121, 2122, 1112
8	2122, 1121, 1112	—	1211, 2122, 1112	2222, 1111	1212, 1211, 2111
9	2121, 1222, 2111	1112	2211, 1122, 2121, 1222, 2111	2111	2212, 2112
10	1221, 2221, 1112	1121, 2122	2211, 1111, 1212, 1211, 2111	1222, 2121	2222, 1111
11	1221, 2221, 1112	—	1221, 2221, 2212, 2112, 1112	—	2211, 1122
12	1222, 2121, 2111	1212, 1211	1121, 2122, 1112	2212, 2112	2212, 2112

THE ASPECTS OF THE HOUSES

The Asc. is aspected by 11, 10, 9 (as ⚹ □ and △) Dexter and by 3, 4, 5 . . . Sinister, and has 7 in opposition.

The Dexter aspect is that which is *contrary* to the natural order of the Houses; it is stronger than the Sinister. So for other Houses. Figures have Friends and Enemies:— ♄: ♃ ☉ ☿ ☽ Friends; ♂ ♀ Enemies. ♃: ♄ ☉ ♀ ☿ ☽; and ♂. ♂: ♀; and ☽ ♄ ☉ ☿. ☉: ♃ ☉ ♀ ☿ ☽; and ♄. ♀: ♃ ☉ ♂ ☿ ☽; and ♄. ☿ : ♄ ♃ ☉ ♀ ☽; and ♂. ☽ : ♃ ☉ ♀ ☿; and ♄ and ♂.

Also figures of 🜂 are sympathetic with those of 🜂, friendly with 🜁 and 🜃; hostile to 🜄.

So ▽ symp. ▽, friendly ⟰ and ⩠, and host. △: ⟰ symp. ⟰, friendly △ and ▽, and host. ⩠. ⩠ symp. ⩠, friendly ▽ and △, and host. ⟰. Again, sign figures are friends to those ⚹ or △, and hostile to those □ or in ☍.

CHAPTER VII

OF THE GENERAL METHOD OF JUDGING A FIGURE

REMEMBER always that if ⸪ or ∴ fall in the Ascendant, the figure is not fit for judgment. Destroy it instantly, and erect a new figure not less than two hours afterwards.

Your figure being thoroughly arranged as on p. 232, note first to what House the demand belongs. Then look for Witnesses and Judge in their special table, and see what is said under the head of the demand. Put this down. Note next what figure falls in the House required (if it spring into other Houses, these too should be considered); *e.g.*, in a question of money stolen, if the figure in 2nd be also in 6th it might show the thief to be a servant in the house. Look next in the Table of Figures in the Houses, and see what the figure signifies in the especial House under consideration. Put this down also. Then by the Table of Aspects (p. 244) note down the figures ⚹ □ △ and ☍, putting good on one side, evil on the other; noting also the strength or weakness, friendliness or hostility to the figure in the House required, of these figures. Then add the meaning of the figure in the 4th, to signify the end of the matter. It may also assist you to form a Reconciler from the figure in the House required and the Judge, noting what figure results and whether it har-monises with one or both by nature (pp. 244, 245). Now con-sider all you have written, and according to the balance of Good and Evil, form your final judgment. Consider also always in money questions where the part of Fortune falls.

Take, *e.g.*, the figure on p. 232, and form a judgment for loss of money in business therefrom.

Tables of Witnesses and Judge say: Moderate.

In 2nd is ∴. Evil, showing obstacle, delay.

Part of Fortune ⊕ is in Asc. with ∴ , showing loss through Querent's own blunders.

∴ springs into no other House; ∴ this does not affect the question.

The figures ✶ and △ of 2nd are ∴, ∴, ∴, and ∴, all good figures and friendly in nature = Well-intentioned help of friends.

The figures □ and ♂ are ∴, ∴, ∴, which are not hostile to ∴; therefore shows opposition not great.

The figure in the 4th is ∴ , which shows a good end, but with anxiety.

Forming a Reconciler, we get ∴ again, a sympathetic figure, but denoting delay = Delay, but helping Querent's wishes.

Adding all together—

  1. Medium;

  2. Evil and obstacles, delay;

  3. Loss through Querent's self;

  4. Strength for evil, medium only;

  5. Well-intentioned aid of friends;

  6. Not much opposition from enemies;

  7. Ending good, but with anxiety;

  8. Delay, but helping Querent's wishes—

we formulate this judgment:

That the Querent's loss in business has been principally owing to his own mismanagement; that he will have a long and hard struggle, but will meet with help from friends; that his obstacles will gradually give way; and that after much anxiety he will eventually recoup himself for his previous losses.

A DESCRIPTION OF
THE CARDS OF THE TAROT

WITH THEIR ATTRIBUTIONS; INCLUDING A
METHOD OF DIVINATION BY THEIR USE

"All divination resembles an attempt by a man born blind to obtain sight by getting blind drunk."

FRA. P.

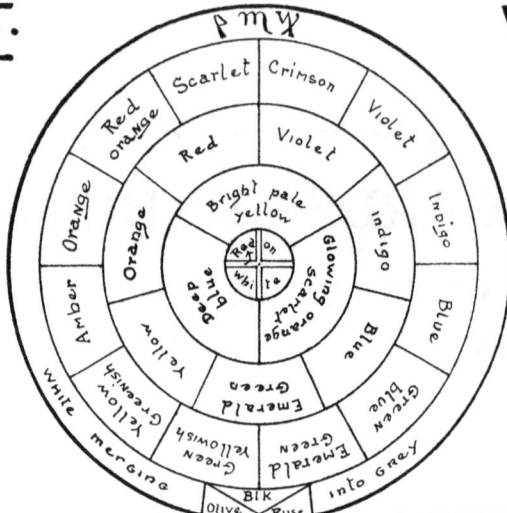

L·I·F·E·   V·I·T·A·

T   A

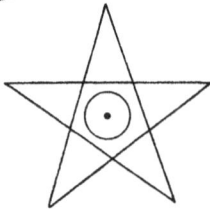

Deep Blue;
Symbols in
Yellow

Red;
Symbols in
Green

Yellow;
Symbols in
Violet

O   P

B·I·O·S·

THE COMPLETE SYMBOL OF THE TAROT

A DESCRIPTION OF
THE CARDS OF THE TAROT

H R U
THE GREAT ANGEL
is
set over the operations of the Secret Wisdom

A καὶ Ω
The First and the Last

"WHAT thou seest, write in a book, and send it unto the Seven Abodes which be in Aushiah."

"And I saw in the Right Hand of Him that Sate upon the Throne a Book, sealed with Seven Seals."

"Who is worthy to open the book, and to loose the Seals thereof?'

S.Y.M.B.O.L.A.   ♀

THE FRONTISPIECE

CONSISTS of a Crux Ansata, which is a form of the Rosy Cross. One arm is scarlet, with the symbols of Leo and the Wand in emerald green.

Another is blue with Eagle and Cup in orange.

A third is yellow, with Aquarius and Dagger in violet.

The last is in the four colours of Malkuth, with Pentacle and Taurus in black.

Ring is white, having at the top the Name of the Great Angel ♐ ♍ ♒ H U A; below cross-bar are Pentagrams, one enclosing Sol and the other enclosing Luna.

The whole space in the ring contains the Rose of 22 Petals bearing the Names of the 22 Keys. In the centre a white circle, and a red cross of four equal arms.

About the whole symbol are the words—

L.I.F.E.   B.I.O.S.   V.I.T.A.,

and the letters—

T. A. P. O., Tarot.

THE TITLES OF THE SYMBOLS

1 THE Ace of Wands is called the Root of the Powers of Fire.

2 The Ace of Cups is called the Root of the Powers of Water.

3 The Ace of Swords is called the Root of the Powers of Air.

4 The Ace of Pentacles is called the Root of the Powers of Earth.

5 The Knight of Wands is "The Lord of the Flame and Lighting: the King of the Spirits of Fire."

6 The Queen of Wands is "The Queen of the Thrones of Flame."

7 The King of Wands is "The Prince of the Chariot of Fire."

8 The Knave of Wands is "The Princess of the Shining Flame: the Rose of the Palace of Fire."

9 The Knight of Cups is "The Lord of the Waves and the Waters: the King of the Hosts of the Sea."

10 The Queen of Cups is "The Queen of the Thrones of the Waters."

11 The King of Cups is "The Prince of the Chariot of the Waters."

12 The Knave of Cups is "The Princess of the Waters: the Lotus of the Palace of the Floods."

13 The Knight of Swords is "The Lord of the Wind and the Breezes: the King of the Spirits of Air."

14 The Queen of Swords is "The Queen of the Thrones of Air."

15 The King of Swords is "The Prince of the Chariot of the Winds."

16 The Knave of Swords is "The Princess of the Rushing Winds: the Lotus of the Palace of Air."

17 The Knight of Pentacles is "The Lord of the Wide and Fertile Land: the King of the Spirits of Earth."

18 The Queen of Pentacles is "The Queen of the Thrones of Earth."

19 The King of Pentacles is "The Prince of the Chariot of Earth."

20 The Knave of Pentacles is "The Princess of the Echoing Hills: the Rose of the Palace of Earth."

NO.	CARD		LORD OF	DECAN	IN
21	5 of Wands		Strife	♄	♌
22	6 „	„	Victory	♃	♌
23	7 „	„	Valour	♂	♌
24	8 „	Pentacles	Prudence	☉	♍
25	9 „	„	Material Gain	♀	♍
26	10 „	„	Wealth	☿	♍
27	2 „	Swords	Peace restored	☽	♎
28	3 „	„	Sorrow	♄	♎
29	4 „	„	Rest from Strife	♃	♎
30	5 „	Cups	Loss in Pleasure	♂	♏
31	6 „	„	Pleasure	☉	♏
32	7 „	„	Illusionary Success	♀	♏
33	8 „	Wands	Swiftness	☿	♐
34	9 „	„	Great Strength	☽	♐
35	10 „	„	Oppression	♄	♐
36	2 „	Pentacles	Harmonious Change	♃	♑
37	3 „	„	Material Works	♂	♑
38	4 „	„	Earthly Power	☉	♑
39	5 „	Swords	Defeat	♀	♒
40	6 „	„	Earned Success	☿	♒
41	7 „	„	Unstable Effort	☽	♒
42	8 „	Cups	Abandoned Success	♄	♓
43	9 „	„	Material Happiness	♃	♓
44	10 „	„	Perfected Success	♂	♓
45	2 „	Wands	Dominion	♂	♈
46	3 „	„	Established Strength	☉	♈
47	4 „	„	Perfected Work	♀	♈
48	5 „	Pentacles	Material Trouble	☿	♉
49	6 „	„	Material Success	☽	♉
50	7 „	„	Success unfulfilled	♄	♉
51	8 „	Swords	Shortened Force	♃	♊
52	9 „	„	Despair and Cruelty	♂	♊
53	10 „	„	Ruin	☉	♊
54	2 „	Cups	Love	♀	♋
55	3 „	„	Abundance	☿	♋
56	4 „	„	Blended Pleasure	☽	♋

255

	THE TWENTY-TWO KEYS OF THE BOOK	LETTER	ATTRI-BUTION
57	0. The Foolish Man — The Spirit of Αἰθήρ	א	⚷
58	1. The Magi-cian — The Magus of Power	ב	☿
59	2. The High-Priestess — The Priestess of the Silver Star	ג	☽
60	3. The Em-press — The Daughter of the Mighty Ones	ד	♀
61	4. The Em-peror — Sun of the Morning, chief among the Mighty	ה	♈
62	5. The Hiero-phant — The Magus of the Eternal	ו	♉
63	6. The Lovers — The Children of the Voice; the Oracles of the Mighty Gods	ז	♊
64	7. The Chariot — The Child of the Powers of the Waters; the Lord of the Triumph of Light	ח	♋
65	11. Fortitude — The Daughter of the Flaming Sword	ט	♌
66	9 .Hermit — The Magus of the Voice of Power, tbe Prophet of the Eternal	י	♍
67	10. The Wheel of Fate — The Lord of the Forces of Life	כ	♃

		THE TWENTY-TWO KEYS OF THE BOOK	LETTER	ATTRI-BUTION
68	8. Justice	The Daughter of the Lords of Truth: the Ruler of the Balance	ל	♎
69	12. The Hanged Man	The Spirit of the Mighty Waters	מ	▽
70	13. Death	The Child of the Great Trans-formers: the Lord of the Gates of Death	נ	♏
71	14. Temperance	The Daughter of the Reconcilers: the Bringer-Forth of life	ס	♐
72	15. The Devil	The Lord of the Gates of Matter: the Child of the Forces of Time	ע	♑
73	16. The Blasted Tower	The Lord of the Hosts of the Mighty	פ	♂
74	17. The Star	The Daughter of the Firmament, the dweller be-tween the Waters	צ	♒
75	18. The Moon	The Ruler of Flux and Reflux: the Child of the Sons of the Mighty	ק	♓

		THE TWENTY-TWO KEYS OF THE BOOK	LETTER	ATTRI-BUTION
76	19. The Sun	The Lord of the Fire of the World	ר	☉
77	20. The Judg-ment	The Spirit of the Primal Fire	ש	⊕ and △
78	21. The Uni-verse	The Great One of the Night of Time	ת	▽ and ♄

Such are the Titles of the
Abodes or Atouts of Thooth;
of the
Mansions of the House of
my
FATHER.

The Descriptions of the Seventy-eight Symbols
of this Book ☊ ; together with
their meanings

OF THE ACES

FIRST in order and importance are the Four Aces, representing the Force of the Spirit, acting in, and binding together, the Four Scales of each Element: and answering to the Dominion of the Letters of the Name in the Kether of each. They represent the Radical Forces.

The Four Aces are said to be placed on the North Pole of the Universe wherein they revolve, governing its revolution; and ruling as the connecting link between Yetzirah and the Material Plane or Universe.

I
THE ROOT OF THE POWERS OF FIRE

Ace of Wands

A WHITE Radiating Angelic Hand, issuing from clouds, and grasping a heavy club, which has three branches in the colours, and with the sigils, of the scales. The Right- and Left-hand branches end respectively in three Flames, and the Centre one in four Flames: thus yielding Ten: the Number of the Sephiroth. Two-and-twenty leaping Flames, or Yodh, surround it, answering to the Paths; of these, three fall below the Right branch for Aleph, Men, and Shin, seven above the Central branch for the double letters; and between it and that of the Right twelve: six above and six below about the Left-hand branch. The whole is a great and flaming Torch. It symbolizes Force—strength, rush, vigour, energy, and it governs, according to its nature, various works and questions.

It implies Natural, as opposed to Invoked, Force.

259

II

THE ROOT OF THE POWERS OF THE WATERS

Ace of Cups or Chalices

A WHITE Radiant Angelic Hand, issuing from clouds, and supporting on the palm thereof a cup, resembling that of the Stolistes.

From it rises a fountain of clear and glistening water: and sprays falling on all sides into clear calm water below, in which grow Lotuses and Water-lilies. The great Letter of the Supernal Mother is traced in the spray of the Fountain.

It symbolizes Fertility—productiveness, beauty, pleasure, happiness, etc.

III

THE ROOT OF THE POWERS OF THE AIR

Ace of Swords

A WHITE Radiating Angelic Hand, issuing from clouds, and grasping the hilt of a sword, which supports a White Radiant Celestial Crown; from which depend, on the right, the olive branch of Peace; and on the left, the palm branch of suffering.

Six Vaus fall from its point. It symbolizes *Invoked*, as contrasted with Natural Force: for it is the Invocation of the Sword. Raised upward, it invokes the Divine crown of Spiritual Brightness, but reversed it is the Invocation of Demonic Force; and becomes a fearfully evil symbol. It represents, therefore, very great power for good or evil, but invoked; and it also represents whirling Force, and strength through trouble. It is the affirmation of Justice upholding Divine Authority; and it may become the Sword of Wrath, Punishment, and Affliction.

IV

THE ROOT OF THE POWERS OF THE EARTH

Ace of Pentacles

A WHITE Radiant Angelic Hand, holding a branch of a Rose Tree, whereon is a large Pentacle, formed of Five concentric circles. The Innermost Circle is white, charged with a red Greek Cross. From this White Centre, Twelve Rays, also white, issue: these terminate at the circumference, making the whole something like an Astrological figure of the Heavens.

It is surmounted by a small circle, above which is a large white Maltese Cross, and with two white wings.

Four Crosses and two buds are shewn. The Hand issueth from the Clouds as in the other three cases.

It represents materiality in all senses, good and evil: and is, therefore, in a sense, illusionary: it shows material gain, labour, power, wealth, etc.

THE SIXTEEN COURT, OR ROYAL CARDS

The Four Kings

THE Four Kings, or "Figures mounted on steeds," represent the Yodh forces of the Name in each Suit: the Radix, Father and commencement of Material Forces, a force in which all the others are implied, and of which they form the development and completion. A force swift and violent in its action, but whose effect soon passes away, and therefore symbolized by a Figure on a Steed riding swiftly, and clothed in complete Armour.

Therefore is the knowledge of the scale of the King so necessary for the commencement of all magical working.

The Four Queens

are seated upon Thrones; representing the Forces of the Hé of the Name in each suit; the Mother and bringer-forth of Material Forces: a force which develops and realizes that of the King: a force steady and unshaken, but not rapid, though enduring. It is therefore symbolized by a Figure seated upon a Throne: but also clothed in Armour.

The Four Princes

These Princes are Figures seated in Chariots, and thus borne forward. They represent the Vau Forces of the Name in each suit: the Mighty Son of the King and Queen, who realizes the influence of both scales of Force. A Prince, the son of a King and Queen, yet a Prince of Princes, and a King of Kings: an Emperor whose effect is at once rapid (though not so swift as that of the Queen) and enduring. It is, therefore, symbolized by a Figure borne in a Chariot, and clothed in Armour. Yet is his power vain and illusionary, unless set in Motion by his Father and Mother.

The Four Princesses

are the Knaves of the Tarot Pack; The Four Princesses or figures of Amazons, standing firmly of themselves: neither riding upon Horses, nor seated upon Thrones, nor borne in Chariots. They represent the forces of the Hé final of the Name in each suit, completing the Influences of the other scales: The mighty and potent daughter of a King and Queen: a Princess powerful and terrible: a Queen of Queens—an Empress—whose effect combines those of the King, Queen, and Prince, at once violent and permanent; therefore symbolized by a Figure standing firmly by itself, only partially draped, and having but little Armour; yet her power existeth

not, save by reason of the others: and then indeed it is mighty
and terrible materially, and is the Throne of the Forces of the
Spirit.

Woe unto whomsoever shall make war upon her, when
thus established!

THE SPHERES OF INFLUENCE OF THE
COURT CARDS OF THE TAROT PACK

THE Princesses rule the Four Parts of the Celestial
Heavens which lie around the north Pole, and above the
respective Cherubic Signs of the Zodiac, and they form the
Thrones of the Powers of the Four Aces.

The twelve cards, the Four Kings, Queens and Princes rule
the dominion of the Celestial Heavens, between the realm of
the Four Princesses and the Zodiac, as is hereafter shewn. And
they, as it were, link together the signs.

V
THE LORD OF THE FLAME AND THE LIGHT-
NING; THE KING OF THE SPIRITS OF FIRE

Knight[1] of Wands

A WINGED Warrior riding upon a black horse with
flaming mane and tail: the horse itself is not winged. The rider
wears a winged helmet (like the old Scandinavian and Gaulish
helmet) with a Rayed Crown, a corslet of scale-mail and
buskins of the same, and a flowing scarlet mantle. Above his
helmet, upon his cuirass, and on the shoulder-pieces and
buskins, he wears as a crest a winged black horse's head. He

---

1   Note that the Kings are now called Knights, and the Princes are now called
Kings. This is unfortunate, and leads to confusion; the Princes may be called
Emperors without harm. Remember only that the horsed figures refer to the
Yod of Tetragrammaton, the charioted figures to the Vau,

grasps a club with flaming ends, somewhat similar to that in the symbol of the Ace of Wands, but not so heavy, and also the sigil of his scale is shown; beneath the rushing feet of his steed are waving flames and fire. He is active—generous— fierce—sudden—impetuous.

If ill dignified, he is evil-minded—cruel—bigoted—brutal. He rules the celestial heavens from above the Twentieth Degree of ♏ to the First Two Decans of ♐: and this includes a part of the Constellation Hercules. (Hercules is always represented with a Club.)

△ of △

King of the Salamanders.

VI

THE QUEEN OF THE THRONES OF FLAME

Queen of Wands

A CROWNED queen with long red-golden hair, seated upon a Throne, with steady flames beneath. She wears a corslet and buskins of scale-mail, which latter her robe discloses. Her arms are almost bare. On cuirass and buskins are leopard's heads winged, and the same symbol surmounteth her crown. At her side is a couchant leopard on which her hands rest. She bears a long wand with a very heavy conical head. The face is beautiful and resolute.

Adaptability, steady force applied to an object, steady rule, great attractive power, power of command, yet liked notwithstanding. Kind and generous when not opposed.

If ill dignified, obstinate, revengeful, domineering, tyrannical, and apt to turn against another without a cause.

She rules the heavens from above the last Decan of ♓ to above the 20° of ♈: including thus a part of Andromeda.

▽ of △

Queen of the Salamanders.

264

VII

THE PRINCE OF THE CHARIOT OF FIRE

King of Wands

A KINGLY Figure with a golden, winged crown, seated on a chariot. He has large white wings. One wheel of his chariot is shewn. He wears corslet and buskins of scale armour decorated with a winged lion's head, which symbol also surmounts his crown. His chariot is drawn by a lion. His arms are bare, save for the shoulder-pieces of the corslet, and he bears a torch or fire-wand, somewhat similar to that of the Zelator Adeptus Minor. Beneath the chariot are flames, some waved, some salient.

Swift, strong, hasty; rather violent, yet just and generous; noble and scorning meanness.

If ill dignified—cruel, intolerant, prejudiced and ill natured.

He rules the heavens from above the last Decan of ♋ to the second Decan of ♌; hence he includes most of Leo Minor.

△ of △

Prince and Emperor of Salamanders.

VIII

THE PRINCESS OF THE SHINING FLAME;
THE ROSE OF THE PALACE OF FIRE

Knave of Wands

A VERY strong and beautiful woman with flowing red-gold hair, attired like an Amazon. Her shoulders, arms, bosom and knees are bare. She wears a short kilt reaching to the knee. Round her waist is a broad belt of scale-mail; narrow at the sides; broader in front and back; and having a winged tiger's head in front. She wears a Corinthian-shaped helmet and crown with a long plume. It also is surmounted by a tiger's head, and the same symbol forms the buckle of her scale-mail

265

buskins. A mantle lined with tiger's skin falls back from her shoulders. Her right hand rests on a small golden or brazen altar ornamented with ram's heads and with Flames of Fire leaping from it. Her left hand leans on a long and heavy club, swelling at the lower end, where the sigil is placed; and it has flames of fire leaping from it the whole way down; but the flames are ascending. This club or torch is much longer than that carried by the King or Queen. Beneath her firmly placed feet are leaping Flames of Fire.

Brilliance, courage, beauty, force, sudden in anger or love, desire of power, enthusiasm, revenge.

If ill dignified, she is superficial, theatrical, cruel, unstable, domineering.

She rules the heavens over one quadrant of the portion around the North Pole.

▽ of △

Princess and Empress of the Salamanders.
Throne of the Ace of Wands.

IX

THE LORD OF THE WAVES AND THE WATERS; THE KING OF THE HOSTS OF THE SEA

Knight of Cups

A BEAUTIFUL, winged, youthful Warrior with flying hair, riding upon a white horse, which latter is not winged. His general equipment is similar to that of the Knight of Wands, but upon his helmet, cuirass and buskins is a peacock with opened wings. He holds a cup in his hand, bearing the sigil of the scale. Beneath his horse's feet is the sea. From the cup issues a crab.

Graceful, poetic, Venusian, indolent, but enthusiastic if roused.

Ill dignified, he is sensual, idle and untruthful.

266

He rules the heavens from above 20° of ♒ to 20° of ♓, thus including the greater part of Pegasus.

△ of ▽

King of Undines and Nymphs.

X

THE QUEEN OF THE THRONES OF THE WATERS

Queen of Cups

A VERY beautiful fair woman like a crowned Queen, seated upon a throne, beneath which is flowing water wherein Lotuses are seen. Her general dress is similar to that of the Queen of Wands, but upon her crown, cuirass and buskins is seen an Ibis with opened wings, and beside her is the same bird, whereon her hand rests. She holds a cup, wherefrom a crayfish issues. Her face is dreamy. She holds a lotus in the hand upon the Ibis.

She is imaginative, poetic, kind, yet not willing to take much trouble for another. Coquettish, good-natured underneath a dreamy appearance. Imagination stronger than feeling. Very much affected by other influences, and therefore more dependent upon dignity than most symbols.

She rules from 20° ♊ to 20° ♋.

▽ of ▽

Queen of Nymphs or Undines.

XI

THE PRINCE OF THE CHARIOT OF THE WATERS

King of Cups

A WINGED Kingly Figure with winged crown seated in a chariot drawn by an eagle. On the wheel is the symbol of a scorpion. The eagle is borne as a crest on his crown, cuirass and buskins. General attire like King of Wands. Beneath his chariot is the calm and stagnant water of a lake. His armour resembles feathers more than scales. He holds in one hand a lotus, and in the other a cup, charged with the sigil of his scale. A serpent issues from the cup, and has its head tending down to the waters of the lake. He is subtle, violent, crafty and artistic; a fierce nature with calm exterior. Powerful for good or evil but more attracted by the evil if allied with apparent Power or Wisdom.

If ill dignified, he is intensely evil and merciless.

He rules from 20° ♎ to 20° ♏.

♈ of ▽

Prince and Emperor of Nymphs or Undines.

XII

THE PRINCESS OF THE WATERS; THE LOTUS
OF THE PALACE OF THE FLOODS

Knave of Cups

A BEAUTIFUL Amazon-like figure, softer in nature than the Princess of Wands. Her attire is similar. She stands on a sea with foaming spray. Away to her right a Dolphin. She wears as a crest a swan with opening wings. She bears in one hand a lotus, and in the other an open cup from which a turtle issues. Her mantle is lined with swansdown, and is of thin floating material.

Sweetness, poetry, gentleness and kindness. Imaginative, dreamy, at times indolent, yet courageous if roused.

When ill dignified she is selfish and luxurious.

She rules a quadrant of the heavens around Kether.

▽ of ▽

Princess and Empress of the Nymphs or Undines
Throne of the Ace of Cups.

XIII
THE LORD OF THE WINDS AND THE BREEZES:
THE KING OF THE SPIRITS OF AIR

Knight of Swords

A WINGED Warrior with crowned Winged Helmet, mounted upon a brown steed. His general equipment is as that of the Knight of Wands, but he wears as a crest a winged six-pointed star, similar to those represented on the heads of Castor and Pollux the Dioscuri, the twins Gemini (a part of which constellation is included in his rule). He holds a drawn sword with the sigil of his scale upon its pommel. Beneath his horse's feet are dark-driving stratus clouds.

He is active, clever, subtle, fierce, delicate, courageous, skilful, but inclined to domineer. Also to overvalue small things, unless well dignified.

If ill dignified, deceitful, tyrannical and crafty.

Rules from 20° ♉ to 20° ♊.

△ of ♎

King of the Sylphs and Sylphides.

XIV
THE QUEEN OF THE THRONES OF AIR

Queen of Swords

A GRACEFUL woman with wavy, curling hair, like a Queen seated upon a Throne and crowned. Beneath the Throne are grey cumulus clouds. Her general attire is as that of the Queen of Wands, but she wears as a crest a winged child's head. A drawn sword in one hand, and in the other a large, bearded, newly severed head of a man.

Intensely perceptive, keen observation, subtle, quick and confident: often persevering, accurate in superficial things, graceful, fond of dancing and balancing.

269

If ill dignified, cruel, sly, deceitful, unreliable, though with a good exterior.

Rules from 20° ♍ to 20° ♎.

▽ of ♎
Queen of the Sylphs and Sylphides.

XV
THE PRINCE OF THE CHARIOT OF THE WINDS

King of Swords

A WINGED King with Winged Crown, seated in a chariot drawn by Arch Fays, represented as winged youths very slightly dressed, with butterfly wings: heads encircled by a fillet with a pentagram thereon: and holding wands surmounted by pentagrams, the same butterfly wings on their feet and fillets. General equipment as the King of Wands: but he bears as a crest a winged angelic head with a pentagram on the brows. Beneath the chariot are grey nimbus clouds. His hair long and waving in serpentine whirls, and whorl figures compose the scales of his armour. A drawn sword in one hand; a sickle in the other. With the sword he rules, with the sickle he slays.

Full of ideas and thoughts and designs, distrustful, suspicious, firm in friendship and enmity; careful, observant, slow, over-cautious, symbolizes *A* and *Ω;* he slays as fast as he creates.

If ill dignified: harsh, malicious, plotting; obstinate, yet hesitating; unreliable.

Rules from 20° ♑ to 20° ♒.

♎ of ♎
Prince and Emperor of the Sylphs and Sylphides.

XVI
THE PRINCESS OF THE RUSHING WINDS:
THE LOTUS OF THE PALACE OF AIR

Knave of Swords

AN AMAZON figure with waving hair, slighter than the Rose of the Palace of Fire. Her attire is similar. The Feet seem springy, giving the idea of swiftness. Weight changing from one foot to another and body swinging around. She is a mixture of Minerva and Diana: her mantle resembles the Ægis of Minerva. She wears as a crest the head of the Medusa with serpent hair. She holds a sword in one hand; and the other rests upon a small silver altar with grey smoke (no fire) ascending from it. Beneath her feet are white clouds.

Wisdom, strength, acuteness; subtlety in material things: grace and dexterity.

If ill dignified, she is frivolous and cunning.

She rules a quadrant of the heavens around Kether.

$$\triangledown \text{ of } \triangle$$

Princess and Empress of the Sylphs and Sylphides.
Throne of the Ace of Wands.

XVII
THE LORD OF THE WIDE AND FERTILE LAND;
THE KING OF THE SPIRITS OF EARTH

Knight of Pentacles

A DARK Winged Warrior with winged and crowned helmet: mounted on a light brown horse. Equipment as the Knight of Wands.

The winged head of a stag or antelope as a crest. Beneath the horse's feet is fertile land with ripened corn. In one hand he bears a sceptre surmounted by a hexagram: in the other a Pentacle like that of the Zelator Adeptus Minor.

Unless very well dignified he is heavy, dull, and material. Laborious, clever, and patient in material matters.

If ill dignified, he is avaricious, grasping, dull, jealous; not very courageous, unless assisted by other symbols.

Rules from above 20° of ♌ to 20° of ♍.

△ of ⛢

King of Gnomes.

XVIII

THE QUEEN OF THE THRONES OF EARTH

Queen of Pentacles

A WOMAN of beautiful face with dark hair; seated upon a throne, beneath which is dark sandy earth. One side of her face is light, the other dark; and her symbolism is best represented in profile. Her attire is similar to that of the Queen of Wands: but she bears a winged goat's head as a crest. A goat is by her side. In one hand she bears a sceptre surmounted by a cube, and in the other an orb of gold.

She is impetuous, kind; timid, rather charming; great-hearted; intelligent, melancholy; truthful, yet of many moods.

If ill dignified she is undecided, capricious, changeable, foolish.

She rules from 20° ♐ to 20° ♑.

▽ of ⛢

The Queen of Gnomes.

XIX

THE PRINCE OF THE CHARIOT OF EARTH

King of Pentacles

A WINGED Kingly Figure seated in a chariot drawn by a bull. He bears as a crest the symbol of the head of the winged bull. Beneath the chariot is land, with many flowers. In the one hand he bears an orb of gold held downwards, and in the other a sceptre surmounted by an orb and cross.

Increase of matter. Increases good or evil, solidifies; practically applies things. Steady; reliable.

If ill dignified he is selfish, animal and material: stupid. In either case slow to anger, but furious if roused.

Rules from 20° ♈ to 20° ♉.

♎ of ♁

Prince and Emperor of the Gnomes.

XX
PRINCESS OF THE ECHOING HILLS: ROSE OF THE PALACE OF EARTH

Knave of Pentacles

A STRONG and beautiful Amazon figure with rich brown hair, standing on grass or flowers. A grove of trees near her. Her form suggests Hebe, Ceres, and Proserpine. She bears a winged ram's head as a crest: and wears a mantle of sheep-skin. In one hand she carries a sceptre with a circular disk: in the other a Pentacle similar to that of the Ace of Pentacles.

She is generous, kind, diligent, benevolent, careful, courageous, persevering, pitiful.

If ill dignified she is wasteful and prodigal. She rules over one quadrant of the heavens around the North Pole of the Ecliptic.

♁ of ♁

Princess and Empress of the Gnomes.
Throne of the Ace of Pentacles.

HEREIN ARE RESUMED THE ESPECIAL CHARACTERISTICS OF THE FOUR COURT CARDS OF THE SUITS

SUITS	CARDS	CRESTS	SYMBOLS	HAIR	EYES
WANDS	King	Winged black horse's head	Black horse, waving flames, club, scarlet cloak	Red-gold	Grey or hazel
	Queen	Leopard's head, winged	Leopard, steady flames, wand with heavy head or end	Red-gold	Blue or brown
	Prince	Lion's head, winged	Waved and salient flames, fire wand of Zelator Adept	Yellow	Blue-grey
	Princess	Tiger's head	Tiger, leaping flames, gold altar, long club, largest at bottom	Red-gold	Blue
CUPS	King	Peacock with opened fan	White horse, crab issuing from cup, sea	Fair	Blue
	Queen	Ibis	Ibis, crayfish issuing from cup, river	Gold-brown	Blue
	Prince	Eagle	Scorpion, eagle; serpent issuing from cup, lake	Brown	Grey or brown
	Princess	Swan	Dolphin lotus, sea with spray, turtle from cup	Brown	Blue or brown
SWORDS	King	Winged hexagram	Winged brown horse, driving clouds, drawn sword	Dark-brown	Dark
	Queen	Winged child's head	Head of man severed, cumulus clouds, drawn sword	Light-brown	Grey
	Prince	Winged Angel's head	Arch fairies winged, whirling hair, nimbi, drawn sword and sickle	Dark	Dark
	Princess	Medusa's head	Silver altar, smoke, clouds, drawn sword	Light-brown	Blue
PENTACLES	King	Winged stag's head	Light-brown horse, ripe cornland, sceptre with hexagram, pentacle as Zelator Adept.	Dark	Dark
	Queen	Winged goat's head	Barren land, fan, light one side only, sceptre with cube, orb of gold	Dark	Dark
	Prince	Winged bull's head	Flowery land, bull, sceptre with orb and cross, orb held downwards	Dark-brown	Dark
	Princess	Winged ram's head	Grass, flowers, grove of trees, sceptre with disk, pentacle like that in ace	Rich brown	Dark

OF THE THIRTY-SIX DECANS

HERE follow the descriptions of the smaller cards of the four suits, thirty-six in number, answering unto the thirty-six Decans of the Zodiac.

Commencing from the sign Aries, the *Central* Decans of each sign follow the order of the Days of the Week. Thus—

CARD	CENTRAL DECAN OF	MEANING	DAY
3 of Wands	♈	Established Strength	☉
6 „ P.	♉	Material Success	☽
9 „ S.	♊	Despair and Cruelty	♂
3 „ C.	♋	Abundance	☿
6 „ W.	♌	Victory	♃
9 „ P.	♍	Material Gain	♀
3 „ S.	♎	Sorrow	♄
6 „ C.	♏	Pleasure	☉
9 „ W.	♐	Great Strength	☽
3 „ P.	♑	Material Works	♂
6 „ S.	♒	Earned Success	☿
9 „ C.	♓	Material Happiness	♃

Being thus the Four Threes, Sixes, and Nines.

The first and third Decans follow the same order: Sunday beginning the First Decan of ♍ and in the Third Decans of ♊ and ♑.

The planets govern respectively Decans with the following Titles—

♄

1.	♌	Strife	5 of Wands.
2.	♎	Sorrow	3 „ Swords.
3.	♐	Oppression	10 „ Wands.
4.	♓	Abundant Success	8 „ Cups.
5.	♉	Success Unfulfilled	7 „ Pentacles.

Or in ♉ ♌ ♎ ♐ ♓ two wands: 1 each of the other suits.

♃

1.	♌	Victory	6 of Wands.
2.	♎	Rest from Strife	4 „ Swords.
3.	♑	Harmonious Change	2 „ Pentacles.
4.	♓	Material Happiness	9 „ Cups.
5.	♊	Shortened Force	8 „ Swords.

Or in ♊ ♌ ♎ ♑ ♓ two swords: 1 each of others.

♂

1.	♌	Valour	7 of Wands.
2.	♏	Loss in Pleasure	5 „ Cups.
3.	♑	Material Works	3 „ Pentacles.
4.	♓	Perfected Success	10 „ Cups.
5.	♈	Dominion	2 „ Wands.
6.	♊	Despair and Cruelty	9 „ Swords.

Or in ♈ ♊ ♌ ♏ ♑ ♓ 2 W. 2 C.: 1 each of others.

One more Decan than the others.

☉

1.	♍	Prudence	8 of Pentacles.
2.	♏	Pleasure	6 „ Cups.
3.	♑	Earthly Power	4 „ Pentacles.
4.	♈	Established Strength	3 „ Wands.
5.	♊	Ruin	10 „ Swords.

Or in ♈ ♊ ♍ ♏ ♑ 2 pentacles: 1 each of others.

♀

1.	♍	Material Gain	9 of Pentacles.
2.	♏	Illusionary Success	7 „ Cups.
3.	♒	Defeat	5 „ Swords.
4.	♈	Perfected Work	4 „ Wands.
5.	♋	Love	2 „ Cups.

Or in ♈ ♋ ♍ ♏ ♒ 2 Cups: 1 each of others.

276

☿

1.	♍	Wealth	10 of Pentacles.
2.	♐	Swiftness	8 „ Wands.
3.	♒	Earned Success	6 „ Swords.
4.	♉	Material Trouble	5 „ Pentacles.
5.	♋	Abundance	3 „ Cups.

Or in ♉ ♋ ♍ ♐ ♒ two Pentacles: 1 of each of the others.

☽

1.	♎	Peace Restored	2 of Swords.
2.	♐	Great Strength	9 „ Wands.
3.	♒	Unstable Effort	7 „ Swords.
4.	♉	Material Success	6 „ Pentacles.
5.	♋	Blended Pleasure	4 „ Cups.

Or in ♉ ♋ ♎ ♐ ♒ two Swords: 1 of each of the others.

There being thirty-six Decans and seven Planets, it follows that one of the latter must rule over one more Decan than the others. This is the Planet Mars, to which are allotted the last Decan of ♓, and the first of ♈, because the long cold of the winter requires a great energy to overcome it, and initiate spring.

And the beginning of the Decanates is from the royal Star of Leo, the great Star Cor Leonis: and therefore is the first Decan that of ♄ in ♌.

Here follow the general meanings of the small cards of the suits, as classified under the nine Sephiroth below Kether.

חכמה The Four Twos symbolize the Powers of the King and Queen just uniting and initiating the Force; but before the Prince and Princess are thoroughly brought into action. Therefore do they generally imply the initiation and fecundation of a thing.

בינה Realization of action owing to the Prince being produced. The central symbol on each card. Action definitely commenced for good or evil.

חסד Perfection, realization, completion: making a matter settled and fixed.

גבורה Opposition, strife and struggle: war; obstacle to the thing in hand. Ultimate success or failure is otherwise shewn.

תפארת Definite accomplishment. Thing carried out.

נצח Generally shew a force transcending the Material Plane: and is like unto a Crown; which, indeed, is powerful, but requireth one capable of wearing it. The Sevens then shew a possible result: which is dependent on the action then taken. They depend much on the symbols that accompany them.

הוד Solitary success: *i.e.* success in the matter for the time being: but not leading to much result apart from the thing itself.

יסוד Very great fundamental force. Executive power, because they restore a firm basis. Powerful for good or evil.

מלכות Fixed, culminated, complete Force, whether good or evil. The matter thoroughly and definitely determined. Ultimating Force.

Follow the particular descriptions of each of the thirty-six cards: with full meanings.

Decan-cards are always modified by the other symbols with which they are in contact.

XXI
THE LORD OF STRIFE

Five of Wands

Two White Radiant Angelic Hands issuant per nubes dexter and sinister. They are clasped together in the grip of the First Order, *i.e.* the four fingers of each right hand crooked into each other, the thumbs meeting above; and they hold, at the same time, by their centres, five wands or torches which are similar unto the wands of a Zelator Adeptus Minor. One wand is upright in the middle; the others cross each other.

Flames leap from the point of junction. Above the middle wand is the sign ♄, and below is that of ♌: thus representing the Decante. Violent strife and boldness, rashness, cruelty, violence, lust, desire, prodigality and generosity; depending on whether the card is well or ill dignified.

Geburah of ' (Quarrelling and fighting).

This Decan hath its beginning from the Royal Star of Leo: and unto it are allotted the two great Angels of the Schemhamphorash והויה and יליאל.

[The proper meaning of the small cards is to be found by making thorough meditation and harmony between these four symbols of each card. It will be seen that this is how the meanings have been done; but the advanced student can go beyond this rude working.]

XXII
THE LORD OF VICTORY

Six of Wands

Two hands in grip as the last, holding six wands crossed three and three. Flames issue from the point of junction. Above and below are short wands with flames issuing, surmounted respectively by the symbols of ♃ and ♌, representing the Decan.

Victory after strife: Love: pleasure gained by labour: carefulness, sociability and avoiding of strife, yet victory therein: also insolence, and pride of riches and success, etc. The whole dependent on the dignity.

Tiphareth of ' (Gain).

Hereunto are allotted the great Angels סיטאל and עלמיה of the Schemhamphorash.

XXIII
THE LORD OF VALOUR

Seven of Wands

Two hands holding by grip six wands, three crossed. A third hand issuing from a cloud at the lower part of the card, holding an upright wand which passes between the others. Flames leap from the point of junction. Above and below the central wand are the symbols of ♂ and ♌, representing the Decan.

Possible victory, depending on the energy and courage exercised; valour; opposition, obstacles and difficulties, yet courage to meet them; quarrelling, ignorance, pretence, and wrangling, and threatening; also victory in small and unimportant things: and influence upon subordinates.

Netzach of ' (Opposition, yet courage).

Therein rule the two great Angels מהשיה and ללהאל of the Schemhamphorash.

XXIV
THE LORD OF PRUDENCE

Eight of Pentacles

A WHITE Radiating Angelic Hand, issuing from a cloud, and grasping a branch of a rose tree, with four white roses thereon, which touch only the four lowermost Pentacles. No rosebuds even, but only leaves, touch the four uppermost disks. All the Pentacles are similar to that of the Ace, but without the Maltese cross and wings. They are arranged like the geomantic figure Populus. Above and below them are the symbols ☉ and ♍ for the Decan.

Over-careful in small things at the expense of great: "Penny wise and pound foolish": gain of ready money in small sums; mean; avaricious; industrious; cultivation of land; hoarding, lacking in enterprise.

Hod of ה (Skill: prudence: cunning).

Therein rule those mighty Angels אכאיה and כהתאל.

XXV
THE LORD OF MATERIAL GAIN

Nine of Pentacles

A WHITE Radiating Angelic Hand, holding a rose branch with nine white roses, each of which touches a Pentacle. The Pentacles are arranged thus ⋮·⋮ : and there are rosebuds on the branches as well as flowers. ♀ and ♍ above and below.

Complete realization of material gain, good, riches; inheritance; covetous; treasuring of goods; and sometimes theft and knavery. The whole according to dignity.

Yesod of ה (Inheritance, much increase of goods).

Herein those mighty Angels הזיאל and אלדיה have rule and dominion.

XXVI
THE LORD OF WEALTH

Ten of Pentacles

AN Angelic Hand, holding by the lower extremity a branch whose roses touch all the Pentacles. No buds, however, are shewn. The symbols of ☿ and ♍ are above and below.

The Pentacles are thus arranged ⋮·⋮ .

Completion of material gain and fortune; but nothing beyond: as it were, at the very pinnacle of success. Old age, slothfulness; great wealth, yet sometimes loss in part; heaviness; dullness of mind, yet clever and prosperous in money transactions.

Malkuth of ה (Riches and wealth).

Herein are לאויה and ההעיה set over this Decan as Angel Rulers.

XXVII

THE LORD OF PEACE RESTORED

Two of Swords or Pikes

Two crossed swords, like the air dagger of a Z.A.M, each held by a White Radiant Angelic Hand. Upon the point where the two cross is a rose of five petals, emitting white rays. At the top and bottom of the card are two small daggers, supporting respectively the symbol ♋ thus, and ♎ representing the Decanate.

Contradictory characters in the same nature, strength through suffering; pleasure after pain. Sacrifice and trouble, yet strength arising therefrom, symbolized by the position of the rose, as though the pain itself had brought forth beauty. Arrangement, peace restored; truce; truth and untruth; sorrow and sympathy. Aid to the weak; arrangement; justice, un-selfishness; also a tendency to repetition of affronts on being pardoned; injury when meaning well; given to petitions; also a want of tact, and asking question of little moment; talkative.

Chokmah of ׳. Quarrel made up, yet still some tension in relations: actions sometimes selfish, sometimes unselfish.

Herein rule the Great Angels יזלאל and מנהאל.

XXVIII

THE LORD OF SORROW

Three of Swords or Spears

Three White Radiating Angelic Hands, issuing from clouds, and holding three swords upright (as though the central sword had struck apart the two others, which were crossed in the preceding symbol): the central sword cuts asunder the rose of five petals, which in the previous symbol grew at the junction of the swords; its petals are falling, and no white rays issue from it.

Above and below the central sword are the symbols of ♄ and ♎.

Disruption, interruption, separation, quarrelling; sowing of discord and strife, mischief-making, sorrow and tears; yet mirth in Platonic pleasures; singing, faithfulness in promises, honesty in money transactions, selfish and dissipated, yet sometimes generous: deceitful in words and repetitions; the whole according to dignity.

Binah of ו (Unhappiness, sorrow, and tears).

Herein rule the Great Angels הריאל and הזמיה as Lords of the Decan.

XXIX
THE LORD OF REST FROM STRIFE

Four of Swords

TWO White Radiating Angelic Hands, each holding two swords; which four cross in the centre. The rose of five petals with white radiations is reinstated on the point of their intersection. Above and below, on the points of two small daggers, are ♃ and ♎, representing the Decanate.

Rest from sorrow; yet after and through it. Peace from and after war. Relaxation of anxiety. Quietness, rest, ease and plenty, yet after struggle. Goods of this life; abundance; modified by dignity as is usual.

Chesed of ו (Convalescence, recovery from sickness; change for the better).

Herein do לאויה and כליאל bear rule.

XXX
THE LORD OF LOSS IN PLEASURE

Five of Cups or Chalices

283

A WHITE Radiating Angelic Hand, holding lotuses or water-lilies, of which the flowers are falling right and left. Leaves only, and no buds, surmount them. These lotus stems ascend between the cups in the manner of a fountain, but no water flows therefrom; neither is there water in any of the cups, which are somewhat of the shape of the magical instrument of the Zelator Adeptus Minor.

Above and below are the symbols of ♂ and ♏ for the Decan.

Death, or end of pleasure: disappointment, sorrow and loss in those things from which pleasure is expected. Sadness, treachery, deceit; ill-will, detraction; charity and kindness ill requited; all kinds of anxieties and troubles from unsuspected and unexpected sources.

Geburah of ה (Disappointment in love, marriage broken off, unkindness of a friend; loss of friendship).

Herein rule לויה and פהליה.

XXXI
THE LORD OF PLEASURE

Six of Chalices

AN Angelic Hand, as before, holds a group of stems of water-lilies or lotuses, from which six flowers bend, one over each cup. From these flowers a white glistening water flows into the cups as from a fountain, but they are not yet full. Above and below are ☉ and ♏ referring to the Decan.

Commencement of steady increase, gain and pleasure; but commencement only. Also affront, detection, knowledge, and in some instances contention and strife arising from un-warranted self-assertion and vanity. Sometimes thankless and presumptuous; sometimes amiable and patient. According to dignity as usual.

Tiphareth of ה (Beginning of wish, happiness, success, or enjoyment).

Therein rule כלכאל and יייאל.

XXXII
THE LORD OF ILLUSIONARY SUCCESS

Seven of Chalices

THE seven cups are arranged as two descending triangles above a point: a hand, as usual, holds lotus stems which arise from the central lower cup. The hand is above this cup and below the middle one. With the exception of the central lower cup, each is overhung by a lotus flower, but no water falls from these into any of the cups, which are all quite empty. Above and below are the symbols of the Decanate ♀ and ♏.

Possible victory, but neutralized by the supineness of the person: illusionary success, deception in the moment of apparent victory. Lying, error, promises unfulfilled. Drunkenness, wrath, vanity. Lust, fornication, violence against women, selfish dissipation, deception in love and friendship. Often success gained, but not followed up. Modified as usual by dignity.

Netzach of ה (Lying, promises unfulfilled; illusion, deception, error; slight success at outset, not retained).

Herein the Angels מלהאל and חהויה rule.

XXXIII
THE LORD OF SWIFTNESS

Eight of Wands or Torches

FOUR White Radiating Angelic Hands (two proceeding from each side) issuant from clouds; clasped in two pairs in the centre with the grip of the First Order. They hold eight wands, crossed four with four. Flames issue from the point of junction. Surmounting the small wands with flames issuing down them, and placed in the centre at the top and bottom of the card respectively, are the symbols of ☿ and ♐ for the Decan.

Too much force applied too suddenly. Very rapid rush, but quickly passed and expended. Violent, but not lasting. Swiftness, rapidity, courage, boldness, confidence, freedom, warfare, violence; love of open air, field-sports, gardens and meadows. Generous, subtle, eloquent, yet somewhat untrustworthy; rapacious, insolent, oppressive. Theft and robbery. According to dignity.

Hod of ' (Hasty communications and messages; swiftness). Therein rule the Angels כתהיה and האאיה.

XXXIV
THE LORD OF GREAT STRENGTH

Nine of Wands or Torches

FOUR hands, as in the previous symbol, holding eight wands crossed four and four; but a fifth hand at the foot of the card holds another wand upright, which traverses the point of junction with the others: flames leap herefrom. Above and below are the symbols ♌ and ♐.

Tremendous and steady force that cannot be shaken. Herculean strength, yet sometimes scientifically applied. Great success, but with strife and energy. Victory, preceded by apprehension and fear. Health good, and recovery not in doubt. Generous, questioning and curious; fond of external appearances: intractable, obstinate.

Yesod of ' (Strength, power, health, recovery from sickness).

Herein rule the Angels ירהאל and שאהיה.

XXXV
THE LORD OF OPPRESSION
Ten of Wands

FOUR hands holding eight wands crossed as before. A fifth hand holding two wands upright, which traverses the junction of the others. Flames issuant. ♄ and ♐.

Cruel and overbearing force and energy, but applied only to material and selfish ends. Sometimes shows failure in a matter, and the opposition too strong to be controlled; arising from the person's too great selfishness at the beginning. Ill-will, levity, lying, malice, slander, envy, obstinacy; swiftness in evil and deceit, if ill dignified. Also generosity, disinterestedness and self-sacrifice, when well dignified.

Malkuth of ☉ (Cruelty, malice, revenge, injustice).

Therein rule רייאל and אומאל.

XXXVI
THE LORD OF HARMONIOUS CHANGE
Two of Disks or Pentacles

TWO wheels, disks or pentacles, similar to that of the Ace. They are united by a green-and-gold serpent, bound about them like a figure of 8. It holds its tail in its mouth. A White Radiant Angelic Hand holds the centre of the whole. No roses enter into this card. Above and below are the symbols of ♃ and ♑. It is a revolving symbol.

The harmony of change, alternation of gain and loss; weakness and strength; everchanging occupation; wandering, discontented with any fixed condition of things; now elated, then melancholy; industrious, yet unreliable; fortunate through prudence of management, yet sometimes unaccountably foolish; alternatively talkative and suspicious. Kind, yet wavering and inconsistent. Fortunate in journeying. Argumentative.

Chokmah of ה (Pleasant change, visit to friends).

Herein the Angels לכבאל and ושריה have rule.

XXXVII
THE LORD OF MATERIAL WORKS

Three of Pentacles

A WHITE-WINGED Angelic Hand, as before, holding a branch of a rose tree, of which two white rosebuds touch and surmount the topmost Pentacle. The Pentacles are arranged in an equilateral triangle. Above and below the symbols ♂ and ♑.

Working and constructive force, building up, creation, erection; realization and increase of material things; gain in commercial transactions, rank; increase of substance, influence, cleverness in business, selfishness. Commencement of matters to be established later. Narrow and prejudiced. Keen in matters of gain; sometimes given to seeking after impossibilities.

Binah of ה (Business, paid employment, commercial transaction).

Herein are יחויה and להחיה Angelic Rulers.

XXXVIII
THE LORD OF EARTHLY POWER

Four of Pentacles

A HAND holding a branch of a rose tree, but without flowers or buds, save that in the centre is one fully blown white rose. Pentacles are disposed as on the points of a square; a rose in its centre. Symbols ☉ and ♑ above and below to represent the Decan.

Assured material gain: success, rank, dominion, earthly power, completed but leading to nothing beyond. Prejudicial, covetous, suspicious, careful and orderly, but discontented. Little enterprise or originality. According to dignity as usual.

Chesed of ה (Gain of money or influence: a present).

Herein do כוזיה and מנדאל bear rule.

XXXIX
THE LORD OF DEFEAT

Five of Swords

Two Rayed Angelic Hands each holding two swords nearly upright, but falling apart of each other, right and left of the card. A third hand holds a sword upright in the centre as though it had disunited them. The petals of the rose, which in the four had been reinstated in the centre, are torn asunder and falling. Above and below are ♀ and ≈ for Decan.

Contest finished and decided against the person; failure, defeat, anxiety, trouble, poverty, avarice, grieving after gain, laborious, unresting; loss and vileness of nature; malicious, slanderous, lying, spiteful and tale-bearing. A busybody and separator of friends, hating to see peace and love between others. Cruel, yet cowardly, thankless and unreliable. Clever and quick in thought and speech. Feelings of pity easily roused, but unenduring.

Geburah of ו (Defeat, loss, malice, spite, slander, evil-speaking).

Herein the Angels אניאל and חעמיה bear rule.

XL
THE LORD OF EARNED SUCCESS

Six of Swords

Two hands, as before, each holding two swords which cross in the centre. Rose re-established thereon. ☿ and ≈

above and below, supported on the points of two short daggers or swords.

Success after anxiety and trouble; self-esteem, beauty, conceit, but sometimes modesty therewith; dominance, patience, labour, etc.

Tiphareth of ו (Labour, work, journey by water).

Ruled by the Great Angels ההעאל and ייאל.

XLI
THE LORD OF UNSTABLE EFFORT

Seven of Swords

TWO Angelic Radiating Hands as before, each holding three swords. A third hand holds up a single sword in the centre. The points of all the swords *just touch* each other, the central sword not altogether dividing them.

The Rose of the previous symbols of this suit is held up by the same hand which holds the central sword: as if the victory were at its disposal. Symbols of ♉ and ♒.

Partial success. Yielding when victory is within grasp, as if the last reserves of strength were used up. Inclination to lose when on the point of gaining, through not continuing the effort. Love of abundance, fascinated by display, given to compliments, affronts and insolences, and to spy upon others. Inclined to betray confidences, not always intentionally. Rather vacillatory and unreliable.

Netzach of ו (Journey by land: in character untrustworthy).

Herein rule the Great Angels ההההאל and מיכאל.

XLII
THE LORD OF ABANDONED SUCCESS

Eight of Chalices

290

A WHITE Radiating Angelic Hand, holding a group of stems of lotuses or water-lilies. There are only two flowers shown, which bend over the two central cups, pouring into them a white water which fills them and runs over into the three lowest, which later are not yet filled. The three ՙՍՙՍՙՍ uppermost are quite empty. At the top and bottom of ՙՍ ՙՍ ՙՍ the card are symbols ♄ and ♓.

Temporary success, but without further results. Thing thrown aside as soon as gained. Not lasting, even in the matter in hand. Indolence in success. Journeying from place to place. Misery and repining without cause. Seeking after riches. Instability.

Hod of ה (Success abandoned; decline of interest).

The Angels ruling are וליה and ילהיה.

XLIII
THE LORD OF MATERIAL HAPPINESS
Nine of Chalices

A WHITE Radiant Angelic Hand, issuing from a cloud holding lotus or water-lilies, one flower of which overhangs each cup; from it a white water pours. Cups are arranged in three rows of 3. ♃ and ♓ above and below.

Complete and perfect realization of pleasure and happiness, almost perfect; self-praise, vanity, conceit, much talking of self, yet kind and lovable, and may be self-denying therewith. High-minded, not easily satisfied with small and limited ideas. Apt to be maligned through too much self-assumption. A good and generous, but sometimes foolish nature.

Yesod of ה (Complete success, pleasure and happiness, wishes fulfilled).

Therein rule the Angels סאליה and עריאל.

XLIV
THE LORD OF PERFECTED SUCCESS

Ten of Cups or Chalices

HAND, as usual, holding bunch of water-lilies or lotuses, whose flowers pour a white water into all the cups, which *all run over.* The uppermost cup is held sideways by a hand, and pours water into the left-hand upper cup. A single lotus flower surmounts the top cup, and is the source of the water that fills it. Above and below the symbols ♂ and ♓.

Permanent and lasting success and happiness, because inspired from above. Not so sensual as "Lord of Material Happiness," yet almost more truly happy. Pleasure, dissipation, debauchery, quietness, peacemaking. Kindness, pity, generosity, wantonness, waste, etc., according to dignity.

Malkuth of ה (Matter settled: complete good fortune).

Herein the Great Angels עשליה and מיהאל rule.

[This is not such a good card as stated. It represents boredom, and quarrelling arising therefrom; disgust springing from too great luxury. In particular it represents drug-habits, the sottish excess of pleasure and the revenge of nature.]

XLV
THE LORD OF DOMINION

Two of Wands

A WHITE Radiating Angelic hand, issuing from clouds, and grasping two crossed wands. Flames issue from the point of junction. On two small wands above and below, with flames of five issuing therefrom, are the symbols of ♂ and ♈ for the Decan.

Strength, domination, harmony of rule and of justice. Boldness, courage, fierceness, shamelessness, revenge, resolution, generous, proud, sensitive, ambitious, refined, restless, turbulent, sagacious withal, yet unforgiving and obstinate.

Chokmah of י (Influence over others, authority, power, dominion).

Therein the Angels והואל and דכיאל bear rule.

XLVI
THE LORD OF ESTABLISHED STRENGTH

Three of Wands

A WHITE Radiating Angelic Hand, as before, issuing from clouds and grasping three wands in the centre (two crossed, the third upright). Flames issue from the point of junction. Above and below are the symbols ☉ and ♈.

Established force, strength, realization of hope. Completion of labour. Success after struggle. Pride, nobility, wealth, power, conceit. Rude self-assumption and insolence. Generosity, obstinacy, etc.

Binah of י (Pride, arrogance, self-assertion).

Herein rule the Angels ההשיה and עממיה.

[This card is much better than as described.]

XLVII
THE LORD OF PERFECTED WORK

Four of Wands

TWO White Radiating Angelic Hands, as before, issuing from clouds right and left of the card and clasped in the centre with the grip of the First Order, holding four wands or torches crossed. Flames issue from the point of junction. Above and below are two small flaming wands, with the symbols of ♀ and ♈ representing the Decan.

Perfection or completion of a thing built up with trouble and labour. Rest after labour, subtlety, cleverness, beauty, mirth, success in completion. Reasoning faculty, conclusions drawn from previous knowledge. Unreadiness, unreliable and unsteady through over-anxiety and hurriedness of action. Graceful in manner, at times insincere, etc.

Chesed of ' (Settlement, arrangement, completion).

Herein are כבאאל and כיתאל Angelic rulers.

XLVIII
THE LORD OF MATERIAL TROUBLE

Five of Pentacles

A WHITE Radiant Angelic Hand issuing from clouds, and holding a branch of the white rose tree, but from which the roses are falling, and leaving no buds behind. Five Pentacles similar to the Ace. Above and below are ☿ and ♉.

Loss of money or position. Trouble about material things. Labour, toil, land cultivation; building, knowledge and acuteness of earthly things, poverty, carefulness, kindness; sometimes money regained after severe toil and labour. Unimaginative, harsh, stern, determined, obstinate.

Geburah of ה (Loss of profession, loss of money, monetary anxiety).

Herein the angels מבהיה and פניאל rule.

XLIX
THE LORD OF MATERIAL SUCCESS

Six of Pentacles

A WHITE Radiant Angelic Hand holding a rose branch with white roses and buds, each of which touches a Pentacle. Pentacles are arranged in two columns of three each ⁝⁝. Above and below are the symbols ♉ and ♉ of the Decan.

Success and gain in material undertakings. Power, influence, rank, nobility, rule over the people. Fortunate, successful, liberal and just.

If ill dignified, may be purse-proud, insolent from excess, or prodigal.

Tiphareth of ה (Success in material things, prosperity in business).

Herein rule the Angels כממיה and יילאל.

L
THE LORD OF SUCCESS UNFULFILLED

Seven of Pentacles

A WHITE Radiating Angelic Hand issuing from a cloud, and holding a white rose branch. Seven Pentacles arranged like the geomantic figure Rubeus. There are only five buds, which overhang, but do not touch the five uppermost Pentacles. Above and below are the Decan symbols, ♄ and ♉ respectively.

Promises of success unfulfilled. (Shewn, as it were, by the fact that the rosebuds do not come to anything.) Loss of apparently promising fortune. Hopes deceived and crushed. Disappointment, misery, slavery, necessity and baseness. A cultivator of land, and yet a loser thereby. Sometimes it denotes slight and isolated gains with no fruits resulting therefrom, and of no further account, though seeming to promise well.

Netzach of ה (Unprofitable speculations and employments; little gain for much labour).

Therein הרתאל and מצראל are ruling Angels.

295

LI

THE LORD OF SHORTENED FORCE

Eight of Swords

FOUR White Radiant Angelic Hands issuing from clouds, each holding two swords, points upwards; all the points touch near the top of the card. Hands issue, two at each bottom angle of the card. The pose of the other sword symbols is re-established in the centre. Above and below are the Decan symbols ♃ and ♊.

Too much force applied to small things: too much attention to detail at the expense of the principal and more important points. When ill dignified, these qualities produce malice, pettiness, and domineering characteristics. Patience in detail of study; great care in some things, counterbalanced by equal disorder in others. Impulsive; equally fond of giving or receiving money or presents; generous, clever, acute, selfish and without strong feeling of affection. Admires wisdom, yet applies it to small and unworthy objects.

Hod of ו (Narrow, restricted, petty, a prison).

Therein rule the Angels ומבאל and יההאל.

LII

THE LORD OF DESPAIR AND CRUELTY

Nine of Swords

FOUR Hands, as in the preceding figure, hold eight swords nearly upright, but with the points falling away from each other. A fifth hand holds a ninth sword upright in the centre, as if it had struck them asunder. No rose at all is shewn, as if it were not merely cut asunder, but utterly destroyed. Above and below are the Decan symbols ♂ and ♊.

Despair, cruelty, pitilessness, malice, suffering, want, loss, misery. Burden, oppression, labour, subtlety and craft, dishonesty, lying and slander.

Yet also obedience, faithfulness, patience, unselfishness, etc. According to dignity.

Yesod of ו (Illness, suffering, malice, cruelty, pain).

Therein do עכואל and מהיאל bear rule.

LIII
THE LORD OF RUIN

Ten of Swords

FOUR Hands holding eight swords, as in the preceding symbol; the points falling away from each other. Two hands hold two swords crossed in the centre, as though their junction had disunited the others. No rose, flower or bud, is shewn. Above and below are ☉ and ♊, representing the Decan.

Almost a worse symbol than the Nine of Swords. Undisciplined, warring force, complete disruption and failure. Ruin of all plans and projects. Disdain, insolence and impertinence, yet mirth and jollity therewith. A marplot, loving to overthrow the happiness of others; a repeater of things; given to much unprofitable speech, and of many words. Yet clever, eloquent, etc., according to dignity.

Malkuth of ו (Ruin, death, defeat, disruption).

Herein the Angels דמביה and מכסאל reign.

LIV
THE LORD OF LOVE

Two of Chalices

A WHITE Radiant Hand, issuant from the lower part of the card from a cloud, holds lotuses. A lotus flower rises above water, which occupies the lower part of the card rising above the hand. From this flower rises a stem, terminating near the top of the card in another lotus, from which flows a sparkling white water, as from a fountain. Crossed on the stem just beneath are two dolphins, Argent and Or, on to which the water falls, and from which it pours in full streams, like jets of gold and silver, into two cups; which in their turn overflow, flooding the lower part of the card. ♀ and ♋ above and below.

Harmony of masculine and feminine united. Harmony, pleasure, mirth, subtlety: but if ill dignified—folly, dissipation, waste, silly actions.

Chokmah of ה (Marriage, love, pleasure).

Therein rule the Angels אועאל and הבויה.

LV

THE LORD OF ABUNDANCE

Three of Chalices

A WHITE Radiating Hand, as before, holds a group of lotuses or water-lilies, from which two flowers rise on either side of, and overhanging the top cup; pouring into it the white water. Flowers in the same way pour white water into the lower cups. All the cups overflow; the topmost into the two others, and these upon the lower part of the card. Cups are arranged in an erect equilateral triangle. ☿ and ♋ above and below.

Abundance, plenty, success, pleasure, sensuality, passive success, good luck and fortune; love, gladness, kindness, liberality.

Binah of ה (Plenty, hospitality, eating and drinking, pleasure, dancing, new clothes, merriment).

Therein the Angels ראהאל and יבמיה are lords.

LVI
THE LORD OF BLENDED PLEASURE

Four of Chalices

FOUR cups: the two upper overflowing into the two lower, which do not overflow. An Angelic Hand grasps a branch of lotus, from which ascends a stem bearing one flower at the top of the card, from which the white water flows into the two upper cups. From the centre two leaves pass right and left, making, as it were, a cross between the four cups. Above and below are the symbols ♌ and ♋ for the Decan.

Success or pleasure approaching their end. A stationary period in happiness, which may, or may not, continue. It does not mean love and marriage so much as the previous symbol. It is too passive a symbol to represent perfectly complete happiness. Swiftness, hunting and pursuing. Acquisition by contention: injustice sometimes; some drawbacks to pleasure implied.

Chesed of ה (Receiving pleasure or kindness from others, but some discomfort therewith).

Therein rule the great Angels הייאל and מומיה.

BRIEF MEANING OF TWENTY-TWO KEYS

0 IF the question refers to spiritual matters, the Fool means idea, thought, spirituality, that which endeavours to transcend Earth. But if question is material, it means folly, stupidity, eccentricity, or even mania.

1 Skill, wisdom, adaptation, craft, cunning, or occult wisdom or power.

2 Change, alternation, increase and decrease, fluctuation; whether for good or evil depends on the dignity.

3 Beauty, happiness, pleasure, success. But with very bad dignity it means luxury, dissipation.

4 War, conquest, victory, strife, ambition.

5 Divine wisdom, manifestation, explanation, teaching, occult force voluntarily invoked.

6 Inspiration (passive, mediumistic), motive power, action.

7 Triumph, victory, health (sometimes unstable).

8 Eternal justice. Strength and force, but arrested as in act of judgment. May mean law, trial, etc.

9 Wisdom from on high. Active divine inspiration. Sometimes "unexpected current."

10 Good fortune, happiness (within bounds). Intoxication of success.

11 Courage, strength, fortitude, power passing on to action. Obstinacy.

12 Enforced sacrifice, punishment, loss, fatal and not voluntary, suffering.

13 Time, age, transformation, change involuntary (as opposed to 18, ♓). Or death, destruction (only latter with special cards). [Specially, a sudden and quite unexpected change.]

14 Combination of forces, realization, action (material effect, good or evil).

15 Materiality, material force, material temptation, obsession.

16 Ambition, fighting, war, courage, or destruction, danger, fall, ruin.

17 Hope, faith, unexpected help. Or dreaminess, deceived hope, etc.

18 Dissatisfaction, voluntary change. Error, lying, falsity, deception. This card is very sensitive to dignity.

19 Glory, gain, riches. With *very* evil cards it means arrogance, display, vanity.

20 Final decision, judgment, sentence, determination of a matter without appeal, *on its plane.*

21 The matter itself. Synthesis, world, kingdom. Usually denotes actual subject of question, and therefore depends entirely on accompanying cards.

[This table is very unsatisfactory. Each card must be most carefully meditated, taking all its correspondences, and a clear idea formed.]

Princes and Queens shew almost always actual men and women connected with the matter.

But the Kings (Knights) sometime represent coming or going of a matter, according as they face.

The Princesses shew opinions, thoughts, ideas, either in harmony with or opposed to, the subject.

A Majority of Wands		Energy, opposition, quarrel.
„	Cups	Pleasure, merriment.
„	Swords	Trouble, sadness, sickness, death.
„	Pentacles	Business, money, possessions.
„	Keys	Strong forces beyond the Querent's control.
„	Court Cards	Society, meetings of many persons.
„	Aces	Strength generally. Aces are always strong cards.

4 Aces	Great power and force.
3 Aces	Riches, success.
4 Kings (Knights)	Swiftness, rapidity.
3 „ „	Unexpected meetings. Knights, in general, shew news.
4 Queens	Authority, influence.
3 Queens	Powerful friends.
4 Princes	Meetings with the great.
3 Princes	Rank and honour.
4 Princesses	New ideas or plans.
3 Princesses	Society of the young.
4 Tens	Anxiety, responsibility.
3 Tens	Buying and selling (commerce).
4 Nines	Added responsibilities.
3 Nines	Much correspondence.
4 Eights	Much news.
3 Eights	Much journeying.
4 Sevens	Disappointments.
3 Sevens	Treaties and compacts.

4 Sixes	Pleasure.
3 Sixes	Gain, success.
4 Fives	Order, regularity.
3 Fives	Quarrels, fights.
4 Fours	Rest, peace.
3 Fours	Industry.
4 Threes	Resolution, determination.
3 Threes	Deceit.
4 Twos	Conferences, conversations.
3 Twos	Reorganization, recommendation.

OF THE DIGNITIES

A CARD is strong or weak, well dignified or ill dignified, according to the cards next to it on either side.

Cards of the same suit on either side strengthen it greatly, for good or evil according to their nature.

Cards of opposite natures on either side weaken it greatly, for either good or evil.

Swords are inimical to Pentacles.

Wands are inimical to Cups.

Swords are friendly with Cups and Wands.

Wands are friendly with Swords and Pentacles.

If a card fall between two other which are mutually contrary, it is not much affected by either.

A METHOD OF DIVINATION BY THE TAROT

[This method is that given to students of the grade Adept Adeptus Minor in the R. R. et A. C. But it has been revised and improved, while certain safeguards have been introduced in order to make its abuse impossible.—O.M.]

303

1 THE Significator.

Choose a card to represent the Querent, using your knowledge or judgment of his character rather than dwelling on his physical characteristics.

2 Take the cards in your left hand. In the right hand hold the wand over them, and say: I invoke thee, I A O, that thou wilt send H R U, the great Angel that is set over the operations of this Secret Wisdom, to lay his hand invisibly upon these consecrated cards of art, that thereby we may obtain true knowledge of hidden things, to the glory of thine ineffable Name. Amen.

3 Hand the cards to Querent, and bid him think of the question attentively, and cut.

4 Take the cards as cut, and hold as for dealing.

First Operation

This shows the situation of the Querent at the time when he consults you.

1 The pack being in front of you, cut, and place the top half to the left.

2 Cut each pack again to the left.

3 These four stack represent I H V H, from right to left.

4 Find the Significator. It be in the ' pack, the question refers to work, business, etc.; if in the ה pack, to love, marriage, or pleasure; if in the ו pack, to trouble, loss, scandal, quarrelling, etc.; if in the ה pack, to money, goods, and such purely material matters.

5 Tell the Querent what he has come for: if wrong, abandon the divination.

6 If right, spread out the pack containing the Significator, face upwards.

Count the cards from him, in the direction in which he faces.

The counting should include the card from which you count.

For Knights, Queens and Princes, count 4.

For Princesses, count 7.

For Aces, count 11.

For small cards, count according to the number.

For trumps, count 3 for the elemental trumps; 9 for the planetary trumps; 12 for the Zodiacal trumps.

Make a "story" of these cards. This story is that of the beginning of the affair.

7 Pair the cards on either side of the Significator, then those outside them, and so on. Make another "story," which should fill in the details omitted in the first.

8 If this story is not quite accurate, do not be discouraged. Perhaps the Querent himself does not know everything. But the main lines ought to be laid down firmly, with correctness, or the divination should be abandoned.

Second Operation
Development of the Question

1 Shuffle, invoke suitably, and let Querent cut as before.

2 Deal cards into twelve stacks, for the twelve astrological houses of heaven.

3 Make up your mind in which stack you ought to find the Significator, *e.g.* in the seventh house if the question concerns marriage, and so on.

4 Examine this chosen stack. If the Significator is not there, try some cognate house. On a second failure, abandon the divination.

5 Read the stack counting and pairing as before.

Third Operation

Further Development of the Question

1 Shuffle, etc., as before.

2 Deal cards into twelve stacks for the twelve signs of the Zodiac.

3 Divine the proper stack and proceed as before.

Fourth Operation

Penultimate Aspects of the Question

1 Shuffle, etc., as before.

2 Find the Significator: set him upon the table; let the thirty-six cards following form a ring round him.

3 Count and pair as before.

[Note that the nature of each Decan is shewn by the small card attributed to it, and by the symbols given in Liber DCCLXXVII, cols. 149–151.]

Fifth Operation

Final Result

1 Shuffle, etc., as before.

2 Deal into ten packs in the form of the Tree of Life.

3 Make up your mind where the Significator should be, as before; but failure does not here necessarily imply that the divination has gone astray.

4 Count and pair as before.

[Note that one cannot tell at what part of the divination the present time occurs. Usually Op. 1 seems to indicate the past history of the question; but not always so. Experience will teach. Sometimes a new current of high help may show the moment of consultation.

I may add that in material matters this method is extremely valuable. I have been able to work out the most complex problems in minute detail. O.M.]

LIBER

ΘΕΣΑΥΡΟΥ ἘΙΔΩΛΩΝ

SVB FIGVRÂ
DCCCCLXIII
(CMLXIII)

צטרת צטרה

Corona, Corolla;
Sic vocatur Malchuth
quando ascendit usque
ad Kether.
The Kabbala.

(The Probationer should learn by heart the chapter
corresponding to the Zodiacal Sign that was rising at
his birth; or, if this be unknown, the chapter "The
Twelvefold Unification of God.")

93	108	123	138	153	168	1	16	31	46	61	76	91
107	122	137	152	167	13	15	30	45	60	75	90	92
121	136	151	166	12	14	29	44	59	74	89	104	106
135	150	165	11	26	28	43	58	73	88	103	105	120
149	164	10	25	27	42	57	72	87	102	117	119	134
163	9	24	39	41	56	71	86	101	116	118	133	148
8	23	38	40	55	70	85	100	115	130	132	147	162
22	37	52	54	69	84	99	114	129	131	146	161	7
36	51	53	68	83	98	113	128	143	145	160	6	21
50	65	67	82	97	112	127	142	144	159	5	20	35
64	66	81	96	111	126	141	156	158	4	19	34	49
78	80	95	110	125	140	155	157	3	18	33	48	63
79	94	109	124	139	154	169	2	17	32	47	62	77

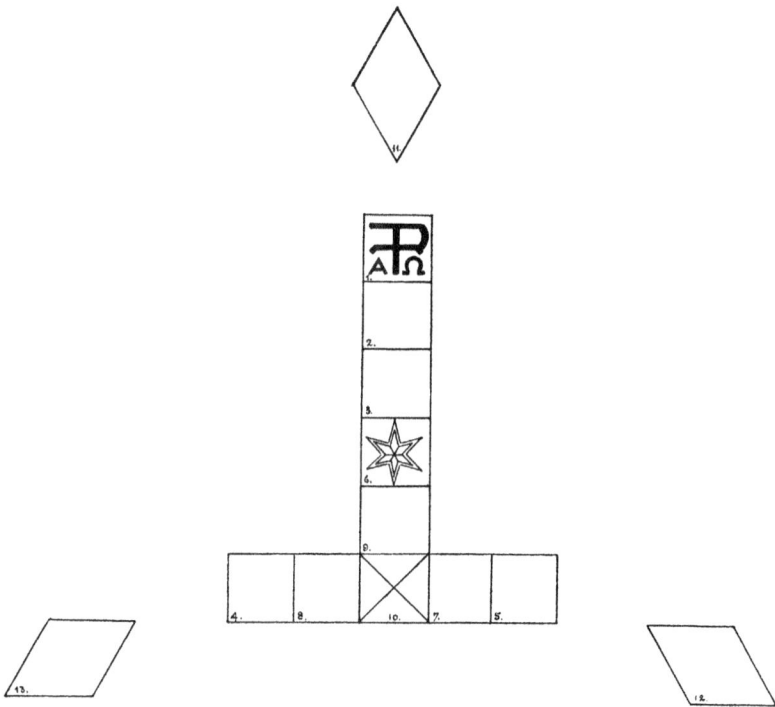

FIG. I.

Triangle of the Universe.

Three veils of the Negative—not yellow: not red; not blue. but therefore symbolised by the "flashing" colours of these three; purple (11): emerald (12) and orange (13). Within their triangle of Yonis is the Lingam touching and filling it. Positive, as they are negative; in the Queen Scale of colour, as they are in the King Scale. Ten are the Emanations of Unity, the parts of that Lingam, in Kether, TARO = 78 = 6 × 13, the Influence of that Unity in the Macrocosrn (Hexagram). The centre of the whole figure is Tiphereth, where is a golden Sun of six rays. Note the reflection of the Yonis to the triad about Malkulh. Also note that the triangle of Yonis is hidden, even as their links are secret. From Malkuth depends the Greek Cross of the Zodiac and their Spiritual Centre (Fig. 2). For Colour Scales see 777.

A∴ A∴

Publication in Class A.

A NOTE UPON LIBER DCCCCLXIII

1 Let the student recite this book, particularly the 169 adorations, unto his Star as it ariseth.

2 Let him seek out diligently in the sky his Star; let him travel thereunto in his Shell; let him adore it unceasingly from its rising even unto its setting by the right adorations, with chants that shall be harmonious therewith.

3 Let him rock himself to and fro in adoration; let him spin around his own axis in adoration; let him leap up and down in adoration.

4 Let him inflame himself in the adoration, speeding from slow to fast, until he can no more.

5 This also shall be sung in open places, as heaths, mountains, woods, and by streams and upon islands.

6 Moreover, ye shall build you fortified places in great cities; caverns and tombs shall be made glad with your praise.

7 Amen.

THE TREASURE-HOUSE OF IMAGES

Here beginneth the Book of
the Meditations on the
Twelvefold Adora-
tion, and the
Unity of
GOD.

𝕿𝖍𝖊 𝕮𝖍𝖆𝖕𝖙𝖊𝖗 𝖐𝖓𝖔𝖜𝖓 𝖆𝖘
𝕿𝖍𝖊 𝕻𝖊𝖗𝖈𝖊𝖕𝖙𝖎𝖔𝖓 𝖔𝖋 𝕲𝖔𝖉
𝖙𝖍𝖆𝖙 𝖎𝖘 𝖗𝖊𝖛𝖊𝖆𝖑𝖊𝖉 𝖚𝖓𝖙𝖔 𝖒𝖆𝖓 𝖋𝖔𝖗 𝖆 𝖘𝖓𝖆𝖗𝖊

◆ ◆ ◆ ◆ ◆   I   ◆ ◆ ◆ ◆ ◆
◆ ◆ ◆ ◆ ◆ adore ◆ ◆ ◆ ◆ ◆
◆ ◆ ◆ ◆ Thee by the ◆ ◆ ◆ ◆
◆ ◆ ◆ ◆ Twelvefold Snare ◆ ◆ ◆ ◆
◆ ◆ ◆ ◆ and by the Unity thereof. ◆ ◆ ◆ ◆

000 In the Beginning there was Naught, and Naught spake unto Naught saying: Let us beget on the Nakedness of Our Nothingness the Limitless, Eternal, Identical, and United: And without will, intention, thought, word, desire, or deed, it was so.

00 Then in the depths of Nothingness hovered the Limitless, as a raven in the night; seeing naught, hearing naught, and understanding naught: neither was it seen, nor heard, nor understood; for as yet Countenance beheld not Countenance.

0 And as the Limitless stretched forth its wings, an un-extended unextendable Light became; colourless, formless, conditionless, effluent, naked, and essential, as a crystalline dew of creative effulgence; and fluttering as a dove betwixt Day and Night, it vibrated forth a lustral Crown of Glory.

1 And out of the blinding whiteness of the Crown grew an Eye, like unto an egg of an humming-bird cherished on a platter of burnished silver.

2 Thus I beheld Thee, O my God, the lid of whose Eye is as the Night of Chaos, and the pupil thereof as the marshalled order of the spheres.

3 For, I am but as a blind man, who wandering through the noontide perceiveth not the loveliness of day; and even as he whose eyes are unenlightened beholdeth not the greatness of this world in the depths of a starless night, so am I who am not able to search the unfathomable depths of Thy Wisdom.

4 For what am I that I durst look upon Thy Countenance, purblind one of small understanding that I am, blindly groping through the night of mine ignorance like unto a little maggot hid in the dark depths of a corrupted corpse?

5 Therefore, O my God, fashion me into a five-pointed star of ruby burning beneath the foundations of Thy Unity, that I may mount the pillar of Thy Glory, and be lost in adoration of the triple Unity of Thy Godhead, I beseech Thee, O Thou who art to me as the Finger of Light thrust through the black clouds of Chaos; I beseech Thee, O my God, hearken Thou unto my cry!

6 Then, O my God, am I not risen as the sun that eateth up ocean as a golden lion that feedeth on a blue-grey wolf? So shall I become one with Thy Beauty, worn upon Thy breast as the Centre of a Sixfold Star of ruby and of sapphire.

7 Yea, O God, gird Thou me upon Thy thigh as a warrior girdeth his sword! Smite my acuteness into the earth, and as a sower casteth his seed into the furrows of the plough, do Thou beget upon me these adorations of Thy Unity, O My Conqueror!

8 And Thou shalt carry me upon Thine hip, O Thou flashing God, as a black mother of the South Country carrieth her babe. Whence I shall reach my lips to Thy pap, and sucking out Thy stars, shed them in these adorations upon the Earth.

9 Moreover, O God my God, Thou who hast cloven me with Thine amethystine Phallus, with Thy Phallus adamantine, with Thy Phallus of Gold and Ivory! thus am I cleft in twain as two halves of a child that is split asunder by the sword of the eunuchs, and mine adorations are divided, and one contendeth against his brother. Unite Thou me even as a split tree that closeth itself again upon the axe, that my song of praise unto Thee may be One Song!

10 For I am Thy chosen Virgin, O my God! Exalt Thou me unto the throne of the Mother, unto the Garden of Supernal Dew, unto the Unutterable Sea!

Amen,

and Amen of Amen,

and Amen of Amen of Amen,

and Amen of Amen of Amen of Amen.

♈ The Chapter known as The Twelvefold Affirmation of God and the Unity thereof

```
✦ ✦ ✦ ✦ ✦       I       ✦ ✦ ✦ ✦ ✦
✦ ✦ ✦ ✦ ✦     adore     ✦ ✦ ✦ ✦ ✦
✦ ✦ ✦ ✦   Thee by the   ✦ ✦ ✦ ✦
✦ ✦ ✦ ✦ Twelve Affirmations ✦ ✦ ✦ ✦
✦ ✦ ✦ ✦ and by the Unity thereof. ✦ ✦ ✦ ✦
```

1 O Thou snow-clad volcan of scarlet fire, Thou flame-crested pillar of fury! Yea, as I approach Thee, Thou departest from me like unto a wisp of smoke blown forth from the window of my house.

2 O Thou summer-land of eternal joy, Thou rapturous garden of flowers! Yea, as I gather Thee, my harvest is but as a drop of dew shimmering in the golden cup of the crocus.

3 O Thou throbbing music of life and death, Thou rhythmic harmony of the world! Yea, as I listen to the echo of Thy voice, my rapture is but as the whisper of the wings of a butterfly.

4 O Thou burning tempest of blinding sand, Thou whirlwind from the depths of darkness! Yea, as I struggle through Thee, through Thee, my strength is but as a dove's down floating forth on the purple nipples of the storm.

5 O Thou crownèd giant among great giants, Thou crimson-sworded soldier of war! Yea, as I battle with Thee, Thou masterest me as a lion that slayeth a babe that is cradled in lilies.

6 O Thou shadowy vista of Darkness, Thou cryptic Book of the fir-clad hills! Yea, as I search the key of Thy house I find my hope but as a rushlight sheltered in the hands of a little child.

7 O Thou great labour of the Firmament, Thou tempest-tossed roaring of the Aires! Yea, as I sink in the depths of

Thine affliction, mine anguish is but as the smile on the lips of a sleeping babe.

8 O Thou depths of the Inconceivable, Thou cryptic, unutterable God! Yea, as I attempt to understand Thee, my wisdom is but as an abacus in the lap of an aged man.

9 O Thou transfigured dream of blinding light, Thou beatitude of wonderment! Yea, as I behold Thee, mine understanding is but as the glimpse of a rainbow through a storm of blinding snow.

10 O Thou steel-girdered mountain of mountains, Thou crested summit of Majesty! Yea, as I climb Thy grandeur, I find I have but surmounted one mote of dust floating in a beam of Thy Glory.

11 O Thou Empress of Light and of Darkness, Thou pourer-forth of the stars of night! Yea, as I gaze upon Thy Countenance, mine eyes are as the eyes of a blind man smitten by a torch of burning fire.

12 O Thou crimson gladness of the midnight, Thou flamingo North of brooding light! Yea, as I rise up before Thee, my joy is but as a raindrop smitten through by an arrow of the Western Sun.

13 O Thou golden Crown of the Universe, Thou diadem of dazzling brightness! Yea, as I burn up before Thee, my light is but as a falling star seen between the purple fingers of the Night.

O Glory be unto Thee through all Time
and though all Space: Glory,
and Glory upon Glory,
Everlastingly. Amen,
and Amen, and
Amen.

♉ The Chapter known as The Twelvefold Renunciation of God and the Unity thereof

◆ ◆ ◆ ◆ ◆   I   ◆ ◆ ◆ ◆ ◆
◆ ◆ ◆ ◆ ◆ adore ◆ ◆ ◆ ◆ ◆
◆ ◆ ◆ ◆ Thee by the ◆ ◆ ◆ ◆
◆ ◆ ◆ ◆ Twelve Renunciations ◆ ◆ ◆ ◆
◆ ◆ ◆ ◆ and by the Unity thereof. ◆ ◆ ◆ ◆

1 O my God, Thou mighty One, Thou Creator of all things, I renounce unto Thee the kisses of my mistress, and the murmur of her mouth, and all the trembling of her firm young breast; so that I may be rolled a flame in Thy fiery embrace, and be consumed in the unutterable joy of Thine everlasting rapture.

2 O my God, Thou Mighty One, Thou Creator of all things, I renounce unto Thee the soft-lipp'd joys of life, and the honey-sweets of this world, and all the subtilities of the flesh; so that I may be feasted on the fire of Thy passion, and be consumed in the unutterable joy of Thine everlasting rapture.

3 O my God, Thou Mighty One, Thou Creator of all things, I renounce unto Thee the ceaseless booming of the waves, and the fury of the storm, and all the turmoil of the wind-swept waters; so that I may drink of the porphyrine foam of Thy lips, and be consumed in the unutterable joy of Thine everlasting rapture.

4 O my God, Thou Mighty One, Thou Creator of all things, I renounce unto Thee the whispers of the desert, and the moan of the simoom, and all the silence of the sea of dust; so that I may be lost in the atoms of Thy Glory, and be consumed in the unutterable joy of Thine everlasting rapture.

5 O my God, Thou Mighty One, Thou Creator of all things, I renounce unto Thee the green fields of the valleys, and the satyr roses of the hills, and the nymph lilies of the meer; so

that I may wander through the gardens of Thy Splendour, and be consumed in the unutterable joy of Thine everlasting rapture.

6 O my God, Thou Mighty One, Thou Creator of all things, I renounce unto Thee the sorrow of my mother, and the threshold of my home, and all the labour of my father's hands; so that I may be led unto the Mansion of Thy Light, and be consumed in the unutterable joy of Thine everlasting rapture.

7 O my God, Thou Mighty One, Thou Creator of all things, I renounce unto Thee the yearning for Paradise, and the dark fear of Hell, and the feast of the corruption of the grave; so that as a child I may be led unto Thy Kingdom, and be consumed in the unutterable joy of Thine everlasting rapture.

8 O my God, Thou Mighty One, Thou Creator of all things, I renounce unto Thee the moonlit peaks of the mountains, and the arrow-shapen kiss of the firs, and all the travail of the winds; so that I may be lost on the summit of Thy Glory, and be consumed in the unutterable joy of Thine everlasting rapture.

9 O my God, Thou Mighty One, Thou Creator of all things, I renounce unto Thee the goatish ache of the years, and the cryptic books, and all the majesty of their enshrouded words; so that I may be entangled in Thy wordless Wisdom, and be consumed in the unutterable joy of Thine everlasting rapture.

10 O my God, Thou Mighty One, Thou Creator of all things, I renounce unto Thee the wine-cups of merriment, and the eyes of the wanton bearers, and all the lure of their soft limbs; so that I may be made drunk on the vine of Thy splendour, and be consumed in the unutterable joy of Thine everlasting rapture.

11 O my God, Thou Mighty One, Thou Creator of all things, I renounce unto Thee the hissing of mad waters, and the trumpeting of the thunder, and all Thy tongues of dancing flame; so that I may be swept up in the breath of Thy nostrils,

and be consumed in the unutterable joy of Thine everlasting rapture.

12 O my God, Thou Mighty One, Thou Creator of all things, I renounce unto Thee the crimson lust of the chase, and the blast of the brazen war-horns, and all the gleaming of the spears; so that like an hart I may be brought to bay in Thine arms, and be consumed in the unutterable joy of Thine everlasting rapture.

13 O my God, Thou Mighty One, Thou Creator of all things, I renounce unto Thee all that Self which is myself, that black sun which shineth in Self's day, whose glory blindeth Thy Glory; so that I may become as a rushlight in Thine abode, and be consumed in the unutterable joy of Thine everlasting rapture.

O Glory be unto Thee through all Time
and though all Space: Glory,
and Glory upon Glory,
Everlastingly. Amen,
and Amen, and
Amen.

The Chapter known as
The Twelvefold Conjuration of God
and the Unity thereof

✦ ✦ ✦ ✦ ✦   I   ✦ ✦ ✦ ✦ ✦
✦ ✦ ✦ ✦ ✦ adore ✦ ✦ ✦ ✦ ✦
✦ ✦ ✦ ✦ Thee by the ✦ ✦ ✦ ✦
✦ ✦ ✦ ✦ Twelve Conjurations ✦ ✦ ✦ ✦
✦ ✦ ✦ ✦ and by the Unity thereof. ✦ ✦ ✦ ✦

1   O Thou Consuming Eye of everlasting light set as a pearl betwixt the lids of Night and Day; I swear to Thee by the formless void of the Abyss, to lap the galaxies of night in darkness, and blow the meteors like bubbles into the frothing jaws of the sun.

2   O Thou ten-footed soldier of blue ocean, whose castle is built upon the sands of life and death; I swear to Thee by the glittering blades of the waters, to cleave my way within Thine armed hermitage, and brood as an eyeless corpse beneath the coffin-lid of the Mighty Sea.

3   O Thou incandescent Ocean of molten stars, surging above the arch of the Firmament; I swear to Thee by the mane-pennoned lances of light, to stir the lion of Thy darkness from its lair, and lash the sorceress of noontide into fury with serpents of fire.

4   O Thou intoxicating Vision of Beauty, fair as ten jewelled virgins dancing about the hermit moon; I swear to Thee by the peridot flagons of spring, to quaff to the dregs Thy chalice of Glory, and beget a royal race before the Dawn flees from awakening Day.

5   O Thou unalterable measure of all things, in whose lap lie the destinies of unborn worlds; I swear to Thee by the balance of Light and Darkness, to spread out the blue vault as a looking-glass, and flash forth therefrom the intolerable lustre of Thy Countenance.

6 O Thou who settest forth the limitless expanse, spanned by wings of thunder above the cosmic strife; I swear to Thee by the voiceless dust of the desert, to soar above the echoes of shrieking life, and as an eagle to feast for ever upon the silence of the stars.

7 O Thou flame-tipped arrow of devouring fire that quiverest as a tongue in the dark mouth of Night; I swear to Thee by the thurible of Thy Glory, to breathe the incense of mine under-standing, and to cast the ashes of my wisdom into the Valley of Thy breast.

8 O Thou ruin of the mountains, glistening as an old white wolf above the fleecy mists of Earth; I swear to Thee by the galaxies of Thy domain, to press Thy lamb's breasts with the teeth of my soul, and drink of the milk and blood of Thy subtlety and innocence.

9 O Thou Eternal river of chaotic law, in whose depths lie locked the secrets of Creation; I swear to Thee by the primal waters of the Deep, to suck up the Firmament of Thy Chaos, and as a volcano to belch forth a Cosmos of coruscating suns.

10 O Thou Dragon-regent of the blue seas of air, as a chain of emeralds round the neck of Space; I swear to Thee by the hexagram of Night and Day, to be unto Thee as the twin fish of Time, which being set apart never divulge the secret of their unity.

11 O Thou flame of the hornèd storm-clouds, that sunderest their desolation, that outroarest the winds; I swear to Thee by the gleaming sandals of the stars, to climb beyond the summits of the mountains, and rend Thy robe of purple thunders with a sword of silvery light.

12 O Thou fat of an hundred fortresses of iron, crimson as the blades of a million murderous swords; I swear to Thee by the smoke-wreath of the volcano, to open the secret shrine of

Thy bull's breast, and tear out as an augur the heart of Thine all-pervading mystery.

13 O Thou silver axle of the Wheel of Being, thrust through the wings of Time by the still hand of Space; I swear to Thee by the twelve spokes of Thy Unity, to become unto Thee as the rim thereof, so that I may clothe me majestically in the robe that has no seam.

O Glory be unto Thee through all Time
and though all Space: Glory,
and Glory upon Glory,
Everlastingly. Amen,
and Amen, and
Amen.

The Chapter known as
The Twelvefold Certitude of God
and the Unity thereof

I
adore
Thee by the
Twelve Certitudes
and by the Unity thereof.

1   O Thou Sovran Warrior of steel-girt valour, whose scimitar is a flame between day and night, whose helm is crested with the wings of the Abyss. I know Thee! O Thou four-eyed guardian of heaven, who kindleth to a flame the hearts of the downcast, and girdeth about with fire the loins of the unarmed.

2   O Thou Sovran Light and fire of loveliness, whose flaming locks stream downwards through the æthyr as knots of lightening deep-rooted in the Abyss. I know Thee! O Thou winnowing flail of brightness, the passionate lash of whose encircling hand scatters mankind before Thy fury as the wind-scud from the stormy breast of Ocean.

3   O Thou Sovran Singer of the revelling winds, whose voice is as a vestal troop of Bacchanals awakened by the piping of a Pan-pipe. I know Thee! O Thou dancing flame of frenzied song, whose shouts, like unto golden swords of leaping fire, urge us onward to the wild slaughter of the Worlds.

4   O Thou Sovran Might of the most ancient forests, whose voice is as the murmur of unappeasable winds caught up in the arms of the swaying branches. I know Thee! O Thou rumble of conquering drums, who lulleth to a rapture of deep sleep those lovers who burn into each other, flame to fine flame.

5   O Thou Sovran Guide of the star-wheeling circles, the soles of whose feet smite plumes of golden fire from the outermost annihilation of the Abyss. I know Thee! O Thou crimson sword of destruction, who chasest the comets from

the dark bed of night, till they speed before Thee as serpent tongues of flame.

6 O Thou Sovran Archer of the darksome regions, who shooteth forth from Thy transcendental crossbow the many-rayed suns into the fields of heaven. I know Thee! O Thou eight-pointed arrow of light, who smiteth the regions of the seven rivers until they laugh like Mænads with snaky thyrsus.

7 O Thou Sovran Paladin of self-vanquished knights, whose path lieth through the trackless forests of time, winding athrough the Byss of unbegotten space. I know Thee! O Thou despiser of the mountains, Thou whose course is as that of a lightening-hoofed steed leaping along the green bank of a fair river.

8 O Thou Sovran Surging of wild felicity, whose love is as the overflowing of the seas, and who makest our bodies to laugh with beauty. I know Thee! O Thou outstrider of the sunset, who deckest the snow-capped mountains with red roses, and strewest white violets on the curling waves.

9 O Thou Sovran Diadem of crownèd Wisdom, whose work knoweth the path of the sylphs of the air, and the black burrowings of the gnomes of the earth. I know Thee! O Thou Master of the ways of life, in the palm of whose hand all the arts lie bounden as a smoke-cloud betwixt the lips of the mountain.

10 O Thou Sovran Lord of primæval Baresarkers, who huntest with dawn the dappled deer of twilight, and whose engines of war are blood-crested comets. I know Thee! O Thou flame-crowned Self-luminous One, the lash of whose whip gathered the ancient worlds, and looseth the blood from the virgin clouds of heaven.

11 O Thou Sovran Moonstone of pearly loveliness, from out whose many eyes flash the fire-clouds of life, and whose breath enkindleth the Byss and the Abyss. I know Thee! O

Thou fountain-head of fierce æthyr, in the pupil of whose brightness all things lie crouched and wrapped like a babe in the womb of its mother.

12 O Thou Sovran Mother of the breath of being, the milk of whose breasts is as the fountain of love, twin-jets of fire upon the blue bosom of night. I know Thee! O Thou Virgin of the moonlit glades, who fondleth us as a drop of dew in Thy lap, ever watchful over the cradle of our fate.

13 O Thou Sovran All-Beholding eternal Sun, who lappest up the constellations of heaven, as a thirsty thief a jar of ancient wine. I know Thee! O Thou dawn-wing'd courtesan of light, who makest me to reel with one kiss of Thy mouth, as a leaf cast into the flames of a furnace.

O Glory be unto Thee through all Time
and though all Space: Glory,
and Glory upon Glory,
Everlastingly. Amen,
and Amen, and
Amen.

The Chapter known as
The Twelvefold Glorification of God
and the Unity thereof

✦ ✦ ✦ ✦ ✦　　　I　　✦ ✦ ✦ ✦ ✦
✦ ✦ ✦ ✦ ✦　adore　✦ ✦ ✦ ✦ ✦
✦ ✦ ✦ ✦　Thee by the　✦ ✦ ✦ ✦
✦ ✦ ✦ ✦　Twelve Glorifications　✦ ✦ ✦ ✦
✦ ✦ ✦ ✦　and by the Unity thereof.　✦ ✦ ✦ ✦

1　O Glory be to Thee, O God my God; for I behold Thee in the Lion Rampant of the dawn: Thou hast crushed with Thy paw the crouching lioness of Night, so that she may roar forth the Glory of Thy Name.

2　O Glory be to Thee, O God my God; for I behold Thee in the lap of the fertile valleys: Thou hast adorned their strong limbs with a robe of poppied corn, so that they may laugh forth the Glory of Thy Name.

3　O Glory be to Thee, O God my God; for I behold Thee in the gilded rout of dancing-girls: Thou hast garlanded their naked middles with fragrant flowers, so that they may pace forth the Glory of Thy Name.

4　O Glory be to Thee, O God my God; for I behold Thee in the riotous joy of the storm: Thou hast shaken the gold-dust from the tresses of the hills, so that they may chaunt forth the Glory of Thy Name.

5　O Glory be to Thee, O God my God; for I behold Thee in the stars and meteors of Night: Thou hast caparisoned her grey coursers with moons of pearl, so that they may shake forth the Glory of Thy Name.

6　O Glory be to Thee, O God my God; for I behold Thee in the precious stones of the black earth: Thou hast lightened her with a myriad eyes of magic, so that she may wink forth the Glory of Thy Name.

7 O Glory be to Thee, O God my God; for I behold Thee in the sparkling dew of the wild glades: Thou hast decked them out as for a great feast of rejoicing, so that they may gleam forth the Glory of Thy Name.

8 O Glory be to Thee, O God my God; for I behold Thee in the stillness of the frozen lakes: Thou hast made their faces more dazzling than a silver mirror, so that they may flash forth the Glory of Thy Name.

9 O Glory be to Thee, O God my God; for I behold Thee in the smoke-veil'd fire of the mountains: Thou hast inflamed them as lions that scent a fallow deer, so that they may rage forth the Glory of Thy Name.

10 O Glory be to Thee, O God my God; for I behold Thee in the countenance of my darling: Thou hast unclothed her of white lilies and crimson roses, so that she may blush forth the Glory of Thy Name.

11 O Glory be to Thee, O God my God; for I behold Thee in the weeping of the flying clouds: Thou hast swelled therewith the blue breasts of the milky rivers, so that they may roll forth the Glory of Thy Name.

12 O Glory be to Thee, O God my God; for I behold Thee in the amber combers of the storm: Thou hast laid Thy lash upon the sphinxes of the waters, so that they may boom forth the Glory of Thy Name.

13 O Glory be to Thee, O God my God; for I behold Thee in the lotus-flower within my heart: Thou hast emblazoned my trumpet with the lion-standard, so that I may blare forth the Glory of Thy Name.

O Glory be unto Thee through all Time
and though all Space: Glory,
and Glory upon Glory,
Everlastingly. Amen,
and Amen, and
Amen.

♍ The Chapter known as The Twelvefold Beseechment of God and the Unity thereof

◆ ◆ ◆ ◆ ◆   I   ◆ ◆ ◆ ◆ ◆
◆ ◆ ◆ ◆ ◆ adore ◆ ◆ ◆ ◆ ◆
◆ ◆ ◆ ◆ Thee by the ◆ ◆ ◆ ◆
◆ ◆ ◆ ◆ Twelve Beseechments ◆ ◆ ◆ ◆
◆ ◆ ◆ ◆ and by the Unity thereof. ◆ ◆ ◆ ◆

1 O Thou mighty God, make me as a fair virgin that is clad in the blue-bells of the fragrant hillside; I beseech Thee, O Thou great God! That I may ring out the melody of Thy voice, and be clothed in the pure light of Thy loveliness: O Thou God my God!

2 O Thou mighty God, make me as a Balance of rubies and jet that is cast in the lap of the Sun; I beseech Thee, O Thou great God! That I may flash forth the wonder of Thy brightness, and melt into the perfect poise of Thy Being: O Thou God, my God!

3 O Thou mighty God, make me as a brown Scorpion that creepeth on through a vast desert of silver; I beseech Thee, O Thou great God! That I may lose myself in the span of Thy light, and become one with the glitter of Thy Shadow: O Thou God, my God!

4 O Thou mighty God, make me as a green arrow of Lightning that speedeth through the purple clouds of Night; I beseech Thee, O Thou great God! That I may wake fire from the crown of Thy Wisdom, and flash into the depths of Thine Understanding: O Thou God, my God!

5 O Thou mighty God, make me as a flint-black goat that pranceth in a shining wilderness of steel; I beseech Thee, O Thou great God! That I may paw one flashing spark from Thy Splendour, and be welded into the Glory of Thy might: O Thou God, my God!

6 O Thou mighty God, make me as the sapphirine waves that cling to the shimmering limbs of the green rocks; I beseech Thee, O Thou great God! That I may chant in foaming music Thy Glory, and roll forth the eternal rapture of Thy Name: O Thou God, my God!

7 O Thou mighty God, make me as a silver fish darting through the vast depths of the dim-peopled waters; I beseech Thee, O Thou great God! That I may swim through the vastness of Thine abyss, and sink beneath the waveless depths of Thy Glory: O Thou God, my God!

8 O Thou mighty God, make me as a white ram that is athirst in a sun-scorched desert of bitterness; I beseech Thee, O Thou great God! That I may seek the deep waters of Thy Wisdom, and plunge into the whiteness of Thine effulgence: O Thou God, my God!

9 O Thou mighty God, make me as a thunder-smitten bull that is drunk upon the vintage of Thy blood; I beseech Thee, O Thou great God! That I may bellow through the universe Thy Power, and trample the nectar-sweet grapes of Thine Essence: O Thou God, my God!

10 O Thou mighty God, make me as a black eunuch of song that is twin-voiced, yet dumb in either tongue; I beseech Thee, O Thou great God! That I may hush my melody in Thy Silence, and swell into the sweet ecstasy of Thy Song. O Thou God, my God!

11 O Thou mighty God, make me as an emerald crab that crawleth over the wet sands of the sea-shore; I beseech Thee, O Thou great God! That I may write Thy name across the shores of Time, and sink amongst the white atoms of Thy Being. O Thou God, my God!

12 O Thou mighty God, make me as a ruby lion that roareth from the summit of a white mountain; I beseech Thee, O Thou great God! That I may echo forth Thy lordship through the hills, and dwindle into the nipple of Thy bounty. O Thou God, my God!

13 O Thou mighty God, make me as an all-consuming Sun ablaze in the centre of the Universe; I beseech Thee, O Thou great God! That I may become as a crown upon Thy brow, and flash forth the exceeding fire of Thy Godhead: O Thou God, my God!

O Glory be unto Thee through all Time
and though all Space: Glory,
and Glory upon Glory,
Everlastingly. Amen,
and Amen, and
Amen.

♎ The Chapter known as The Twelvefold Gratification of God and the Unity thereof

✦ ✦ ✦ ✦ ✦   I   ✦ ✦ ✦ ✦ ✦
✦ ✦ ✦ ✦ ✦ adore ✦ ✦ ✦ ✦ ✦
✦ ✦ ✦ ✦ Thee by the ✦ ✦ ✦ ✦
✦ ✦ ✦ ✦ Twelve Gratifications ✦ ✦ ✦ ✦
✦ ✦ ✦ ✦ and by the Unity thereof. ✦ ✦ ✦ ✦

1 O Thou green-cloaked Mænad in labour, who bearest beneath Thy leaden girdle the vintage of Thy kisses; release me from the darkness of Thy womb, so that I may cast off my infant wrappings and leap forth as an armed warrior in steel.

2 O Thou snake of misty countenance, whose braided hair is like a fleecy dawn of swooning maidens; hunt me as a fierce wild boar through the skies, so that Thy burning spear may gore the blue heavens red with the foaming blood of my frenzy.

3 O Thou cloudy Virgin of the World, whose breasts are as scarlet lilies paling before the sun; dandle me in the cradle of Thine arms, so that the murmur of Thy voice may lull me to a sleep like a pearl lost in the depths of a silent sea.

4 O Thou wine-voiced laughter of fainting gloom, who art as a naked faun crushed to death between millstones of thunder; make me drunk on the rapture of Thy song, so that in the corpse-clutch of my passion I may tear the cloud-robe from off Thy swooning breast.

5 O Thou wanton cup-bearer of madness, whose mouth is as the joy of a thousand thousand masterful kisses; intoxicate me on Thy loveliness, so that the silver of Thy merriment may revel as a moon-white pearl upon my tongue.

6 O Thou midnight Vision of Whiteness, whose lips are as pouting rosebuds deflowered by the deciduous moon; tend me as a drop of dew in Thy breast, so that the dragon of Thy gluttonous hate may devour me with its mouth of adamant.

7 O Thou effulgence of burning love, who pursueth the dawn as a youth pursueth a rose-lipped maiden; rend me with the fierce kisses of Thy mouth, so that in the battle of our lips I may be drenched by the snow-pure fountains of Thy bliss.

8 O Thou black bull in a field of white girls, whose foaming flanks are as starry night ravished in the fierce arms of noon; shake forth the purple horns of my passion, so that I may dissolve as a crown of fire in the bewilderment of Thine ecstasy.

9 O Thou dread arbiter of all men, the hem of whose broidered skirt crimsoneth the white battlements of Space; bare me the starry nipple of Thy breast, so that the milk of Thy love may nurture me to the lustiness of Thy virginity.

10 O Thou thirsty charioteer of Time, whose cup is the hollow night filled with the foam of the vintage of day; drench me in the shower of Thy passion, so that I may pant in Thine arms as a tongue of lightning on the purple bosom of night.

11 O Thou opalescent Serpent-Queen, whose mouth is as the sunset that is bloody with the slaughter of day; hold me in the crimson flames of Thine arms, so that at Thy kisses I may expire as a bubble in the foam of Thy dazzling lips.

12 O Thou Odalisque of earth's palace, whose garments are scented and passionate as spring flowers in sunlit glades; roll me in the sweet perfume of Thy hair, so that Thy tresses of gold may anoint me with the honey of a million roses.

13 O Thou manly warrior amongst youths, whose limbs are as swords of fire that are welded in the furnace of war; press Thy cool kisses to my burning lips, so that the folly of our passion may weave us into the Crown of everlasting Light.

O Glory be unto Thee through all Time
and though all Space: Glory,
and Glory upon Glory,
Everlastingly. Amen,
and Amen, and
Amen.

♏ The Chapter known as The Twelvefold Denial of God and the Unity thereof

✦ ✦ ✦ ✦ ✦   I   ✦ ✦ ✦ ✦ ✦
✦ ✦ ✦ ✦ ✦   adore   ✦ ✦ ✦ ✦ ✦
✦ ✦ ✦ ✦ Thee by the ✦ ✦ ✦ ✦
✦ ✦ ✦ ✦ Twelve Denials ✦ ✦ ✦ ✦
✦ ✦ ✦ ✦ and by the Unity thereof. ✦ ✦ ✦ ✦

1   O Thou God of the Nothingness of All Things!

Thou who art neither the Formless breath of Chaos; nor the exhaler of the ordered spheres:

O Thou who art not the cloud-cradled star of the morning; nor the sun, drunken upon the mist, who blindeth men!

I deny Thee by the powers of mine understanding;

Guide me in the unity of Thy might, and lead me to the fatherhood of Thine all-pervading Nothingness;

for Thou art all and none of these in the fullness of Thy Not-Being.

2   O Thou God of the Nothingness of All Things!

Thou who art neither the vitality of worlds; nor the breath of star-entangled Being:

O Thou who art not horsed 'mid the centaur clouds of night; nor the twanging of the shuddering bowstring of noon!

I deny Thee by the powers of mine understanding;

Throne me in the unity of Thy might, and stab me with the javelin of Thine all-pervading Nothingness;

for Thou art all and none of these in the fullness of Thy Not-Being.

3   O Thou God of the Nothingness of All Things!

Thou who art neither the Pan-pipe in the forest; nor life's blue sword wrapped in the cloak of death:

O Thou who art not found amongst the echoes of the hills; nor in the whisperings that wake within the valleys!

I deny Thee by the powers of mine understanding;

Crown me in the unity of Thy might, and flash me as a scarlet tongue into Thine all-pervading Nothingness;

for Thou art all and none of these in the fullness of Thy Not-Being.

4 O Thou God of the Nothingness of All Things!

Thou who art neither the Crown of the flaming storm; nor the opalescence of the Abyss:

O Thou who art not a nymph in the foam of the sea; nor a whirling devil in the sand of the desert!

I deny Thee by the powers of mine understanding;

Bear me in the unity of Thy might, and pour me forth from out the cup of Thine all-pervading Nothingness;

for Thou art all and none of these in the fullness of Thy Not-Being.

5 O Thou God of the Nothingness of All Things!

Thou who art neither the formulator of law; nor the Cheat of the maze of illusion:

O Thou who art not the foundation-stone of existence; nor the eagle that broodeth upon the egg of space!

I deny Thee by the powers of mine understanding;

Swathe me in the unity of Thy might, and teach me wisdom from the lips of Thine all-pervading Nothingness;

for Thou art all and none of these in the fullness of Thy Not-Being.

6 O Thou God of the Nothingness of All Things!

Thou who art neither the fivefold root of Nature; nor the fire-crested helm of her Master:

O Thou who art not the Emperor of Eternal Time; nor the warrior shout that rocketh the Byss of Space!

I deny Thee by the powers of mine understanding;

Raise me in the unity of Thy might, and suckle me at the swol'n breasts of Thine all-pervading Nothingness;

for Thou art all and none of these in the fullness of Thy Not-Being.

7   O Thou God of the Nothingness of All Things!

Thou who art neither the golden bull of the heavens; nor the crimsoned fountain of the lusts of men:

O Thou who reclinest not upon the Waggon of Night; nor restest Thine hand upon the handle of the Plough!

I deny Thee by the powers of mine understanding;

Urge me in the unity of Thy might, and drench me with the red vintage of Thine all-pervading Nothingness;

for Thou art all and none of these in the fullness of Thy Not-Being.

8   O Thou God of the Nothingness of All Things!

Thou who art neither the starry eyes of heaven; nor the forehead of the crowned morning;

O Thou who art not perceived by the powers of the mind; nor grasped by the fingers of Silence or of Speech!

I deny Thee by the powers of mine understanding;

Robe me in the unity of Thy might, and speed me into the blindness of Thine all-pervading Nothingness;

for Thou art all and none of these in the fullness of Thy Not-Being.

9   O Thou God of the Nothingness of All Things!

Thou who art neither the forge of Eternity; nor the thunder-throated womb of Chaos:

O Thou who art not found in the hissing of the hail-stones; nor in the rioting of the equinoctial storm!

I deny Thee by the powers of mine understanding;

Bring me to the unity of Thy might, and feast me on honeyed manna of Thine all-pervading Nothingness;

for Thou art all and none of these in the fullness of Thy Not-Being.

10   O Thou God of the Nothingness of All Things!

Thou who art neither the traces of the chariot; nor the pole of galloping delusion:

O Thou who art not the pivot of the whole Universe; nor the body of the woman-serpent of the stars!

I deny Thee by the powers of mine understanding;

Lead me in the unity of Thy might, and draw me unto the threshold of Thine all-pervading Nothingness;

for Thou art all and none of these in the fullness of Thy Not-Being.

11 O Thou God of the Nothingness of All Things!

Thou who art neither the moaning of a maiden; nor the electric touch of fire-thrilled youth:

O Thou who art not found in the hardy kisses of love; nor in the tortured spasms of madness and of hate!

I deny Thee by the powers of mine understanding;

Weight me in the unity of Thy might, and roll me in the poised rapture of Thine all-pervading Nothingness;

for Thou art all and none of these in the fullness of Thy Not-Being.

12 O Thou God of the Nothingness of All Things!

Thou who art neither the primal cause of causes; nor the soul of what is, or was, or will be:

O Thou who art not measured in the motionless balance; nor smitten by the arrow-flights of man!

I deny Thee by the powers of mine understanding;

Shield me in the unity of Thy might, and reckon me aright in the span of Thine all-pervading Nothingness;

for Thou art all and none of these in the fullness of Thy Not-Being.

13 O Thou God of the Nothingness of All Things!

Thou who art neither the breathing influx of life; nor the iron ring i' the marriage feast of death:

O Thou who art not shadowèd forth in the songs of war; nor in the tears or lamentations of a child!

I deny Thee by the powers of mine understanding;

Sheathe me in the unity of Thy might, and kindle me with the grey flame of Thine all-pervading Nothingness;

for Thou art all and none of these in the fullness of Thy Not-Being.

O Glory be unto Thee through all Time
and though all Space: Glory,
and Glory upon Glory,
Everlastingly. Amen,
and Amen, and
Amen.

The Chapter known as
The Twelvefold Rejoicing of God
and the Unity thereof

<pre>
✦ ✦ ✦ ✦ ✦   I   ✦ ✦ ✦ ✦ ✦
✦ ✦ ✦ ✦ ✦   adore   ✦ ✦ ✦ ✦ ✦
✦ ✦ ✦ ✦   Thee by the   ✦ ✦ ✦ ✦
✦ ✦ ✦ ✦ Twelve Rejoicings ✦ ✦ ✦ ✦
✦ ✦ ✦ ✦ and by the Unity thereof. ✦ ✦ ✦ ✦
</pre>

1   Ah! but I rejoice in Thee, O Thou my God;

Thou seven-rayed rainbow of perfect loveliness;

Thou light-rolling chariot of sunbeams;

Thou fragrant scent of the passing storm:

Yea, I rejoice in Thee, Thou breath of the slumbering valleys;

O Thou low-murmuring ripple of the ripe cornfields!

I rejoice, yea, I shout with gladness! till, as the mingling blushes of day and night, my song weaveth the joys of life into a gold and purple Crown, for the Glory and Splendour of Thy Name.

2   Ah! but I rejoice in Thee, O Thou my God;

Thou zigzagged effulgence of the burning stars;

Thou wilderment of indigo light;

Thou grey horn of immaculate fire:

Yea, I rejoice in Thee, Thou embattled cloud of flashing flame;

O Thou capricious serpent-head of scarlet hair!

I rejoice, yea, I shout with gladness! till my roaring filleth the wooded mountains, and like a giant forceth the wind's head through the struggling trees, in the Glory and Splendour of Thy Name.

3   Ah! but I rejoice in Thee, O Thou my God;

Thou silken web of emerald bewitchment;

Thou berylline mist of marshy meers;

338

Thou flame-spangled fleece of seething gold:

Yea, I rejoice in Thee, Thou pearly dew of the setting moon;

O Thou dark purple storm-cloud of contending kisses!

I rejoice, yea, I shout with gladness! till all my laughter, like enchaunted waters, is blown as an iris-web of bubbles from the lips of the deep, in the Glory and Splendour of Thy Name.

4   Ah! but I rejoice in Thee, O Thou my God;

Thou who broodest on the dark depths of the deep;

Thou lap of the wave-glittering sea;

Thou bright vesture of the crested floods:

Yea, I rejoice in Thee, Thou native splendour of the Waters;

O Thou fathomless Abyss of surging joy!

I rejoice, yea, I shout with gladness! till the mad swords of my music smite the hills, and rend the amethyst limbs of Night from the white embrace of Day, at the Glory and Splendour of Thy Name.

5   Ah! but I rejoice in Thee, O Thou my God;

Thou cloud-hooded bastion of the stormy skies;

Thou lightning anvil of angel swords;

Thou gloomy forge of the thunderbolt:

Yea, I rejoice in Thee, Thou all-subduing Crown of Splendour;

O Thou hero-souled helm of endless victory!

I rejoice, yea, I shout with gladness! till the mad rivers rush roaring through the woods, and my re-echoing voice danceth like a ram among the hills, for the Glory and Splendour of Thy Name.

6   Ah! but I rejoice in Thee, O Thou my God;

Thou opalescent orb of shattered sunsets;

Thou pearly boss on the shield of light;

Thou tawny priest at the Mass of lust:

Yea, I rejoice in Thee, Thou chalcedony cloudland of light;

O Thou poppy-petal floating upon the snowstorm!

I rejoice, yea, I shout with gladness! till my frenzied words rush through the souls of men, like a blood-red bull through a white herd of terror-stricken kine, at the Glory and Splendour of Thy Name.

7 Ah! but I rejoice in Thee, O Thou my God;
Thou unimperilled flight of joyous laughter;
Thou eunuch glaive-armed before joy's veil;
Thou dreadful insatiable One:
Yea, I rejoice in Thee, Thou lofty gathering-point of Bliss;
O Thou bridal-bed of murmuring rapture!

I rejoice, yea, I shout with gladness! till I tangle the black tresses of the storm, and lash the tempest into a green foam of twining basilisks, in the Glory and Splendour of Thy Name.

8 Ah! but I rejoice in Thee, O Thou my God;
Thou coruscating star-point of Endlessness;
Thou inundating fire of the Void;
Thou moonbeam cup of eternal life:
Yea, I rejoice in Thee, Thou fire-sandalled warrior of steel;
O Thou bloody dew of the field of slaughter and death!

I rejoice, yea, I shout with gladness! till the music of my throat smiteth the hills as a crescent moon waketh a nightly field of sleeping comets, at the Glory and Splendour of Thy Name.

9 Ah! but I rejoice in Thee, O Thou my God;
Thou jewel-work of snow on the limbs of night;
Thou elaboration of oneness;
Thou shower of universal suns:
Yea, I rejoice in Thee, Thou gorgeous, Thou wildering one;
O Thou great lion roaring over a sea of blood!

I rejoice, yea, I shout with gladness! till the wild thunder of my praise breaketh down, as a satyr doth a babe, the nine and ninety gates of Thy Power, in the Glory and Splendour of Thy Name.

10 Ah! but I rejoice in Thee, O Thou my God;

Thou ambrosia-yielding rose of the World;

Thou vaulted dome of effulgent light;

Thou valley of venomous vipers:

Yea, I rejoice in Thee, Thou dazzling robe of the soft rain-clouds;

O Thou lion-voiced up-rearing of the goaded storm!

I rejoice, yea, I shout with gladness! till my rapture, like unto a two-edged sword, traceth a sigil of fire and blasteth the banded sorcerers, in the Glory and Splendour of Thy Name.

11 Ah! but I rejoice in Thee, O Thou my God;

Thou Crown of unutterable loveliness;

Thou feather of hyalescent flame;

Thou all-beholding eye of brightness:

Yea, I rejoice in Thee, Thou resplendent everlasting one:

O Thou vast abysmal ocean of foaming flames!

I rejoice, yea, I shout with gladness! till the stars leap like white coursers from the night, and the heavens resound as an army of steel-clad warriors, at the Glory and Splendour of Thy Name.

12 Ah! but I rejoice in Thee, O Thou my God;

Thou star-blaze of undying expectation;

Thou ibis-throated voice of silence;

Thou blinding night of understanding:

Yea, I rejoice in Thee, Thou white finger of Chaotic law;

O Thou creative cockatrice twined amongst the waters!

I rejoice, yea, I shout with gladness! till my cries stir the night as the burnished gold of a lance thrust into a poisonous dragon of adamant, for the Glory and Splendour of Thy Name.

13 Ah! but I rejoice in Thee, O Thou my God;

Thou self-luminous refulgent Brilliance;

Thou eye of light that hath no eyelid;

Thou turquoise-studded sceptre of deed:

Yea, I rejoice in Thee, Thou white furnace womb of Energy;

O Thou spark-whirling forge of the substance of the worlds;

I rejoice, yea, I shout with gladness! till I mount as a white beam unto the crown, and as a breath of night melt into the golden lips of Thy dawn, in the Glory and Splendour of Thy Name.

O Glory be unto Thee through all Time
and though all Space: Glory,
and Glory upon Glory,
Everlastingly. Amen,
and Amen, and
Amen.

The Chapter known as The Twelvefold Humiliation of God and the Unity thereof

✦ ✦ ✦ ✦ ✦   I   ✦ ✦ ✦ ✦ ✦
✦ ✦ ✦ ✦ ✦ adore ✦ ✦ ✦ ✦ ✦
✦ ✦ ✦ ✦ Thee by the ✦ ✦ ✦ ✦
✦ ✦ ✦ ✦ Twelve Humiliations ✦ ✦ ✦ ✦
✦ ✦ ✦ ✦ and by the Unity thereof. ✦ ✦ ✦ ✦

1 O my God, behold me fully and be merciful unto me, as I humble myself before Thee; for all my searching is as a bat that seeks some hollow of night upon a sun-parched wilderness.

2 O my God, order me justly and be merciful unto me, as I humble myself before Thee; for all my thoughts are as a dust-clad serpent wind at noon that danceth through the ashen grass of law.

3 O my God, conquer me with love and be merciful unto me, as I humble myself before Thee; for all the striving of my spirit is as a child's kiss that struggles through a cloud of tangled hair.

4 O my God, suckle me with truth and be merciful unto me, as I humble myself before Thee; for all my agony of anguish is but as a quail struggling in the jaws of an hungry wolf.

5 O my God, comfort me with ease and be merciful unto me, as I humble myself before Thee; for all the toil of my life is but as a small white mouse swimming through a vast sea of crimson blood.

6 O my God, entreat me gently and be merciful unto me, as I humble myself before Thee; for all my toil is but as a threadless shuttle of steel thrust here and there in the black loom of night.

7 O my God, fondle me with kisses and be merciful unto me, as I humble myself before Thee; for all my desires are as

dewdrops that are sucked from silver lilies by the throat of a young god.

8 O my God, exalt me with blood and be merciful unto me, as I humble myself before Thee; for all my courage is but as the fang of a viper that striketh at the rosy heel of dawn.

9 O my God, teach me with patience and be merciful unto me, as I humble myself before Thee; for all my knowledge is but as the refuse of the chaff that is flung to the darkness of the void.

10 O my God, measure me rightly and be merciful unto me, as I humble myself before Thee; for all my praise is but as a single letter of lead lost in the gilded scriptures of the rocks.

11 O my God, fill me with slumber and be merciful unto me, as I humble myself before Thee; for all my wakefulness is but as a cloud at sunset that is like a snake gliding through the dew.

12 O my God, kindle me with joy and be merciful unto me, as I humble myself before Thee; for all the strength of my mind is but as a web of silk that bindeth the milky breasts of the stars.

13 O my God, consume me with fire and be merciful unto me, as I humble myself before Thee; for all mine understanding is but as a spider's thread drawn from star to star of a young galaxy.

O Glory be unto Thee through all Time
and though all Space: Glory,
and Glory upon Glory,
Everlastingly. Amen,
and Amen, and
Amen.

The Chapter known as
The Twelvefold Lamentation of God
and the Unity thereof

I
adore
Thee by the
Twelve Lamentations
and by the Unity thereof.

1 O woe unto me, my God, woe unto me; for all my song is as the dirge of the sea that moans about a corpse, lapping most mournfully against the dead shore in the darkness. Yet in the sob of the wind do I hear Thy name, that quickeneth the cold lips of death to life.

2 O woe unto me, my God, woe unto me; for all my praise is as the song of a bird that is ensnared in the network of the winds, and cast adown the drowning depths of night. Yet in the faltering notes of my music do I mark the melody of universal truth.

3 O woe unto me, my God, woe unto me; for all my works are as a coiled-up sleeper who hath overslept the day, even the dawn that hovereth as a hawk in the void. Yet in the gloom of mine awakening do I see, across the breasts of night, Thy shadowed form.

4 O woe unto me, my God, woe unto me; for all my labours are as weary oxen laggard and sore stricken with the goad, ploughing black furrows across the white fields of light. Yet in the scrawling trail of their slow toil do I descry the golden harvest of Thine effulgence.

5 O woe unto me, my God, woe unto me; for all the hope of my heart hath been ravished as the body of a virgin that is fallen into the hands of riotous robbers. Yet in the outrage of mine innocence do I disclose the clear manna of Thy purity.

6 O woe unto me, my God, woe unto me; for all the passion of my love is mazed as the bewildered eyes of a youth, who should wake to find his belovèd fled away. Yet in the crumpled couch of lust do I behold as an imprint the sigil of Thy name.

7 O woe unto me, my God, woe unto me; for all the joy of my days lies dishonoured as the spangle-veil'd Virgin of night torn and trampled by the sun-lashed stallions of Dawn. Yet in the frenzy of their couplings do I tremble forth the pearly dew of ecstatic light.

8 O woe unto me, my God, woe unto me; for all the aspirations of my heart ruin as in time of earthquake the bare hut of an hermit that he hath built for prayer. Yet from the lightning-struck tower of my reason do I enter Thy house that Thou didst build for me.

9 O woe unto me, my God, woe unto me; for all my joy is as a cloud of dust blown athwart a memory of tears, even across the shadowless brow of the desert. Yet as from the breast of a slave-girl do I pluck the fragrant blossom of Thy Crimson Splendour.

10 O woe unto me, my God, woe unto me; for all the feastings of my flesh have sickened to the wormy hunger of the grave, writhing in the spasms of indolent decay. Yet in the maggots of my corruption do I shadow forth sunlit hosts of crowned eagles.

11 O woe unto me, my God, woe unto me; for all my craft is as an injured arrow, featherless and twisted, that should be loosed from its bowstring by the hands of an infant. Yet in the wayward struggling of its flight do I grip the unwavering courses of Thy wisdom.

12 O woe unto me, my God, woe unto me; for all my faith is as a filthy puddle in the sinister confines of a forest, splashed by the wanton foot of a young gnome. Yet like a wildfire

through the trees at nightfall do I divine the distant glimmer of Thine Eye.

13 O woe unto me, my God, woe unto me; for all my life sinks as the western Sun that struggles in the strangling arms of Night, flecked over with the starry foam of her kisses. Yet in the very midnight of my soul do I hold as a scarab the signet of Thy name.

O Glory be unto Thee through all Time
and though all Space: Glory,
and Glory upon Glory,
Everlastingly. Amen,
and Amen, and
Amen.

♓ The Chapter known as
The Twelvefold Bewilderment of God
and the Unity thereof

```
✦  ✦  ✦  ✦  ✦      I      ✦  ✦  ✦  ✦  ✦
✦  ✦  ✦  ✦  ✦   adore   ✦  ✦  ✦  ✦  ✦
✦  ✦  ✦  ✦  Thee by the    ✦  ✦  ✦  ✦
✦  ✦  ✦  ✦  Twelve Bewilderments  ✦  ✦  ✦  ✦
✦  ✦  ✦  ✦  and by the Unity thereof. ✦  ✦  ✦  ✦
```

1   O what art Thou, O God my God, Thou snow-browed storm that art whirled up in clouds of flame?

O Thou red sword of the thunder!

Thou great blue river of ever-flowing Brightness, over whose breasts creep the star-bannered vessels of night!

O how can I plunge within Thine inscrutable depths, and yet with open eye be lost in the pearly foam of Thine Oblivion?

2   O what art Thou, O God my God, Thou eternal incarnating immortal One?

O Thou welder of life and death!

Thou whose breasts are as the full breasts of a mother, yet in Thy hand Thou carriest the sword of destruction!

O how can I cleave the shield of Thy might as a little wanton child may burst a floating bubble with the breast-feather of a dove?

3   O what art Thou, O God my God, Thou mighty worker laden with the dust of toil?

O Thou little ant of the earth!

Thou great monster who infuriatest the seas, and by their vigour wearest down the strength of the cliffs!

O how can I bind Thee in a spider's web of song, and yet remain one and unconsumèd before the raging of Thy nostrils?

4   O what art Thou, O God my God, Thou forked tongue of the purple-throated thunder?

O Thou silver sword of lightning!

Thou who rippest out the fire-bolt from the storm-cloud, as a sorcerer teareth the heart from a black kid!

O how can I possess Thee as the dome of the skies, so that I may fix the keystone of my reason in the arch of Thy forehead?

5 O what art Thou, O God my God, Thou amber-scal'd one whose eyes are set on columns?

O Thou sightless seer of all things!

Thou spearless warrior who urgest on Thy steeds and blindest the outer edge of darkness with Thy Glory!

O how can I grasp the whirling wheels of Thy splendour, and yet be not smitten into death by the hurtling fury of Thy chariot?

6 O what art Thou, O God my God, Thou red fire-fang that gnawest the blue limbs of night?

O Thou devouring breath of flame!

Thou illimitable ocean of frenzied air, in whom all is one, a plume cast into a furnace!

O how can I dare to approach and stand before Thee, for I am but as a withered leaf whirled away by the anger of the storm?

7 O what art Thou, O God my God, Thou almighty worker ungirded of slumber?

O Thou Unicorn of the Stars!

Thou tongue of flame burning above the firmament, as a lily that blossometh in the drear desert!

O how can I pluck Thee from the dark bed of Thy birth, and revel like a wine-drenched faun in the banqueting-house of Thy Seigniory?

8 O what art Thou, O God my God, Thou dazzler of the deep obscurity of day?

O Thou golden breast of beauty!

Thou shrivelled udder of the storm-blasted mountains, who no longer sucklest the babe-clouds of wind-swept night!

O how can I gaze upon Thy countenance of eld, and yet be not blinded by the black fury of Thy dethronèd Majesty?

9 O what art Thou, O God my God, Thou seraph-venom of witch-vengeance enchaunted?

O Thou coiled wizardry of stars!

Thou one Lord of life triumphant over death, Thou red rose of love nailed to the cross of golden light!

O how can I die in Thee as sea-foam in the clouds, and yet possess Thee as a frail white mist possessess the stripped limbs of the Sun?

10 O what art Thou, O God my God, Thou soft pearl set in a bow of effulgent light?

O Thou drop of shimmering dew!

Thou surging river of bewildering beauty who speedest as a blue arrow of fire beyond, beyond!

O how can I measure the poisons of Thy limbeck, and yet be for ever transmuted in the athanor of Thine understanding?

11 O what art Thou, O God my God, Thou disrober of the darkness of the Abyss?

O Thou veil'd eye of creation!

Thou soundless voice who, for ever misunderstood, rollest on through the dark abysms of infinity!

O how can I learn to sing the music of Thy name, as a quivering silence above the thundering discord of the tempest?

12 O what art Thou, O God my God, Thou teeming desert of the abundance of night?

O Thou river of unquench'd thirst!

Thou tongueless one who lickest up the dust of death and casteth it forth as the rolling ocean of life!

O how can I possess the still depths of Thy darkness, and yet in Thine embrace fall asleep as a child in a bower of lilies?

13 O what art Thou, O God my God, Thou shrouded one veiled in a dazzling effulgence?

O Thou centreless whorl of Time!

Thou illimitable abysm of Righteousness, the lashes of whose eye are as showers of molten suns!

O how can I reflect the light of Thine unity, and melt into Thy Glory as a cloudy chaplet of chalcedony moons?

O Glory be unto Thee through all Time
and though all Space: Glory,
and Glory upon Glory,
Everlastingly. Amen,
and Amen, and
Amen.

𝕿𝖍𝖊 𝕮𝖍𝖆𝖕𝖙𝖊𝖗 𝖐𝖓𝖔𝖜𝖓 𝖆𝖘
𝕿𝖍𝖊 𝕿𝖜𝖊𝖑𝖛𝖊𝖋𝖔𝖑𝖉 𝖀𝖓𝖎𝖋𝖎𝖈𝖆𝖙𝖎𝖔𝖓 𝖔𝖋 𝕲𝖔𝖉
𝖆𝖓𝖉 𝖙𝖍𝖊 𝖀𝖓𝖎𝖙𝖞 𝖙𝖍𝖊𝖗𝖊𝖔𝖋

I
adore
Thee by the
Twelve Unifications
and by the Unity thereof.

1 O Thou Unity of all things: as the water that poureth through the fingers of my hand, so art Thou, O God my God. I cannot hold Thee, for Thou art everywhere; lo! though I plunge into the heart of the ocean, there still shall I find Thee, Thou Unity of Unities, Thou Oneness, O Thou perfect Nothingness of Bliss!

2 O Thou Unity of all things: as the hot fire that flameth is too subtle to be held, so art Thou, O God my God. I cannot grasp Thee, for Thou art everywhere; lo! though I hurl me down the scarlet throat of a volcano, there still shall I find Thee, Thou Unity of Unities, Thou Oneness, O Thou perfect Nothingness of Bliss!

3 O Thou Unity of all things: as the moon that waneth and increaseth in the heavens, so art Thou, O God my God. I cannot stay Thee; for Thou art everywhere; lo! though I devour Thee, as a dragon devoureth a kid, there still shall I find Thee, Thou Unity of Unities, Thou Oneness, O Thou perfect Nothingness of Bliss!

4 O Thou Unity of all things: as the dust that danceth over the breast of the desert, so art Thou, O God my God. I cannot seize Thee, for Thou art everywhere; lo! though I lick up with my tongue the bitter salt of the plains, there still shall I find Thee, Thou Unity of Unities, Thou Oneness, O Thou perfect Nothingness of Bliss!

5 O Thou Unity of all things: as the air that bubbleth from the dark depths of the waters, so art Thou, O God my God. I cannot catch Thee, for Thou art everywhere; lo! though I net Thee as a goldfish in a kerchief of silk, there still shall I find Thee, Thou Unity of Unities, Thou Oneness, O Thou perfect Nothingness of Bliss!

6 O Thou Unity of all things: as the cloud that flitteth across the white horns of the moon, so art Thou, O God my God. I cannot pierce Thee, for Thou art everywhere; lo! though I tangle Thee in a witch-gossamer of starlight, there still shall I find Thee, Thou Unity of Unities, Thou Oneness, O Thou perfect Nothingness of Bliss!

7 O Thou Unity of all things: as the star that travelleth along its appointed course, so art Thou, O God my God. I cannot rule Thee, for Thou art everywhere; lo! though I hunt Thee across the blue heavens as a lost comet, there still shall I find Thee, Thou Unity of Unities, Thou Oneness, O Thou perfect Nothingness of Bliss!

8 O Thou Unity of all things: as the lightning that lurketh in the heart of the thunder, so art Thou, O God my God. I cannot search Thee, for Thou art everywhere; lo! though I wed the flaming circle to the enshrouded square, there still shall I find Thee, Thou Unity of Unities, Thou Oneness, O Thou perfect Nothingness of Bliss!

9 O Thou Unity of all things: as the earth that holdeth all precious jewels in her heart, so art Thou, O God my God. I cannot spoil Thee, for Thou art everywhere; lo! though I burrow as a mole in the mountain of Chaos, there still shall I find Thee, Thou Unity of Unities, Thou Oneness, O Thou perfect Nothingness of Bliss!

10 O Thou Unity of all things: as the pole-star that burneth in the centre of the night, so art Thou, O God my God. I cannot hide Thee, for Thou art everywhere; lo! though I turn from

Thee at each touch of the lodestone of lust, there still shall I find Thee, Thou Unity of Unities, Thou Oneness, O Thou perfect Nothingness of Bliss!

11 O Thou Unity of all things: as the blue smoke that whirleth up from the altar of life, so art Thou, O God my God. I cannot find Thee, for Thou art everywhere; lo! though I inter Thee in the sarcophagi of the damned, there still shall I find Thee, Thou Unity of Unities, Thou Oneness, O Thou perfect Nothingness of Bliss!

12 O Thou Unity of all things: as a dark-eyed maiden decked in crimson and precious pearls, so art Thou, O God my God. I cannot rob Thee, for Thou art everywhere; lo! though I strip Thee of Thy gold and scarlet raiment of Self, there still shall I find Thee, Thou Unity of Unities, Thou Oneness, O Thou perfect Nothingness of Bliss!

13 O Thou Unity of all things: as the sun that rolleth through the twelve mansions of the skies, so art Thou, O God my God. I cannot slay Thee, for Thou art everywhere; lo! though I lick up the Boundless Light, the Boundless, and the Not, there still shall I find Thee, Thou Unity of Unities, Thou Oneness, O Thou perfect Nothingness of Bliss!

O Glory be unto Thee through all Time
and though all Space: Glory,
and Glory upon Glory,
Everlastingly. Amen,
and Amen, and
Amen.

The Chapter known as The Hundred and Sixty=Nine Cries of Adoration and the Unity thereof

✦ ✦ ✦ ✦ ✦   I   ✦ ✦ ✦ ✦ ✦
✦ ✦ ✦ ✦ ✦ adore ✦ ✦ ✦ ✦ ✦
✦ ✦ ✦ ✦ Thee by the ✦ ✦ ✦ ✦
✦ ✦ ✦ ✦ Hundred and Sixty- ✦ ✦ ✦ ✦
✦ ✦ ✦ ✦ Nine Cries of Adoration ✦ ✦ ✦ ✦
✦ ✦ ✦ ✦ and by the Unity thereof. ✦ ✦ ✦ ✦

O Thou Dragon-prince of the air, that art drunk on the blood of the sunsets! I adore Thee, Evoe! I adore Thee, IAO!

O Thou Unicorn of the storm, that art crested above the purple air! I adore Thee, Evoe! I adore Thee, IAO!

O Thou burning sword of passion, that art tempered on the anvil of flesh! I adore Thee, Evoe! I adore Thee, IAO!

O Thou slimy lust of the grave, that art tangled in the roots of the tree! I adore Thee, Evoe! I adore Thee, IAO!

O Thou smoke-shrouded sword of flame, that art en-sheathed in the bowels of earth! I adore Thee, Evoe! I adore Thee, IAO!

O Thou scented grove of wild vines, that art trampled by the white feet of love! I adore Thee, Evoe! I adore Thee, IAO!

O Thou golden sheaf of desires, that art bound by a fair wisp of poppies! I adore Thee, Evoe! I adore Thee, IAO!

O Thou molten comet of gold, that art seen through the wizard's glass of Space! I adore Thee, Evoe! I adore Thee, IAO!

O Thou shrill song of the eunuch, that art heard behind the curtain of shame! I adore Thee, Evoe! I adore Thee, IAO!

O Thou bright star of the morning, that art set betwixt the breasts of night! I adore Thee, Evoe! I adore Thee, IAO!

O Thou lidless eye of the world, that art seen through the sapphire veil of space! I adore Thee, Evoe! I adore Thee, IAO!

O Thou smiling mouth of the dawn, that art freed from the laughter of the night! I adore Thee, Evoe! I adore Thee, IAO!

O Thou dazzling star-point of hope, that burnest over oceans of despair! I adore Thee, Evoe! I adore Thee, IAO!

O Thou naked virgin of love, that art caught in a net of wild roses! I adore Thee, Evoe! I adore Thee, IAO!

O Thou iron turret of death, that art rusted with the bright blood of war! I adore Thee, Evoe! I adore Thee, IAO!

O Thou bubbling wine-cup of joy, that foamest like the cauldron of murder! I adore Thee, Evoe! I adore Thee, IAO!

O Thou icy trail of the moon, that art traced in the veins of the onyx! I adore Thee, Evoe! I adore Thee, IAO!

O Thou frenzied hunter of love, that art slain by the twisted horns of lust! I adore Thee, Evoe! I adore Thee, IAO!

O Thou frozen book of the seas, that art graven by the swords of the sun! I adore Thee, Evoe! I adore Thee, IAO!

O Thou flashing opal of light, that art wrapped in the robes of the rainbow! I adore Thee, Evoe! I adore Thee, IAO!

O Thou purple mist of the hills, that hideth shepherds from the wanton moon! I adore Thee, Evoe! I adore Thee, IAO!

O Thou low moan of fainting maids, that art caught up in the strong sobs of love! I adore Thee, Evoe! I adore Thee, IAO!

O Thou fleeting beam of delight, that lurkest within the spear-thrusts of dawn! I adore Thee, Evoe! I adore Thee, IAO!

O Thou golden wine of the sun, that art poured over the dark breasts of night! I adore Thee, Evoe! I adore Thee, IAO!

O Thou fragrance of sweet flowers, that art wafted over blue fields of air! I adore Thee, Evoe! I adore Thee, IAO!

O Thou mighty bastion of faith, that withstandest all the breachers of doubt! I adore Thee, Evoe! I adore Thee, IAO!

O Thou silver horn of the moon, that gorest the red flank of the morning! I adore Thee, Evoe! I adore Thee, IAO!

O Thou grey glory of twilight, that art the hermaphrodite triumphant! I adore Thee, Evoe! I adore Thee, IAO!

O Thou thirsty mouth of the wind, that art maddened by the foam of the sea! I adore Thee, Evoe! I adore Thee, IAO!

O Thou couch of rose-leaf desires, that art crumpled by the vine and the fir! I adore Thee, Evoe! I adore Thee, IAO!

O Thou bird-sweet river of Love, that warblest through the pebbly gorge of Life! I adore Thee, Evoe! I adore Thee, IAO!

O Thou golden network of stars, that art girt about the cold breasts of Night! I adore Thee, Evoe! I adore Thee, IAO!

O Thou mad whirlwind of laughter, that art meshed in the wild locks of folly! I adore Thee, Evoe! I adore Thee, IAO!

O Thou white hand of Creation, that holdest up the dying head of Death! I adore Thee, Evoe! I adore Thee, IAO!

O Thou purple tongue of Twilight, that dost lap up the lucent milk of Day! I adore Thee, Evoe! I adore Thee, IAO!

O Thou thunderbolt of Science, that flashest from the dark clouds of Magic! I adore Thee, Evoe! I adore Thee, IAO!

O Thou red rose of the Morning, that glowest in the bosom of the Night! I adore Thee, Evoe! I adore Thee, IAO!

O Thou flaming globe of Glory, that art caught up in the arms of the sun! I adore Thee, Evoe! I adore Thee, IAO!

O Thou silver arrow of hope, that art shot from the arc of the rainbow! I adore Thee, Evoe! I adore Thee, IAO!

O Thou starry virgin of Night, that art strained to the arms of the morning! I adore Thee, Evoe! I adore Thee, IAO!

O Thou sworded soldier of life, that art sucked down in the quicksands of death! I adore Thee, Evoe! I adore Thee, IAO!

O Thou bronze blast of the trumpet, that rollest over emerald-tipped spears! I adore Thee, Evoe! I adore Thee, IAO!

O Thou opal mist of the sea, that art sucked up by the beams of the sun! I adore Thee, Evoe! I adore Thee, IAO!

O Thou red worm of formation, that art lifted by the white whorl of love! I adore Thee, Evoe! I adore Thee, IAO!

O Thou mighty anvil of Time, that outshowerest the bright sparks of life! I adore Thee, Evoe! I adore Thee, IAO!

O Thou red cobra of desire, that art unhooded by the hands of girls! I adore Thee, Evoe! I adore Thee, IAO!

O Thou curling billow of joy, whose fingers caress the limbs of the world! I adore Thee, Evoe! I adore Thee, IAO!

O Thou emerald vulture of Truth, that art perched upon the vast tree of life! I adore Thee, Evoe! I adore Thee, IAO!

O Thou lonely eagle of night, that drinkest at the moist lips of the moon! I adore Thee, Evoe! I adore Thee, IAO!

O Thou wild daughter of Chaos, that art ravished by the strong son of law! I adore Thee, Evoe! I adore Thee, IAO!

O Thou ghostly night of terror, that art slaughtered in the blood of the dawn! I adore Thee, Evoe! I adore Thee, IAO!

O Thou poppied nectar of sleep, that art curled in the still womb of slumber! I adore Thee, Evoe! I adore Thee, IAO!

O Thou burning rapture of girls, that disport in the sunset of passion! I adore Thee, Evoe! I adore Thee, IAO!

O Thou molten ocean of stars, that art a crown for the forehead of day! I adore Thee, Evoe! I adore Thee, IAO!

O Thou little brook in the hills, like an asp betwixt the breasts of a girl! I adore Thee, Evoe! I adore Thee, IAO!

O Thou mighty oak of magic, that art rooted in the mountain of life! I adore Thee, Evoe! I adore Thee, IAO!

O Thou sparkling network of pearls, that art woven of the waves by the moon! I adore Thee, Evoe! I adore Thee, IAO!

O Thou wanton sword-blade of life, that art sheathèd by the harlot call'd Death! I adore Thee, Evoe! I adore Thee, IAO!

O Thou mist-clad spirit of spring, that art unrob'd by the hands of the wind! I adore Thee, Evoe! I adore Thee, IAO!

O Thou sweet perfume of desire, that art wafted through the valleys of love! I adore Thee, Evoe! I adore Thee, IAO!

O Thou sparkling wine-cup of light, whose foaming is the heart's blood of the stars! I adore Thee, Evoe! I adore Thee, IAO!

O Thou silver sword of madness, that art smitten through the midden of life! I adore Thee, Evoe! I adore Thee, IAO!

O Thou hooded vulture of night, that art glutted on the entrails of day! I adore Thee, Evoe! I adore Thee, IAO!

O Thou pearl-grey arch of the world, whose keystone is the ecstasy of man! I adore Thee, Evoe! I adore Thee, IAO!

O Thou silken web of movement, that art blown through the atoms of matter! I adore Thee, Evoe! I adore Thee, IAO!

O Thou rush-strewn threshold of joy, that art lost in the quicksands of reason! I adore Thee, Evoe! I adore Thee, IAO!

O Thou wild vision of Beauty, but half seen betwixt the cusps of the moon! I adore Thee, Evoe! I adore Thee, IAO!

O Thou pearl cloud of the sunset, that art caught up in a murderer's hand! I adore Thee, Evoe! I adore Thee, IAO!

O Thou rich vintage of slumber, that art crushed from the bud of the poppy! I adore Thee, Evoe! I adore Thee, IAO!

O Thou great boulder of rapture, that leapest adown the mountains of joy! I adore Thee, Evoe! I adore Thee, IAO!

O Thou breather-out of the winds, that art snared in the drag-net of reason! I adore Thee, Evoe! I adore Thee, IAO!

O Thou purple breast of the storm, that art scarred by the teeth of the lightning! I adore Thee, Evoe! I adore Thee, IAO!

O Thou Pillar of phosphor foam, that Leviathan spouteth from's nostrils! I adore Thee, Evoe! I adore Thee, IAO!

O Thou song of the harp of life, that chantest forth the perfection of death! I adore Thee, Evoe! I adore Thee, IAO!

O Thou veilèd beam of the stars, that art tangled in the tresses of night! I adore Thee, Evoe! I adore Thee, IAO!

O Thou flashing shield of the sun, as a discus hurled by the hand of Space! I adore Thee, Evoe! I adore Thee, IAO!

O Thou ribald shout of laughter, that echoest among the tombs of death! I adore Thee, Evoe! I adore Thee, IAO!

O Thou unfailing cruse of joy, that art filled with the tears of the fallen! I adore Thee, Evoe! I adore Thee, IAO!

O Thou burning lust of the moon, that art clothed in the mist of the ocean! I adore Thee, Evoe! I adore Thee, IAO!

O Thou one measure of all things, that art Dam of the great order of worlds! I adore Thee, Evoe! I adore Thee, IAO!

O Thou frail virgin of Eden, that art ravished to the abode of Hell! I adore Thee, Evoe! I adore Thee, IAO!

O Thou dark forest of wonder, that art tangled in a gold web of dew! I adore Thee, Evoe! I adore Thee, IAO!

O Thou tortured shriek of the storm, that art whirled up through the leaves of the woods! I adore Thee, Evoe! I adore Thee, IAO!

O Thou dazzling opal of light, that flamest in the crumbling skull of space! I adore Thee, Evoe! I adore Thee, IAO!

O Thou red knife of destruction, that art sheathed in the bowels of order! I adore Thee, Evoe! I adore Thee, IAO!

O Thou storm-drunk breath of the winds, that pant in the bosom of the mountains! I adore Thee, Evoe! I adore Thee, IAO!

O Thou loud bell of rejoicing, that art smitten by the hammer of woe! I adore Thee, Evoe! I adore Thee, IAO!

O Thou red rose of the sunset, that witherest on the altar of night! I adore Thee, Evoe! I adore Thee, IAO!

O Thou bright vision of sunbeams, that burnest in a flagon of topaz! I adore Thee, Evoe! I adore Thee, IAO!

O Thou virgin lily of night, that sproutest between the lips of a corpse! I adore Thee, Evoe! I adore Thee, IAO!

O Thou blue helm of destruction, that art winged with the lightnings of madness! I adore Thee, Evoe! I adore Thee, IAO!

O Thou voice of the heaving seas, that tremblest in the grey of the twilight! I adore Thee, Evoe! I adore Thee, IAO!

O Thou unfolder of heaven, red-winged as an eagle at sunrise! I adore Thee, Evoe! I adore Thee, IAO!

O Thou curling tongue of red flame, athirst on the nipple of my passion! I adore Thee, Evoe! I adore Thee, IAO!

O Thou outrider of the sun, that spurrest the bloody flanks of the wind! I adore Thee, Evoe! I adore Thee, IAO!

O Thou dancer with gilded nails, that unbraidest the star-hair of the night! I adore Thee, Evoe! I adore Thee, IAO!

O Thou moonlit pearl of rapture, clasped fast in the silver hand of the Dawn! I adore Thee, Evoe! I adore Thee, IAO!

O Thou wanton mother of love, that art mistress of the children of men! I adore Thee, Evoe! I adore Thee, IAO!

O Thou crimson fountain of blood, that spoutest from the heart of Creation! I adore Thee, Evoe! I adore Thee, IAO!

O Thou warrior eye of the sun, that shooteth death from the berylline Byss! I adore Thee, Evoe! I adore Thee, IAO!

O Thou Witch's hell-broth of hate, that boilest in the white cauldron of love! I adore Thee, Evoe! I adore Thee, IAO!

O Thou Ribbon of Northern Lights, that bindest the elfin tresses of night! I adore Thee, Evoe! I adore Thee, IAO!

O Thou red sword of the Twilight, that art rusted with the blood of the noon! I adore Thee, Evoe! I adore Thee, IAO!

O Thou sacrificer of Dawn, that wearest the chasuble of sunset! I adore Thee, Evoe! I adore Thee, IAO!

O Thou bloodshot eye of lightning, glowering beneath the eyebrows of thunder! I adore Thee, Evoe! I adore Thee, IAO!

O Thou four-square Crown of Nothing, that circlest the destruction of worlds! I adore Thee, Evoe! I adore Thee, IAO!

O Thou bloodhound whirlwind of lust, that art unleashed by the first kiss of love! I adore Thee, Evoe! I adore Thee, IAO!

O Thou wondrous chalice of light, uplifted by the Mænads of Dawn! I adore Thee, Evoe! I adore Thee, IAO!

O Thou fecund opal of death, that sparklest through a sea of mother-of-pearl! I adore Thee, Evoe! I adore Thee, IAO!

O Thou crimson rose of the Dawn, that art fastened in the dark locks of Night! I adore Thee, Evoe! I adore Thee, IAO!

O Thou pink nipple of Being, thrust deep into the black mouth of Chaos! I adore Thee, Evoe! I adore Thee, IAO!

O Thou vampire Queen of the Flesh, wound as a snake around the throats of men! I adore Thee, Evoe! I adore Thee, IAO!

O Thou tender nest of dove's down, built up betwixt the hawk's claws of the Night! I adore Thee, Evoe! I adore Thee, IAO!

O Thou concubine of Matter, anointed with love-nard of Motion! I adore Thee, Evoe! I adore Thee, IAO!

O Thou flame-tipp'd bolt of Morning, that art shot out from the crossbow of Night! I adore Thee, Evoe! I adore Thee, IAO!

O Thou frail blue-bell of Moonlight, that art lost in the gardens of the Stars! I adore Thee, Evoe! I adore Thee, IAO!

O Thou tall mast of wreck'd Chaos, that art crowned by the white lamp of Cosmos! I adore Thee, Evoe! I adore Thee, IAO!

O Thou pearly eyelid of Day, that art closed by the finger of Evening! I adore Thee, Evoe! I adore Thee, IAO!

O Thou wild anarch of the Hills, pale glooming above the mists of the Earth! I adore Thee, Evoe! I adore Thee, IAO!

O Thou moonlit peak of pleasure, that art crowned by viper tongues of forked flame! I adore Thee, Evoe! I adore Thee, IAO!

O Thou wolfish head of the winds, that frighteth the snow-white lamb of winter! I adore Thee, Evoe! I adore Thee, IAO!

O Thou dew-lit nymph of the Dawn, that swoonest in the satyr arms of the Sun! I adore Thee, Evoe! I adore Thee, IAO!

O Thou mad abode of kisses, that art lit by the fat of murdered fiends! I adore Thee, Evoe! I adore Thee, IAO!

O Thou sleeping lust of the Storm, that art flame-gorg'd as a flint full of fire! I adore Thee, Evoe! I adore Thee, IAO!

O Thou soft dew of the Evening, that art drunk up by the mist of the Night! I adore Thee, Evoe! I adore Thee, IAO!

O Thou wounded son of the West, that gushest out Thy blood on the heavens! I adore Thee, Evoe! I adore Thee, IAO!

O Thou burning tower of fire, that art set up in the midst of the seas! I adore Thee, Evoe! I adore Thee, IAO!

O Thou unvintageable dew, that art moist upon the lips of the Morn! I adore Thee, Evoe! I adore Thee, IAO!

O Thou silver crescent of love, that burnest over the dark helm of War! I adore Thee, Evoe! I adore Thee, IAO!

O Thou snow-white ram of the Dawn, that art slain by the lion of the noon! I adore Thee, Evoe! I adore Thee, IAO!

O Thou crimson spear-point of life, that art thrust through the dark bowels of Time! I adore Thee, Evoe! I adore Thee, IAO!

O Thou black waterspout of Death, that whirlest, whelmest the tall ship of Life! I adore Thee, Evoe! I adore Thee, IAO!

O Thou mighty chain of events, that art strained betwixt Cosmos and Chaos! I adore Thee, Evoe! I adore Thee, IAO!

O Thou towering eagre of lust, that art heaped up by the moon-breasts of youth! I adore Thee, Evoe! I adore Thee, IAO!

O Thou serpent-crown of green light, that art wound round the dark forehead of Death! I adore Thee, Evoe! I adore Thee, IAO!

O Thou crimson vintage of Life, that art poured into the jar of the Grave! I adore Thee, Evoe! I adore Thee, IAO!

O Thou waveless Ocean of Peace, that sleepest beneath the wild heart of man! I adore Thee, Evoe! I adore Thee, IAO!

O Thou whirling skirt of the stars, that art swathed round the limbs of the Æthyr! I adore Thee, Evoe! I adore Thee, IAO!

O Thou snow-white chalice of Love, thou art filled up with the red lusts of Man! I adore Thee, Evoe! I adore Thee, IAO!

O Thou fragrant garden of Joy, firm-set betwixt the breasts of the morning! I adore Thee, Evoe! I adore Thee, IAO!

O Thou pearly fountain of Life, that spoutest up in the black court of Death! I adore Thee, Evoe! I adore Thee, IAO!

O Thou brindle hound of the Night, with thy nose to the sleuth of the Sunset! I adore Thee, Evoe! I adore Thee, IAO!

O Thou leprous claw of the ghoul, that coaxest the babe from its chaste cradle! I adore Thee, Evoe! I adore Thee, IAO!

O Thou assassin word of law, that art written in ruin of earthquakes! I adore Thee, Evoe! I adore Thee, IAO!

O Thou trembling breast of the night, that gleamest with a rosary of moons! I adore Thee, Evoe! I adore Thee, IAO!

O Thou Holy Sphinx of rebirth, that crouchest in the black desert of death! I adore Thee, Evoe! I adore Thee, IAO!

O Thou diadem of the suns, that art the knot of this red web of worlds! I adore Thee, Evoe! I adore Thee, IAO!

O Thou ravished river of law, that outpourest the arcanum of Life! I adore Thee, Evoe! I adore Thee, IAO!

O Thou glimmering tongue of day, that art sucked into the blue lips of Night! I adore Thee, Evoe! I adore Thee, IAO!

O Thou Queen-Bee of Heaven's hive, that smearest thy thighs with honey of Hell! I adore Thee, Evoe! I adore Thee, IAO!

O Thou scarlet dragon of flame, enmeshed in the web of a spider! I adore Thee, Evoe! I adore Thee, IAO!

O Thou magic symbol of light, that art frozen on the black book of blood! I adore Thee, Evoe! I adore Thee, IAO!

O Thou swathed image of Death, that art hidden in the coffin of joy! I adore Thee, Evoe! I adore Thee, IAO!

O Thou red breast of the sunset, that pantest for the ravishment of Night! I adore Thee, Evoe! I adore Thee, IAO!

O Thou serpent of malachite, that baskest in a desert of turquoise! I adore Thee, Evoe! I adore Thee, IAO!

O Thou fierce whirlpool of passion, that art sucked up by the mouth of the sun! I adore Thee, Evoe! I adore Thee, IAO!

O Thou green cockatrice of Hell, that art coiled around the finger of Fate! I adore Thee, Evoe! I adore Thee, IAO!

O Thou lambent laughter of fire, that art wound round the heart of the waters! I adore Thee, Evoe! I adore Thee, IAO!

O Thou gorilla blizzard Air, that tearest out Earth's tresses by the roots! I adore Thee, Evoe! I adore Thee, IAO!

O Thou reveller of Spirit, that carousest in the halls of Matter! I adore Thee, Evoe! I adore Thee, IAO!

O Thou red-lipped Vampire of Life, that drainest blood from the black Mount of Death! I adore Thee, Evoe! I adore Thee, IAO!

O Thou little lark of Beyond, that art heard in the dark groves of knowledge! I adore Thee, Evoe! I adore Thee, IAO!

O Thou summer softness of lips, that glow hot with the scarlet of passion! I adore Thee, Evoe! I adore Thee, IAO!

O Thou pearly foam of the grape, that art flecked with the roses of love! I adore Thee, Evoe! I adore Thee, IAO!

O Thou frenzied hand of the seas, that unfurlest the black Banner of Storm! I adore Thee, Evoe! I adore Thee, IAO!

O Thou shrouded book of the dead, that art sealed with the seven souls of man! I adore Thee, Evoe! I adore Thee, IAO!

O Thou writhing frenzy of love, that art knotted like the grid-flames of Hell! I adore Thee, Evoe! I adore Thee, IAO!

O Thou primal birth-ring of thought, that dost encircle the thumb of the soul! I adore Thee, Evoe! I adore Thee, IAO!

O Thou blind flame of Nothingness, as a crown upon my brow! I adore Thee, Evoe! I adore Thee, IAO!

O Glory be unto Thee through all Time
and though all Space: Glory,
and Glory upon Glory,
Everlastingly. Amen,
and Amen, and
Amen.

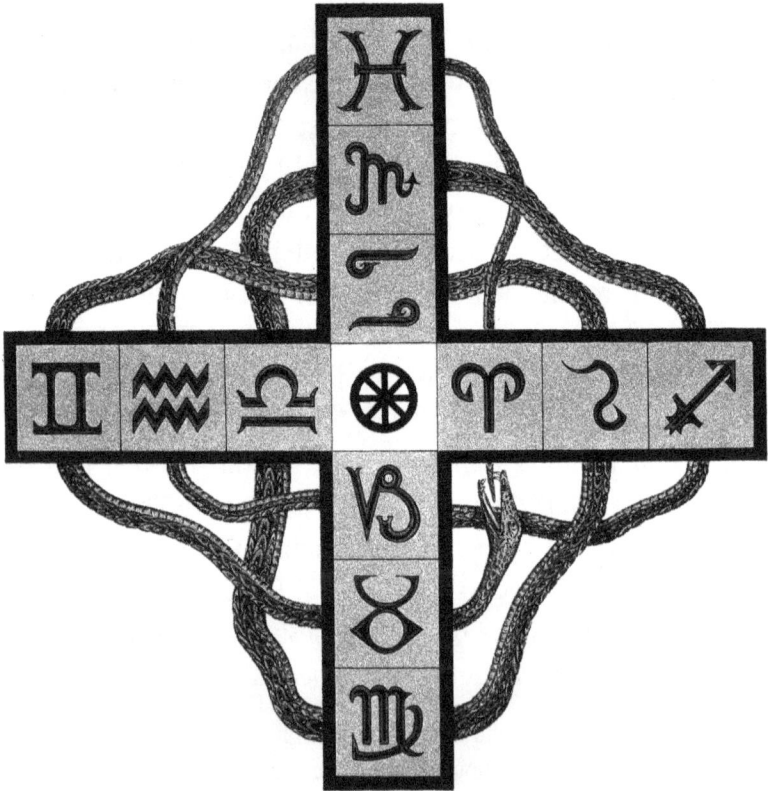

FIG. 2.
The Greek Cross of the Zodiac.

♈. Emerald on Scarlet.   ♎. Scarlet on Emerald.
♉. Greenish Blue on Orange-Red.   ♏. Orange-Red on Greenish Blue.
♊. Royal Blue on Orange.   ♐. Orange on Royal Blue.
♋. Indigo on Amber.   ♑. Amber on Indigo.
♌. Violet on Greenish Yellow.   ♒. Greenish Yellow on Violet.
♍. Crimson on Yellow-Green   ♓. Yellow-Green on Crimson.

Spirit. Black on White.
Serpent. Azure, with Golden Scales.
Border. Gold.

The Chapter known as The Unconsciousness of God that is hidden from man for a sign

<pre>
✦ ✦ ✦ ✦ ✦   I   ✦ ✦ ✦ ✦ ✦
✦ ✦ ✦ ✦ ✦   adore   ✦ ✦ ✦ ✦ ✦
✦ ✦ ✦ ✦   Thee by the   ✦ ✦ ✦ ✦
✦ ✦ ✦ ✦ Twelvefold Sign ✦ ✦ ✦ ✦
✦ ✦ ✦ ✦ and by the Unity thereof. ✦ ✦ ✦ ✦
</pre>

12 The Light of my Life is as the light of two moons, one rising and the other setting, one increasing and the other waning; the one growing fat as the other groweth lean, like a paunchy thief sucking dry a skin of amber wine. Yet though the light of the first devoureth the light of the second, nevertheless the light of the second disgorgeth the light of the first, so that there is neither the desire of light nor the need of light—all being as a woven twilight of day and night, a madness of mingling moons. Yet I behold!

11 Now mine eyes are seven, and are as stars about a star; and the lids of mine eyes are fourteen, two to each eye. Also have I seven arms to do the bidding of the seven eyes; and each arm hath an hand of three fingers, so that I may rule the great ocean and burn it up with the Spirit of Flame, and that I may drown the fire in the Abode of the Waters. Thus I am rendered naked; for neither flame nor water can clothe me; therefore am I as a breath of wind blown over an Earth of Adamant, that knoweth neither sorrow nor rejoicing; then do I abide as a River of Light between the Night of Chaos and the Day of Creation.

10 Two are the moons of my madness, like the horns on the head of a goat. And between them burneth a pyramid of flame, which consumeth neither but blindeth both, so that the one beholdeth not the other. Notwithstanding, when the one is lost in the water, and the other is burnt up in the flame, they

become united in the form of a woman fashioned of Earth and of Air, who without husband is yet mother of many sons.

9 Now the Sons are in truth but one Son; and the one Son but a daughter draped and never naked; for her mother is naked, therefore is she robed. And she is called the Light of my Love, for she is concealed and cannot be seen, as the Sun burneth over her and drowneth her in fire, whilst below her surgeth the sea, whose waves are as flames of water. When thou hast licked up the ocean thou shalt not see her because of the fire; and when thou hast swallowed the Sun surely shall the waters be driven from thee, so that though the fire be thine the water hath slipped thee, as a dog its leash. Yet the path is straight.

8 Along it shalt thou journey, and then shalt thou learn that the fear of death is the blood of the world. So the woman dressed herself in the shrouds of the dead, and decked herself with the bones of the fallen; and all feared her, therefore they lived. But she feared life; therefore she wove a dew-moon in her tangled hair as a sign of the fickleness of Death, and wept tears of bitter sorrow that she should live in the blossom of her youth. And her tears crept like scorpions down her cheeks, and sped away in the darkness like serpents; and for each serpent came there an eagle which did carry it away.

7 "Why weep?" said the Balance swinging to the left. "Why laugh?" said the Balance swinging to the right. "Why not remain still?" answered the Hand that held the Balance. And the Balance replied: "Because on my right laughs Death and on my left weeps a Virgin."

6 Then the voice of the Hand said to the girl: "Why weep?" And the maid answered: "Because Death maketh jest of my life." Then the Hand stayed the Balance, and at once the girl saw that she was Death, and that Death that had sat opposite

her was in truth a motherless babe. So she took the child she had conceived in the arms of fear, and went her way laughing.

5 And the infant grew strong; yet its strength was in its weakness; and though to look at it from before was to look upon a man-child, from behind it was a little girl with golden hair. Now, when the child wished to tempt a maid he faced and approached her; and when the child wished to tempt a man she turned her back on him and fled.

4 But one day the child met, at the self-same hour, Love; and the man, seeing a woman, approached her eagerly, and the woman, seeing a man, fled, so that he might capture her. Thus it came about that the child met the child and wondered, not knowing that the child had lost the child. So it was that they walked side by side.

3 Then that part of the child that was man loved and lusted for that part of the child that was woman; and each knew not that each was the other, and felt that they were two and yet one, nevertheless one and yet two. And when one said: "Who art thou?" the other answered at the self-same moment: "Who am I?"

2 Soon becoming perplexed if I were Thou, or if Thou were I, it came about that the I mingled with the Thou, and the Thou with the I, so that six added to ten became sixteen, which is felicity; for it is the interplay of the elements. Four are the elements that make man, and four are the elements that make woman. Thus was the child reborn.

1 But though the man ruleth the woman, and the woman ruleth the man, the Child ruleth both its mother and father, and being five is Emperor over the kingdom of their hearts. To its father it giveth four, and to its mother it giveth four, yet it remaineth five, for it hath of its father an half and of its mother an half; but in itself it is equal to both its father and its mother; for it is father of fathers and mother of mothers.

0 Therefore is it One Whole, and not two halves; and being One is Thirteen, which is called Nothing when it is All-things.

.

Amen
without lie,
and Amen of Amen,
and Amen of Amen of Amen.

A SYLLABUS OF THE OFFICIAL INSTRUCTIONS OF A∴ A∴ HITHERTO PUBLISHED

THE publications of the A∴ A∴ divide themselves into four classes.[1]

Class "A" consists of books of which may be changed not so much as the style of a letter: that is, they represent the utterance of an Adept entirely beyond the criticism of even the Visible Head of the Organization.

Class "B" consists of books or essays which are the result of ordinary scholarship, enlightened and earnest.

Class "C" consists of matter which is to be regarded rather as suggestive than anything else.

Class "D" consists of the Official Rituals and Instructions.

[Class "E" consists of manifestos, broadsheets, epistles and other public statements.]

Some publications are composite, and pertain to more than one class.

CLASS "A" PUBLICATIONS

LIBER I.—*Liber B vel Magi.*

This is an account of the Grade of Magus, the highest grade which it is ever possible to manifest in any way whatever upon this plane. Or so it is said by the Masters of the Temple.

---

1   [Fifth class added later. All post-*Equinox* additions enclosed in square brackets.]

LIBER VII.—*Liber Liberi vel Lapidis Lazvli, Advmbratio Kabbalæ Ægyptiorvm Svb Figvrâ VII*, being the Voluntary Emancipation of a certain Exempt Adept from his Adeptship. These are the Birth Words of a Master of the Temple.

The nature of this book is sufficiently explained by its title. Its seven chapters are referred to the seven planets in the following order: Mars, Saturn, Jupiter, Sol, Mercury, Luna, Venus.

LIBER X.—*Liber Porta Lucis.*

This book is an account of the sending forth of the Master by the A∴ A∴ and an explanation of his mission.

LIBER XXVII.—*Liber Trigrammaton*, being a book of Trigrams of the Mutations of the TAO with the YIN and the YANG.

An account of the cosmic process: corresponding to the Stanzas of DZYAN in another system.

LIBER LXV.—*Liber Cordis cincti serpente.*

An account of the relations of the Aspirant with his Holy Guardian Angel. This book is given to Probationers, as the attainment of the Knowledge and Conversation of the Holy Guardian Angel is the Crown of the Outer College. Similarly Liber VII is given to Neophytes, as the grade of Master of the Temple is the next resting-place, and Liber CCXX to Zelator, since that carries him to the highest of all possible grades. Liber XXVII is given to the Practicus, as in this book is the ultimate foundation of the highest theoretical Qabalah, and Liber DCCCXIII to the Philosophus, as it is the foundation of the highest practical Qabalah.

LIBER LXVI.—*Liber Stellæ Rubeæ.* A secret ritual, the Heart of IAO-OAI, delivered unto V.V.V.V.V. for his use in a certain matter of *Liber Legis*, and written down under the figure LXVI.

This book is sufficiently described by the title.

LIBER XC.—*Liber Tzaddi vel Hamus Hermeticus Sub Figurâ XC.*

An account of Initiation, and an indication as to those who are suitable for the same.

LIBER CLVI.—*Liber Cheth vel Vallum Abiegni Sub Figurâ CLVI.*

This book is a perfect account of the task of the Exempt Adept, considered under the symbols of a particular plane, not the intellectual.

LIBER CCXX.—*Liber L. vel Legis Sub Figurâ CCXX as delivered by LXXVIII unto DCLXVI.*[2]

This book is the foundation of the New Æon, and thus of the whole of our Work.

LIBER CCXXXI.—*Liber Arcanorum τῶν Atv τοῦ Tahvti Quas Vidit Asar in Amennti Sub Figurâ CCXXXI. Liber Carcerorum τῶν Qliphoth cum suis Geniis. Adduntur Sigilla et Nomina Eorum.*

This is an account of the cosmic process so far as it is indicated by the Tarot Trumps.

LIBER CCCLXX.—*Liber A'ash vel Capricorni Pneumatici Sub Figurâ CCCLXX.*

Contains the true secret of all practical magick.

LIBER CD.—*Liber Tav vel Kabbalæ Trium Literarum Sub Figurâ CD.*

A graphic interpretation of the Tarot on the plane of initiation.

LIBER DCCCXIII.—*vel Ararita Sub Figurâ DLXX.*

This book is an account of the Hexagram and the method of reducing it to the Unity, and Beyond.

---

2   [Later renamed *Liber AL vel Legis*. The subsequently recovered Holograph MS. was designated Liber XXXI and is considered its own "Holy Book."]

CLASS "A–B"

[LIBER CDXV.—*Opus Lutetianum. The Paris Working.*]

LIBER CDXVIII.—*Liber XXX ÆRUM vel Sæculi. Being of the Angels of the thirty ÆTHYRS, the Vision and the Voice.*

Besides being the classical account of the thirty Æthyrs and a model of all visions, the cries of the Angels should be regarded as accurate, and the doctrine of the function of the Great White Brotherhood understood as the foundation of the Aspiration of the Adept. The account of the Master of the Temple should in particular be taken as authentic.

The instruction in the 8th Æthyr pertains to Class D, *i.e.* it is an Official Ritual, and the same remarks apply to the account of the proper method of invoking Æthyrs given in the 18th Æthyr.

CLASSES "A" and "B"

LIBER CMLXIII.—Θησαυροῦ Ἐιδώλων. *The Treasure-House of Images.*

[A superb collection of Litanies appropriate to the Signs of the Zodiac.] Only the short note pertains to Class A.

CLASS "B"

LIBER VI.—*Liber O vel Manus et Sagittæ.*

The instructions given in this book are too loose to find place in the Class D publications.

Instructions given for elementary study of the Qabalah, Assumption of God forms, Vibration of Divine Names, the Rituals of Pentagram and Hexagram, and their uses in production and invocation, a method of attaining astral visions so-called, and an instruction in the practice called Rising on the Planes.

LIBER IX.—*Liber E vel Exercitiorum.*

This book instructs the aspirant in the necessity of keeping a record. Suggests methods of testing physical clairvoyance. Gives instruction in Asana, Pranayama and Dharana, and advises the application of tests to the physical body, in order that the student may thoroughly understand his own limitations.

[LIBER XXI.—Kh*ing* K*ang* K*ing. The Classic of Purity,* by Ko Hsuen.

A Taoist classic put into rhyme. A new translation from the Chinese by the Master Therion.[3]]

LIBER XXX.—*Liber Libræ.*

An elementary course of morality suitable for the average man.

LIBER LVIII.

This is an article on the Qabalah in the Temple of Solomon the King, *Equinox V.*

LIBER LXI.—*Liber Causæ.* The Preliminary Lection, including the History Lection.

Explains the actual history of the origin of the present movement. Its statements are accurate in the ordinary sense of the world. The object of the book is to discount Mythopœia.

LIBER LXIV.—*Liber Israfel,* formerly called *Anubis.*

An instruction in a suitable method of preaching.

[LIBER LXXI.—*The Voice of the Silence, the Two Paths, the Seven Portals.*

By H. P. Blavatsky, with an elaborate commentary by Frater O. M.]

---

3 [Crowley's "translations" of the Yî King and Tao Teh King also belong here, the *caveat* being that both remained unpublished for decades after his death. See the Curriculum following.]

LIBER LXXVIII.

A description of the Cards of the Tarot with their attributions, including a method of divination by their use.

LIBER LXXXIV.—*vel CHANOKH.*

A brief abstraction of the Symbolic representation of the Universe derived by Dr. John Dee through the Scrying of Sir Edward Kelly. Its publication is at present incomplete.

LIBER XCVI.—*Liber Gaias.*

A Handbook of Geomancy. Gives a simple and fairly satisfactory system of Geomancy.

[LIBER CVI.—*Concerning Death.*

A Treatise on the Nature of Death, and the proper attitude to be taken towards it.]

[LIBER CXI.—*Liber Aleph. The Book of Wisdom or Folly.*

An extended and elaborate commentary on the Book of the Law, in the form of a letter from the Master Therion to his magical son. Contains some of the deepest secrets of initiation, with a clear solution of many cosmic and ethical problems.]

[LIBER CLXV.—*A Master of the Temple.*

The record of a man who actually attained by the system taught by the A∴ A∴]

LIBER D.—*Liber Sepher Sephiroth.*

A dictionary of Hebrew words arranged according to their numerical value.

LIBER DXXXVI.—Βατραχοφρενοβοοκοσμομαχία.

An instruction in expansion of the field of the mind.

LIBER DCCLXXVII.—*vel Prolegomena Symbolica Ad Systemam Sceptico-Mysticæ Viæ Explicandæ, Fundamentum Hieroglyphicum Sanctissimorum Scientæ Summæ.*

A tentative table of correspondences between various religious symbols.

LIBER DCCCLXVIII.—*Liber Viarum Viæ.*

A graphic account of magical powers classified under the Tarot trumps.

LIBER CMXIII.—*Liber Viæ Memoriæ.* תישארב

Gives methods of attaining the magical memory or memory of past lives, and an insight into the function of the aspirant in this present life.

CLASS "C"

LIBER XXXIII.

An account of A∴ A∴ first written in the language of his period by the Councillor von Eckartshausen, and now revised and rewritten in the Universal Cipher.

An elementary suggestive account of the work of the Order in its relation to the average man. The preliminary paper of M∴ M∴ M∴ may be classed with this.

LIBER XLI.—*Thien TAO* (in Konx Om Pax).

An advanced study of Attainment by the method of equilibrium on the ethical plane.

LIBER LV.—*The Chymical Jousting of Brother Perardua.*

An account of the Magical and Mystic Path in the language of Alchemy.

LIBER LIX.—*Across the Gulf.*

A fantastic account of a previous incarnation. Its principal interest is that its story of the overthrowing of Isis by Osiris may help the reader to understand the meaning of the over-throwing of Osiris by Horus in the present Æon.

LIBER LXVII.—*The Sword of Song.*

A critical study of various philosophies. An account of Buddhism.

Liber XCV.—*The Wake World* (in Konx Om Pax).

A poetical allegory of the relations of the soul and the Holy Guardian Angel.

Liber CXLVIII.—*The Soldier and the Hunchback.*

An essay on the method of equilibrium on the intellectual plane.

Liber CXCVII.—*The High History of Good Sir Palamedes the Saracen Knight and of his following of the Questing Beast.*

A poetic account of the Great Work, and enumeration of many obstacles.

Liber CCXLII.—*Aha!*

An exposition in poetic language of several of the ways of attainment and the results obtained.

Liber CCCXXXIII.—*The Book of Lies falsely so-called.*

This book deals with many matters on all planes of the very highest importance. It is an official publication for Babes of the Abyss, but is recommended even to beginners as highly suggestive. Its Chapters XXV, XXXVI and XLIV are in Class D.

Liber CCCXXXV.—*Adonis.*

This gives an account in poetic language of the struggle of the human and divine elements in the consciousness of man, giving their harmony following upon the victory of the latter.

Liber CDLXXIV.—*Liber Os Abysmi vel Daath.*

An instruction in a purely intellectual method of entering the Abyss.

Liber DCCCLX.—*John St. John.*

A model of what a magical record should be, so far as accurate analysis and fullness of description are concerned.

Liber MMCMXI.—*A Note on Genesis.*

A model of Qabalistic ratiocination.

CLASS "D"

LIBER III.—*Liber Jugorum.*
An instruction for the control of speech, action and thought.

LIBER VIII.—*See* CDXVIII.

LIBER XI.—*Liber N V.*
An instruction for attaining Nuit.

LIBER XIII.—*Graduum Montis Abiegni.*
An account of the task of the Aspirant from Probationer to Adept.

[LIBER XV.—*Ecclesiæ Gnosticæ Catholicæ Canon Missæ.*
Represents the original and true pre-Christian Christianity.]

LIBER XVI.—*Liber Turris vel Domus Dei.*
An instruction for attainment by the direct destruction of thoughts as they arise in the mind.

LIBER XVII.—*Liber I A O.*
Gives three methods of attainment through a willed series of thoughts.

This book has not been published. It is the active form of Liber H H H. The article "Energized Enthusiasm" is an adumbration of this book.

LIBER XXV.
This is the chapter called the "Star Ruby" in the *Book of Lies.* It is an improved form of the "lesser" ritual of the Pentagram.

LIBER XXVIII.—*Liber Septem Regum Sanctorum.*
A ritual of Initiation bestowed on certain selected Probationers.

LIBER XXXVI.—*The Star Sapphire.*
Is Chapter XXXVI of the *Book of Lies,* giving an improved ritual of the Hexagram.

LIBER XLIV.—*The Mass of the Phœnix.*
This is Chapter XLIV of the *Book of Lies.* An instruction in a simple and exoteric form of Eucharist.

LIBER C.—*Liber* כף

[The Book of the Unveiling of the Sangraal wherein it is spoken of the Wine of the Sabbath of the Adepts.[4]] Has not been, and at present will not be, published.

LIBER CXX.—*Liber Cadaveris.*
The Ritual of Initiation of a Zelator.

LIBER CLXXV.—*Astarte vel Liber Berylli.*
An instruction in attainment by the method of devotion.

LIBER CLXXXV.—*Liber Collegii Sancti.*
Being the tasks of the Grades and their Oaths proper to Liber XIII. This is the official Paper of the various grades. It includes the Task and Oath of a Probationer.

LIBER CC.—*Resh vel Helios.*
An instruction for adorations of the Sun four times daily, with the object of composing the mind to meditation and of regularizing the practices.

LIBER CCVI.—*Liber R V vel Spiritus.*
Full instruction in Pranayama.

LIBER CCCLXI.—*Liber H H H.*
Gives three methods of attainment through a willed series of thoughts.

LIBER CDXII.—*A vel Armorum.*
An instruction for the preparation of the Elemental Instruments.

LIBER CDLI.—*Liber Siloam.*
Not yet published. A direct method of inducing trance.

LIBER DLV.—*Liber H A D.*
An instruction for attaining Hadit.

---

4   [Eventually, all the higher degree papers of the O.T.O. found themselves on this list, whereas no further A∴ A∴ rituals or instructions appear to have been issued.]

LIBER DCLXXI.—*Liber Pyramidos.*

The ritual of the initiation of a Neophyte. It includes sub-rituals numbered from 672 to 676.

[LIBER DCCC.—*Liber Samekh. Theurgia Goëtia Summa (Congressus cum Dæmone).*

The ritual employed by the Beast 666 for the Attainment of the Knowledge and Conversation of his Holy Guardian Angel during the Semester of His performance of the Operation of the Sacred Magick of Abramelin the Mage.]

LIBER DCCCXXXI.—*Liber I O D,* formerly called VESTA.

An instruction giving three methods of reducing the manifold consciousness to the Unity.

LIBER   .—*Liber Collegii Interni.*
Not yet published.

[CLASS "E"]

LIBER II.—*The Message of the Master Therion.*

Explains the essense of the new Law in a very simple manner.

LIBER CL.—*De Lege Libellum.*

A further explanation of the Book of the Law, with special reference to the Powers and Privileges conferred by its acceptance.

LIBER CCC.—*Khabs am Pekht.*

A special instruction for the Promulgation of the Law. This is the first and most important duty of every Aspirant of whatever grade. It builds up in him the character and Karma which forms the Spine of Attainment.

LIBER DCCCXXXVII.—*The Law of Liberty.*

A further explanation of the Book of the Law in reference to certain ethical problems.

A NOTE EXPLAINING WHY EACH NUMBER
HAS BEEN GIVEN TO EACH BOOK

LIBER

I. I is the number of the Magus in the Tarot.

III. Refers to the threefold method given, and to the Triangle as a binding force.

VII. Refers to the 7 chapters, and to the fact that the number 7 is peculiarly suitable to the subject of the Book.

VIII. The Tarot card numbered 8, the Charioteer, the bearer of the Holy Graal, represents the Holy Guardian Angel.

IX. Refers to Yesod. The foundation, because the elementary practices recommended in the book are the foundation of all the work.

X. Porta Lucis, the Gate of Light, is one of the titles of Malkuth, whose number is X.

XI. A concentration of the title N V, whose value is 56, and 6 and 5 are 11. (See CCXX. I, i. and II, i.)

XIII. The number of Achad=Unity, and the title is perhaps intended to show that all paths of attainment are essential.

XVI. The key of the Tarot numbered XVI is the Lightning Struck Tower.

XVII. I A O adds up to 17.

XXV. The square of 5, this being a ritual of the Pentagram.

XXVII. The number of permutations of 3 things taken 3 at a time, and (of course) the cube of 3.

XXX. 30 is the letter Lamed, which is Justice in the Tarot, referred to Libra.

XXXIII. This number was given on Masonic grounds.

LIBER

XXXVI. The square of 6, this book being the ritual of the Hexagram.

XLIV. From דם blood, because blood is sacrificed, also because the God Adored is Horus, who gave 44 as his special number. See *Equinox VII*, 376.

LV. The mystic number of Malkuth and of נה ornament; a number generally suitable to the subject of the book.

LVIII. חן Grace, a secret title of the Qabalah. See Sepher Sephiroth.

LIX.

LXI. See Sepher Sephiroth. The allusion is to the fact that this book forms an introduction to the series.

LXIV. A number of Mercury.

LXV. The number of Adonai.

LXVI. The sum of the first 11 numbers. This book relates to Magic, whose Key is 11.

LXVII. The number of זין a sword.

LXXVIII. The number of cards in the Tarot pack.

LXXXIV. Enumeration of the name Enoch.

XC. Tzaddi means a fish-hook. "I will make you fishers of men."

XCV. The number of מלכה "queen," attributed to Malkuth.

XCVI. The total number of points in the 16 figures.

C. Enumeration of the letter Kappa spelt in full. K and Φ are the initials of magical instruments referred to in the text.

CXX. See Rosicrucian Symbolism.

CXLVIII. מאזנים The Balances.

LIBER

CLVI. Babalon, to whom the book refers. See Sepher Sephiroth.

CLXXV. The number of Venus or Astarte.

CLXXXV.

CXCVII. Number of Z O O N, "Beast."

CC. The number of ר the Sun.

CCVI. The number of R V, referred to in the text.

CCXX. The number of the Verses in the three chapters of the Book. It has, however, an enormous amount of symbolism; in particular it combines the 10 Sephiroth and 22 Paths; 78 is איאס. For 666 vide Sepher Sephiroth.

CCXXXI. Sum of the numbers [0 + 1 + ….. + 20 + 21] printed on the Tarot Trumps.

CCXLII. "Aha!" spelt in full.

CCCXXXIII. The number of Choronzon.

CCCXXXV. The Numeration of Adonis in Greek.

CCCXLI. The Sum of the 3 Mothers of the Alphabet.

CCCLXX. עש Creation.

CD. From the large Tau ת in the diagram.

CDXII. Numeration of בית Beth, the letter of the Magus of the Tarot, whose weapons are here described.

CDXVIII. Vide Sepher Sephiroth. Used for this book because the final revelation is the Lord of the Æon.

CDLI. The number of שילעאם Siloam.

CDLXXIV. The number of Daath.

D. The number of ὁ ἀριθμὸς the Greek word for Number.

DXXXVI. The number of the מסלות the sphere of the Fixed Stars.

LIBER

DLV.   H a d   fully expanded; thus הה, אלף, דלת; compare 11 where N u is fully contracted.

DLXX.

DCLXXI.   From תרעא, the Gate, and the spelling in full of the name Adonai.

DCCLXXVII.   See Sepher Sephiroth.

DCCCVIII.   The number of the name נחשתן.

DCCCXI.   The number of I A O in Greek.

DCCCXIII.   See Sepher Sephiroth.

DCCCXXXI.   Φαλλὸς.

DCCCLX.   The number of 'Ιων "John."

DCCCLXVIII.   נתיבות Paths.

CMXIII.   Berashith, the Beginning, spelt backwards in the title to illustrate the development of the magical memory.

CMLXIII.   Achad spelt fully; see Sepher Sephiroth.

MMDCDXI.   Berashith spelt with Capital B as in Genesis i. 1.

CURRICULUM
OF A∴ A∴

Do what thou wilt shall be the whole of the Law.

In order to facilitate the study of The Official Instructions and other publications of the A∴ A∴, the Præmonstrator of the Order now issues a series of courses corresponding to the various grades. The grades themselves represent magical and mystical progress, corresponding to which will be grades of studentship representing intellectual progress, and an examination in each such grade must be passed before the equivalent magical grade is officially conferred.

It must be understood that the highest occult attainments are possible even to people who have no intellectual knowledge whatever. But this has been in the past a source of great iniquity, as it represents an overdevelopment of one organ of the Nature at the expense of others.

It is the particular object of the A∴ A∴ to see to it that progress is orderly and thorough. It must further be stated that although certain books have been chosen for particular study, the student is not thereby absolved from the general study of all of them. For it is important to him to make from the beginning a comprehensive effort to understand the entire system, first, because it is desirable that he should choose his practices from the whole armoury at his disposal, and, also, because as he advances he must be to some extent familiar with all these practices, so that he may be fitted to instruct those entrusted to his guidance.

COURSE I.

GENERAL READING.

SECTION 1.—*Books for Serious Study:*[1]

THE EQUINOX. The standard Work of Reference in all occult matters. The Encyclopædia of Initiation.

LIBER ABA (Book 4). A GENERAL ACCOUNT in elementary terms of magical and mystical powers. In four parts: (1) Mysticism. (2) Magical Theory. (3) Magical Practice. (4) The Law.

COLLECTED WORKS OF A. CROWLEY. These works contain many mystical and magical secrets, both stated clearly in prose, and woven into the robe of sublimest poesy.

*THE YÎ KING. (S. B. E. Series, Oxford University Press.) The "Classic of Changes"; gives the initiated Chinese system of Magick.[2]

*THE TAO TEH KING. (S. B. E. Series.) gives the initiated Chinese system of Mysticism.[2]

*TANNHÄUSER, by A. Crowley. An allegorical drama concerning the Progress of the Soul; the Tannhäuser story slightly remodelled.

*THE UPANISHADS. (S. B. E. Series.) The Classical Basis of Vedantism, the best-known form of Hindu Mysticism.

*THE BHAGAVAD-GITA. A dialogue in which Krishna, the Hindu "Christ," expounds a system of Attainment.

*THE VOICE OF THE SILENCE, by H. P. Blavatsky, with an elaborate commentary by Frater O. M.

*THE GOËTIA. The most intelligible of the mediaeval rituals of Evocation. Contains also the favorite Invocation of the Master Therion.[3]

*THE SHIVA SANHITA. A famous Hindu treatise on certain physical practices.

*THE HATHAYOGA PRADIPIKA. Similar to The Shiva Sanhita.

---

1   [Items with an asterisk (*) previously listed in Liber IX. Additions mostly either works of fiction (Section 2) or pertain ostensibly to the mysteries of the O.T.O.]

2   [Crowley's "translation" included in Liber CCVII as Class B.]

3   [Eventually designated by Crowley as Class B.]

*ERDMANN'S "HISTORY OF PHILOSOPHY." A compendious account of philosophy from the earliest times. Most valuable as a general education of the mind.

*THE SPIRITUAL GUIDE OF MOLINOS. A simple manual of Christian mysticism.

*THE STAR OF THE WEST. (Captain Fuller.) An introduction to the study of the Works of Aleister Crowley.

*THE DHAMMAPADA. (S. B. E. Series, Oxford University Press.) The best of the Buddhist classics.

*THE QUESTIONS OF KING MILINDA. (S. B. E. Series.) Technical points of Buddhist dogma, illustrated by dialogues.

*VARIETIES OF RELIGIOUS EXPERIENCE. (James.) Valuable as showing the uniformity of mystical attainment.

*KABBALA DENUDATA, von Rosenroth: also the Kabbalah Unveiled, by S. L. Mathers. The text of the Kabalah, with commentary. A good elementary introduction to the subject.

*KONX OM PAX. Four invaluable treatises and a preface on Mysticism and Magick.

THE PISTIS SOPHIA. An admirable introduction to the study of Gnosticism.

THE ORACLES OF ZOROASTER. An invaluable collection of precepts mystical and magical.

THE DREAM OF SCIPIO, by Cicero. Excellent for its Vision and its Philosophy.

THE GOLDEN VERSES OF PYTHAGORAS, by Fabre d'Olivet. An interesting study of the exoteric doctrines of this Master.

THE DIVINE PYMANDER, by Hermes Trismegistus. Invaluable as bearing on the Gnostic Philosophy.

THE SECRET SYMBOLS OF THE ROSICRUCIANS, reprint of Franz Hartmann. An invaluable compendium.

SCRUTINIUM CHYMICUM, by Michael Maier. One of the best treatises on alchemy.

SCIENCE AND THE INFINITE, by Sidney Klein. One of the best essays written in recent years.

TWO ESSAYS ON THE WORSHIP OF PRIAPUS, by Richard Payne Knight. Invaluable to all students.

THE GOLDEN BOUGH, by J. G. Frazer. The Text-Book of Folk Lore. Invaluable to all students.

THE AGE OF REASON, by Thomas Paine. Excellent, though elementary, as a corrective to superstition.

RIVERS OF LIFE, by General Forlong. An invaluable text-book of old systems of initiation.

THREE DIALOGUES, by Bishop Berkeley. The Classic of subjective idealism.

ESSAYS OF DAVID HUME. The Classic of Academic Scepticism.

FIRST PRINCIPLES, by Herbert Spencer. The Classic of Agnosticism.

PROLEGOMENA, by Emanuel Kant. The best introduction to Metaphysics.

THE CANON. The best text-book of Applied Qabalah.

THE FOURTH DIMENSION, by H. Hinton. The text-book on this subject.

THE ESSAYS OF THOMAS HENRY HUXLEY. Masterpieces of philosophy, as of prose.

The object of this course of reading is to familiarize the student with all that has been said by the Great Masters in every time and country. He should make a critical examination of them; not so much with the idea of discovering where truth lies, for he cannot do this except by virtue of his own spiritual experience, but rather to discover the essential harmony in those varied works. He should be on his guard against partisanship with a favourite author. He should familiarize himself thoroughly with the method of mental equilibrium, endeavouring to contradict any statement soever, although it may be apparently axiomatic.

The general object of this course, besides that already stated, is to assure sound education in occult matters, so that when spiritual illumination comes it may find a well-built temple. Where the mind is strongly biased towards any special theory, the result of an illumination is often to inflame that portion of the mind which is thus overdeveloped, with the result that the aspirant, instead of becoming an Adept, becomes a bigot and fanatic.

The A∴ A∴ does not offer examination in this course, but recommends these books as the foundation of a library.

SECTION 2.—*Other books, principally fiction, of a generally suggestive and helpful kind:*

ZANONI, by Sir Edward Bulwer Lytton. Valuable for its facts and suggestions about Mysticism.

A STRANGE STORY, by Sir Edward Bulwer Lytton. Valuable for its facts and suggestions about Magick.

THE BLOSSOM AND THE FRUIT, by Mabel Collins. Valuable for its account of the Path.

PETRONIUS ARBITER. Valuable for those who have wit to understand it.

THE GOLDEN ASS, by Apuleius. Valuable for those who have wit to understand it.

LE COMTE DE GABALIS. Valuable for its hints of those things which it mocks.

THE RAPE OF THE LOCK, by Alexander Pope. Valuable for its account of elementals.

UNDINE, by de la Motte Fouqué. Valuable as an account of elementals.

BLACK MAGIC, by Marjorie Bowen. An intensely interesting story of sorcery.

LE PEAU DE CHAGRIN, by Honoré de Balzac. A magnificent magical allegory.

NUMBER NINETEEN, by Edgar Jepson. An excellent tale of modern magic.

DRACULA, by Bram Stoker. Valuable for its account of legends concerning vampires.

SCIENTIFIC ROMANCES, by H. Hinton. Valuable as an introduction to the study of the Fourth Dimension.

ALICE IN WONDERLAND, by Lewis Carroll. Valuable to those who understand the Qabalah.

ALICE THROUGH THE LOOKING GLASS, by Lewis Carroll. Valuable to those who understand the Qabalah.

THE HUNTING OF THE SNARK, by Lewis Carroll. Valuable to those who understand the Qabalah.

THE ARABIAN NIGHTS, translated by either Sir Richard Burton or John Payne. Valuable as a storehouse of oriental magick-lore.

MORTE D'ARTHUR, by Sir Thomas Mallory. Valuable as a storehouse of occidental magick-lore.

THE WORKS OF FRANÇOIS RABELAIS. Invaluable for Wisdom.

THE KASIDAH, by Sir Richard Burton. Valuable as a summary of philosophy.

THE SONG CELESTIAL, by Sir Edwin Arnold. "The Bhagavad-Gita" in verse.

THE LIGHT OF ASIA, by Sir Edwin Arnold. An account of the attainment of Gotama Buddha.

THE ROSICRUCIANS, by Hargrave Jennings. Valuable to those who can read between the lines.

THE REAL HISTORY OF THE ROSICRUCIANS, by A. E. Waite. A good vulgar piece of journalism on the subject.

THE WORKS OF ARTHUR MACHEN. Most of these stories are of great magical interest.

THE WRITINGS OF WILLIAM O'NEILL (BLAKE). Invaluable to all students.

THE SHAVING OF SHAGPAT, by George Meredith. An excellent allegory.

LILITH, by George MacDonald. A good introduction to the Astral.

LÀ-BAS, by J. K. Huysmans. An account of the extravagances caused by the Sin-complex.

THE LORE OF PROSERPINE, by Maurice Hewlett. A suggestive enquiry into the Hermetic Arcanum.

EN ROUTE, by J. K. Huysmans. An account of the follies of Christian mysticism.

SIDONIA THE SORCERESS, by Wilhelm Meinhold.

THE AMBER WITCH, by Wilhelm Meinhold.

These two tales are highly informative.

MACBETH; MIDSUMMER NIGHT'S DREAM; THE TEMPEST, by W. Shakespeare. Interesting for traditions treated.

REDGAUNTLET, by Sir Walter Scott. Also one or two other novels. Interesting for traditions treated.

ROB ROY, by James Grant. Interesting for traditions treated.

THE MAGICIAN, by W. Somerset Maugham. An amusing hotchpot of stolen goods.

THE BIBLE, by various authors unknown. The Hebrew and Greek Originals are of Qabalistic value. It contains also many magical apologues, and recounts many tales of folk-lore and magical rites.

KIM, by Rudyard Kipling. An admirable study of Eastern thought and life. Many other stories by this author are highly suggestive and informative.

For Mythology, as teaching Correspondences:

Books of Fairy Tales generally.
Oriental Classics generally.
Sufi Poetry generally.
Scandinavian and Teutonic Sagas generally.
Celtic Folk-Lore generally.

This course is of general value to the beginner. While it is not to be taken, in all cases, too seriously, it will give him a general familiarity with the mystical and magical tradition, create a deep interest in the subject, and suggest many helpful lines of thought.

It has been impossible to do more, in this list, than to suggest a fairly comprehensive course of reading.

COURSE II.

The basis of our whole work is the Book of the Law. It is essential for every Probationer to study this book and those which are directly connected with it, as commentaries:[4]

LIBER CCXX.—*Liber L. vel Legis* Sub Figurâ CCXX, as delivered by XCIII. unto DCLXVI. This book is the foundation of the New Æon, and thus of the whole of our Work.

†LIBER II.—*The Message of the Master Therion.* It explains the essence of the New Law in a very simple manner.

†LIBER DCCCXXXVII.—*The Law of Liberty.* This is a further explanation of the Book of the Law in reference to certain ethical problems.

†LIBER CL.—*De Lege Libellum.* A further explanation of the Book of the Law, with special reference to the Powers and Privileges conferred by its acceptance.

†LIBER CXI.—(*ALEPH.*) *The Book of Wisdom or Folly.* An extended and elaborate commentary on the Book of the Law, in the form of a letter from the Master Therion to his magical son.

†LIBER X.—*Liber Porta Lucis.* This book is an account of the sending forth of the Master by the A∴ A∴ and an explanation of his mission.

†LIBER XC.—*Liber TZADDI vel Hamus Hermeticus,* Sub Figurâ XC. An account of Initiation, and an indication as to those who are suitable for the same.

†LIBER CDXVIII.—*Liber XXX ÆRUM vel Sæculi.* Being of the Angels of the thirty Æthyrs the Vision and the Voice.

Besides being the classical account of the thirty Æthyrs and a model of all visions, the cries of the Angels should be regarded as accurate, and the doctrine of the function of the Great White Brotherhood understood as the foundation of the Aspiration of the Adept. The account of the Master of the Temple should in particular be taken as authentic.

---

4   [Items with a dagger (†) unique to the particular course in this curriculum; items with a double dagger (‡) also prescribed by Liber CLXXXV at the same stage.]

393

The instruction in the 8th Æthyr pertains to Class D, *i.e.* it is an Official Ritual, and the same remarks apply to the account of the proper method of invoking Æthyrs given in the 18th Æthyr.

†‡LIBER LXV.—*Liber Cordis Cincti Serpente.* An account of the relations of the Aspirant with his Holy Guardian Angel. This book is given to Probationers, as the attainment of the Knowledge and Conversation of the Holy Guardian Angel is the Crown of the Outer College. Similarly Liber VII. is given to Neophytes, as the grade of Master of the Temple is the next resting-place, and Liber CCXX. to Zelator, since that carries him to the highest of all possible grades. Liber XXVII. is given to the Practicus, as in this book is the ultimate foundation of the highest theoretical Qabalah, and Liber DDCCXIII. to the Philosophus, as it is the foundation of the highest practical Qabalah.

LIBER VI.—*Liber O vel Manus et Sagittæ.* The instructions given in this book are too loose to find place in the Class D publications.

Instructions given for elementary study of the Qabalah, Assumption of God forms, Vibration of Divine Names, the Rituals of Pentagram and Hexagram, and their uses in production and invocation, a method of attaining astral visions so called, and an instruction in the practice called Rising on the Planes.

LIBER IX.—*Liber E vel Exercitiorum.* This book instructs the aspirant in the necessity of keeping a record. Suggests methods of testing physical clairvoyance. Gives instruction in Asana, Pranayama and Dharana, and advises the application of tests to the physical body, in order that the student may thoroughly understand his own limitations

†LIBER XXX.—*Liber Libræ.* An elementary course of morality suitable for the average man.

†‡LIBER LXI.—*Liber Causæ.* The Preliminary Lection, including the History Lection. Explains the actual history of the origin of the present movement. Its statements are accurate in the ordinary sense of the word. The object of the book is to discount Mythopœia.

†LIBER XXXIII.—An account of A∴ A∴ first written in the language of his period by the Councillor von Eckarthausen, and now revised and rewritten in the Universal Cipher.

†LIBER XXV.—This is the chapter called the "Star Ruby" in the *Book of Lies*. It is an improved form of the "lesser" ritual of the Pentagram.

†LIBER CC.—*Resh vel Helios.* An instruction for adoration of the Sun four times daily, with the object of composing the mind to meditation and of regularizing the practices.

†LIBER CCC.—A SPECIAL INSTRUCTION for the Promulgation of the Law. This is the first and most important duty of every Aspirant of whatever grade. It builds up in him the Character and Karma which form the Spine of Attainment.

LIBER ABA (Book 4). A GENERAL ACCOUNT in elementary terms of magical and mystical powers. In four parts: (1) Mysticism (2) Magical Theory (3) Magical Practice (4) The Law.

†LIBER CCVII.—*Syllabus.* An enumeration of the Official Publications of the A∴ A∴ with a brief description of the contents of each book.

This course of reading will furnish the Probationer with a thorough general knowledge of the whole system of Attainment, and of the practices tending to this goal, so that he may choose freely as to what way he will take in his Beginning. For this is always left by the A∴ A∴ to his Free Will; They only begin to advise and criticize him on the information supplied to Them by himself in the Magical Record which he prepares for Their Instruction.

COURSE III.

The following books are officially appointed for the study of the Neophyte:

LIBER CCXX.—*Liber L. vel Legis* Sub Figurâ CCXX, as delivered by XCIII. unto DCLXVI. This book is the foundation of the New Æon, and thus of the whole of our Work.

†‡LIBER VII.—*Liber Liberi vel Lapidis Lazvli, Advmbratio Kabbalæ Ægyptiorvm* Sub Figurâ VII., being the Voluntary Emancipation of a certain Exempt Adept from his Adeptship. These are the Birth Words of a Master of the Temple.

The nature of this book is sufficiently explained by its title. Its seven chapters are referred to the seven planets in the following order: Mars, Saturn, Jupiter, Sol, Mercury, Luna, Venus.

‡LIBER VI.—*Liber O vel Manus et Sagittæ.* The instructions given in this book are too loose to find place in the Class D publications.

Instructions are given for elementary study of the Qabalah, Assumption of God-forms, Vibration of Divine Names, the Rituals of Pentagram and Hexagram, and their uses in protection and invocation, a method of attaining astral visions so called, and an instruction in the practice called Rising on the Planes.

LIBER IX.—*Liber E vel Exercitiorum.* This book instructs the aspirant in the necessity of keeping a record. Suggests methods of testing physical clairvoyance. Gives instruction in Asana, Pranayama and Dharana, and advises the application of tests to the physical body, in order that the student may thoroughly understand his own limitations.

†LIBER XCVI.—*Liber Gaias.* A Handbook of Geomancy. Gives a simple and fairly satisfactory system of Geomancy.

†LIBER LXXVIII. A description of the Cards of the Tarot with their attributions, including a method of divination by their use.

†‡LIBER CDXII.—*A vel Armorum.* An instruction for the preparation of the Elemental Instruments.

†LIBER CDLXXIV.—*Liber Os Abysmi vel* DAATH. An instruction in a purely intellectual method of entering the Abyss.

LIBER DCCCXI.—*Energized Enthusiasm.*

This course is specially adapted to the Task of this Grade, the Attainment of Control of the Body of Light, development of Intuition, et cetera.

COURSE IV.

The Zelator will be examined in the following books:

‡LIBER CCXX.—*Liber L. vel Legis* Sub Figurâ CCXX, as delivered by XCIII. unto DCLXVI. This book is the foundation of the New Æon, and thus of the whole of our Work.

†LIBER CMLXIII.—Θησαυρού Ειδώλων. *The Treasure House of Images.* This Book is a superb collection of Litanies ap-propriate to the Signs of the Zodiac.

†LIBER CMXIII.—*Liber Viæ Memoriæ.* Gives methods for attaining the magical memory or memory of past lives, and an insight into the function of the aspirant in this present life.

†LIBER III.—*Liber Jugorum.* An instruction for the control of speech, action and thought.

†LIBER XIII.—*Graduum Montis Abiegni.* An account of the task of the Aspirant from Probationer to Adept.

†‡LIBER XVII.—*Liber I A O.* Gives three methods of attain-ment through a willed series of thoughts.

This book has not been published. It is the active form of Liber H H H. The article "Energized Enthusiasm" is an adumbration of this book.

†LIBER XXXVI.—*The Star Sapphire.* Is Chapter XXXVI. of the *Book of Lies,* giving an improved ritual of the Hexagram.

†LIBER CLXXXV.—*Liber Collegii Sancti.* Being the tasks of the Grades and their Oaths proper to Liber XIII. This is the official paper of the various grades. It includes the Task and Oath of a Probationer.

†LIBER CCVI.—*Liber R V vel Spiritus.* Full instruction in Prana-yama.

†‡LIBER CCCLXI.—*Liber H H H.* Gives three methods of attain-ment through a willed series of thoughts

†LIBER CCCXXXIII.—*The Book of Lies falsely so-called.* This book deals with many matters on all planes of the very highest importance. It is an oflicial publication for Babes of the Abyss, but is recommended even to beginners as highly suggestive. Its Chapters XXV, XXXVI, and XLIV are in Class D.

LIBER DCCCXI.—*Energized Enthusiasm.*

This course is specially adapted to the Task of this Grade, the Attainment of Hatha-Yoga.

COURSE V.

The Practicus will be examined in the following books:

Liber CCXX.—*Liber L. vel Legis* Sub Figurâ CCXX, as delivered by XCIII. unto DCLXVI. This book is the foundation of the New Æon, and thus of the whole of our Work.

†‡Liber XXVII.—*Liber Trigrammaton,* being a book of Trigrams of the Mutations of the Tao with the Yin and the Yang.

An account of the cosmic process: corresponding to the Stanzas of Dzyan in another system.

†Liber CCXXXI.—*Liber Arcanorum τῶν Atv τοῦ Tahvti Quas Vidit Asar in Amennti Sub Figurâ CCXXXI. Liber Carcerorum τῶν Qliphoth cum suis Geniis. Adduntur Sigilla et Nomina Eorum.*

This is an account of the cosmic process so far as it is indicated by the Tarot Trumps.

†Liber CD.—*Liber Tav vel Kabbalæ Trium Literarum* Sub Figurâ CD. A graphic interpretation of the Tarot on the plane of initiation.

†‡Liber LVIII. This is an article on the Qabalah in the Temple of Solomon the King, *Equinox V.*

†Liber LXIV.—*Liber Israfel,* formerly called *Anubis.* An instruction in a suitable method of preaching.

†Liber LXXXIV.—*vel Chanokh.* A brief abstraction of the Symbolic representation of the Universe derived by Dr. John Dee through the Scrying of Sir Edward Kelly. Its publication is at present incomplete.

†Liber DXXXVI.—Βατραχοφρενοβοοκοσμομαχία.
An instruction in expansion of the field of the mind.

†‡Liber D.—*Liber Sepher Sephiroth.* A dictionary of Hebrew words arranged according to their numerical value. This is an Encyclopædia of the Holy Qabalah, which is a Map of the Universe, and enables man to attain its Perfect Understanding.

‡LIBER DCCLXXVII.—*vel Prolegomena Symbolica Ad Systemam Sceptico-Mysticæ Viæ Explicandæ, Fundamentum Hieroglyphicum Sanctissimorum Scientæ Summæ.*

A complete Dictionary oi the Correspondences of all magical elements, re-printed with extensive additions, making it the only standard comprehensive book of reference ever published. It is to the language of Occultism what Webster or Murray is to the English language.[5]

†LIBER LXVII.—*The Sword of Song.* A critical study of various philosophies. An account of Buddhism.

†LIBER MMCMXI.—*A Note on Genesis.* A model of Qabalistic ratiocination.

This course is specially adapted to the Task of this Grade, the Attainment of Gñana Yoga.

COURSE VI.

The Philosophus will be examined in the following books:

LIBER CCXX.—*Liber L. vel Legis* Sub Figurâ CCXX, as delivered by XCIII. unto DCLXVI. This book is the foundation of the New Æon, and thus of the whole of our Work.

†‡LIBER DCCCXIII.—*vel Ararita* Sub Figurâ DLXX. This book is an account oi the Hexagram and the method of reducing it to the Unity, and Beyond.

†LIBER LV.—*The Chymical Jousting of Brother Perardua.* An account of the Magical and Mystic Path in the language oi Alchemy.

†LIBER LIX.—*Across the Gulf.* A fantastic account of a previous incarnation. Its principal interest is that its story oi the overthrowing of Isis by Osiris may help the reader to understand the meaning of the overthrowing of Osiris by Horus in the present Æon.

†LIBER CXCVII.—*The High History of Good Sir Palamedes* the Saracen Knight and of his following of the Questing Beast. A poetic account of the Great Work, and enumeration of many obstacles.

---

5   [Compare with the somewhat more modest description in Liber CCVII.]

†LIBER CCXLII.—*AHA!* An exposition in poetic language of several of the ways of attainment and the results obtained.

†LIBER CCCXXXV.—*Adonis.* This gives an account in poetic language of the struggle of the human and divine elements in the consciousness of man, giving their harmony following upon the victory of the latter.

†LIBER XVI.—*Liber Turris vel Domus Dei.* An instruction for attainment by the direct destruction of thoughts as they arise in the mind.

†‡LIBER CLXXV.—*Astarte vel Liber Berylli.* An instruction in attainment by the method of devotion, or Bhakta-Yoga.

†LIBER XLVI.—*The Key of the Mysteries.* A Translation by Frater O. M. of the masterpiece of Eliphas Levi.

This course is specially adapted to the Task of this Grade, the Attainment of Bhakta-Yoga.

COURSE VII.

The Dominus Liminis will be examined in the following books:

LIBER CCXX.—*Liber L. vel Legis* Sub Figurâ CCXX, as delivered by XCIII. unto DCLXVI. This book is the foundation of the New Æon, and thus of the whole of our Work.

†LIBER XCV.—*The Wake World* (in Konx Om Pax). A poetical allegory of the relations of the soul and the Holy Guardian Angel.

†LIBER DCCCLX.—*John St. John.* A model of what a magical record should be, so far as accurate analysis and fullness of description are concerned.

†LIBER VIII.—*See* CDXVIII.

†LIBER XI.—*Liber N V.* An instruction for attaining Nuit.

†LIBER DLV.—*Liber H A D.* An instruction for attaining Hadit.

†LIBER DCCCXXXI.—*Liber I O D,* formerly called *VESTA.* An instruction giving three methods of reducing the manifold consciousness to the Unity.

This course is specially adapted to facilitate the Task proper to the Grade of Adeptus Minor, the Attainment of Raja-Yoga and of the Knowledge and Conversation of the Holy Guardian Angel.

COURSE VIII.

LIBER CCXX.—*Liber L. vel Legis* Sub Figurâ CCXX, as delivered by XCIII. unto DCLXVI. This book is the foundation of the New Æon, and thus of the whole of our Work.

†LIBER I.—*Liber B vel Magi.* This is an account of the Grade of Magus, the highest grade which it is ever possible to manifest in any way whatever upon this plane. Or so it is said by the Masters of the Temple.

†LIBER LXVI.—*Liber Stellæ Rubeæ.* A secret ritual, the Heart of IAO-OAI, delivered into V.V.V.V.V. for his use in a certain matter of Liber Legis, and written down under the figure LXVI.

†LIBER CLVI.—*Liber Cheth vel Vallum Abiegni* Sub Figurâ CLVI. This book is a perfect account of the task of the Exempt Adept, considered under the symbols of a particular plane, not the intellectual.

†LIBER XLIV.—*The Mass of the Phœnix.* A Ritual of the Law.[6]

†LIBER XLI.—*Thien Tao* (in Konx Om Pax). An Essay on Attainment by the Way of Equilibrium.

†LIBER DCCCLXVIII.—*Liber Viarum Viæ.* A graphic account of magical powers classified under the Tarot Trumps.

Course VIII. publications are specially suited to the grade of Major Adept, whose task is the attainment of the full Magical Power. It is highly desirable that Aspirants to this grade should have attained the 9th degree O.T.O., in which case much secret knowledge is offered them besides that openly published. The methods of examination for the Inner College differ therefore from those employed in the Outer.

---

6   [Compare with the entirely different description in Liber CCVII.]

Additional publications will be referred, as they are issued, to the proper course.

The Exempt Adept will possess a thorough knowledge of all these courses, and present a thesis of his own, as a general Epitome of his own Attainment as reflected in the sphere of the Mind.

Love is the law, love under will.

www.ingramcontent.com/pod-product-compliance
Lightning Source LLC
Chambersburg PA
CBHW021824270326
41932CB00007B/331